Archaeology of Frankish Church Councils, AD 511–768

Medieval Law and Its Practice

VOLUME 6

Archaeology of Frankish Church Councils, AD 511–768

By
Gregory I. Halfond

BRILL

LEIDEN • BOSTON
2010

This book is printed on acid-free paper.

Library of Congress Cataloging-in-Publication Data

Halfond, Gregory I.
Archaeology of Frankish Church Councils, AD 511–768 / by Gregory I. Halfond.
p. cm. -- (Medieval law and its practice, ISSN 1873–8176 ; v. 6)
Includes bibliographical references and index.
ISBN 978-90-04-17976-9 (hardback : alk. paper)
1. Councils and synods--France--History. 2. France--Church history--To 987. I. Title. II. Series.

BR200.H35 2009
262'.524409021--dc22

2009033918

ISSN 1873-8176
ISBN 978 90 04 17976 9

PRINTED IN THE NETHERLANDS

CONTENTS

CONTENTS

PREFACE

> The processes of nature can therefore be properly described as sequences of mere events, but those of history cannot. They are not processes of mere events but processes of actions, which have an inner side, consisting of processes of thought; and what the historian is looking for is these processes of thought. All history is the history of thought.
> –R. G. Collingwood, *The Idea of History*

As R. G. Collingwood eloquently argues in his classic unfinished work, *The Idea of History* (1946), what matters to a historian are not events per se, but rather human thoughts manifested in events. In so doing, Collingwood draws a comparison between the geologist and the archaeologist. In examining the same rock strata, the former is concerned fundamentally with chronology, i.e., the order of events, as dictated by the physical evidence. The latter, however, views this same evidence "as artifacts serving human purposes and thus expressing a particular way in which men have thought about their own life."[1] The latter's work is thus "historical," while the former's is "quasi-historical." Archaeology, by Collingwood's definition, is "history in which the sources used…are not pre-existing narratives of the events into which the historian is inquiring."[2] The absence of narrative forces a historian working with archaeological evidence to apply an overtly Baconian methodology of questioning in order to interpret these artifacts in a historical manner.

The following is a work of institutional history. As such, its purpose is to explicate the functions and procedures of an administrative body in order to determine its importance to the community it serves. Institutional history, particularly of a period in which the survival of documents coincides only sporadically with the needs of the historian, requires the scholar to consult a wide variety of sources, most of which

[1] R. G. Collingwood, *The Idea of History* (Oxford: Clarendon Press, 1946), 212.

[2] R. G. Collingwood, *An Autobiography* (Oxford: Oxford University Press, 1939), 133. On archaeology's place in Collingwood's philosophy of history, see W. J. van der Dussen, *History as a Science: The Philosophy of R. G. Collingwood* (The Hague: Martinus Nijhoff Publishers, 1981), 201–53. Collingwood made little distinction between the methodological and the philosophical principles that guided his work in archaeology and history respectively.

are not directly concerned with the institution being studied or the questions being posed. In such cases, they are more akin to Collingwood's archaeological sources than to traditional literary ones, lacking a germane narrative to question or critique. They contain narratives to be sure, but narratives little concerned with the institution as such. This study's title, therefore, is not intended to suggest a Foucaultian approach to the evidence, or the analysis of physical objects recovered from the strata of the earth. Rather, it is a reflection of an effort to construct a narrative of institutional history from isolated shards of evidence while avoiding the "scissors and paste" methodology despised by Collingwood.

The institution under consideration here is the ecclesiastical council, as it appeared in the Frankish kingdoms between Clovis' convocation of the First Council of Orléans in 511 and the royal coronation of Charlemagne in 768. Church councils as a phenomenon have not been neglected by other historians of the Early Middle Ages. Few, however, have looked beyond the legislation composed during the course of these meetings, and have examined the nature of the institution that produced it. This scholarly lacuna has left unanswered a number of fundamental questions about the role of synods in the *regnum Francorum*, not least of all the uncertain legal status of the conciliar canons and the extent of royal control over the church and its councils. These questions and others are addressed in this study, which has been conceived as a monograph rather than as a handbook.

Additionally, I place a special emphasis on contextualizing the Frankish councils within the physical, political, legal, and religious world in which they gathered. This perspective allows conclusions to be drawn about the broader social significance of the councils in what otherwise would have been a mere bureaucratic history. Whenever possible, I draw attention to the individuals behind the institution. A council is a collective body of men, who, despite their willingness to subsume their identities within the greater corporate body, still bring to the meeting their own histories, agendas, and personalities. Although many of the prelates and clerics who attended the Frankish councils are known to us merely as names, and their distinct identities are lost to history, I emphasize throughout this study the reality of their individuality. Indeed, their "individual reflective acts of thought" (to use Collingwood's terminology) before and during meetings are what made each and every council and its agenda unique, and thus are of fundamental importance to this study.

What follows is a revised version of a doctoral dissertation defended at the University of Minnesota in 2007. There are numerous individuals to whom I owe a large debt of gratitude for helping me to see this project through to completion. The members of my doctoral committee—Bernard S. Bachrach, Ruth Karras, Michael Lower, George Sheets, and James Tracy—were extraordinarily generous with their time and advice, and were very patient with an anxious young graduate student. Special thanks are due to my adviser, Bernard S. Bachrach, whose devotion to the study of history has inspired generations of students. His probing questions, encyclopedic knowledge of sources and scholarship, and constant encouragement made this project possible. I would also like to thank Paul Fouracre, Felice Lifshitz, and Joseph Goering for their helpful comments on individual chapters, and Kathy Kaiser for her copyediting. It was Paul Hyams and Danuta Shanzer who initially triggered my interest in the Early Middle Ages, and both continue to serve as sources of support and inspiration. At Framingham State College, Jon Huibregtse, Brad Nutting, Tom Krainz, Richard Allen, Nick Racheotes, and Bridgette Sheridan have been welcoming and supportive colleagues. Neil Conrad and the other librarians at Whittemore Library have tirelessly sought out dozens of obscure publications for use in this project. Dave Merwin and Kathryn Fatherley have generously provided the map that appears at the end of this volume. For their friendship and encouragement, I would like to thank Edward Snyder, Christopher Marshall, and Matthew Lundquist. Finally, I owe the largest debt of gratitude to my family: Jay and Gayle Halfond, Rebecca Halfond, Murray and Jeanne Halfond, and my loving wife, Larissa, to whom this book is dedicated.

ABBREVIATIONS

AASS	*Acta Sanctorum* (online database)
CCSL	*Corpus Christianorum: Series Latina* (Turnhout)
ChLa	*Chartae Latinae Antiquiores*, vols. 13–19 (Olten)
DLH	Gregory of Tours, *Decem Libri Historiarum* (Hanover)
MGH	*Monumenta Germaniae Historica* (Berlin, Hanover, and Leipzig)
AA	*Auctores Antiquissimi*
SRG	*Scriptores Rerum Germanicarum*
SRM	*Scriptores Rerum Merovingicarum*
SS	*Scriptores (Folio)*
PL	*Patrologia Latina*, ed. J. P. Migne (Paris)
SC	*Sources Chrétiennes* (Paris)

Note on Translations

All translations are my own, unless explicitly stated otherwise. For the texts of the Frankish conciliar canons, I have relied on the standard editions of Charles de Clercq (CCSL 148A) and Albert Werminghoff (MGH Leges III, Tomus 2). For the pre-Frankish Gallic councils, I have consulted the edition of Charles Munier (CCSL 148).

INTRODUCTION

A ROMAN INSTITUTION IN A POST-ROMAN WORLD*

A Gallo-Roman Institution

In the year AD 742, Saint Boniface (ca. 675–754) composed a letter to the newly elected Pope Zacharias (r. 741–52), in which he informed the pontiff that "old men report that the Franks have not held a synod for eighty years."[1] Although the English bishop was exaggerating by a good four decades, he communicated an unambiguous message: it was reprehensible that the Frankish bishops were so lax in their duties as to neglect meeting collectively with their brethren for the better part of a century. Such an appalling state of affairs could only suggest a serious state of degeneration among the Frankish episcopacy. For Boniface, the solution to the problem was obvious: new ecclesiastical councils needed to be held in order to correct the abuses of the past decades, with himself, naturally, presiding.[2] It was the good fortune of Boniface that the sons of the Frankish *maior domus* Charles Martel (688–741), Carloman (d. 755) and Pippin III (ca. 714–68), agreed, and enthusiastically sponsored a series of "reform" councils beginning in the 740s.[3]

---

* A different version of this introductory chapter was published before as "Cum Consensu Omnium: Frankish Church Councils from Clovis to Charlemagne" in *History Compass*, Volume 5, February issue (Oxford: Wiley-Blackwell, 2007). It has been reprinted with the permission of the publisher.

[1] Boniface, *S. Bonifatii et Lulli Epistolae*, MGH Epistolarum III, ed. Ernst Dümmler (Berlin: Weidmann, 1892), no. 50.

[2] In this same letter (no. 50), Boniface tells the pope that he already has received permission from Carloman to hold a council in the eastern half of the Frankish kingdom.

[3] Timothy Reuter, "Kirchenreform und Kirchenpolitik im Zeitalter Karl Martells: Begriffe und Wirklichkeit," in *Karl Martell in seiner Zeit*, ed. Jörg Jarnut, Ulrich Nonn, and Michael Richter (Sigmaringen, Germany: Jan Thorbecke Verlag, 1994), 35–59, has argued that it would be anachronistic to apply the word *reform* to the eighth-century councils. C.f. M. A. Claussen, *The Reform of the Frankish Church: Chrodegang of Metz and the Regula Canonicorum in the Eighth Century* (Cambridge: Cambridge University Press, 2004), who employs the term liberally. Peter Brown, *The Making of Western Christendom*, 2nd ed. (Oxford: Blackwell, 2003), 437–40, prefers the more precise term *correctio*. On the idea of reform in early medieval Europe, see Julia Barrow, "Ideas and Applications of Reform," in *The Cambridge History of Christianity*, vol. 3, ed. Thomas F. X. Noble and Julia M. H. Smith (Cambridge: Cambridge University Press, 2008), 345–62.

In doing so, the two *principes* were addressing the immediate concern of consolidating their political positions in the wake of their father's death.[4] But in their convocation of church councils they also were following a long tradition that characterized secular involvement in church affairs in the *regnum Francorum*.

Certainly, ecclesiastical councils had been held in Gaul prior to the establishment of Frankish royal power. Between 314 and 506, more than thirty synods were convoked in the Gallic provinces.[5] Nor were the Franks innovators in permitting the *princeps* a role in their convocation and discussions. This practice dated back to the reign of the first Christian Roman emperor, Constantine I (r. 306–37), under whose watchful eye the ecumenical Council of Nicaea met in AD 325. Constantine also was responsible for the convocation of the first Gallo-Roman synod, held in Arles in 314 at the will of the *piissimus imperator*, who intended for it to settle the Donatist controversy tearing apart the African church at that time.[6] Neither Constantine nor his imperial or Frankish successors hesitated to instigate conciliar business and, indeed, viewed it as their prerogative. What is more, the majority of ecclesiastics in both the Roman and Frankish eras did not question this privilege.[7]

[4] Paul Fouracre, *The Age of Charles Martel* (Harlow: Pearson Education Ltd., 2000), 169–70.

[5] They were Arles (314), Cologne (346), Arles (353), Béziers (356), Paris (360–1), Valence (374), Bordeaux (384), Unknown (385/6), Trier (386), Nîmes (394/6), Turin (398), Beziers (ca. 421), Unknown (429), Riez (439), Unknown (440), Orange (441), Vaison (442), Unknown (ca. 444), Arles (449), Arles (449/50), Unknown (450), Lerins (ca. 451), Arles (451/2), Vienne (451/2), Angers (453), Tours (461), Unknown (463), Vannes (ca. 465), Lyons (ca. 469), Arles (ca. 470), Lyons (ca. 470), Agde (506), and possibly the so-called Second Council of Arles (442/506), on which see Ralph Mathisen, "The Second Council of Arles and the Spirit of Compilation and Codification in Late Roman Gaul," *Journal of Early Christian Studies* 5, no. 4 (1997): 511–54. Discussion of all of the preceding councils can be found in Ralph Mathisen, *Ecclesiastical Factionalism and Religious Controversy in Fifth-Century Gaul* (Washington, DC: Catholic University of America Press, 1989). For a quantitative analysis of the Gallo-Roman councils, see Peter Gassmann, "Der Episkopat in Gallien im 5. Jahrhundert" (Ph.D. diss., Rheinischen Friedrich Wilhelms Universität zu Bonn, 1977), 260–3. On the continuity between the fourth- and fifth-century Gallic councils with those held under the Franks, see Hans Barion, *Das fränkisch-deutsche Synodalrecht des Frühmittelalters* (Bonn: Ludwig Röhrscheid Verlag, 1931), 202; J. M. Wallace-Hadrill, *The Frankish Church* (Oxford: Clarendon Press, 1983), 107; William M. Daly, "Clovis: How Barbarian, How Pagan?" *Speculum* 69, no. 3 (1994): 657.

[6] Arles (314), Preface. All citations of the Gallo-Roman councils (pre-511) are from *Concilia Galliae A.314–A.506*, ed. Charles Munier, CCSL 148 (Turnhout, Belgium: Brepols, 1963).

[7] Jean Gaudemet, *La formation du droit séculier et du droit de l'Eglise aux IVe et Ve siècles* (Paris: Sirey, 1957), 136, notes that not even Pope Leo the Great contested the right of the Roman emperors to convoke councils.

When Carolingian-era clerics memorialized ecumenical councils of the Roman period, they made no effort to minimize the role of the emperors in these meetings, and, in fact, emphasized it. Illustrations of the Councils of Nicaea and Ephesus (431) in a ninth-century Northern Italian canonical collection, for example, depict deferent clerics presenting their canons to haloed emperors, sitting in majesty.[8]

Imperial participation in conciliar life had benefits for both the church and the state. It was ordinary, for example, for councils to request secular assistance to enforce their rulings, a tradition that continued well after the end of Roman rule in the West. In return, conciliar participants had to accept some level of imperial involvement in their deliberations, although the nature of that involvement sometimes can be difficult to assess, and certainly varied according to the circumstances under which a given council was held.[9] In some cases, the emperors' aid in the enforcement of conciliar decisions took the form of adopting ecclesiastical legislation as the basis for their own *constitutiones*.[10] Later, the Frankish kings often would consult canons in scripting their own edicts.

The Frankish councils also owed a number of their procedures and documentary *formulae* to Roman antecedents.[11] Most scholars today accept that synods held throughout the post-imperial West adopted much of their protocol from the procedures of Roman administrative bodies. Whether the Roman senate itself was the direct source of

[8] Jean Hubert, Jean Porcher, and W. F. Volbach, *Europe in the Dark Ages*, trans. Stuart Gilbert and James Emmons (London: Thames and Hudson, 1969), 143–4 (Vercelli, Biblioteca Capitolare, CLXV).

[9] Brigitte Basdevant-Gaudemet, "Les évêques, les papes, et les princes dans la vie conciliaire en France du IVe au XIIe siècle," *Revue historique de droit français et étranger* 69 (1991): 3–4; Ramsay MacMullen, *Voting About God in Early Church Councils* (New Haven: Yale University Press, 2006), 67–74. Timothy Barnes, *Athanasius and Constantius* (Cambridge, MA: Harvard University Press, 1993), 165–75, has argued that the old scholarly paradigm of *kaiserliche Synodalgewalt* is misleading, noting that councils often met independently of imperial convocation and input, and that even Constantine denied himself the right to annul conciliar rulings. Although Barnes neglects the influence of indirect government pressure, he is right to emphasize that councils did not serve as mere mouthpieces for the imperial will in the later Roman empire.

[10] Gaudemet, *La formation du droit séculier et du droit de l'Église*, 143.

[11] Jürgen Hannig, *Consensus Fidelium* (Stuttgart: Anton Hiersemann, 1982), 64–79, demonstrates how councils served as an intermediary in the transference of Roman notions and formulas of *consensus* to the Frankish kingdoms. On the councils' transmission of the *cum…convenissemus* formula to Merovingian *placita*, see Peter Classen, "Kaiserreskript und Königsurkunde, Diplomatische Studien zum römische-germanischen Kontinuitätsproblem, II. Teil," *Archiv für Diplomatik* 2 (1956): 69–70.

inspiration is less clear.[12] Regardless, the influence of secular procedures of governance on church councils is not surprising. After all, the episcopal participants of both the Gallo-Roman and early Frankish synods, by and large, were the members of prominent Roman aristocratic families, well versed in the traditions of office holding.[13] Many

[12] The argument that the procedures of the Roman senate influenced conciliar practices in Late Antiquity has been made by, among others, Heinrich Gelzar, *Ausgewählte kleine Schriften* (Leipzig: B. G. Teubner, 1907), 144; Pierre Batiffol, "Le règlement des premiers conciles africains," *Bulletin d'ancienne littérature et d'archéologie chrétiennes* 3 (1913): 3–19; Hermann Josef Sieben, *Die Konzilsidee in der Alten Kirche* (Paderborn, Germany: Ferdinand Schöningh, 1979), 476–82; Elisabeth Herrmann, *Ecclesia in Re Publica: Die Entwicklung der Kirche von pseudostaatlicher zu staatlich inkorporierter Existenz* (Frankfurt: Peter Lang, 1980), 61–70; Hamilton Hess, *The Early Development of Canon Law and the Council of Serdica* (Oxford: Oxford University Press, 2002), 24–9; MacMullen, *Voting About God in Early Church Councils*, 18–9. Others recognize the Roman administrative influence, while preferring to see municipal or provincial assemblies as the direct sources of it: Cyrille Vogel, "Primatialité et synodalite dans l'Église locale durant la période anteniceene," in *Aspects de l'orthodoxie: Structures et spiritualité* (Paris: Presses Universitaires de France, 1981), 61–3; P. R. Amidon, "The Procedures of Cyprian's Councils," *Vigiliae Christianae* 37 (1983): 328–39; Hannig, *Consensus Fidelium*, 72. Jean Gaudemet, in turn, has argued that although councils probably borrowed from the procedures of imperial institutions, no body was the lone source of influence: Jean Gaudemet, *L'Église dans l'Empire Romain (IVe–Ve siècles)* (Paris: Sirey, 1958), 451–2; Gaudemet, *La formation du droit séculier et du droit de l'Eglise*, 135–6. On Roman senatorial procedures, see the classic account of Theodor Mommsen, *Römisches Staatsrecht* (Graz: Akademische Druck- u. Verlagsanstalt, 1952–3), III.951–1003.

[13] On the aristocratic nature of the Gallic episcopate, as well as the existence of episcopal dynasties, see Louis Duchesne, *L'Eglise au VI siècle* (Paris: Fontemoing and Co., E. de Boccard, Successeur, 1925), 524; Henry G. J. Beck, *The Pastoral Care of Souls in South-East France During the Sixth Century* (Rome: Apud Aedes Universitatis Gregorianae, 1950), 6; Martin Heinzelmann, *Bischofsherrschaft in Gallien* (Munich: Artemis Verlag, 1976); Edward James, *The Origins of France: From Clovis to the Capetians, 500–1000* (New York: St. Martin's Press, 1982), 49–63; Ian Wood, "The Ecclesiastical Politics of Merovingian Clermont," in *Ideal and Reality in Frankish and Anglo-Saxon Society*, ed. Patrick Wormald, Donald Bullough, and Roger Collins (Oxford: Basil Blackwell, 1983), 37–40; Raymond Van Dam, *Leadership and Community in Late Antique Gaul* (Berkeley: University of California Press, 1985), 133–4, 203–12, 228–9; Reinhold Kaiser, "Les évêques et leurs pouvoirs," in *La Neustrie: Les pays au nord de la Loire de Dagobert à Charles le Chauve (VIIe-IXe siècles)*, ed. Patrick Périn and Laure-Charlotte Feffer (Rouen: Musées et Monuments Départementaux de Seine-Maritime, 1985), 99–101; Patrick Geary, *Before France and Germany: The Creation and Transformation of the Merovingian World* (Oxford: Oxford University Press, 1988), 123–35; Martin Heinzelmann, "Prosopographie et recherche de continuité historique: L'exemple des V–VII siècles," *Mélanges de l'École française de Rome: Moyen Age-Temps Modernes* 100, no. 1 (1988): 233–4; Ralph Mathisen, *Roman Aristocrats in Barbarian Gaul* (Austin: University of Texas Press, 1993), 89–104; Martin Heinzelmann, "L'aristocratie et les évêchés entre Loire et Rhin jusqu'à la fin du VII siècle," in *La christianisation des pays entre Loire et Rhin (IV–VII siècle)*, ed. Pierre Riché (Paris: Éditions

were conversant in secular law and court procedures, and brought this knowledge and experience with them to their ecclesiastical careers.[14]

The organization of the Frankish church itself was based on a provincial system installed by the former imperial government. With the end of Roman rule in Gaul, metropolitan bishops assumed the responsibilities of provincial governors, and suffragans took on much of the responsibility for governing their individual *civitates*.[15] By the late fifth century, ecclesiastical governance in Gaul was already deeply intertwined with imperial administration, procedures, and influence. The Frankish kings, desirous to imitate their imperial predecessors, made no effort to diminish the Roman character of the church they inherited.[16] Still, the church council was not an imperial invention per se. Over the course of the second and third centuries, bishops and lower clerics had gathered independently to discuss issues of contention within and between individual Christian communities. But it was only with Christianity's new protected status under the Christian emperors, in combination with the rise of larger and more powerful Christian communities after AD 313 that "an epoch of intense conciliar life" was able to flourish during the

du Cerf, 1993), 75–90; Ian Wood, *The Merovingian Kingdoms: 450–751* (London: Longman Group, 1994), 79. On the participation of episcopal dynasties in Gallic conciliar life, see J. Champagne and R. Szramkiewicz, "Recherches sur les conciles des temps mérovingiens," *Revue historique de droit français et étranger* 49 (1971): 27; c.f. Wallace-Hadrill, *The Frankish Church*, 108–9.

[14] Caroline Humfress, *Orthodoxy and the Courts in Late Antiquity* (Oxford: Oxford University Press, 2007), 212.

[15] James, *The Origins of France*, 49–63; Jill Harries, "Church and State in the *Notitia Galliarum*," *The Journal of Roman Studies* 68 (1978): 34.

[16] The Frankish kings' desire to imitate their imperial predecessors is well established. See, e.g., Paul Hinschius, *Kirchenrecht* (Berlin: I. Guttentag, 1869–97), III.539–40; Charles de Clercq, *La législation religieuse franque de Clovis à Charlemagne (507–814)* (Louvain, Belgium: Bureaux du Recueil Bibliothèque de Université, 1936), 99; Jean Gaudemet, *Les sources du droit de l'Eglise en Occident* (Paris: Éditions du Cerf/Editions du C.N.R.S., 1985), 108; Martin Heinzelmann, "Bischof und Herrschaft vom spätantiken Gallien bis zu den karolingischen Hausmeiern: Die institutionellen Grundlagen," in *Herrschaft und Kirche*, ed. Friedrich Prinz (Stuttgart: Anton Hiersemann, 1988), 34–5; 68–70; Jean Heuclin, "Le Concile d'Orléans de 511, un premier concordat?" in *Clovis: Histoire et mémoire*, ed. Michel Rouche (Paris: Presses de l'Université de Paris-Sorbonne, 1997), 436; Elisabeth Magnou-Nortier, "Existe-t-il une géographie gaulois des courants de pensée dans le clergé de Gaule au VIe siècle?" in *Grégoire de Tours et l'espace gaulois*, ed. Nancy Gauthier and Henry Galinié (Tours: Revue Archéologique du Centre de la France, 1997), 148–9; Daly, "Clovis: How Barbarian, How Pagan," 656; Jean Durliat, *Les finances publiques de Dioclétien aux Carolingiens (284–889)* (Sigmaringen, Germany: Jan Thorbecke Verlag, 1990), 141.

fourth and fifth centuries.[17] Despite the retreat of the Roman central government in Gaul in the latter half of this period, the Gallo-Roman conciliar epoch reached its zenith in the hundred years leading up to the establishment of the Frankish *regnum,* particularly under the supervision of the bishops of Arles, notably Hilary (429–49) and Caesarius (502–42).[18]

The influence of Caesarius on Frankish conciliar tradition was especially strong. His conciliar activities commenced with the Visigothic-sponsored Council of Agde (in 506), which he presided over. But competition for control of southern Gaul disrupted his efforts to legislate not only on a grand scale, but even on a provincial one, as constantly changing political borders threatened the integrity of traditional Roman administrative and ecclesiastical units. But, thanks to an Ostrogothic military offensive against the Burgundians in 523, Caesarius was able to gain control over the entire province of Arles. Exercising his authority as metropolitan and papal vicar, he convoked, in quick succession, half a dozen provincial synods in the mid-520s and early 530s. In these councils, Caesarius and his suffragans discussed a wide range of issues, including pastoral care, clerical discipline, liturgy, and, most influentially, the Augustinian conception of Divine Grace.[19] Although Caesarius would never attend a Frankish council personally, his suffragans would, bringing with them knowledge of administrative and legislative traditions to which they were contributors.[20] Thus, when Clovis the Frank convoked his own council in 511 at Orléans, he was engaging in an activity with deep roots in Gallo-Roman custom.

[17] Gaudemet, *Les sources du droit de l'Eglise en Occident*, 41. Hess, *The Early Development of Canon Law*, 6–8, notes that the second-century gatherings cannot be considered councils because they met at a time in which monepiscopal governance was still in its infancy. On the pre-Nicene synods, see Joseph Fischer and Adolf Lumpe, *Die Synoden von den Anfängen bis zum Vorabend des Nicaenums* (Paderborn, Germany: Ferdinand Schöningh, 1997).

[18] Barion, *Das fränkisch-deutsche Synodalrecht des Frühmittelalters*, 7–8. On the activities of Hilary, see Mathisen, *Ecclesiastical Factionalism and Religious Controversy in Fifth-Century Gaul*, 101–72. The Franks took over Arles in AD 536, thereby weakening Caesarius' influence over the Gallic church. On the effects of this gravitational shift in power, see William Klingshirn, *Caesarius of Arles: The Making of a Christian Community in Late Antique Gaul* (Cambridge: Cambridge University Press, 1994), 244–72.

[19] On Caesarius' conciliar activities and their context, see ibid., 136–45.

[20] Ibid., 258–9.

Clovis, the *Novus Constantinus*, convoked the First Council of Orléans four years after his defeat of Alaric II (r. 484–507), the king of the Visigoths, at the Battle of Vouillé.[21] Clovis' convocation was not merely a symbolic act of *imitatio imperii*. He intended for his council to assist in the integration of newly conquered southern *civitates* into his northern Gallic *regnum*. Of the cities of the south, only those not yet securely under Frankish rule lacked representation at his council. The northern bishops, who attended Clovis' synod in somewhat greater numbers, were more recent appointees than their southern counterparts, many of whom took their seats during the reign of the Arian Alaric. Some of the northerners, in fact, may have been gifted their seats by the Frankish king himself.[22] It was a southerner, however, Bishop Cyprian of Bordeaux, who served as council president, perhaps in recognition of the seniority and experience of the southern prelates.

The *civitas* where the bishops met would become over the following decades a standard meeting place for major interprovincial councils, but at the time of the First Council of Orléans its participation in Gallic conciliar business was negligible.[23] Clovis' choice of location seems to have had more to do with the status of Orléans as a frontier city, lying between the Frankish kingdom and the annexed Visigothic provinces.[24] The Frankish king did not travel to Orléans personally to participate in the council's deliberations, but he—at least in part—established its agenda, and he put his *auctoritas* behind its decisions.[25] These decisions drew upon canonical precedents both recent and ancient, and addressed issues raised by the unification of the Gallic church under Frankish rule. The convocation of the first Frankish council thus was informed by both Roman tradition and the concerns of the day. In all subsequent synods, tradition and innovation would be similarly linked.

[21] For the application of this epithet to Clovis, see Gregory of Tours, *Decem Libri Historiarum*, MGH SRM I, 1, ed. Bruno Krusch and Wilhelm Levison (Hanover: Hahn, 1937–51), II.31.

[22] Heuclin, "Le Concile d'Orléans de 511," 439–40; Odette Pontal, *Histoire des conciles mérovingiens* (Paris: Éditions du Cerf, 1989), 56.

[23] Evurtius of Orléans possibly attended the Council of Valence in 374. Declopetus of Orléans' subscription is attached to the *acta* of the pseudo-council of Cologne (346).

[24] Pontal, *Histoire des conciles mérovingiens*, 50; Heuclin, "Le Concile d'Orléans de 511," 438.

[25] Orléans (511), Preface.

What, then, was the nature of the institution adopted by Clovis and his successors? On the most basic level, councils were the meetings held among the church leadership, either on the diocesan, provincial, interprovincial, or ecumenical level. They could be convoked by secular and ecclesiastical leaders alike, and were attended by a mix of bishops, clerics, monks, and occasionally laymen, depending on the geographic representation and agenda of the meeting. In the Gallic sources, *synodus* and *concilium* are used interchangeably to describe ecclesiastical assemblies, although modern scholars occasionally apply the former term to smaller gatherings.[26] The agendas of these councils were usually multifaceted. One important task, particularly at the larger meetings, was the composition of ecclesiastical legislation.[27] Through the course of deliberation, the attendees produced a series of decisions known as *canones,* which were intended to define the rules of church life. In his *Etymologiae*, Bishop Isidore of Seville (ca. 560–636) defines a *canon* as a *regula,* a word that originally meant "measuring stick," but which came to denote an instruction on how to live a proper life (*recte*).[28] The Frankish councils, too, employed this definition.[29] In the ecclesiastical context, *canones* were the legislative expressions of

[26] Adolf Lumpe, "Zur Geschichte der Wörter *Concilium* und *Synodus* in der antiken christlichen Latinität," *Annuarium Historiae Conciliorum* 2, no. 1 (1970): 1–21. Lumpe does not dismiss Matti Sainio's theory that originally the two terms may once have meant the opposite of what they mean today, but observes that "the mixture of both expressions occurred very early" (7). For Sainio's theory, see Matti Antero Sainio, *Semasiologische Untersuchungen: Über die Entstehung der christlichen Latinität* (Helsinki: Finnische Literaturgesellschaft, 1940), 69 f. Isidore of Seville, writing in the early seventh century, defined both terms in the sense of a gathering: Isidore of Seville, *Etymologiae*, ed. W. M. Lindsay (Oxford: Clarendon Press, 1911), VI.16.11–2. On diocesan synods in the Carolingian and post-Carolingian periods, see Joseph Avril, "L'institution synodale et la législation épiscopale de temps carolingiens au IVe Concile de Latran," *Revue d'histoire de l'Eglise de France* 89, no. 223 (2003): 273–307.

[27] In contrast to the Gallo-Roman, Merovingian, and Visigothic synods, all of which engaged in canonical legislating, only a handful of Anglo-Saxon councils are known to have issued canonical acts: Catherine Cubitt, *Anglo-Saxon Church Councils c. 650–850* (London: Leicester University Press, 1995), 62–3.

[28] Isidore of Seville *Etymologiae* VI.16.1.

[29] References to *regula canonum, canonum regulas,* and *canonum regulis* can be found in Lyons (567/70), c. 5; Clichy (626/7), Preface; and St. Jean de Losne (673/5), c. 21, respectively. The authors of the Frankish canonical records also refer to their own decisions as *regulae* on a number of occasions, e.g., Arles (524), c. 3; Orléans (538), Preface; Orléans (541), c. 2; Orléans (549), cc. 10 and 18; Clichy (626/7), Preface. There are also numerous references to *ecclesiasticae regulae:* e.g., Arles (524), Preface; Carpentras (527), Acts; Orléans (533), c. 7; Clermont (535), Preface; Orléans (541), c. 38; Paris (614), c. 3; Unknown (c. 614), c. 1.

the unified church or, to be more precise, churches. They drew their authority from their connection to the enduring canonical tradition, the consensus of the conciliar participants, and (practically speaking) from the willingness of civil and religious authorities to recognize them as binding.[30] The Frankish councils published their canonical *acta* in what is known as the "*placuit*-form," a Roman-derived documentary *formula* characterized by a preface (*praefatio*) containing details of the synod's assemblage; canons introduced by traditional legal phrases, such as *ut, si quis, placuit nobis, statuimus, decrevimus, constituimus,* and *censuimus*; and an appended list of participant subscriptions.[31]

Although Frankish sources frequently distinguish their *canones* from secular *leges,* their tendency to place these two words in opposition to each other is suggestive of the close relationship between ecclesiastical and secular legislation in this period.[32] Further evidence of this relationship is seen in the frequent citations of Roman imperial edicts by the Frankish councils,[33] the adoption of canonical precedents

---

[30] The relation of conciliar *auctoritas* to tradition (*paradosis*) dates back to Bishop Athanasius of Alexandria (ca. 293–373) and his efforts to champion the authority of the Council of Nicaea (325), on which see Sieben, *Die Konzilsidee in der Alten Kirche,* 62–3. Vincent of Lerins and Pope Leo the Great, in turn, emphasized the importance of *consensus* (intra-ecclesiastical and with tradition) for conciliar authority, on which see Sieben, *Die Konzilsidee in der Alten Kirche,* 103–70. On the importance tradition and consensus vis-à-vis synods, see also Klaus Oehler, "Der Consensus Omnium als Kriterium der Wahrheit in der antiken Philosophie und der Patristik," *Antike und Abendland* 10 (1961): 121–2; Barion, *Das fränkisch-deutsche Synodalrecht des Frühmittelalters,* 97–110; Karl Morrison, *Tradition and Authority in the Western Church: 300–1140* (Princeton: Princeton University Press, 1969), 4–5, 195–7; Hannig, *Consensus Fidelium,* 64–79; Rachel L. Stocking, *Bishops, Councils, and Consensus in the Visigothic Kingdom, 589–633* (Ann Arbor: University of Michigan Press, 2000), 1–25; Hess, *The Early Development of Canon Law,* 29–33. The debate over secular involvement in conciliar legislating is discussed in detail in subsequent chapters. I will note here only that Jean Gaudemet, *Église et cité: Histoire du droit canonique* (Paris: Cerf/Montchrestien, 1994), 227, downplays the importance of secular enforcement.

[31] Hess, *The Early Development of Canon Law,* 69–72. Hess sees a direct relationship between the *placuit*-form and the *liber sententiarum* of the Roman senate.

[32] See, e.g., Orléans (511), c. 1; Mâcon (581/3), c. 16; Mâcon (585), cc. 9 and 14; Guntram, *Edictum,* in *Capitularia Regum Francorum,* ed. Alfred Boretius, MGH Leges II.1 (Hanover: Hahn, 1883), 10–12; Gregory of Tours *Decem Libri Historiarum* V.18. The similarity between conciliar and secular legal *formulae,* e.g., the traditional conditional phrase *si quis,* is also suggestive of the relationship between the two bodies of law; on this, see Hannig, *Consensus Fidelium,* 67–8.

[33] On which, see Jean Gaudemet, "Survivances romaines dans le droit de la monarchie franque du Vème au Xème siècle," in *La formation du droit canonique médiéval* (London: Variorum, 1980), II.164–8. The overwhelming majority of references to secular *leges* by the Frankish councils are to Roman, rather than to Frankish, law. See, e.g., Orléans (511), cc. 1 and 23; Orléans (541), c. 13; Orléans (549), c. 7; Tours (567), cc. 21

by secular legislators,[34] and the number of Frankish manuscripts that include both secular and canonical legislation.[35] Nevertheless, despite the collaborative relationship between lay and canon law, tensions between the two systems remained a constant throughout the Merovingian era.[36] A potential means of defusing this tension emerged under the early Carolingians, whereby the *princeps* took unprecedented responsibility for legislating on church matters. But this plan relied too heavily on royal strength and episcopal subservience to be a practical long-term solution, and the relationship between canon and secular law remained in flux into the High Middle Ages.

Issuing canons, however, was but one function of Gallo-Roman and Frankish church councils. These assemblies also played an important judicial role.[37] Councils investigated charges against transgressors of canonical standards, occasionally going so far as to hand the wrongdoer over to the secular authorities for punishment. Bishop

---

and 22; Mâcon (581/3), c. 16; Mâcon (585), c. 9. It is not always possible to identify the legal compilations consulted by the conciliar attendees, although Paul Mikat, *Die Inzestgesetzgebung der merowingisch-fränkischen Konzilien (511–626/27)* (Paderborn, Germany: Ferdinand Schöningh, 1994), 57–8, 125–6, and 130–1, has suggested that bishops at the Councils of Orléans (538), Tours (567), and Mâcon (585) all had recourse to the late-fourth-century *Lex Dei* (or *Collatio Legum Mosaicarum*). On the transmission of the *Lex Dei* in this period, see Robert M. Frakes, "The Manuscript Tradition of the *Lex Dei*," *Zeitschrift der Savigny-Stifung für Rechtsgeschichte* 124 (2007): 290–304.

[34] Chlothar II, for example, drew upon fourteen canons of the Council of Paris (614) for his edict of the same year: Chlothar II *Edictum*, in *Capitularia Regum Francorum*, nos. 1–4, 6–7, 10, and 18. Similarly, the *Leges Alamannorum* requires parricides and fratricides to be judged "according to the canons": *Leges Alamannorum*, ed. Karl Lehmann and Karl August Eckhardt, 2nd ed., MGH Leges V.1 (Hanover: Hahn, 1966), XL.

[35] Gaudemet, "Survivances romaines," 169–73; Mark Vessey, "The Origins of the Collectio Sirmondiana: A New Look at the Evidence," in *The Theodosian Code*, ed. Jill Harries and Ian Wood (Ithaca, NY: Cornell University Press, 1993), 178–99. There are a number of Frankish manuscripts, particularly from the Carolingian era, which contain both capitularies and conciliar canons, e.g., Paris, Bibliothèque Nationale, Lat. 1455, Vatican Vat. Lat. 3827, and Vatican Vat. Lat. 5751. For the contents of those manuscripts containing Frankish capitularies, see Hubert Mordek, *Bibliotheca Capitularium Regum Francorum Manuscripta* (Munich: Monumenta Germaniae Historica, 1995). Rosamond McKitterick, *The Carolingians and the Written Word* (Cambridge: Cambridge University Press, 1989), 48–55, has also noted the existence of Carolingian-era manuscripts containing both conciliar canons and the *Lex Salica*, e.g., Warsaw Quart. 480, Berne 442, Leiden lat. Q.119, and Bibliothèque Nationale lat. 3182.

[36] See, e.g., Lyons (567/70), c. 2, and Paris (614), c. 12, both of which declare those donations made to the church by clerics through wills not written in accordance with the *legum secularium* to be irrevocable.

[37] Humfress, *Orthodoxy and the Courts in Late Antiquity*, 208–11, notes a secular influence on the development of synodal judicial procedures.

Gregory of Tours (ca. 538–94) describes in extensive detail a number of such synodal trials in the course of his *Decem Libri Historiarum*, including the Council of Paris (577), where Bishop Praetextatus of Rouen was tried for plotting against King Chilperic (r. 561–84), and a synod held in Clermont-Ferrand between the years of 584 and 591, which investigated whether Bishop Ursicinus of Cahors had illegally annexed parishes from the diocese of Rodez.[38]

Gregory had firsthand experience with conciliar judicial proceedings.[39] Gregory, born Georgius Florentius in Clermont, was the scion of a distinguished senatorial family whose members held an impressive number of episcopal seats in sixth-century Gaul.[40] Gregory states in his *Histories* that all but five bishops of the *civitas* of Tours were his relations.[41] But this fact made it no less difficult for him to maintain his position as head of the church of Tours and chief patron of the cult of Saint Martin.[42] In the year 580, Gregory was summoned to appear before a council at King Chilperic's palace at Berny-Rivière, and accused of making slanderous remarks about the king's wife, Fredegund, and Bishop Bertram of Bordeaux. According to Gregory's own account, his troubles first began when his nemesis, Leudast, became *comes* of Tours. Leudast provoked the bishop by attending church fully armed, stealing ecclesiastical property, and imposing physical punishments on clerics charged with crimes. Leudast allied himself with some of Gregory's own disloyal clerics, promising one the bishopric if they did away with Gregory. Meanwhile, according to Gregory, other enemies in the court of Chilperic were also plotting against him. Several of

---

[38] Gregory of Tours *Decem Libri Historiarum* V.18 and VI.38.

[39] Councils with judicial components to their agendas include Lyons (518/9), Carpentras (527), Marseilles (533), Orléans (549), Paris (551/2); Brittany (552), Saintes (561/7), Lyons (567/70), Paris (573), Paris (577), Chalon (579), Saintes (579), Berny (580), Lyons (581), Auvergne (584/91), Troyes (585), Mâcon (585), Unknown 2 (588), Unknown 1 (589), Sorcy (589), Poitiers (589/90), Auvergne (590), Verdun/Metz (590), Chalon (602/4), Mâcon (626/7), Orléans (639/41), Chalon (647/53), Arles (648/50), Mâlay-le-Roi (677), Unknown (ca. 677/9), and Soissons (744). Examples of questionable reliability or conciliar status include Unknown (ca. 538), Lyons (572/3), Tours (ca. 580), Unknown (late seventh century), Rouen (711/5), Unknown (745), and Constance (758/9).

[40] On Gregory's family, see Martin Heinzelmann, *Gregory of Tours: History and Society in the Sixth Century*, trans. Christopher Carroll (Cambridge: Cambridge University Press, 2001), 11–28.

[41] Gregory of Tours *Decem Libri Historiarum* V.49.

[42] Wood, *The Merovingian Kingdoms*, 87.

the king's officials attempted to convince Gregory to flee the city of Tours in anticipation of an invasion by Chilperic's brother, Guntram (r. 561–92). Chilperic ordered the entire matter to be investigated by a synod. Before the meeting opened, Gregory's disloyal cleric, the subdeacon Riculf, reported his superior's unfaithfulness to the royal family. Despite the power and planning of his enemies, Gregory was saved, he claimed, due to popular support and the goodwill of his episcopal colleagues. Riculf later revealed under torture that the real target of the conspiracy had been Fredegund. Once she was removed from power, Clovis, Chilperic's son by another wife, planned to take the throne and promote Leudast to *dux*.[43] As Gregory's experiences attest, conciliar judicial hearings could involve more than trivial intra-ecclesiastical disputes; sometimes high matters of state were determined in the synodal setting.

A third function of church councils was the issuing or confirming of grants and privileges to monastic and clerical foundations, sometimes at the request of a convoking monarch. The Council of Orléans (549), for example, confirmed the foundation and stipulated the protection of a hospice (*xenodochium*) at Lyons endowed by King Childebert I (r. 511–58) and his wife.[44] Similarly, King Guntram requested that the Council of Valence (583/5) confirm those donations that he and his family had made to the basilicas of Saint Marcel at Chalon and Saint Symphorian at Autun.[45] In conjunction with the Council of Paris of 614, King Chlothar II (r. 584–629) issued an edict in which he ordered *iudices* not to disturb properties with immunity.[46] Likewise, the Council of Saint-Jean-de-Losne (673/5) confirmed previously granted monastic privileges,[47] while the Pippinid Council of Ver (755) declared that the immunities of churches had to be respected.[48] These examples are merely a sampling of seventh- and eighth-century councils that granted such privileges.[49]

---

[43] Gregory of Tours *Decem Libri Historiarum* V.48–9.

[44] Orléans (549), c. 15.

[45] Valence (583/5), Conciliar Acts.

[46] Chlothar II *Edictum*, in *Capitularia Regum Francorum*, no. 14. Chlothar also confirmed and granted immunities in his *Praeceptio*, in *Capitularia Regum Francorum*, nos. 11–2.

[47] Saint-Jean-de-Losne (673/5), c. 14.

[48] Ver (755), c. 19.

[49] See also the grant of the Council of Clichy (636/7) to the monastery of Rebais: Fredegar, *Chronica*, MGH SRM II, ed. Bruno Krusch (Hanover: Hahn, 1888), IV.78;

Additionally, surviving seventh- and eighth-century episcopal privileges are likely indicative of actions taken by synods.[50] These documents record the grants of exemptions and privileges to monastic institutions under the names of individual bishops. Like conciliar acts, they are endorsed with episcopal subscriptions.[51] Whether or not these documents reflect conciliar meetings, however, remains contested.[52] Apparent corroborating references to these 'pseudo-synods' are not sure evidence, as the authors of these other sources may have assumed the existence of the meetings based on their knowledge of the subscription lists. Additionally, several of the episcopal subscriptions

Vita Agili Abbatis Resbacensis, AASS Aug. VI, ch. 28. Also, the Councils of Paris and Clichy (653/4) granted privileges to Saint Denis: *Die Urkunden der Merowinger*, ed. Carlrichard Brühl, Theo Kölzer, Martina Hartmann, and Andrea Stieldorf (Hanover: Hahn, 2001), no. 85. The Council of Rouen (688/9), whose veracity has been questioned, may have granted them to Fontenelle: *Vita Ansberti*, MGH SRM V, ed. Bruno Krusch (Hanover: Hahn, 1910), ch. 18. And the Council of Compiegne (757), under the direction of Chrodegang of Metz (712–66), granted them to the monastery at Gorze: *Concilia Aevi Karolini*, ed. Albert Werminghoff, MGH: Legum, sectio III, tomus 2, part 1 (Hanover: Hahn, 1906–8), 59–63.

[50] Eugen Ewig identifies fifteen privileges composed between 637 and 728: Bishop Burgundofaro of Meaux to the Monastary of Rebais (Clichy, 636/7), Audobert of Paris to Saint-Maur-des-Fosses (Unknown, 645), Landricius of Paris to Saint-Denis (Paris, 654), Emmo of Sens to Saint-Colombe (Unknown, 660), Emmo of Sens to Saint-Pierre-le-Vif (Mâlay-le-Roi, 660), Audomarus of Therouanne to Saint-Omer (Sithiu, 663), Numerianus of Trier to Saint-Die (Unknown, 663/75), Berthefridus of Amiens to Corbie (Chatou, 664), Drauscius of Soissons to Notre-Dame in Soissons (Soissons, 667), Aredius of Vaison to Groseaux (Unknown, 683), Aiglibertus of Le Mans to Notre-Dame in Le Mans (Le Mans, 683), Bertoendus of Chalons to Montier-en-Der (Rheims, 692), Privilege to Saint-Colombe (Sens, 695), Agerardus of Chartres to Notre-Dame of Blois (Chatou, 696), Widegernus of Strasbourg to Murbach (Strasbourg, 728). There are additional eighth-century privileges, e.g., Flavigny (719 and 722), but as testaments or *formulae* they do not suggest councils, and Ewig does not count them. On these fifteen privileges, see Eugen Ewig, "Beobachtungen zu den Klosterprivilegien des 7. und frühen 8. Jahrhunderts," in *Spätantikes und fränkisches Gallien*, ed. Hartmut Atsma (Munich: Artemis Verlag, 1979), II.411–26; Eugen Ewig, "Beobachtungen zu den Bischofslisten der merowingischen Konzilien und Bischofsprivilegien," in *Spätantikes und fränkisches Gallien*, ed. Hartmut Atsma (Munich: Artemis Verlag, 1979), II.427–55; Odette Pontal, *Die Synoden im Merowingerreich* (Paderborn, Germany: Ferdinand Schöningh, 1986), 204–12.

[51] Ewig, "Beobachtungen zu den Bischofslisten," 427–55. Charters have been taken as evidence for councils in other parts of the former Roman Empire as well. See, e.g., Cubitt, *Anglo-Saxon Church Councils c. 650–850*, 205–34.

[52] Odette Pontal, who includes these privileges in the original German edition of her *Synoden im Merowingerreich*, chooses to leave them out, with no explanation, in the second French edition. These privilege-meetings are also not included in the most recent German edition of the Gallic councils: Josef Limmer, *Konzilien und Synoden im spätantiken Gallien von 314 bis 696 nach Christi Geburt* (Frankfurt am Main: Peter Lang, 2004).

appended to these charters appear to have been collected after the fact.[53] The weight of the evidence, however, supports the connection between these documents and actual councils. Even if some invitees were unable to attend a meeting, it would have been highly inefficient to have the resulting charter carted about from city to city in order to assemble all of the required subscriptions. Additionally, several of the privileges reveal an attention to the rank order of the subscribing metropolitans.[54] The autograph signatures in the privileges that survive in original copies, e.g., King Clovis II's confirmation of Bishop Landricius of Paris' grant to Saint-Denis (654) and Bishop Agerardus of Chartres' privilege for Notre-Dame of Blois (696), likewise suggest that the documents were signed during meetings.[55] The suggestion that a council may have been invented by concerned beneficiaries who had knowledge of the original privilege-charter does not undermine the likelihood that a meeting of bishops took place to witness the signing of the document. Finally, although the privilege charters are vague about the nature of these meetings, their convocation, scheduling, locations, attendance, and agendas are comparable to those of contemporary synods.[56]

Although the Frankish councils engaged in all of the activities outlined above, it is rare that we can reconstruct a given meeting's entire agenda. In some cases, our total evidence for a council consists of a single canonical record, judicial decision, or privilege-charter. This has led some scholars to distinguish between "legislative," "judicial," and "political" councils.[57] The problem with this classification system is that it assigns councils to artificial, even anachronistic, categories for the convenience of historians. The majority of Frankish councils met with more complex agendas than can be summarized by such vague terms as "legislative," "judicial," or "political." Far preferable to this identification scheme is the classic terminology introduced by Paul Hinschius in the third volume of his immense *Kirchenrecht* (1869–97).

---

[53] Pontal, *Die Synoden im Merowingerreich*, 211–2.

[54] Ewig, "Beobachtungen zu den Bischofslisten," 445–6.

[55] *Chartae Latinae Antiquiores*, ed. Albert Bruckner and Robert Marichal (Olten, Switzerland: Urs Graf Verlag, 1954–2004), vol. 13, nos. 558 and 580.

[56] Ewig, "Beobachtungen zu den Bischofslisten," 439–40 and 451.

[57] See, in this regard, especially Pontal, *Histoire des conciles mérovingiens*. This is ironic, because Pontal herself acknowledges that "rigorous classification" was not pursued in the Early Middle Ages (p. 14). A similar observation can be found in Gaudemet, *Église et cité*, 223–4.

Hinschius identified ecclesiastical councils as either (1) general or ecumenical councils; (2) provincial and plenary councils (i.e., representative bodies of major ecclesiastical units); (3) interprovincial, national, and imperial councils (i.e., representative bodies of ecclesiastical units greater than individual provinces); or (4) diocesan synods.[58] The benefit of the Hinschius classification system is that it does not force a council into a predetermined category that could oversimplify its agenda. Unfortunately, the Hinschius system has not always been consistently applied, which has resulted in confusion in the scholarly tradition.[59] In this book, I employ the Hinschius classifications, as they seem to me the most easily applicable to the Frankish context.

Turning from qualitative to quantitative categorization: How many church councils took place in the Frankish *regnum* from Clovis' first in Orléans in 511 to the accession of Charlemagne to the throne in 768? No two scholars have compiled identical tallies. In most cases, the number hovers between seventy and eighty.[60] I have identified seventy-nine councils as authentic in appendix A. This number does not include those councils whose authenticity has been either contested or invalidated, such as the Councils of Agaune (515/23), Tournai (520), Rheims (ca. 626), and Utrecht (697), which are listed in appendix B. Certainly, councils were held for which no documentary evidence survives. It would stretch credulity to argue that it was mere coincidence that those decades in which Gregory of Tours, the most prolific and detailed narrator of sixth-century life in Gaul, was bishop (573–94) saw the most concentrated conciliar activity in Frankish history. Indeed, twenty-seven percent of the sixty-six Merovingian synods identified by Odette Pontal in her handbook devoted to these councils fall within this period.

[58] Hinschius, *Kirchenrecht*, III.328. On the difficulties of terminological classification in the Carolingian period, see Wilfried Hartmann, "Zu einigen Problemen der karolingischen Konzilsgeschichte," *Annuarium Historiae Conciliorum* 9, no. 1 (1977): 12–15.

[59] For example, in his stimulating history of the Frankish church, J. M. Wallace-Hadrill eschews consistency in labeling councils, and employs, among other terms, "provincial," "local," "national," "regional," and "metropolitical" to identify council types: Wallace-Hadrill, *The Frankish Church*, 94–5.

[60] Pontal, for example, lists sixty-two councils for the Merovingian period in the first edition of *Synoden im Merowingerreich* and sixty-six in the second. Hartmann lists thirteen councils (not including Roman and Italian synods) for the years between 740 and 768 in his *Die Synoden der Karolingerzeit im Frankenreich und in Italien* (Paderborn, Germany: Ferdinand Schöningh, 1989).

It is clear that our knowledge of councils, especially those that issued no surviving legislation, is heavily determined by the quantity and detail of our sources.[61] Partly for this reason, it is sometimes assumed that more church councils were held in the sixth century than in the seventh.[62] In fact, if we take into account the episcopal privileges of the late seventh century, it is clear that there was no considerable drop in conciliar activity in the latter century.[63] Additionally, the councils of the seventh century demonstrate remarkable institutional continuity with those held a century earlier, even if fewer of their canons survive. Their surviving acts reveal no major revolutions in protocol, episcopal representation, or legislative concerns.[64] As in the previous century, conciliar attendees shaped their legislative agendas in accordance with decisions made at earlier meetings, particularly those convoked by the same monarch. This was a particular necessity when a king's territory was composed of several geographically distinct regions, as was sometimes the case in the seventh century. This certainly was true for those councils held under the auspices of Chlothar II—Paris (614), Unknown (ca. 614), and Clichy (626/7)—whose acts demonstrate a coordinated effort to legislate on a common agenda of canonical concerns.[65] Thus, legislative agendas continued to reflect both local concerns and royal interests. As for the geographic representation of the councils of the seventh century, the ever-changing political situation continued to influence the invitation of bishops. For example, the subscription list of the Council of Chalon-sur-Saône (647/53) reflects the political

[61] Wilfried Hartmann, "Konzilien und Geschichtsschreibung in karolingischer Zeit," in *Historiographie im frühen Mittelalter*, ed. Anton Scharer and Georg Scheibelreiter (Vienna: R. Oldenbourg, 1994), 481–98.

[62] See, e.g., the list of councils provided in Pontal, *Histoire des conciles mérovingiens*, 374.

[63] Taking into account the episcopal privileges, eighty-four councils can be identified for the sixth and seventh centuries combined. Roughly thirty-seven of these (forty-four percent) assembled in the seventh century.

[64] For those seventh-century councils with surviving subscription lists, an average of thirty-four bishops attended. Compare this with the data compiled by Champagne and Szramkiewicz, "Recherches sur les conciles des temps mérovingiens," 16. On the legislative agendas of these meetings, see Pontal, *Histoire des conciles mérovingiens*, 205–23.

[65] A similar effort can be seen in the legislative acts of the Councils of Bordeaux (662/75) and Saint-Jean-de-Losne (673/5), both convoked on the orders of Childeric II. On the agendas of the latter two councils, see the observations of Pontal, *Histoire des conciles mérovingiens*, 223; Wood, *The Merovingian Kingdoms*, 229.

unification of Neustria and Burgundy.[66] But political borders were always a factor in determining provincial representation at synods. The seventh century did witness a growing partiality for holding church councils in conjunction with royal assemblies, gatherings collectively known as *concilia mixta*.[67] Although councils continued to meet without royal involvement, the growing popularity of the *concilia mixta* model in the seventh and eighth centuries was a natural outgrowth of the participation of Roman emperors, and later barbarian kings, in conciliar business.

Frankish Councils in Historiographical Tradition

Considering the mass of detail that Gregory of Tours provides on conciliar procedures, it is surprising that those modern scholars who have looked at councils in the Frankish era have focused largely upon those that issued canons, at the expense of those synods known only through

[66] Chalon-sur-Saône (647/53), Subscriptions. On the reflection of political borders in seventh-century subscription lists, see Champagne and Szramkiewicz, "Recherches sur les conciles des temps mérovingiens," 14–5.

[67] On the prominence of this model during the early Pippinid era, see Wilfried Hartmann, "Laien auf Synoden der Karolingerzeit," *Annuarium Historiae Conciliorum* 10, no. 2 (1978): 257. In this era, synods become increasingly indistinguishable from the ecclesiastical division of the royal assembly. This problem is partially terminological, as it is often difficult to tell from a given literary context whether the word *synodus* is referring to a church council, a royal assembly, or an ecclesiastical division of said assembly. On the difficulty of distinguishing between these references, as well as the blending of institutions, see Brunner, *Deutsche Rechtsgeschichte*, II.424–5; Erich Seyfarth, *Fränkische Reichsversammlungen unter Karl dem Grossen und Ludwig dem Frommen* (Borna-Leipzig: Buchdruckerei Robert Noske, 1910), 1–10; François Louis Ganshof, "The Church and the Royal Power in the Frankish Monarchy under Pippin III and Charlemagne," in *The Carolingians and the Frankish Monarchy: Studies in Carolingian History*, trans. Janet Sondheimer (Ithaca, NY: Cornell University Press, 1971), 207; Jean Imbert, "Le pouvoir législatif dans l'Eglise carolingienne," *L'année canonique* 17 (1973): 592; Hartmann, "Zu einigen Problemen der karolingischen Konzilsgeschichte," 13–4; Hartmann, "La transmission et l'influence du droit synodal carolingien," 486; Hartmann, *Die Synoden der Karolingerzeit*, 5; Jean Imbert, *Les temps carolingiens: L'Église les institutions* (Paris: Editions Cujas, 1994), I.134; Philippe Depreux, "L'expression statutum est a domno rege et sancta synodo annonçant certains dispositions du capitulaire Francfort (794)," in *Das Frankfurter Konzil von 794: Kristallisationspunkt karolingischer Kultur*, ed. Rainer Berndt (Mainz, Germany: Selbstverlag der Gesellschaft für Mittelrheinische Kirchengeschichte, 1997), 87–92; Mayke De Jong, "Charlemagne's Church," in *Charlemagne: Empire and Society*, ed. Joanna Story (Manchester: Manchester University Press, 2005), 109–10. See also Edgar Loening, who distinguishes Merovingian national councils from *concilia mixta*: Loening, *Geschichte des deutschen Kirchenrechts*, II. 138–43.

auxiliary sources, such as narrative histories, chronicles, charters, and hagiographies. This was not always the case. During the classical period of conciliar studies, which stretched from Jacques Merlin's first collection of 1524 through the publication of Giovanni Domenico Mansi's thirty-one-volume *Sacrorum Conciliorum Nova et Amplissima Collectio* between the years of 1759 and 1798, the primary objective of scholars such as Jacques Sirmond (pub. 1629), Philippe Labbe and Gabriel Crossart (pub. 1671–2), Jean Hardouin (pub. 1714–5), and Nicola Coleti (pub. 1728–33) was to locate any and all references to ecclesiastical councils in the manuscripts of European libraries.[68] The fruits of their labors—more than a dozen mammoth, multivolume compilations—were published between the sixteenth century and the eighteenth century.[69]

Mansi's compilation of the councils embodies both the successes and shortcomings of this long-term project. Mansi lists more Frankish councils than any previous (or subsequent) compilation. Unfortunately, the level of critical scholarship in his edition is not up to modern standards, and a number of the councils that he presents as authentic have been dismissed as creative anachronisms by subsequent editors and scholars. Still, the frequent citation of Mansi by modern historians is indicative of breadth of his collection, despite the publication of modern critical editions and translations of Catholic church councils.

Beginning with the publication of Friedrich Maassen's *Concilia aevi Merovingici* in 1893, and Albert Werminghoff's *Concilia aevi Karolini* in 1906, both as part of the ongoing *Monumenta Germaniae Historica* project, a heretofore-unprecedented emphasis was placed by scholars on the canonical *acta* of the Gallic councils, which for the first time were available in accessible and reliable critical editions. Although both Maassen and Werminghoff included relevant excerpts from narrative, hagiographical, and diplomatic sources, these references were relatively sparse when compared with those cited by Mansi. This new emphasis on the conciliar acts themselves encouraged the publication of what remains the classic survey of Frankish religious legislation, Charles de

[68] On the history of Mansi and his predecessors, see Henri Quentin, *Jean-Dominique Mansi et les grandes collections conciliaires* (Paris: E. Leroux, 1900). A short but useful synopsis also can also be found in Richard Kay, "Mansi and Rouen: A Critique of the Conciliar Collections," *The Catholic Historical Review* 52, no. 2 (1966): 155–8. Both Quentin and Kay reject the notion that these early collections were essentially complete and reliable.

[69] On the relevant compilations, see Pontal, *Histoire des conciles mérovingiens*, 28–9.

Clercq's *La législation religieuse franque de Clovis à Charlemagne* (1936), which examined canonical legislation in conjunction with royal edicts and monastic rules. De Clercq took a chronological approach to his sources, providing for each council both a discussion of its historical context, as well as a detailed analysis of the canons.[70] Since the publication of de Clercq's book in 1936, other scholars, supported by the critical editions of the *MGH*, the *Corpus Christianorum*, the *Sources Chrétiennes*, and other series, have looked in detail at a variety of topics of interest to the Frankish legislators, such as liturgy,[71] political theology,[72] property rights,[73] social welfare,[74] Jewish policy,[75] the survival of paganism,[76] and other assorted issues.[77] This ongoing interest in the legislative decrees of the Frankish councils is due, in no small

[70] De Clercq, *La législation religieuse franque*, 1–155.

[71] Matthieu Smyth, "Les canons conciliaires de la Gaule, témoins des responsabilités liturgiques épiscopales en Occident," *Revue de droit canonique* 49, no. 2 (1999): 259–77.

[72] Aloys Suntrup, *Studien zur politischen Theologie im frühmittelalterlichen Okzident* (Münster: Ascherendorff, 2001).

[73] M. R. Mayeux, "Les biens de l'Eglise considérés comme patrimoine des pauvres à travers les conciles occidentaux du VIe siècle," in *Inspiration religieuse et structures temporelles* (Paris: Les Éditions Ouvrières, 1948), 139–209; Elisabeth Magnou-Nortier, "A propos des rapports entre l'Eglise et l'etat franc: La lettre synodale au Roi Théodebert (535)," in *Societa, Istituzioni, Spiritualita: Studi in Onore di Cinzio Violante*, vol. 1 (Spoleto: Centro Italiano di Studi Sull'alto Medioevo, 1994), 519–34.

[74] Mayeux, "Les biens de l'Eglise considérés comme patrimoine des pauvres," 139–209; Walter Ullmann, "Public Welfare and Social Legislation in the Early Medieval Councils," *Studies in Church History* 7 (1971): 1–39.

[75] Bernard Bachrach, *Early Medieval Jewish Policy* (Minneapolis: University of Minnesota Press, 1977), 44–65; Walter Pakter, "Les esclaves chrétiens des juifs: Troisième Concile d'Orléans (538)," *Archives Juives* 21, nos. 1–2 (1985): 3–4; Paul Mikat, *Die Judengesetzgebung der merowingisch-fränkischen Konzilien* (Opladen, Germany: Westdeutscher Verlag, 1995); Friedrich Lotter, "La crainte du prosélytisme et la peur du contact: Les juifs dans les actes des synodes mérovingiens," in *Clovis: Histoire et mémoire*, ed. Michel Rouche (Paris: Presses de l'Université de Paris-Sorbonne, 1997), 849–79; Christof Geisel, *Die Juden im Frankenreich* (Frankfurt am Main: Peter Lang, 1998), 98–230.

[76] E. J. Jonkers, "Die Konzile und einige Formen alten Volksglaubens im fünften und sechsten Jahrhundert," *Vigiliae Christianae* 22, no. 1 (1968): 49–53; Odette Pontal, "Survivances païennes, superstitions et sorcellerie au Moyen Age d'après les décrets des conciles et synodes," *Annuarium Historiae Conciliorum* 27/8 (1995–6): 129–36.

[77] Brigitte Basdevant-Gaudemet, "L'évêque, d'après la législation de quelques conciles mérovingiens," in *Clovis: Histoire et mémoire*, ed. Michel Rouche (Paris: Presses de l'Université de Paris-Sorbonne, 1997), 471–94; Brigitte Basdevant-Gaudemet, "La Bible dans les canons des conciles mérovingiens, " in *Bibel und Recht: Rechtshistorisches Kolloquium 9–13. Juni 1992*, ed. Jörn Eckert, Hans Hattenhauer, and Brigitte Basdevant-Gaudemet (Frankfurt: P. Lang, 1994), 51–67; Jean Gaudemet, "A propos du C. 12 du Concile de Mâcon (1er Novembre 583)," *Mémoires de la Société pour l'histoire du droit*

part, to their usefulness as indicators of the beliefs and policies of the ecclesiastical elite. Although we may not always be able to assume their enforcement, the canons certainly offer invaluable insight into the minds of their authors and the historical contexts in which they formulated their policies.

At the same time that the first modern critical editions of the Frankish councils were going to press, the traditional method of conciliar scholarship, in the mode of Mansi and his predecessors, gave a final glorious gasp in the form of Karl Joseph Von Hefele's *Conciliengeschichte* (1873–90), which remains a useful source of information about individual councils.[78] Also available in an English edition and in an expanded French edition,[79] Hefele's work proposed to trace ecclesiastical conciliar history from its very beginnings, providing transcriptions and summaries of the conciliar records of all known councils in both the eastern and western halves of the former Roman Empire. Although monumental in its breadth, Hefele's work nevertheless has been justly criticized for its lack of critical analysis.[80] This problem was partially rectified in the French edition (1907–52) by its editor, Henri Leclercq, who buttressed the series' scholarly apparatus with additional citations, a bibliography, and a critical discussion of the dating, locations, and authenticity of individual councils. Still, because of its age, the information contained in Hefele's survey can never be assumed to reflect the current *status questionis* for a given synod.

Even those nineteenth- and early-twentieth-century scholars who took a more consciously critical approach than Hefele and his continuators to the Frankish councils were hampered in their efforts by their

---

et des institutions des anciens pays bourguignons comtois et romands 13 (1950/1): 277–82; Paul Mikat, *Die Inzestverbote des Dritten Konzils von Orléans (538): Ein Beitrag zur Geschichte des Frankischen Eherechts* (Opladen, Germany: Westdeutscher Verlag, 1993); Mikat, *Die Inzestgesetzgebung der merowingisch-fränkischen Konzilien (511–626/27)*; Catherine R. Peyroux, "Canonists Construct the Nun: Church Law and Women's Monastic Practice in Merovingian France," in *Law, Society, and Authority in Late Antiquity*, ed. Ralph Mathisen (Oxford: Oxford University Press, 2001), 242–55.

[78] On the uncritical approach of Hefele and his continuators toward Mansi's corpus, see Kay, "Mansi and Rouen: A Critique of the Conciliar Collections," 157–8.

[79] Karl Joseph Von Hefele, *Conciliengeschichte* (Freiburg im Breisgau: Herder, 1873–90). English edition: *A History of the Councils of the Church*, trans. William R. Clark (Edinburgh: T. and T. Clark, 1883–96); French edition: *Histoire des conciles d'après les documents originaux*, trans. H. Leclercq (Paris: Letouzey et Ané, 1909).

[80] See, e.g., Richard Kay, review of *Histoire des conciles mérovingiens*, by Odette Pontal, *Speculum* 67, no. 4 (1992): 1030–2.

reliance on the Mansian corpus.[81] The foremost among these were the prodigious turn-of-the-century German legal and ecclesiastical historians Edgar Loening, Paul Hinschius, Heinrich Brunner, and Albert Hauck.[82] In an important shift in focus, these scholars concerned themselves less with individual councils and their legislation than with defining their collective role vis-à-vis a Frankish *Landeskirche*.[83] In particular, the related issues of royal involvement in conciliar life and the legal status of synodal canons dominated their discussions. But the most important contribution of this group effort was to shift the focus away from conciliar canons and back to the councils themselves.

Unfortunately, only a few twentieth-century historians followed in their wake. The most important successor to this group was Hans Barion, whose *Das fränkisch-deutsche Synodalrecht des Frühmittelalters* (1931) remained the only book-length study of the Frankish councils until the publication of *Die Synoden im Merowingerreich* by Odette Pontal in 1986. Barion's monograph, whose scope includes the post-Carolingian German councils, is rarely cited today beyond a handful of specialists. Adopting the prevailing German framework of a Frankish national church, Barion argued that royal synods would have been necessary regardless of Clovis' decision to convoke the Council of Orléans in 511.[84] The Merovingian kings, according to Barion, did not govern the church directly; rather, they allowed the Gallic bishops to do so through the institution of national synods.[85] Barion argued that these councils took over those functions that the monarchy was unwilling or unable to perform, but with royal approval.[86] Kings could put the power of the royal

[81] Kay, "Mansi and Rouen: A Critique of the Conciliar Collections," 159.

[82] Edgar Loening, *Geschichte des deutschen Kirchenrechts* (Strasbourg: Verlag Karl J. Trübner, 1878); Paul Hinschius, *Kirchenrecht* (Berlin: I. Guttentag, 1869–97); Heinrich Brunner, *Deutsche Rechtsgeschichte*, 2nd ed. (Munich: Duncker and Humblot, 1906–28); Albert Hauck, *Kirchengeschichte Deutschlands*, 8th ed. (Berlin: Akademie Verlag, 1954). One can also include in this group Rudolph Sohm, *Kirchenrecht* (Leipzig and Munich: Verlag von Duncker and Humblot, 1892–1923).

[83] The paradigm of a Frankish *Landeskirche* is also adopted by, among others, Richard Weyl, *Das fränkische Staatskirchenrecht zur Zeit der Merovinger* (Breslau: Verlag von Wilhelm Keobner, 1888; reprint, Aalen, Germany: Scientia Verlag, 1970); Hans von Schubert, *Staat und Kirche in den arianischen Königreichen und im Reiche Chlodwigs* (Munich and Berlin: Druck und Verlag von R. Oldenbourg, 1912); Karl Voigt, *Staat und Kirche von Konstantin dem Grossen bis zum Ende der Karolingerzeit* (Stuttgart: W. Kohlhammer, 1936); and recently Sieben, *Die Konzilsidee in der Alten Kirche*, 501–10.

[84] Barion, *Das fränkisch-deutsche Synodalrecht*, 201–2.

[85] Ibid., 233.

[86] Ibid., 251–2.

government behind canons, but they could not take away their ecclesiastical authority.[87] Barion's arguments have not ended the debate on royal involvement in Frankish councils. Some scholars have argued that the participation of the kings largely ended with their convocation of the councils, or at the very least that they usually chose not to concern themselves directly with issues of church discipline or dogma.[88] Others have held that royal involvement depended heavily upon the specific circumstances and issues at hand.[89] Still others have stressed the monarchy's role in confirming conciliar canons, thereby bestowing their presumed legal force.[90] One recent scholar has even suggested that the Frankish kings were so deeply involved in the legislative process that conciliar and secular law cannot easily be distinguished in the sixth century.[91]

With the exception of a few shorter studies, the most influential of which is discussed later, Barion's book remained the last word on the Frankish councils as an institution until the inauguration of Walter Brandmüller's *Konziliengeschichte* series fifty years later. Intended to supplant the work of Hefele and Leclercq, the relevant volumes are *Die Synoden im Merowingerreich* by Odette Pontal (1986) and *Die Synoden der Karolingerzeit im Frankenreich und in Italien* by Wilfried Hartmann (1989). Both handbooks update Hefele and Leclercq by summarizing the ongoing debates, usually involving dating or authenticity, surrounding individual councils. They also survey the legislation produced by those councils whose acts survive. Hartmann was the natural choice to compose the Carolingian volume, having already published a plethora of revealing shorter studies on the topic.[92] Pontal was a less obvious

---

[87] Ibid., 245–6.

[88] Duchesne, *L'Eglise au VI siècle*, 528; Basdevant-Gaudemet, "Les évêques, les papes, et les princes," 7; Pontal, *Histoire des conciles mérovingiens*, 252.

[89] DeClercq, *La législation religieuse franque de Clovis à Charlemagne*, 6, 99, 104; Eugen Ewig, *Die Merowinger und das Frankenreich* (Stuttgart: W. Kohlhammer, 1988), 104–5; Pontal, *Histoire des conciles mérovingiens*, 299, 300–1.

[90] See, e.g. Hinschius, *Kirchenrecht*, III.542–3; Weyl, *Das fränkische Staatskirchenrecht*, 21–5; Barion, *Das fränkisch-deutsche Synodalrecht*, 233–52; Ewig, *Die Merowinger und das Frankenreich*, 104–5; Gaudemet, *Église et cité*, 156; Olivier Guillot, "La justice dans le royaume franc à l'epoque mérovingienne," *Settimane di Studio del Centro Italiano di Studi Sull'Alto Medioevo* 42, no. 2 (1994): 662 ff. Karl Voigt, in contrast, has argued that the Merovingian kings did not so much confirm the decisions of councils as use them for precedents in issuing their own legislation: *Staat und Kirche*, 250–4.

[91] Wood, *The Merovingian Kingdoms*, 106; Ian Wood, "Incest, Law, and the Bible in Sixth-Century Gaul," *Early Medieval Europe* 7, no. 3 (1998): 293.

[92] He was also the editor of the third (and eventually fourth) volume of the Monumenta Germaniae Historica's edition of the Carolingian councils: *Die Konzilien*

selection, as her previous work had focused on French synods of a later period. Nevertheless, her book, which subsequently was translated into French as *Histoire des conciles mérovingiens*, quickly became a standard work. Many of Pontal's conclusions are indeed insightful, in particular her argument that the Gallic bishops were dealing in their councils with real worries that affected their church and their society.[93] She asserts that to see conciliar legislation as somehow isolated from social realities would be to misunderstand entirely the function of the Frankish councils. This is an argument I elaborate upon in this study.

Although Barion's, Pontal's, and Hartmann's works are the only book-length studies of the Frankish councils as an institution, there are a small number of important shorter studies, several of them focusing on the surviving canonical record subscription lists.[94] The most important of these is J. Champagne and R. Szramkiewicz's "Recherches sur les conciles des temps mérovingiens" (1971), which took the first truly systematic quantitative approach to the conciliar evidence. The authors tallied, among other things, the level of participation in the twenty-two interprovincial synods with subscription lists that were held between the years 511 and 695, the attendance of metropolitan bishops at these councils, and the most heavily represented provinces during the course of this period. Thanks to Champagne and Szramkiewicz's work, we now can evaluate with greater accuracy the comparative size of a given council and the character of its participants. Some have already taken their lead, and applied similar methods to particular regions of Francia.[95] Nevertheless, the selectivity of

der Karolingischen Teilreiche, 843–859, ed. Wilfried Hartmann, MGH: Legum, Sectio III, Tomus 3 (Hanover: Hahn, 1984); *Die Konzilien der Karolingischen Teilreiche, 860–874*, ed. Wilfried Hartmann, MGH: Legum, Sectio III, Tomus 4 (Hanover: Hahn, 1998).

[93] Pontal, *Histoire des conciles mérovingiens*, 305. For a similar conclusion, see Roger Collins, "Law and Ethnic Identity in the Western Kingdoms in the Fifth and Sixth Centuries," in *Medieval Europeans*, ed. Alfred P. Smyth (New York: St. Martin's Press, 1998), 17.

[94] See, e.g., Woldemar Lippert, "Die Verfasserschaft der Canon gallischer Concilien des V. und VI. Jahrhunderts," *Neues Archiv der Gesellschaft für ältere deutsche Geschichtskunde* 14 (1889): 9–58; Bertold Bretholz, "Die Unterschriften den gallischen Concilien des 6. und 7. Jahrhunderts," *Neues Archiv der Gesellschaft für ältere deutsche Geschichtskunde* 18 (1892): 529–47; Champagne and Szramkiewicz, "Recherches sur les conciles des temps mérovingiens," 5–49; Ralph Mathisen, "Episcopal Hierarchy and Tenure in Office in Late Roman Gaul: A Method for Establishing Dates of Ordination," *Francia* 17/1 (1990): 125–40.

[95] See, e.g., Fabienne Cardot, *L'espace et le pouvoir: Étude sur l'Austrasie mérovingienne* (Paris: Publications de la Sorbonne, 1987), 142–7 (especially chart on p. 147).

Champagne and Szramkiewicz's test group, which excludes the dozens of councils whose acts either do not survive or never existed, should make one wary about applying their findings without qualification.

Along with the aforementioned studies of conciliar legislation and institutional history, a number of scholars, particularly continental historians, have looked closely at the procedures by which this legislation was collected and disseminated through canonical collections and ultimately became part of medieval canon law. The fruits of their labors have taken the form of narrative histories, studies of individual collections, and manuscript bibliographies. The classic work in the first category remains Paul Fournier and Gabriel Le Bras' *Histoire des collections canoniques en Occident* (1931), which traces in two volumes the history of canonical collections up through the compilation of Gratian's *Decretum* (ca. 1140).[96] Although much work has been done on individual collections since their book's publication,[97] many of Fournier and Le Bras' general conclusions, such as their observation that Gallic canonical manuscript production began shifting northward in the latter half of the sixth century, continue to mark, with some modifications, the state of the question.[98]

Among the numerous works in the second category, Hubert Mordek's *Kirchenrecht und Reform im Frankenreich: Die Collectio Vetus Gallica, die älteste systematische Kanonessammlung des fränkischen Gallien* (1975) is arguably the most significant contribution to the study of canonical collections in the past half century.[99] Ostensibly an edition of and commentary on the influential anthology known as the *Vetus Gallica*, Mordek's study offers a wealth of information on the compilation of canonical collections during the Merovingian period. Although Mordek is not greatly concerned with church councils per se, his work is arguably the most successful to date in demonstrating how conciliar legislation was preserved, disseminated, and eventually turned into

[96] Paul Fournier and Gabriel Le Bras, *Histoire des collections canoniques en occident depuis les Fausses Décrétales jusqu'au Décret de Gratien* (Paris: Recueil Sirey, 1931).

[97] An up-to-date bibliography of these shorter studies can be found in Lotte Kéry, ed., *Canonical Collections of the Early Middle Ages (ca. 400–1140)* (Washington, DC: The Catholic University of America Press, 1999).

[98] Fournier and Le Bras, *Histoire des collections canoniques en Occident*, I.44.

[99] Hubert Mordek, *Kirchenrecht und Reform im Frankenreich: Die Collectio Vetus Gallica, die älteste systematische Kanonessammlung des fränkischen Gallien* (Berlin: Walter de Gruyter, 1975). For a summary of Mordek's findings concerning the *Vetus Gallica*, see also Hubert Mordek, "Die Collectio Vetus Gallica, die älteste systematische Kanonensammlung des fränkischen Gallien," *Francia* 1 (1973): 45–61.

legal precedent for future councils, an issue too often glossed over by scholars of canonical collection production.[100] Mordek, additionally, traces how this single collection went through a series of redactions and proved enormously popular for a local anthology, thus ensuring the dissemination of those conciliar decisions contained within its pages.[101]

Among the works in the third category,[102] Friedrich Maassen's *Geschichte der Quellen und der Literatur des canonischen Rechts* (1870) still holds a place of considerable prominence.[103] Unlike *Histoire des collections canoniques en Occident*, it provides detailed information on the contents of canonical compilations, making it a crucial source for those interested in the transmission of any given council's decisions. Although Maassen's byzantine organization scheme, with its layers of cross-references, makes his book difficult to use, his work remains the best source for information on individual collections, short of the original manuscripts. Maassen's work has recently been complemented, although not superseded, by Lotte Kéry's extremely valuable *Canonical Collections of the Early Middle Ages* (1999), which contains more up-to-date bibliographical and manuscript information on individual canonical collections. Kéry, however, does not include any details on

---

[100] See also Wilfried Hartmann, "Die Konzilien in der vorgratianischen Zeit des Kirchenrechts," in *Proceedings of the Ninth International Congress of Medieval Canons Law*, ed. Peter Landau and Joers Mueller (Vatican City: Biblioteca Apostolica Vaticana, 1997), 259–86; Wilfried Hartmann, "La transmission et l'influence du droit synodal carolingien," *Revue historique de droit français et étranger* 63 (1985): 483–97. A few scholars have also looked in detail at Gratian's inclusion of Gallic councils in his *Decretum*: Yves Le Roy, "Les conciles gaulois et le Décret de Gratien," *Revue historique de droit français et étranger* 62 (1984: 553–75; Isolde Schröder, "Zur Rezeption merowingischer Konzilskanones bei Gratian," in *Papsttum, Kirche und Recht im Mittelalter: Festschrift für Horst Fuhrmann zum 65. Geburtstag*, ed. Hubert Mordek (Tübingen, Germany: Max Niemeyer, 1991), 233–50.

[101] Additionally, Mordek has demonstrated both here and elsewhere the role that canonical collections played in the context of individual church councils: *Kirchenrecht und Reform im Frankenreich*, 66–70 (re the Council of Clichy); "Bischofsabsetzung in spätmerowingischer Zeit: Justelliana, Bernensis, und das Konzil von Mâlay (677)," in *Papsttum, Kirche und Recht im Mittelalter: Festschrift für Horst Fuhrmann zum 65. Geburtstag*, ed. Hubert Mordek (Tübingen, Germany: Max Niemeyer, 1991), 31–53.

[102] Other useful bibliographic works on canonical collections are Alphonse Van Hove's *Prolegomena*, Commentum Lovaniense in Codicem Iuris Canonici, vol. I, tom. I (Mechelen: H. Dessain, 1945) and Alphonso Stickler's *Historia Iuris Canonici Latini* (Torino: Pontificium Athenaeum Salesianum, 1950), both of which provide brief descriptions of the major collections.

[103] Friedrich Maassen, *Geschichte der Quellen und der Literatur des canonischen Rechts* (Graz: Akademische Druck-U. Verlagsanstalt, 1870).

the contents of these collections. This lacuna has been addressed in part by a software database of the contents of systematic canonical collections compiled by Linda Fowler-Magerl, *Clavis Canonum: Selected Canon Law Collections Before 1140* (2005), the organization of which improves considerably upon Maassen's difficult reference book.[104]

The great mass of scholarship that has been done in the past century on Gallic conciliar legislation and canonical collections is due in no small part to the desire of scholars to explain the origins of medieval canon law. As important as this project is, it does not focus enough attention on the institution itself that served as the foundation for later developments. Unlike the Carolingian era, which has benefited greatly from the copious penetrating studies of Hartmann in particular, the Merovingian and early Pippinid periods have lacked the sustained attention of any one scholar since the early twentieth century.

An Institutional Approach

The purpose of this book is to examine the history of Frankish councils from the reign of King Clovis I to the ascension of Charlemagne to the throne in AD 768, a period marked by fundamental institutional continuity. The political transformations of Late Antiquity undeniably affected Frankish conciliar life. However, the heavy emphasis placed by the episcopate upon tradition, combined with the desire of the Frankish monarchs to imitate their imperial predecessors, encouraged the endurance of traditional practices. Institutional and legislative innovations did take place between the reigns of Clovis and Charlemagne, but to focus only on them would obscure the larger picture: most of the major transformations in synodal life in Frankish Gaul were not abrupt developments, but rather lengthy processes that grew directly out of a common Roman heritage.

Continuities, therefore, are stressed in this study. But although the Frankish council was an institution with firm roots in the Roman past, individual meetings were uniquely influenced by the physical, political, and social realities of contemporary life. This means that it is impossible to understand or interpret canonical pronouncements apart from the immediate historical contexts that necessitated their

---

[104] Linda Fowler-Magerl, *Clavis Canonum: Selected Canon Law Collections Before 1140* (Hanover: Hahn, 2005).

enactment. For this reason, the sources for this study consist not simply of the canons themselves, but also contemporary or near-contemporary narrative histories, hagiographies, epistles, capitularies, formularies, and charters, some of which have been underutilized in examining conciliar history. I discuss these sources, their difficulties, and their insights, in chapter 1.

Among the meetings examined in this study are those councils that took place in Gaul in the decades immediately following the establishment of the *regnum Francorum,* but in territory not yet conquered by the Merovingians, i.e., Burgundy and Provence. This decision is warranted by the fact that both the Burgundian synods and those held under the auspices of Caesarius of Arles, met, like their Frankish counterparts, in accordance with Gallo-Roman tradition. Additionally, many of their decisions were later subsumed in Frankish canonical custom, thereby ensuring their close relation to Frankish legislative norms. The one exception to this policy is the Visigothic Council of Narbonne of 589, which took place at a time when the Visigoths were already on the way to developing an independent conciliar tradition.[105]

Geography and politics deeply informed conciliar business in the Frankish kingdoms. And the physical world—in all of its complexity and diversity—also influenced the protocol of conciliar convocation, travel arrangements, and rules of order, as well as the publication and dissemination of canonical decisions. Chapter 2 of this study situates the Frankish councils within their physical environment, thereby emphasizing both their connection to the world outside the meeting hall, as well as the amount of planning, time, and hardships that participating bishops had to endure for the sake of gathering with their brethren. Such an exertion of effort is highly suggestive of the

[105] The Visigothic councils of Toledo have received more scholarly attention as an institution than those of Francia. For the most recent interpretation of their history, see Rachel Stocking, *Bishops, Councils, and Consensus in the Visigothic Kingdom* (Ann Arbor: University of Michigan Press, 2000). The relevant *Konziliengeschichte* volume, however, contains the most thorough analysis of these synods: José Orlandis and Domingo Ramos-Lissón, *Die Synoden auf der Iberischen Halbinsel biz zum Einbruch des Islam (711)* (Paderborn, Germany: Ferdinand Schöningh, 1981). Although the Visigothic councils, like the Frankish synods, had Roman origins, they developed into a distinct institution by the middle of the seventh century. Furthermore, as Edward James, "Septimania and its Frontier: An Archaeological Approach," in *Visigothic Spain: New Approaches*, ed. Edward James (Oxford: Clarendon Press, 1980), 223–41, has shown, there also was in Southern Gaul a "political polarization between Frank and Visigoth (or, more pertinently, between Aquitanian and Septimanian)" (241).

importance of conciliar activities for the Frankish episcopate. Although the evidence that I present in this chapter is drawn from a broad geographic and chronological context, I have made no attempt to reconstruct a composite (and consequently fictional) "Ur-council."

Although one of this study's major themes is institutional continuity, this is in no way meant to deny the extraordinary legislative innovation that went on during this period, despite the predominance of a handful of frequent issues of discussion. Chapter 3 offers evidence that the repetition of similar concerns by the Frankish councils over the course of the sixth, seventh, and eighth centuries is not indicative of a detachment from contemporary realities. On the contrary, conciliar concerns were not static at all, and were inseparably tied to real-world concerns. This becomes apparent in a case study of what was one of the most worldly of the Frankish councils' concerns: the protection of church property. Other legislative issues—such as the councils' anxiety over the status of Jews in the Frankish kingdoms—reveal a similar willingness to innovate when previous measures have proven to be ineffective.

Chapter 4 addresses the enforcement of conciliar legislation. Manuscripts and other evidence suggest that Gallic clerics and laymen had a reasonable understanding of canonical expectations. However, whether their behavior reflected this understanding is a question that we can answer only rarely, and arguably one that distracts us from the more important question of the legality of canonical legislation in the Frankish kingdoms. Ecclesiastical and secular sources alike reveal that conciliar canons were considered to be enforceable prescriptive rules during the Merovingian period, although they were not considered identical with secular *leges*.[106] This status quo began to change in the middle of the eighth century, when the introduction of royal capitularies as the primary method of disseminating canons rendered previous distinctions between ecclesiastical and secular law obsolete. This process culminated in the reign of Charlemagne, by which time the *Rex Francorum* had became the primary legislator for his church.

Chapter 5 reevaluates the place of the Frankish councils within the greater context of the development of medieval canon law. Between the sixth and twelfth centuries, the Frankish canons were copied into

[106] On conciliar canons as prescriptive declarations, see Judith Evans Grubbs, *Law and Family in Late Antiquity: The Emperor Constantine's Marriage Legislation* (Oxford: Clarendon Press, 1995), 77–8.

a plethora of local canonical collections, which, in turn, influenced the compilation of additional collections and conciliar decisions.[107] However, with the compilation of Gratian's *Concordia Discordantium Canonum*,[108] canon law achieved a hitherto-unrealized form and stability. In chapter 5, I examine both the processes by which conciliar canons were transcribed, compiled, and disseminated in canonical collections, and the extent to which their authors saw them as part of a larger body of ecclesiastical law. The Frankish canons, in fact, maintained their authoritative force for canon lawyers of the High Middle Ages, who were separated by centuries from the time of composition. These lawyers included many of these canons in their own compilations of canon law, but the price of survival was the loss (or radical change) of original authorial intent.

This study concludes in chapter 6 with a discussion of institutional continuity and change in conciliar practices over the course of the sixth, seventh, and eighth centuries. Despite important institutional and legislative innovations between 511 and 768, the prevailing continuities necessitate looking at this period as a unified epoch. Frankish councils certainly adapted as circumstances warranted, but even their transformative experiences took place in the context of their Gallo-Roman origins.

Conciliar evidence has been, and continues to be, heavily mined for evidence by scholars of the Frankish kingdoms. However, it is impossible to adequately evaluate this material unless we first understand the institution and individuals who fashioned it. The council also stood at the center of the complex relationship between the Frankish monarchy and the church; the methods by which the council took account of the interests of both parties, thereby providing a forum for compromise, are arguably as important as the decisions themselves. In returning the focus of conciliar studies to the source of the legislation, we can better understand both the canons themselves and the society that produced them.

---

[107] According to Schröder, "Zur Rezeption merowingischer Konzilskanones bei Gratian," 233–4, 174 out of 504 Merovingian-era canons were transcribed into important canonical collections. Some 51 of these canons were included in Gratian's *Decretum*. Thus, "more than a tenth of the [Merovingian] conciliar decisions became part of the *Corpus Iuris Canonici*." C.f. Pontal, who counts 44 Merovingian canons in the *Corpus Iuris Canonici*, not including those from pseudo-councils: *Histoire des conciles mérovingiens*, 305.

[108] On the compositional history of Gratian's *Decretum*, see Anders Winroth, *The Making of Gratian's Decretum* (Cambridge: Cambridge University Press, 2000). Winroth demonstrates that the *Decretum* was composed in two distinct stages, both completed between the years 1139 and 1158.

CHAPTER 1

SOURCES OF CONCILIAR HISTORY

Editions

In the most recent Latin edition of the Merovingian councils, the entire documentary yield of these meetings fills a mere 326 pages.[1] Among the documents included are canonical *acta,* judicial decisions, and epistles. However, even those councils whose acts survive are not represented in the edition by their entire written output. Some lack subscription lists, others a record of their judicial decisions, and still others their convocation letters.[2] Although the documents that do survive allow us to infer the existence of some of those that have been lost, the incomplete nature of the surviving Frankish conciliar corpus is regrettable. Still, the evidence that does survive is not insignificant, and arguably not sufficiently appreciated for its quantity and variety. Therefore, before embarking on an examination of the institutional modus operandi of the Frankish councils, we ought first to survey this surviving evidence in all of its diversity in order to appreciate both its value and its deficiencies.

Modern scholars who reference the Frankish councils largely derive their source material from one of the modern editions and translations that began to appear in the late nineteenth century. Most of these were published as volumes in larger series, such as the *Monumenta Germaniae Historica*, the *Corpus Christianorum*, and the *Sources Chrétiennes*, and concentrated on the literary products of the councils themselves rather than secondary references to their activities.[3]

---

[1] I.e., Charles de Clercq, ed., *Concilia Galliae: A.511–A.695*, CCSL 148A (Turnhout, Belgium: Brepols, 1963).

[2] Gunther Gottlieb, "Die formalen Bestandteile in der Überlieferung der gallischen Konzilien des 4. und 5. Jahrhunderts," *Annuarium Historiae Conciliorum* 16, no. 2 (1984): 254–5.

[3] Along with the Latin editions of Maassen, Werminghoff, and De Clercq, there have been two modern translations of the Merovingian-era councils: Jean Gaudemet and Brigitte Basdevant-Gaudemet, eds., *Les canons des conciles mérovingiens (VIe–VIIe siècles)*, SC 353–4 (Paris: Editions du Cerf, 1989); and Limmer, ed., *Konzilien und Synoden im spätantiken Gallien von 314 bis 696 nach Christi Geburt.*

The first two of these editions—Friedrich Maassen's *Concilia aevi Merovingici* (1893) and Albert Werminghoff's *Concilia aevi Karolini* (1906)—contained fifty-four and ten councils, respectively, from the period under examination (511–768).[4] Neither volume included all of those synods found in Mansi's collection, nor all secondary references to conciliar proceedings. For example, there is an apparent reference in the Carolingian Third Continuation of Fredegar's *Chronica* to a council of bishops and priests that met in Bourges during the reign of King Pippin I.[5] The context of this reference makes it difficult to say whether *consilio* indicates a conciliar meeting. Pippin may have simply spent his Christmas holidays in Bourges "on the advice of his bishops and priests."[6] Mansi, however, includes a Council of Bourges (767–8) in his collection.[7] Werminghoff does not. In a similar case, Mansi interprets subscriptions to the papal synod of 680 as evidence of a Frankish council the previous year: "Felix humilis episcopus Arelatensis, legatus venerabilis synodi per Galliarum provincias constitutae."[8] It has been suggested that the passage should read "synodus per Galliarum provincias constituta," and, therefore, it is not a reference to a distinct Gallic meeting.[9] Maassen, in any case, makes no mention of a council.

Although both of these examples involve ambiguous references, there are other instances in which an incontrovertible reference to a council is disregarded by modern editors. For example, neither Maassen nor Charles de Clercq—the latter having published the now-standard Latin edition of the Merovingian councils in 1963 for the *Corpus*

[4] This tally excludes the Roman synods included by Werminghoff in his edition.

[5] Fredegar (Continuator), *Chronica*, MGH SRM II, ed. Bruno Krusch (Hanover: Hahn, 1888), ch. 50.

[6] This is the sense of Wallace-Hadrill's translation of the passage: Fredegar, *The Fourth Book of the Chronicle of Fredegar*, trans. J. M. Wallace-Hadrill (London: Thomas Nelson and Sons Ltd., 1960), 118. Michael McCormick, "Pippin III, the Embassy of Caliph al Mansur, and the Mediterranean World," in *Der Dynastiewechsel von 751*, ed. Matthias Becher and Jorg Jarnut (Münster: Scriptorium, 2004), 228–9, translates this passage "by counsel of the bishops and priests," although he notes that "in this part of the *Continuations*, *consilium* refers to the king consulting with his grandees or to a plan." For additional examples of both *episcopi* and *sacerdoti* offering advice to kings, see, e.g., Soissons (744), Preface and c. 2.

[7] Giovanni Domenico Mansi, ed., *Sacrorum Conciliorum Nova et Amplissima Collectio* (Paris: H. Welter, 1901–27; orig. 1759–98), XII.678–9.

[8] Ibid., XI.175–6.

[9] Hefele and Leclercq, *Histoire des conciles d'après les documents originaux*, III.1.476. Rudolph Riedinger's edition of the acts of the Third Council of Constantinople maintains the original wording: *Concilium Universale Constantinopolitanum Tertium* (Berlin: Walter de Gruyter, 1984), I.149.

Christianorum series—include the text of an epistle composed by Bishop Mappinus of Rheims in 550, in which the prelate gives his reasons for not attending a council in Toul convoked by King Theudebald of Austrasia (r. 547–55).[10] Similarly, neither editor mentions an entry from the *Annales Mettenses Priores* for the year 692, which credits Mayor Pippin II (d. 714) with convening a synod for the sake of "churches, orphans, and widows."[11] Both editors also fail to include those councils whose convocation is certain but whose actual assembly is not. They do not provide entries, for example, for the subsequent synods convoked during the closing sessions of the Councils of Mâcon (585), Chalon-sur-Saône (647/53), or Saint-Jean-de-Losne (673/5).[12] Pope Gregory the Great's (r. 590–604) tireless efforts to get a council convened to correct clerical abuses in the Frankish church likewise go unmentioned.[13] Additionally, the editors neglect a rescheduled synod, originally convoked by Bishop Sulpicius of Bourges (d. 646/7) sometime between the years of 630 and 643.[14] Nor do they list councils that were summoned but were aborted before they could meet, such as one scheduled to assemble in Troyes in 585 on the orders of Kings Guntram and Childebert II (r. 575–96), but which the bishops of Childebert's kingdom refused to attend.[15]

Finally, Maassen, De Clercq, and Werminghoff do not include contested or pseudo-councils in their editions, with the lone exception of the so-called Council of Rheims (626/7). Hefele and Lerclercq had taken note of many of these questionable meetings, and helpfully summarized the then-scholarly consensus on their authenticity. Odette Pontal, too, in her *Histoire des conciles mérovingiens*, includes a brief section on several disputed synods. However, no comprehensive catalog has ever been produced, and one would need to consult dozens of sources to learn of all relevant references. Included as an appendix to

---

[10] *Epistolae Austrasicae*, MGH Epistolarum III, ed. Wilhelm Gundlach (Berlin: Weidmann, 1892), no. 11.

[11] *Annales Mettenses Priores*, ed. Bernhard Simson (Hanover: Hahn, 1905), entry for 692.

[12] Mâcon (585), c. 20; Chalon (647/53), Epistle to Theudorius of Arles; St. Jean-de-Losne (673/75), c. 11. On the convocation of synods by synods, see chapter 2.

[13] Gregory I, *Registrum Epistularum*, CCSL 140, vol. 1–2, ed. Dag Norberg (Turnhout: Brepols, 1972), V.58–60, VIII.4, IX.214, IX.216, IX.219–20, IX.223.

[14] Desiderius of Cahors, *Epistulae S. Desiderii Cadurcensis*, ed. Dag Norberg (Uppsala: Almquist and Wiksell, 1961), II.16.

[15] Gregory of Tours *Decem Libri Historiarum* VIII.13. Another example of a canceled council can be found in Desiderius of Cahors *Epistulae S. Desiderii Cadurcensis* II.17.

this study is a register of fifty-one contested or fictional councils, the most complete compiled to date.[16] Its importance lies both in the insight that these references provide for their authors' understanding of Frankish conciliar practices (both contemporary and anachronistic), as well as in the potential authenticity of some of these meetings. At the very least, there are a number of assemblies whose genuineness or conciliar status remains in question.

For example, Gregory of Tours records that the royal pretender, Gundovald (d. 585) convoked a meeting of bishops in Bordeaux ca. 584/5 to elect the priest Faustianus as bishop of Dax.[17] The position had already been promised to the *comes* Nicetius by the now-deceased King Chilperic. But Gundovald, in an effort to assert his own legitimacy, had undertaken to invalidate all of Chilperic's written orders. Gundovald was supported halfheartedly in his efforts by Bishop Bertram of Bordeaux, who, despite his duty as a metropolitan, refused to personally ordain Faustianus for fear of later repercussions, claiming that his bleary eyes bothered him too much to allow him to perform the ceremony. So the ordination was carried out instead by Bishop Palladius of Saintes. Despite the fact that Gundovald's actions were in clear *imitatio* of Merovingian convocation procedures, few modern scholars have identified this meeting as a council.[18]

Similarly, according to the *Vita Cuniberti* (ninth century or later), King Dagobert I (r. 623–39) convoked a council in order to appoint Cunibert (ca. 625–63) bishop of Cologne.[19] The late date of the *Vita* strengthens the probability that this story is a creative anachronism. Nevertheless, the appointment procedures described in the passage would not have been out of place in early-seventh-century Francia.[20] A similar example can be found in the two ninth-century versions of

---

[16] I also have included in this list those councils attested to only by non-contemporary sources, regardless of their appearance in modern editions, e.g., Sens (594/614). I also have included the episcopal privileges discussed in the introduction.

[17] Gregory of Tours *Decem Libri Historiarum* VII.31.

[18] Gundovald's meeting is identified as a council by Bernard Bachrach, *Anatomy of a Little War: A Diplomatic and Military History of the Gundovald Affair (568–586)* (Boulder: Westview Press, 1994), 99–100.

[19] Maurice Coens, ed., "Les vies de Saint Cunibert et la tradition manuscrite," *Annalecta Bollandiana* 47 (1929): ch. 3.

[20] Heribert Müller, "Kunibert von Köln," *Rheinische Lebensbilder* 12 (1991): 12–3. The *Formulary of Marculf* preserves a series of *formulae* detailing the election procedure, in which the king plays no small role: *Marculfi Formularum*, ed. Alf Uddholm (Uppsala: Eranos Förlag, 1952), I.5–7.

the *Vita Galli Confessoris*, written by Wetti and Walahfrid Strabo, both based on a fragmentary template of debated authenticity.[21] According to the *Vitae*, Duke Gunzo (or Cunzo) of Alamannia convoked a *synodus* of bishops and laymen in Constance so that Gallus might be elected bishop of that *civitas*. The synod lasted three days, and Gallus refused the appointment on the grounds that, as a peregrine monk, he could not be elected bishop. In his place, the deacon Johannes was chosen on the saint's recommendation.[22] The questionable veracity of the *Vitae Galli* has much to do with the council's absence from modern editions and studies of Frankish councils. But it may also be that the unusual setting of this account, Alamannia, contributed to its neglect. These three examples are just a sampling of neglected councils of questionable and dubious authenticity. Not only are most of these absent from modern editions and translations of the Frankish councils, but a substantial number of them do not even appear in the comprehensive handbooks of Pontal and Hartmann.[23]

The deficiencies of modern editions are due largely to their editors' focus on those documents issued by, or in relation to, a council, at the expense of secondary references from contemporary sources that mention ecclesiastical meetings. It is true that these passages are not ignored entirely. Both Maassen and De Clercq, for example, include excerpts from hagiographical *vitae*,[24] Gregory of Tours' *Historiae*,[25] Fredegar's *Chronica*,[26] and one royal diploma.[27] Werminghoff, for his

[21] On the controversy surrounding the oldest version of the *Vita Galli*, see Hagen Keller, "Fränkische Herrschaft und alemannisches Herzogtum im 6. und 7. Jahrhundert," *Zeitschrift für die Geschichte des Oberrheins* 85 (1976): 1–30.

[22] Wetti, *Vita Galli Confessoris*, MGH SRM IV, ed. Bruno Krusch (Hanover: Hahn, 1902), ch. 24; Walahfrid Strabo, *Vita Galli Confessoris*, MGH SRM IV, ed. Bruno Krusch (Hanover: Hahn, 1902), ch. 24.

[23] See, e.g., the Councils of Tournai (520), Unknown (ca. 538), Bordeaux (584/5), Cologne (ca. 626), Paris (632), Constance (ca. 635/40), Unknown (679), Arles (ca. 682), Meaux (690), Utrecht (697), Liege (708/56), Tongres (708/56), Rouen (711/15), Utrecht (719), Strasbourg (728), Germania (746), Mainz (753/4), Les Estinnes (756), Constance (758/9), and Bourges (767/8).

[24] They cite the *Vita Caesarii* re Valence (ca. 528), the *Vita Betharii* re Sens (594/614), the *Vita Desiderii* re Chalon (602/4), the *Vita Eustasii* re Mâcon (626/7), the *Vita Agili* re Clichy (636), the *Vita Eligii* re Orléans (639/41), the *Vita Leudegarii* re Unknown (ca. 677/9), and the *Gesta Episcoporum Autissiodorensium* re Auxerre (692/6).

[25] They cite the *Historiae* re the Councils of Saintes (561/7), Paris (577), Chalon (579), Berny (580), Lyons (581), Auvergne (584/91), Unknown 2 (588), Unknown 1 (589), Sorcy (589), Poitiers (589/90), Metz (590), and Auvergne (590).

[26] They cite Fredegar re the Council of Chalon (602/4).

[27] They cite Diploma no. 122 of Theuderic III re Mâlay-le-Roi (677).

part, includes a handful of epistles and Chrodegang of Metz's privilege to the monastery of Gorze.[28] Still, the number of important secondary references that these editors ignore is considerable. In subsequent chapters, for example, I refer on a number of occasions to Gregory of Tours' important account of the Second Council of Mâcon (585), which neither Maassen nor De Clercq deemed worthy of inclusion in their editions. For those interested primarily in the legislative pronouncements of the Frankish councils, the editorial work of Maassen, De Clercq, and Werminghoff is immensely helpful, and likely sufficient; for those, however, interested in the councils as functioning institutions, their publications do not tell the full story.

Conciliar Documentation

Before examining in detail the sources that these editors neglect, we ought to first note those that they include (the manuscripts from which they derive are discussed in chapter 5). Besides the handful of short excerpts from independent sources, the material contained in the editions of Maassen, De Clercq, and Werminghoff falls into three major categories: canons, conciliar *acta* of a non-legislative nature, and epistles. Between the years 511 and 768, councils held all over Frankish Gaul and Germania issued more than six hundred canons, which dealt with such issues of concern as clerical discipline, episcopal rights and jurisdiction, and the management of ecclesiastical property. Forty of these canons dealt specifically with conciliar protocol and legislation, in particular the necessity of holding regular provincial councils and proper synodal judicial procedures.[29] Although their normative nature, as well as chronological and geographic diversity, renders the canons problematic sources of evidence of actual conciliar procedures, they still provide

[28] Besides a short citation from a letter of Hincmar of Rheims concerning Les Estinnes (743), Werminghoff provides in full only the epistles of Boniface and Zacharias re Unknown (747). He provides the text for Chrodegang's privilege in his entry for the Council of Compiègne (757).

[29] Epaone (517), c. 1; Orléans (533), cc. 1–2; Clermont (535), c. 1; Orléans (538), cc. 1, 22–4; Orléans (541), cc. 6 and 37; Orléans (549), cc. 17–8 and 23; Eauze (551), c. 7; Arles (554), c. 1; Tours (567), cc. 1–2 and 7–9; Mâcon (585), cc. 9 and 20; Auxerre (585/605), c. 7; Paris (614), cc. 1 and 4; Clichy (626/7), cc. 4, 6, and 27; Chalon (647/53), cc. 1–2; St. Jean de Losne (673/5), cc. 11 and 21; Germania (742), cc. 1 and 4; Soissons (744), c. 1; Ver (755), cc. 4–5, 8, 13, and 17. See also Chalon (647/53), Preface; Pippin *Capitulary of 754/5*, in *Capitularia Regum Francorum*, no. 3.

insight into a distinctly Frankish understanding of conciliar activities. For instance, a number of these proclamations clarify the appellate judicial function of church councils, which allows us to contextualize better the many secondary references to conciliar trials. Although we can never assume that all clerics disputing with their bishop had recourse to a synodal hearing, the canonical regulations demonstrate that, at the very least, the Frankish episcopate, as a body, approved of collegiate oversight of an individual prelate's disciplinary policies.

But although the canons themselves are a problematic source for conciliar procedures, the documents that transmitted them are absolutely invaluable in this regard. These canonical *acta*, as copied into contemporary or nearly contemporary systematic canonical collections, contain evidence of the convocation, location, date, royal involvement, and agendas of individual synods. From a comparison of chronologically and geographically diverse acts, we can conclude much about the protocol of Frankish councils. Additionally, the subscription lists attached to these documents, as the work of Champagne and Szramkiewicz has shown, are invaluable for the evidence they provide on conciliar attendance. Not only do they permit us to draw quantitative conclusions about participation in Frankish synods, they also can serve as the basis for prosopographical analyses of the attendees. Although biographical information is lacking for the majority of Gallo-Frankish bishops for our period, "leading names" (*leitnamen*) can be taken as evidence of lineages between individuals with identical or similar names. Certainly, onomastic similarities alone are not sure proof of familial relationships, but they are nevertheless important clues.[30] In the conciliar context, prosopography is especially useful for identifying preexisting relationships and communities whose existence might affect a meeting's composition, agenda, or rapport with royal authorities.

[30] On the use of *leitnamen* as evidence of familial relationships, see Karl F. Werner, "Important Noble Families in the Kingdom of Charlemagne," in *The Medieval Nobility*, ed. and trans. Timothy Reuter (New York: North Holland Publishing, 1979), 149–50; Constance Bouchard, *Those of My Blood: Constructing Noble Families in Medieval Francia* (Philadelphia: University of Pennsylvania Press, 2001), 7–10. On prosopographical methodology, see also K. F. Werner, "Liens de parenté et noms de personne: Un problème historique et méthodologique," in *Famille et parenté dans l'occident médiéval*, ed. Georges Duby and Jacques Le Goff (Rome: École française de Rome, 1977), 13–18, 25–34; Heinzelmann, "Prosopographie et recherche de continuité historique," 227–39; George Beech, "Prosopography," in *Medieval Studies: An Introduction*, 2nd ed., ed. James M. Powell (Syracuse: Syracuse University Press, 1992), 185–226.

Take, for example, the twenty-one bishops who, on the orders of King Guntram, attended a synod in Mâcon in the month of November, sometime between the years 581 and 583. These men were not strangers. Eight had attended a council together in Paris in 573, and another eight attended one in Lyons in May 583.[31] Subsequently, nine of them attended the Council of Valence (583/5), and eighteen either participated in, or sent representatives to, the Second Council of Mâcon in 585.[32] A number of these bishops also were members of an intimate group of episcopal supporters of King Guntram.[33] Priscus of Lyons, for example, had been the king's *domesticus,* and Flavius of Chalon-sur-Saône had served him only a few years earlier as a *referendarius.*[34] In 586, Guntram ordered Artemius of Sens to travel to the court of Chlothar II to investigate the murder of Bishop Praetextatus, and Namatius of Orléans went on a diplomatic mission to the Bretons in the following year.[35] Flavius of Chalon and Syagrius of Autun accompanied the king on his journey to Paris for the baptism of Chlothar II in 591.[36] Hagiographical tradition also reports that Syagrius of Autun acted as

[31] The names of Priscus of Lyons, Syagrius of Autun, Gallomagnus of Troyes, Aunacharius of Auxerre, Hesychius of Grenoble, Silvester of Besançon, Victor of Saint-Paul-Trois-Châteaux, and Heraclius of Digne are found among the subscriptions to the Council of Paris (573). The names of Priscus of Lyons, Syagrius of Autun, Hesychius of Grenoble, Evantius of Vienne, Ragnoaldus of Valence, Eusebius of Mâcon, Agricola of Nevers, and Flavius of Chalon are found in those attached to the acts of the Council of Lyons (583).

[32] Priscus of Lyons, Evantius of Vienne, Hesychius of Grenoble, Ragnoaldus of Valence, Eusebius of Mâcon, Flavius of Chalon, Pappus of Apt, Artemius of Vaison, and Martianus of Tarentaise also attended the Council of Valence (583/5). Priscus of Lyons, Evantius of Vienne, Artemius of Sens, Syagrius of Autun, Aunacharius of Auxerre, Hesychius of Grenoble, Silvester of Besançon, Ragnoaldus of Valence, Heraclius of Digne, Eusebius of Mâcon, Namicius of Orléans, Agricola of Nevers, Mummolus of Langres, Flavius of Chalon, and Hiconius of Maurienne attended the Second Council of Mâcon (585). Artemius of Vaison, Pappus of Apt, and Martianus of Tarentaise sent representatives there.

[33] Gregory Halfond, "All the King's Men: Episcopal Political Loyalties in the Merovingian Kingdoms," *Medieval Prosopography* (forthcoming).

[34] Priscus' service is recorded in his epitaph; see Louis Duchesne, *Fastes épiscopaux de l'ancienne Gaule* (Paris: Albert Fontemoing, 1907–15), II.168. Gregory of Tours *Decem Libri Historiarum* V.45 mentions Flavius' former secular office. Fredegar *Chronica* III.89 suggests that Flavius was a supporter of Gundovald, a claim that the editors of the *PLRE* rightly dispute: J. R. Martindale, ed., *The Prosopography of the Later Roman Empire,* vols. 2–3 (Cambridge: Cambridge University Press, 1992), IIIA.487. Flavius was elected bishop in 580.

[35] Gregory of Tours *Decem Libri Historiarum* VIII.31, IX.18.

[36] Ibid., X.28.

an intermediary between various supplicants and King Guntram.[37] Additionally, the *Gesta Episcoporum Autissiodorensium* offers the chronologically unlikely suggestion that Bishop Aunacharius of Auxerre was raised in King Guntram's palace.[38] Close relations with the king had their dividends: When Bishop Victor of Saint-Paul-Trois-Châteaux was excommunicated by his fellow bishops for forgiving attackers sent by his enemies, Bishops Sagittarius of Gap and Salonius of Embrun, without first getting the approval of those prelates who had joined him in pressing charges, he was pardoned only after King Guntram personally interceded on his behalf.[39]

Along with their conciliar and political duties, the bishops at Mâcon interacted in a variety of other contexts as well. During a conference with King Guntram, Bishops Syagrius, Aunacharius, Agricola of Nevers, and Hesychius of Grenoble coauthored an official response to Bishop Gundegisel of Bordeaux's report of a monastic rebellion in Poitiers (589–90).[40] According to his biography in the *Gesta Episcoporum Autissiodorensium*, Aunacharius received his clerical training with the guidance of Syagrius of Autun.[41] Several of the Mâcon attendees were also members of the circle surrounding Bishop Nicetius of Lyons (fl. 552–73), who, besides wielding considerable political and religious influence, was also the great-uncle of Gregory of Tours.[42] Gregory tells us in his biography of Nicetius that Syagrius and Gallomagnus of Troyes witnessed miracles performed by the bishop.[43] Nicetius' successor, Priscus, however, was not quite so enamored with his illustrious

[37] *Vita Rusticulae sive Marciae Abbatissae Arelatensis*, MGH SRM IV, ed. Bruno Krusch (Hanover: Hahn, 1902), ch. 3.

[38] *Gesta Episcoporum Autissiodorensium*, ed. and trans. Michel Sot, Guy Lobrichon, and Monique Goullet (Paris: Belles Lettres, 2002), ch. 19. Aunacharius is said to have been ordained the same year that Guntram became king: 561 (see the editors' note, 106). See also, however, the comments of Wolfert S. Van Egmond, *Conversing with Saints: Communication in Pre-Carolingian Hagiography from Auxerre* (Turnhout: Brepols, 2006), 70–1, on the difficulty of calculating the true length of Aunacharius' episcopacy.

[39] Gregory of Tours *Decem Libri Historiarum* V.20.

[40] Ibid., IX.41. Chlothild, who claimed to be the daughter of King Charibert, led her fellow nuns in an uprising against their abbess, Leubovera. On this revolt, see Ibid., IX.39–43.

[41] *Gesta Episcoporum Autissiodorensium*, ch. 19. See also *Vita Sancti Aunarii Episcopi Autissiodorensis*, AASS Sept. VII, ch. 3 (a possible source).

[42] Gregory of Tours *Decem Libri Historiarum* V.5. Artemius of Sens and Artemius of Vaison may even have been relations of Nicetius, whose mother was named Artemia.

[43] Gregory of Tours, *Liber Vitae Patrum*, MGH SRM I.2, ed. Bruno Krusch (Hanover: Hahn, 1885), VIII.8, VIII.10.

predecessor. According to Gregory, Priscus and his wife, Susanna, harassed and even murdered some of Nicetius' former associates, and attempted to give away the saint's cloak after his death.[44] Priscus, it seems, was attempting to destroy any potential relics that could be associated with a cult of worship around the future saint.

That the Mâcon bishops were collectively members of an existing aristocracy is confirmed by the spare familial information available. For example, the author of the *Gesta Episcoporum Autissiodorensium* describes Aunacharius of Auxerre, the son of Pastor and Ragnoara of Orléans, as being "[de] genere nobilissimus."[45] Additionally, we know that Aunacharius was not the only member of his immediate family to gain a powerful ecclesiastical position. His brother was Bishop Austrinus of Orléans, and his sister Austregilde was the mother of Bishop Lupus of Sens.[46] We can similarly infer the prominent status of Gallomagnus of Troyes from the marriage of his daughter Palatina to Bodegiselus, an Austrasian *dux*.[47] Syagrius of Autun, if he may be identified as a member of the famous Syagrii *gens*, possessed an even more impressive heritage, stretching back to the self-styled *Rex Romanorum* Syagrius (fl. 465–87), who was defeated in battle by Clovis in 486, and earlier still to two late-fourth-century Gallo-Roman consuls, both named Flavius Syagrius.[48] Syagrius' episcopal superior, Priscus of Lyons, similarly came from a distinguished family: his epitaph explicitly states that he was of "progenie clarus."[49] We may also infer the high social status of Namatius of Orléans and Flavius of Chalon from descriptions of them as prominent landowners.[50]

---

[44] Gregory of Tours *Liber Vitae Patrum* VIII.5; Gregory of Tours *Decem Libri Historiarum* IV.36.

[45] *Gesta Episcoporum Antissiodorensium*, ch. 19. The same parental names are given in the *Vita Sancti Aunarii Episcopi Autissiodorensis*, ch. 1.

[46] *Gesta Episcoporum Autissiodorensium*, ch. 19.

[47] Martindale, ed., *The Prosopography of the Later Roman Empire*, IIIA.501. Martindale cites Fortunatus' dedication of a poem to "Palatina filia Galli Magni episcopi" as evidence of this relationship: Venantius Fortunatus, *Opera Poetica*, MGH AA IV.1, ed. Friedrich Leo (Berlin: Weidmann, 1881–5), VII.6.

[48] For Syagrius *Rex*, see Karl F. Stroheker, *Der senatorische Adel im spatantiken Gallien* (Tübingen: Alma Mater Verlag, 1948), 221–2; Martindale, ed., *The Prosopography of the Later Roman Empire*, II.1041–2; Martin Heinzelmann, "Gallische Prosopographie, 260–527," *Francia* 10 (1982): 699. For Flavius Syagrius, see A. H. M. Jones, J. R. Martindale, and J. Morris, eds., *The Prosopography of the Later Roman Empire I* (Cambridge: Cambridge University Press, 1971), 862–3; Heinzelmann, "Gallische Prosopographie, 260–527," 699.

[49] Duchesne, *Fastes épiscopaux de l'ancienne Gaule*, II.168.

[50] Gregory of Tours *Decem Libri Historiarum* IX.18; *Vita Nicetii Episcopi Lugdunensis*, MGH SRM III, ed. Bruno Krusch (Hanover: Hahn, 1896), 7. The identification of the

Some of these men were, no doubt, members of long-standing episcopal dynasties. Hesychius of Grenoble, for example, was possibly a member of the lineage descended from Hesychius of Vienne (middle to late fifth century), the father of Bishop Avitus of Vienne (ca. 460–518), and the patriarch of an important episcopal dynasty.[51] Additionally, we perhaps can associate Priscus of Lyons with the illustrious line of Priscus Valerianus, an early-to-middle-fifth-century *praefectus praetorio*, which had links to the metropolitical capital of Lyons through Eucherius of Lyons (early to middle fifth century).[52] It also has been suggested that Evantius of Vienne was a member of the Eventii family, which supplied a number of distinguished secular and ecclesiastical officeholders throughout this period.[53] It is even a possibility that some of the bishops assembled at Mâcon in 581/3 were related to one another, albeit distantly, through familial and matrimonial ties, as the families of the Agricolae, Avitii, and Priscii were linked through blood and marriage.[54] Thus, if we assume that Agricola of Nevers, Hesychius of Grenoble, and Priscus of Lyons were members of the families that bear these names, they must have shared some measure of kinship.

These hypotheses of family relationships, when taken in conjunction with the Mâcon attendees' verifiable personal data, reveal that the majority of bishops at this council were members of a socially and politically prominent aristocracy, bound together by family, office, and socioeconomic background, an observation that can be extended to conciliar attendees in general. The bishops at Mâcon were not strangers. They were members of a common sociopolitical class, and served in a common provincial hierarchy. They attended multiple councils together, and shared links to the royal court. And in none of these ways

---

wealthy landowner Flavius mentioned in the *Vita Nicetii* with Flavius of Chalon is not certain. See Martindale, ed., *The Prosopography of the Later Roman Empire*, IIIA.487.

[51] On the Avitii family, see the introduction to Danuta Shanzer and Ian Wood's *Avitus of Vienne: Letters and Selected Prose* (Liverpool: Liverpool University Press, 2002), 4–5. On Hesychius of Vienne, see also Heinzelmann, "Gallische Prosopographie, 260–527," 624. On Avitus of Vienne, see Ibid., 568.

[52] For the relation between Priscus Valerianus and Eucherius of Lyons, see Mathisen, *Ecclesiastical Factionalism and Religious Controversy in Fifth-Century Gaul*, 79. Priscus Valerianus was also a relation of Emperor Eparchius Avitus, who, in turn, was related to the Apollonarii family. See Martindale, ed., *The Prosopography of the Later Roman Empire*, II.1142–3.

[53] Mathisen, *Ecclesiastical Factionalism and Religious Controversy in Fifth-Century Gaul*, 28, note 5.

[54] See *stemmatae* 14–18 (especially 14) in Martindale, ed., *The Prosopography of the Later Roman Empire*, II.1317–20.

were the attendees of the Council of Mâcon unique. Although our knowledge of individual conciliar attendees is limited, there is much we can say about them as a body. Furthermore, we can better understand conciliar decisions when we have some familiarity with their authors and their class interests.

Canons, however, were not the only form that conciliar decisions took during this period. Two other common document types to be issued by councils were judicial decisions and ecclesiastical privileges. We noted in the previous chapter the routine use of councils as judicial tribunals. Although our knowledge of tribunal processes derives primarily from narrative or epistolary sources, we do possess several conciliar judicial decisions in their original articulation. These documents, however, do not necessarily follow a universal form. For example, in the year 533, Caesarius of Arles convoked a council in Marseilles to investigate the "many shameful and dishonest" deeds of Bishop Contumeliosus of Riez.[55] Following the suspect's confession and sentencing, the council issued a written account detailing the charges and penalties imposed. This document is very similar to canonical *acta* of the *placuit*-form. Among other features, it begins with a "cum…convenissemus" introductory clause, and concludes with the date of the assembly and the subscriptions of the attendees.[56] A very similar report was issued twenty years later by the Council of Paris (552), which met on the orders of Childebert I to investigate charges against Bishop Saffaracus of Paris.[57] It, too, replicated the traditional *placuit*-form of Frankish canonical records.

On other occasions, judicial decisions were announced as canons[58] or as epistles.[59] The Council of Chalon-sur-Saone (647/53), in fact, did both. This Neustro-Burgundian council was convoked in the name of the underage king, Clovis II, and its agenda included both legislative and judicial matters. In the final canon of its published *acta*, the council records the deposition of two bishops, Agapius and Bobo, both of the *civitas* of Digne.[60] The council dealt generally with the issue of two

[55] Marseilles (533), Conciliar Acts.

[56] It is interesting to note that the consular year is provided, a detail lacking in subsequent Frankish conciliar documents.

[57] Paris (551/2), Conciliar Acts.

[58] See, e.g., Lyons (518/23), c. 1; Chalon (647/53), c. 20; Soissons (744), c. 2.

[59] See, e.g., Carpentras (527), Epistle to Agricius of Antibes; Paris (573), Epistles to Egidius of Rheims and Sigibert I; Chalon (647/53), Epistle to Theodorius of Arles.

[60] Chalon (647/53), c. 20.

bishops sharing the same seat in another ruling, but singled out Agapius and Bobo in its twentieth canon for their many transgressions of canon law.[61] The same council also sent a letter to the absent Bishop Theodorius of Arles to inform him that he was suspended from his episcopal duties on account of his many canonical transgressions until another council should meet. The letter clearly states that if Theodorius had attended the Council of Chalon, he would have been disciplined there.[62] Finally, when a synod such as the Council of Mâlay-le-Roi (677)- convoked by King Theuderic III (r. 673, 675–91)—met in the king's presence, it had the option of publishing its judicial ruling in the form of a royal diploma, thus adding royal force to its verdict.[63]

Grants of ecclesiastical privileges similarly took a number of different forms. Sometimes they were granted or confirmed in the form of canons contained within the *acta*,[64] and on other occasions separate documents were produced. The latter could take the form of either standard *placuit*-form acts—e.g., the Council of Valence (583/5)—or charters. It was noted in the previous chapter how many of these charters are not explicit as to whether they were composed in a conciliar context. Some, however, are more forthright about their origins, such as a royal diploma issued by Clovis II (r. 639–57) in 654, which states that the king confirmed privileges granted to St. Denis "cum consilio pontefecum et inlustrium virorum nostorum procerum."[65] Although we might read *consilio* here as "advice," the presence of the subscriptions of at least fourteen bishops and two deacons indicates that the diploma was issued by a mixed council of clerics and laymen.[66] Similarly, in Chrodegang of Metz's grant to the monastery of Gorze in 757, it is noted explicitly that the charter was issued by a synod in the palace of Compiègne.[67] Admittedly, the failure of some charters to indicate the context of their composition, combined with the formulaic nature of such documents, makes them problematic sources for

[61] Ibid., c. 4.

[62] Ibid., Epistle to Theodorius.

[63] *Die Urkunden der Merowinger*, no. 122.

[64] See, e.g., Orléans (549), c. 15; Saint-Jean-de-Losne (673/5), c. 14; Ver (755), c. 19.

[65] *Die Urkunden der Merowinger*, no. 85.

[66] See, e.g., Hefele and Leclercq, *Histoire des conciles d'après les documents originaux*, III.1.296 (see also note 2 for additional references); Pontal, *Histoire des conciles mérovingiens*, 226.

[67] Werminghoff, ed., *Concilia aevi Karolini*, I.63.

conciliar protocol.[68] Nevertheless, they do provide insight into a sometimes-underappreciated synodal function.

Secondary References to Conciliar Activity

Although conciliar documents can provide important evidence of what transpired during the course of meetings, this information is often skeletal, offering little in the way of detail or color. For this, we must turn to contemporary sources written neither by nor for a council. Narrative sources in a variety of genres—history, poetry, epistolography, and hagiography—provide important evidence of contextualizing individual councils.[69] In particular, they provide otherwise-unavailable physical details, such as travel difficulties, the implications of a royal presence at a council, and the violent confrontations that sometimes arose during proceedings. Many, although not all, of these references were cited or transcribed by Mansi and Hefele. Neither editor, however, made an effort to contextualize them, or offer the critical analysis requisite for evaluating them as evidence of conciliar procedure in the *regnum Francorum*. Their evidentiary value, in fact, is tremendous, but so are the interpretive challenges that they pose. Several important examples of such references follow.

Historical works, including narrative histories, chronicles, and annals, are perhaps our most valuable sources for conciliar procedures. Of these, none are more important than Bishop Gregory of Tours' *Decem Libri Historiarum*, written ca. 585–94.[70] The *Histories* are

[68] The prevalence of forgeries is also problematic. See, for example, the forged foundation document for the monastery of Saint Maurice at Agaune, which can be found in Maxime Reymond, "La charte de Saint Sigismond pour Saint-Maurice d'Agaune 515," *Zeitschrift für Schweizerische Geschichte* 6 (1926): 3–6. Although Reymond argues that the forgery is based on lost original documents, subsequent scholars have dismissed this theory: Jean-Marie Theurillat, "L'Abbaye de Saint-Maurice d'Agaune des origines à la réforme canoniale, 515 – 830," *Vallesia* 9 (1954): 1–128; Ian Wood, "Prelude to Columbanus: The Monastic Achievement in the Burgundian Territories," in *Columbanus and Merovingian Monasticism*, ed. Howard B. Clarke and Mary Brennan (Oxford: B.A.R., 1981), 15–8. Nevertheless, the council recorded in the forgery is mentioned in Fredegar *Chronica* IV.1. On the controversy surrounding the so-called Council of Agaune, see appendix B.

[69] I have purposely left out of this discussion conciliar *ordines*, which are discussed in the next chapter.

[70] On the work's compositional history, see Alexander C. Murray, "Chronology and the Composition of the *Histories* of Gregory of Tours," *Journal of Late Antiquity* 1, no. 1 (2008): 157–96.

particularly informative about the decades in which Gregory held his episcopal office, and they offer several detailed descriptions of conciliar proceedings, some of which Gregory witnessed personally, or learned of secondhand. His account of the Second Council of Mâcon (585), for example, provides some fascinating particulars totally absent from the council's published acts. Gregory explains how King Guntram, who convoked the synod, used it to punish those bishops who had sided with the royal pretender Gundovald against him. According to his account,

> Faustianus, who had been ordained bishop of Dax on the order of Gundovald, was removed from office on the conditition that Bertram, Orestes, and Palladius, who had blessed him, should feed him and supply him with one hundred *aurei* every year....Bishop Ursicinus of Cahors [too] was excommunicated, for the reason that he publically confessed to receiving Gundovald.[71]

Gregory also describes a debate that took place between the attending bishops over whether the word *homo* included, by implication, *mulier*, and a rather underwhelming poetic recitation by Bishop Praetextatus of Rouen, newly returned from exile.[72] Gregory also describes a fight that broke out between the servants of the conciliar president, Priscus of Lyons, and those of Duke Leudegisel, who presumably was in attendance as well. Priscus, we are told, was forced to empty out his own pockets in order to settle the dispute.[73]

Alas, there are no historians comparable to Gregory for the remainder of the Merovingian period. For the late sixth and seventh centuries (584–642), our most valuable historical source is Fredegar's *Chronica* (ca. 660).[74] But Fredegar, who may have been a lay aristocrat writing from a Burgundian or Austrasian perspective, offers far scantier details than Gregory about the actual business of councils, and by no means includes references to all of the meetings held in the years that he was writing.[75] Moreover, he mentions only those councils convoked on royal command, showing no interest in provincial synods. The anonymous

[71] Gregory of Tours *Decem Libri Historiorum* VIII.20.
[72] Ibid.
[73] Ibid.
[74] Ian Wood, "Fredegar's Fables," in *Historiographie im frühen Mittelalter*, ed. Anton Scharer and Georg Scheibelreiter (Vienna: R. Oldenbourg, 1994), 359–66; Roger Collins, *Fredegar*, Authors of the Middle Ages IV.2 (Aldershot: Variorum, 1996).
[75] He ignores, or is ignorant of, the Councils of Mâcon (626/7), Bourges (ca. 630/43), and Orléans (639/41).

Neustrian author of the *Liber Historiae Francorum* (ca. 727), who takes the narrative of Merovingian political history up through 721, shows little interest in purely ecclesiastical matters, and ignores church councils altogether.[76] His neglect, in no small way, helps to account for the conciliar "black hole" of the early eighth century. For the middle of the eighth century, the Carolingian *Annales Mettenses Priores* and *Annales Regni Francorum* demonstrate considerably more interest in conciliar business. Their focus, however, is entirely on those councils convoked by members of the Pippinid family, particularly those in which the *principes* are said to have played a role.[77] Although the uneven chronological and geographical distribution of our evidence prevents us from ever achieving a comprehensive view of conciliar life in all places and times in the Frankish kingdoms, sources in a variety of non-historical genres at least allow us to fill in some of the gaps.[78] These sources, too, are unevenly distributed, but are especially important for locations and periods in which we are underserved by our historical narratives, such as charters and hagiographical *vitae* for late-seventh-century Neustria and Boniface's correspondence for early-eighth-century Germania. But

---

[76] On the *Liber Historiae Francorum*, see Richard Gerberding, *The Rise of the Carolingians and the Liber Historiae Francorum* (Oxford: Clarendon Press, 1987). See pages 31–2 on the author's lack of interest in ecclesiastical affairs.

[77] See, e.g., Unknown (689), Düren (748), Compiègne (757), and Gentilly (767). On these councils, see appendix A. On the *Annales Mettenses Priores* as pro-Carolingian propaganda, see Yitzhak Hen, "The Annals of Metz and the Merovingian Past," in *The Uses of the Past in the Early Middle Ages*, ed. Yitzhak Hen and Matthew Innes (Cambridge: Cambridge University Press, 2000), 175–90; Paul Fouracre and Richard Gerberding, eds., *Late Merovingian France* (Manchester: Manchester University Press, 1996), 330–49. On the *Annales Regni Francorum* as Carolingian "official history," see Rosamond McKitterick, *Charlemagne* (Cambridge: Cambridge University Press, 2008), 31–56.

[78] References to councils in historical works include Gregory of Tours *Decem Libri Historiarum* IV.4, IV.6–7, IV.26, IV.36, IV.47, V.18, V.20, V.27, V.36, V.49, VI.1, VI.38–9, VII.17, VII.31, VIII.20, IX.20, IX.32, IX.37, IX.39–43, X.8, X.15–7, X.19–20; Fredegar *Chronica* IV.1, IV.24, IV.78; *Gesta Episcoporum Autissiodorensium* chs. 19, 24; Flodoard of Rheims, *Historiae Remensis Ecclesiae*, MGH Scriptores 36 (Hanover: Hahn, 1998), I.16, II.5, II.7; Marius of Avenches, *Chronica*, ed. and trans. Justin Favrod (Lausanne: Cahiers Lausannois d'Histoire Médiévale, 1993), entry for 579; *Annales Mettenses Priores*, ed. Bernhard Simson (Hanover: Hahn, 1905), entries for 692, 748, 757, 767; *Annales Regni Francorum*, MGH SRG I, ed. Friedrich Kurz (Hanover: Hahn, 1895), entries for 757, 767; Ado of Vienne, *Sancti Adonis Chronicon*, PL 123, ed. J. P. Migne (Paris: Garnier Brothers, 1879), entry for 767; Odorannus of Sens, *Chronicon*, PL 142, ed. J. P. Migne (Paris: Garnier Brothers, 1880), entry for 675; Pseudo-Anastasius Bibliothecario (Peter the Deacon), *Epitome Chronica Casinensis*, Rerum Italicarum Scriptores II, ed. Lodovico Antonio Muratori (Milan: Typographia Societatis Palatinae, 1723–51), II.1, p. 355.

such sources can also provide additional information on better-known periods, and even on councils known otherwise through historical accounts.

Returning to the Second Council of Mâcon, it is regrettable that the text of Bishop Praetextatus' poem has not survived, so that we might judge for ourselves its literary worth. But this was not the only verse to be recited aloud at a synod. Surviving in a collection of his literary works is Venantius Fortunatus' panegyric to King Chilperic, performed on the occasion of Gregory of Tours' trial at the Council of Berny (580).[79] Fortunatus, at the time he composed this poem, was in a difficult position. Gregory was his good friend, a patron, and a frequent correspondent in both prose and verse. But Fortunatus, an Italian émigré, was a court poet who relied upon royal favor and patronage to earn a living, and on this occasion the king, whose praises he was to sing, was the very person prosecuting his comrade. Fortunatus decided to deliver the panegyric, putting a particular emphasis on the king's commendable sense of justice:

> What shall I say of your administration of justice, o prince? No-one fares badly with you if he truly seeks justice, for in your honest speech are held the scales of just measure and the course of justice runs straight. Truth is not hindered, falsehood and error settle nothing, deceit flees before your judgment, and order returns.[80]

Following Bishop Bertram of Bordeaux's examination of the defendant, Chilperic, who had become aware of the degree of support Gregory enjoyed both among the conciliar attendees and the crowds gathered outside the villa, chose to play the role of *bonus rex*, and left it up to the assembled bishops whether to call witnesses or allow Gregory to clear himself through an oath. The attendees, not surprisingly, sided with their fellow bishop, and Gregory, having given his oath, returned—relieved—to his diocese. Although we shall never know what role, if

---

[79] Venantius Fortunatus *Opera Poetica* IX.1. For literary and historical interpretations of this poem, see Brian Brennan, "The Career of Venantius Fortunatus," *Traditio* 41 (1985): 74–5; Judith George, "Poet as Politician: Venantius Fortunatus' Panegyric to King Chilperic," *Journal of Medieval History* 15:1 (1989): 5–18; Judith George, *Venantius Fortunatus: A Latin Poet in Merovingian Gaul* (Oxford: Clarendon Press, 1992), 48–57; Simon Coates, "Venantius Fortunatus and the Image of Episcopal Authority in Late Antique and Early Merovingian Gaul," *English Historical Review* 115, no. 464 (2000): 1135–6.

[80] Venantius Fortunatus *Opera Poetica* IX.1.85–90, as translated by Judith George, *Venantius Fortunatus: Personal and Political Poems* (Liverpool: Liverpool University Press, 1995), 77.

any, Fortunatus' poem played in Chilperic's decision not to pursue the case, which had serious implications for the stability of his kingdom, its contents nevertheless elucidate the close, yet often difficult, relationship between cross and crown. Gregory wrote his account of the trial, in part, as an *exemplum* of the sorts of abuses this relationship could encourage, while Chilperic intended that this same event illustrate the cooperative ideal of episcopal–state relations. We will have numerous occasions in the pages to come to observe the implications of this complicated relationship for Frankish conciliar life.

Fortunatus' poem is a fascinating and unique document. The epistolary evidence of conciliar practices, in contrast, is comparatively abundant.[81] The modern editors of the councils include in their volumes most of those missives written to or by a sitting council, including the few surviving letters of convocation, but there are many others just as valuable. Of particular importance for this study are the copious epistles of St. Boniface, which detail conciliar activities in mid-eighth-century Germania. Boniface (formerly Wynfrid), an Englishman by birth, was not merely an observer of conciliar activity, but a proponent and participant as well. He had spent his early years in England, at the monasteries of Exeter and Nursling, before his missionary zeal compelled him to travel to the Continent, initially to Frisia, and later to Thuringia, Hesse, Saxony, and Bavaria. He was encouraged in his missionary efforts by the papacy, which awarded him with the office of bishop in 722 and archbishop in 732. He also received the support and protection of the powerful Frankish mayor Charles Martel, whose sons would later encourage Boniface's proposed *correctio* of the Frankish church.[82] Boniface's letters provide a unique window into both his successes and disappointments in pursuing this holy project.

The introduction began with an allusion to one of Boniface's most famous letters, his complaint to Pope Zacharias about the lax morals of

[81] See, e.g., De Clercq, ed., *Concilia Galliae: A.511–A.695*, 22–4, 50–2, 66–9, 86–97, 111–2, 195–9, 212–7, 309–10; Werminghoff, ed., *Concilia aevi Karolini*, 45–50; Avitus of Vienne, *Opera*, MGH AA VI.2, ed. Rudolf Peiper (Berlin: Weidmann, 1883), no. 30; *Epistolae Austrasicae*, no. 11; *Epistolae aevi Merowingici Collectae*, MGH Epistolarum III, ed. Wilhelm Gundlach (Berlin: Weidmann, 1892), nos. 3, 16; Columbanus, *Columbae sive Columbani Abbatis Luxoviensis et Bobbiensis Epistolae*, MGH Epistolarum III, ed. Wilhelm Gundlach (Berlin: Weidmann, 1892), no. 2; Desiderius of Cahors *Epistulae S. Desiderii Cadurcensis*, nos. II.16–7; Boniface *S. Bonifatii et Lulli Epistolae*, nos. 44, 45, 50, 51, 56, 59, 60, 61, 62, 77, 78, 80; Gregory I *Registrum Epistularum*, nos. IX.214, IX.216, IX.219–20.

[82] Boniface *S. Bonifatii et Lulli Epistolae*, no. 22.

the Frankish episcopate. Although this particular letter is discussed again in detail in chapter 6, it is worth summarizing here as an example of the sorts of information that personal correspondence can provide. Boniface had corresponded frequently with Pope Zacharias' predecessors, so sending a letter of introduction on the occasion of the new pope's election was not an unexpected gesture. Nevertheless, one cannot help but wonder what Zacharias' initial reaction was upon receiving such a lengthy and rather pompous missive, especially with the papal throne barely warm. After a perfunctory welcome and congratulations to the new pontiff, Boniface gets down to business. He informs the pope of several already-enacted reforms, including his establishment of three new dioceses in Germania, and requests that Zacharias confirm the legitimacy of his actions.[83] Boniface then informs the pontiff that Carloman, the *dux Francorum*, had requested that he convoke a synod in his portion of the Frankish kingdom. It is here that Boniface shares with the pope the dubious gossip that "old men report that the Franks have not held a synod for eighty years." He requests a special grant of papal authority to reform the Frankish church and to punish offenders of canonical tradition, and reminds Pope Zacharias of his own appointment as apostolic legate. Boniface concludes his letter by asking the pope to correct the same abuses in Rome that he is combating in the *regnum Francorum*.[84] Boniface's correspondence—despite its mix of arrogance, self-righteousness, holy indignation, and piety—offers invaluable insight into the mind of one of the guiding lights of mid-eighth-century Frankish conciliar life, albeit one not native to Francia. From his outsider's perspective, we can see the difficulties in imposing spiritual ideals on temporal realities.

One can note a similar perspective in the correspondence of the Irish *peregrinus* Columbanus (543–615), who was at least as self-assured and high-minded as Boniface.[85] Like Boniface, Columbanus was deeply critical of the Frankish church. Unlike Boniface, he did not engage in local conciliar affairs with state-endorsed authority, despite the support he initially received from the Merovingian monarchy. Nor,

[83] In his reponse to Boniface's letter, the pope agreed to his request, but warned the bishop that in the future he should consider whether locations such as those selected really merited their own bishops (Boniface *S. Bonifatii et Lulli Epistolae*, no. 51). The pope also criticized Boniface's request to appoint his own sucessor while alive.

[84] Boniface *S. Bonifatii et Lulli Epistolae*, no. 50.

[85] On Columbanus' literary corpus, see Michael Lapidge, ed. *Columbanus: Studies of the Latin Writings* (Woodbridge: Boydell Press, 1997).

at the time of this engagement, was his base of operations in Gaul particularly underserved by the Frankish ecclesiastical establishment, at least compared with Germania.[86] In the early years of the first decade of the seventh century (ca. 603/4), Columbanus learned that a council had been convoked in response to his activities and preaching, ostensibly to settle the debate he had provoked over the proper date for celebrating Easter.[87] Easter observance, however, was not the council's sole concern, as Columbanus had angered many local bishops with his lack of deference for conciliar precedent regarding episcopal oversight of monastic houses.[88] The Irish monk, therefore, chose not to appear in what was certain to be a hostile environment, and instead sent a letter by messenger to the assembled body of bishops. In his letter, Columbanus commends the synodal attendees for congregating, but suggests, somewhat condescendingly, that they ought to be meeting on a more regular basis. It is true that we know of no provable councils held between the time of Columbanus' arrival in Burgundy and this synod, although this certainly does not mean that none were held, nor that Columbanus' criticisms were legitimate.[89]

In his letter, the Irishman goes on to praise God that it was on his account that the Frankish bishops decided to convoke a council, and begs them to use this occasion to discuss matters beyond his own dispute with them.[90] Like Boniface a century and a half later, Columbanus disapproved of the general character of the Frankish episcopate, which he considered to be spiritually lax, and he was not timid about

[86] On Columbanus' activities in Francia, see Pierre Riché, "Columbanus, His Followers, and the Merovingian Church," in *Columbanus and Merovingian Monasticism*, ed. Howard B. Clarke and Mary Brennan (Oxford: B.A.R., 1981), 59–72; Friedrich Prinz, "Columbanus, the Frankish Nobility, and the Territories East of the Rhine," in *Columbanus and Merovingian Monasticism*, ed. Howard B. Clarke and Mary Brennan (Oxford: B.A.R., 1981), 73–87; Donald Bullough, "The Career of Columbanus," in *Columbanus: Studies of the Latin Writings*, ed. Michael Lapidge (Woodbridge: Boydell Press, 1997), 1–28; T. M. Charles-Edwards, *Early Christian Ireland* (Cambridge: Cambridge University Press, 2000), 344–90.

[87] Bullough, "The Career of Columbanus," 10, 13–4, suggests that this council may be identifiable with Chalon (602/4), which deposed Bishop Desiderius of Vienne. Hefele and Leclercq, *Histoire des conciles d'après les documents originaux*, III.1.245–6, argue that the council is identical with Sens (594/614).

[88] Wallace-Hadrill, *The Frankish Church*, 65–66.

[89] *Vita Betharii Episcopi Carnoteni*, MGH SRM III, ed. Bruno Krusch (Hanover: Hahn, 1896), ch. 11, reports that a council was held in Sens sometime between 594 and 614, but this work is of a late date.

[90] Columbanus *Columbae sive Columbani Abbatis Luxoviensis et Bobbiensis Epistolae*, no. 2.

expressing his opinion. But despite his disparaging insinuations about the negligent conciliar habits of the bishops, Columbanus chose not to grace an actual council with his presence, a council that had been convoked to deal with his own activities, no less. The irony of the situation is that despite the ill will that he had engendered among many members of the Frankish episcopacy, it was by no means universally united against him, and it is even possible that the council chose not to condemn him or his activities.[91] Certainly, over the course of the next century, the Frankish church permitted the Irish monk's influence to permeate Gallic monasticism, although not necessarily at the expense of alternate traditions.[92] Furthermore, a Burgundian council held ca. 626/7 on the orders of King Chlothar II voted to support Columbanus' monastic rule as practiced under Abbot Eusthasius of Luxeuil.[93] Although Columbanus' letter tells us at least as much about the personality of its author as the state of affairs it purports to describe, like Boniface's correspondence, it offers a unique view of Frankish conciliar practices from the outside in. It reminds us that their rulings were neither universally admired nor always met the standards, realistic or not, of non-Frankish observers.

Although epistolary sources are very useful for their capacity to provide information about the personalities and opinions of contemporary participants and observers of the Merovingian and Pippinid era synods, they do not always allow us to appreciate the role that these synods played in the larger spiritual world of the Frankish kingdoms. For this, we may turn to hagiographical sources. These edifying texts, besides offering invaluable glimpses of local color, discuss councils within a spiritual, rather than a mere administrative, context. The conciliar proceedings serve as a stage for the saintly performer to demonstrate his piety. In some cases, the saint and his allies use this platform to confront heretics face-to-face. In Hincmar of Rheims' ninth-century *Vita Sancti Remigii*, Bishop Remigius of Rheims (d. 533), the baptizer

[91] Charles-Edwards, *Early Christian Ireland*, 369.

[92] E.g. the Benedictine tradition: Friedrich Prinz, *Frühes Mönchtum im Frankenreich* (Munich: R. Oldenbourg, 1965), 263–92.

[93] Jonas of Bobbio, *Vitae Columbani Abbatis Discipulorumque Eius Libri Duo Auctore Iona*, MGH SRM IV, ed. Bruno Krusch (Hanover: Hahn, 1902), ch. II.9. On the Council of Mâcon (626/7), see Pontal, *Histoire des conciles mérovingiens*, 225; Charles-Edwards, *Early Christian Ireland*, 364–9; Felice Lifshitz, *The Name of the Saint: The Martyrology of Jerome and Access to the Sacred in Francia, 627–827* (Notre Dame: University of Notre Dame Press, 2006), 16–19; Wood, *The Merovingian Kingdoms*, 194–7.

of Clovis, successfully disputes with an Arian bishop.[94] Similarly, in Jonas of Bobbio's *Vita Eusthasi Abbatis Luxouiensis* (ca. 640), Columbanus' disciple, Abbot Eusthasius of Luxeuil (d. 629), defends his master's rule at a council at Mâcon (626/7) against the monk (and former referendary) Agrestius and his allies.[95] In the eighth-century edition of the *Vita Eligii*, Eligius (d. 660), then a palace official, learns that a foreign heretic has begun preaching in Auxerre. Thereupon, "along with Audoin and other Catholic men…he uncovered and made public all appearances of this plague. He did not desist from warning the bishops and the *optimates* until an episcopal council met on the order of the *princeps* [Clovis II] in the city of Orléans." At the synod, a bishop is able to demolish the heretic's arguments.[96]

The holy man does not always fare so well at the council, however. In his *vita* of Desiderius of Vienne (d. 606/7), the Visigothic king Sisebut describes how Brunhild (d. 613) and her grandson Theuderic II (r. 596–613) convinced a woman of ill repute, ironically named Justa, to accuse the bishop before a council of forcing himself sexually upon her. Sisebut describes how "those presiding [over the council], following their predetermined scheme, handed down with daring recklessness an unjust sentence against the innocent man, whom they punished by removing him from office and sending him into exile to an island monastery."[97] He later would be executed. Although the broad details of Desiderius' martyrdom are not in question, Sisebut's narrative is certainly a literary construction, and probably one with a political agenda. It is uncertain whether Sisebut was intent on stirring up anti-Frankish sentiment in Visigothic Spain or Gaul, promoting himself at the expense of his political rivals, or appealing to Chlothar II, Brunhild's executioner.[98] What is clear is that he embellished a real event—the

---

[94] Hincmar of Rheims, *Vita Remigii Episcopi Remensis*, MGH SRM III, ed. Bruno Krusch (Hanover: Hahn, 1896), ch. 21. See also Flodoard of Rheims *Historia Ecclesiae Remensis* I.16.

[95] Jonas of Bobbio *Vitae Columbani Abbatis Discipulorumque Eius Libri Duo Auctore Iona*, ch. II.9.

[96] *Vita Eligii Episcopi Noviomagensis*, MGH SRM IV, ed. Bruno Krusch (Hanover: Hahn, 1902), ch. I.35.

[97] Sisebut, *Vita vel Passio Sancti Desiderii Episcopi Viennensis*, MGH SRM III, ed. Bruno Krusch (Hanover: Hahn, 1896), ch. 4. C.f. Fredegar *Chronica* IV.24; *Passio Sancti Desiderii Episcopi Viennensis II*, MGH SRM III, ed. Bruno Krusch (Hanover: Hahn, 1896), chs. 7–8.

[98] For various readings, see Jacques Fontaine, "King Sisebut's Vita Desiderii and the Political Function of Visigothic Hagiography," in *Visigothic Spain: New Approaches*, ed. Edward James (Oxford: Clarendon Press, 1980), 93–129; Andrew Fear, "The Ghost of

Council of Chalon (602/4)—in an effort to discredit those who condemned Desiderius, and, by extension, their royal masters.

Another hagiographical work with a clear political agenda is the *Passio Leudegarii* (ca. 680), which relates how the Neustrian mayor Ebroin (d. 680), in the name of King Theuderic III, had the holy man brought before a council on charges of plotting the murder of King Childeric II (r. 662–75). Leudegar had originally received his episcopal appointment to the seat of Autun ca. 662 on the order of Queen Balthild, the widow of King Clovis II. After the queen's forced retirement to the monastery of Chelles ca. 664/5, tensions between Ebroin and his political rivals, including Leudegar, worsened.[99] In 673, upon the death of Balthild's son, Chlothar III (r. 657–73), Ebroin chose her other son, Theuderic III, to take his brother's place on the Neustrian throne. Leudegar and his faction engineered a coup against the king and his mayor, and gave the crown to Theuderic's brother, Childeric II. Ebroin's life, we are told, was spared through the intervention of Leudegar.[100] But Leudegar himself soon fell out with the new king, and was locked up in the monastery of Luxeuil, where Ebroin had earlier been incarcerated and tonsured. However, Childeric and his pregnant wife were assassinated in 675, allowing the former bishop and mayor, as well as Theuderic III, to return to public life. Ebroin soon had the upper hand on Leudegar, and had the bishop deposed, as well as physically mutilated.[101] The mayor convoked a council to discredit and eliminate his opponent once and for all. When Leudegar refused to confess his guilt, the conciliar attendees "tore off his tunic from upon his head, and the impious tyrant [i.e., Ebroin] ordered that he [Leudegar] be handed over to a man named Chrodebert, who was then Count of the Palace, and that he be executed by the sword."[102]

In both the *Passio Leudegarii* and the *Vita Sancti Desiderii*, a corrupt state and a corrupt clergy are depicted as working in tandem to bring down an untainted holy man. In neither case, however, was the real

Saint Desiderius," *La Corónica* 29, no. 2 (2001): 79–93; Wood, *The Merovingian Kingdoms*, 173.

[99] Passio Leudegarii Episcopi et Martyris Augustodunensis I, MGH SRM V, ed. Bruno Krusch (Hanover: Hahn, 1910), ch. 4.

[100] *Ibid.*, chs. 5–6.

[101] *Ibid.*, chs. 15–32.

[102] *Passiones Leudegarii Episcopi et Martyris Augustodunensis* I.33 and II.16–7. These complicated events are clearly summarized by Fouracre and Gerberding, *Late Merovingian France*, 21–3.

man politically naïve. Both works were composed by authors whose agendas went beyond simply promoting a cult of sanctity, and who engaged in both character rehabilitation and character assassination.[103] And—as in the letters of Columbanus and Boniface, written before and after the trial of Leudegar, respectively—the authors comment on the moral state of the Frankish episcopate by focusing on its conciliar activities. Although the spiritual and political programs of these *vitae* necessitate our treating their perspectives critically, both accounts emphasize the role the Frankish royal government played in ecclesiastical assemblies, an issue to which we will return frequently in later chapters. Both emphasize, too, the judicial function these assemblies served, and the quite real ability of kings and their officials to influence or corrupt hearings.

Hagiographical narratives, by employing councils as the stages for spiritual dramas, add an otherworldly dimension to these proceedings, reminding us of their broader significance for the religious health of the Frankish kingdoms. Nevertheless, despite the insight that *vitae* can provide into the religious *mentalité* of the period, the late composition of many texts forces us to draw upon them for evidence only with extreme care. The fictionalizing elements of hagiographical literature are problematic enough; anachronistic fabrications only add to the difficulties they pose.[104] Already noted, for example, was the hesitancy of modern editors to include the references to councils found in the *vitae* of Cunibert and Gallus. In both of these texts, the genuineness of the events is difficult to gauge, but neither describes events that are easily provable to be anachronistic. In other late texts, however, conciliar descriptions are more obviously creative interpolations. In the hodgepodge *Vita Dagoberti III*, which scholars have dated to numerous periods between the ninth and eleventh centuries, there is an account of a council that Dagobert (r. 711–15/6) supposedly held in the city of Rouen. We are told that the king himself attended the proceedings and, while there, mediated a dispute between Abbot Hugo of Fontanelle and the *maior domus* Childericus.[105] There are a number of problems

---

[103] On the *Passio Leudegarii*, see Paul Fouracre, "Merovingian History and Merovingian Hagiography," *Past and Present* 127 (1990): 13–21. On the *Vita Desiderii*, see note 98.

[104] Ian Wood, "Forgery in Merovingian Hagiography," in *Monumenta Germaniae Historica: Schriften* 33, Fälschungen im Mittelalter V (1988): 369–84.

[105] *Vita Dagoberti III Regis Francorum*, MGH SRM II, ed. Bruno Krusch (Hanover: Hahn, 1888), ch. 8.

with this account. The *vita* draws heavily upon the language and content of earlier compositions, such as the *Annales Mettenses Priores* and the *Gesta Abbatum Fontanellensium*. In both the *Annales Mettenses* and the *Vita Dagoberti*, for instance, we read that the synods met for the benefit of the church, orphans, and widows ("de utilitatibus ecclesiarum, orfanorum, ac viduarum").[106] Also, the reference to Abbot Hugo is problematic, because he is believed not to have taken office officially until after Dagobert's death (ca. 723).[107] In addition, the mayor Childericus is an invention.[108] And finally, there is the problem of the identity of the title character himself: the author of the *vita* conflates Dagobert III with Dagobert II (r. 676–9).[109] Thus, the "evidence" that the *Vita Dagoberti* offers for Frankish conciliar procedures is questionable at best, dubious at worst. In general, the inherent difficulty of drawing upon hagiographical sources for certain types of information necessitates evaluating each text individually and critically. Although the vast number of *vitae* published in the volumes of the *Monumenta Germaniae Historica* and the *Acta Sanctorum* present a methodological minefield for the modern scholar to traverse, rewards are there, and many of these texts can add vibrancy and color to an otherwise rather lifeless view of conciliar infrastructure and protocol.[110]

---

[106] *Annales Mettenses Priores*, entry for 692.

[107] *Gesta Abbatum Fontanellensium*, ed. and trans. Pascal Pradié (Paris: Les Belles Lettres, 1999), ch. 4.

[108] *Vita Dagoberti III Regis Francorum*, p. 516, note 5.

[109] On the *Vita Dagoberti*, see Alain Dierkens, "Note sur un passage de la Vita Dagoberti: Dagobert II et le domaine de Biesme," *Revue belge de philologie et d'histoire* 62, no. 2 (1984): 259–70; Claude Carozzi, "La Vie de Saint Dagobert de Stenay: Histoire et hagiographie," *Revue belge de philologie et d'histoire* 62, no. 2 (1984): 225–58.

[110] Among the other relevant hagiographical references, reliable and problematic alike, are Gregory of Tours, *Liber Vitae Patrum*, MGH SRM I.2, ed. Bruno Krusch (Hanover: Hahn, 1885), VI.5; Baudonivia, *Vita Sanctae Radegundis Liber II*, MGH SRM II, ed. Bruno Krusch (Hanover: Hahn, 1888), ch. 15; Venantius Fortunatus, *Vita Albini Episcopi Andegavensis*, MGH AA IV.2, ed. Bruno Krusch (Berlin: Weidmann, 1885), ch. XVIII; Ludger of Münster, *Vita Sancti Gregorii Trajectensis*, AASS OSB III.2, ed. Jean Mabillon (Venice: Sebastian Coleti and Joseph Bettinelli,1733–8), ch. 9; Pseudo-Marcellinus, *Vita Suuiberti*, Scriptores Brunsvicensium II, ed. Wilhelm Leibnitz (Hanover: N. Foersteri, 1707–11), II.222–42; *Vita Agili Abbatis Resbacensis*, AASS Aug. VI, ch. 5; *Vita Ansberti Episcopi Rotomagensis*, MGH SRM V, ed. Bruno Krusch (Hanover: Hahn, 1910), ch. 18; *Vita Aviti Episcopi Viennensis*, MGH AA VI.2, ed. Rudolph Peiper (Hanover: Hahn, 1883), ch. 2; *Vita Baboleni*, Recueil des Historiens des Gaules et de la France III, ed. Martin Bouquet (Paris: V. Palmé, 1804–1904), 569D; *Vita Betharii Episcopi Carnoteni*, MGH SRM III, ed. Bruno Krusch (Hanover: Hahn, 1896), ch. 11; *Vita Caesari Episcopi Arelatensis*, MGH SRM III, ed. Bruno Krusch (Hanover: Hahn, 1896), ch. I.60; *Vita Dalmatii Episcopi Ruteni*, MGH SRM III, ed.

The references to councils beyond the authoritative modern editions are thus plentiful, albeit hugely variable in their detail and authenticity. To treat them as missing jigsaw pieces in a larger reconstructive effort, however, would be methodologically dishonest. One of the fundamental arguments of this book is that councils cannot be detached from their immediate historical context and still be understood. The same holds true for the texts that describe them. These, too, were written in different places and times, and by different authors with very different agendas. A description of conciliar activity written in the sixth century often has very different assumptions than one written in the ninth century. Similarly, a document composed in Provence and one written in the Rhineland might reflect differing traditions. Nevertheless, continuities in practice dominate these sources, and are all the more significant for their stability across time and space. Although the fragmentary nature of our evidence certainly complicates any analysis of conciliar procedures, careful use of what survives can tell us a great deal more about the institutional operations of the Frankish councils than was previously assumed. In the next chapter, I draw upon this vast array of evidence to reconstruct the physical world of these ecclesiastical assemblies.

Bruno Krusch (Hanover: Hahn, 1896), ch. 7; *Vita Faronis Episcopi Meldensis*, MGH SRM V, ed. Bruno Krusch (Hanover: Hahn, 1910), ch. 110; *Vita Melanii Episcopi Redonici*, MGH SRM III, ed. Bruno Krusch (Hanover: Hahn, 1896), ch. 4; *Vita Nivardi Episcopi Remensis*, MGH SRM V, ed. Bruno Krusch (Hanover: Hahn, 1910), ch. 7; *Vita Tertia Bonifatii*, in *Vitae Sancti Bonifatii*, ed. Wilhelm Levison (Hanover: Hahn, 1905), ch. 7; *Vita Quarta Bonifatii Auctore Moguntino*, in *Vitae Sancti Bonifatii*, ed. Wilhelm Levison (Hanover: Hahn, 1905), ch. 7; Walahfrid Strabo, *Vita Othmari*, MGH SS II, ed. George Pertz (Hanover: Hahn, 1829), ch. 4–6.

CHAPTER 2

THE PHYSICAL WORLD OF THE FRANKISH COUNCILS

In the year 590, the Austrasian king Childebert II ordered the bishops of his realm, who were scheduled to hold a synod in the city of Verdun that October, to travel to Metz the following month to officiate in a judicial hearing against Bishop Egidius of Rheims, who had been accused of treason. There were torrential rainstorms that fall, which turned the roads to mud and caused the rivers to overflow their banks. These were far from ideal traveling conditions, and the Austrasian bishops were in no mood to leave the comforts of their own *civitates*. Nevertheless, they were compelled by the royal command to brave the elements and participate in the trial.[1]

Gregory of Tours is our source for these events, and his account offers an important reminder that the reality of conciliar participation was neither as tidy nor as undemanding as suggested by the surviving canonical *acta*. The standard *cum...convenissemus* formula that introduces many conciliar acts obscures the effort and planning that allowed bishops to come together as a united body.[2] From the composition of letters of convocation to the protocol of the meeting itself, the holding of an ecclesiastical synod was a complex matter, and one that was deeply affected by the world outside the meeting hall.

Preliminaries

All councils, regardless of size or agenda, began with the decision that circumstances demanded the collective deliberation of the bishops. Who made this decision, and what these circumstances were, could vary considerably. Between 511 and 768, sixteen conciliar acts in prefatory statements explicitly credit their convocation to the reigning

[1] Gregory of Tours *Decem Libri Historiarum* X.19. On Egidius and his involvement in political conspiracies, see Bachrach, *Anatomy of a Little War*, 48–9, 78–81, 107–8.

[2] Variations of this formula can be found in the *praefationes* of the acts of the Councils of Arles (524), Orange (529), Marseilles (533), Orléans (533), Clermont (535), Orléans (538), Orléans (541), Paris (552), Lyons (567/70), Mâcon (581/3), Valence (583/5), Paris (614), Clichy (626/7), and Bordeaux (662/76).

princeps.[3] We know from secondary references of at least thirty more councils convoked on royal authority.[4] The frequency of royal convocations has encouraged some scholars to assume that royal approval was required for the holding of a synod.[5] Besides at least twenty-nine

[3] Orléans (511), Preface: "Cum autore Deo ex evocatione gloriosissimi regi Clothovechi in Aurelianensi urbe fuisset concilium summorum antestitum congregatum"; Orléans (533), Preface: "Cum ex praeceptione gloriosissimus regum…convenimus"; Clermont (535), Preface: "Cum…consentiente domno nostro gloriosissimo piissimove regi Theudebertho in Arverna urbe sancta synodus convenisset"; Orléans (549), Preface: "Cum clementissimus princeps domnus triumphorum titulis invictissimus Childbertus rex pro amore sacrae fidei et statu religionis in Aurelianensi urbe congragasset in unum Domini sacerdotes"; Paris (551/2), Preface: "Cum in urbe Parissius ad invitationem domini regis gloriosissimi Childeberthi venissimus"; Tours (567), Preface: "Quapropter Christo auspice in Turonica civitate consilio concordante iuxta coniventiam gloriosissimi domni Chariberthi regis adnuentis coadunati"; Mâcon (581/3), Preface: "Cum ad iniunctionem gloriosissimi domni Guntramni Regis tam pro causis publicis pro necessitatibus pauperum in urbe Matiscensi nostra mediocritas convenisset"; Valence (583/5), Conciliar Acts: "Cum in urbe Valentina iuxta imperium gloriosissimi domini Guntramni regis nostra mediocritas pro diversis pauperum querimoniis convenisset"; Paris (614), Preface: "Cum…ex evocatione gloriosissimi principis domni Hlotharii regis in synodali concilio convenissemus"; Clichy (626/7), Preface: "Suggerente gloriosissimo atque piissimo domno Hlothario rege…venissemus"; Chalon (647/53), Preface: "[E]x evocatione vel ordinatione gloriosissimi domni Chlodovei regis pro zelo religionis vel ortodoxae fidei dilectione in Cabillonense urbe in ecclesia sancti Vincenti pariter conglobati"; Bordeaux (662/76), Preface: "Cum…per iussorium gloriosi principis Childericis regis convenissemus"; St. Jean-de-Losne (673/5), Preface: "[I]n praesentia gloriosissimi principis nostri domni Childerici regis congregate eramus"; Germania (742), Preface: "Ego Karlmannus, dux et princeps Francorum...cum consilio servorum Dei et optimatum meorum episcopos, qui in regno meo sunt, cum presbiteris et concilium et synodum pro timore Christi congregavi"; Soissons (744), Preface: "Dum plures non habeatur incognitum, qualiter nos in Dei nomine una cum consensu episcoporum sive sacerdotum vel servorum Dei consilio seu comitibus et obtimatibus Francorum conloqui apud Suessionis civitas synodum vel concilio facere decrevimus: quod ita in Dei nomine et fecimus"; Ver (755), Preface: "Ideoque gloriosissimus atque religiosus inluster vir, Francorum rex Pippinus, universos paene Galliarum episcopos adgregari fecit ad concilium Vernus palatio publico, recuperare aliquantisper cupiens institute canonica." The Council of Ascheim (756) addresses the Bavarian Duke Tassilo in its preface: "Domino gloriossimo duce nostro Tassiloni maxime congregatio iura synodali per presentes eulogias in Christo salutem dirigitur."

[4] I.e., Toul (550), Metz (550/5), Lyons (567/70), Paris (573), Paris (577), Chalon (579), Berny (580), Lyons (581), Troyes (585), Mâcon (585), Unknown 1 (588), Unknown 2 (588), Unknown 1 (589), Unknown 2 (589), Poitiers (589/90), Verdun/Metz (590), Chalon (602/4), Mâcon (626/7), Clichy (636), Orléans (639/41), Clichy (654), Unknown (675), Mâlay-le-Roi (677), Unknown (ca. 677/9), Unknown (689) [by Pippin II], Les Estinnes (743), Düren (748), Compiègne (757), Gentilly (767), and most certainly Orléans (538), Orléans (541), Verberie (756), and Attigny (762), even though royal convocation is not explicitly stated. Those councils whose authenticity is questionable have not been included in this tally.

[5] E.g., Hauck, *Kirchengeschichte Deutschlands*, I.164–5; Voigt, *Staat und Kirche*, 248; Ewig, *Merowinger und das Frankenreich*, 104–5. Others have seen the king's absolute

identifiable councils that bear no mark of royal convocation,[6] the earliest claim that royal approval was requisite for conciliar convocation dates only to the middle seventh century, when an irate King Sigibert III (r. 632–56) complained in a letter to Bishop Desiderius of Cahors that he had recently learned from his *fideles* that a council had been scheduled for the Kalends of September (ca. 643) without his knowledge:

> Since it was hidden from our previous notice, it has been agreed with our *proceres* that a *synodalis concilius* may not assemble in our kingdom without our knowledge, nor on the *Kalends* of September may any meeting of *sacerdotes* occur of which we are unaware that pertains to our rule. Afterwards, if we are informed in advance at an opportune time, whether on account of ecclesiastical affairs or the *regni utilitas*, we will not refuse to allow it to meet under the reasonable condition that, as we have said, we are informed first.[7]

It is ironic that this unprecedented claim for monarchical privilege should come from a young king who had so recently (639) been humiliated in battle by Duke Radulf of Thuringia, and whose palace mayor, Grimoald, would place his own son on the throne following the king's death.[8] It has been plausibly suggested that Grimoald himself was responsible for the composition of this letter.[9] Certainly, in the seventh century, the Frankish nobility began to demonstrate an intense interest

right of approval as limited to national, as opposed to provincial, councils, e.g., Loening, *Geschichte des deutschen Kirchenrechts*, II.204–5; Weyl, *Das fränkische Staatskirchenrecht zur Zeit der Merovinger*, 17–9, 25–6; Barion, Das *fränkisch-deutsche Synodalrecht*, 222–3.

[6] I.e., Lyons (516), Epaone (517), Lyons (518/9), Arles (524), Carpentras (527), Valence (528), Orange (529), Vaison (529), Marseilles (533), Eauze (551), Brittany (ca. 552), Arles (554), Paris (556/73), Saintes (ca. 558/61), Saintes (561/7), Saintes (579), Lyons (583), Auvergne (584/91), Auxerre (585/605), Sorcy (589), Auvergne (590), Unknown (ca. 614), Bourges (ca. 630/43), Bourges (ca. 643), Arles (648/60), Paris (653), Nantes (655/8), Autun (ca. 662/76), and Auxerre (692/6). Although Orléans (538), Orléans (541), Verberie (756), and Attigny (762) bear no explicit marks of monarchical convocation, circumstances strongly suggest that they were convoked by royal authority. Those councils whose authenticity or conciliar status have been questioned have not been included in this tally.

[7] Desiderius of Cahors *Epistulae S. Desiderii Cadurcensis* II.17.

[8] For the former event, see Fredegar *Chronica* IV.87. For the latter, see *Liber Historiae Francorum*, MGH SRM II, ed. Bruno Krusch (Hanover: Hahn, 1888), 43. On Radulf and Grimoald, see Martindale, ed., *The Prosopography of the Later Roman Empire*, IIIB.1075, IIIA.556.

[9] Pierre Gérard, *Histoire des Francs d'Austrasie*, 2d ed. (Bruxelles: J. Rosez, 1865), I.359.

in participating in the convocation process.[10] Regardless of the letter's true authorship, its claims were both unprecedented and unique in the Merovingian period. As in the Roman imperial era, secular powers often did instigate, officially or unofficially, a council's convocation, but this was not a mandated practice. It was not until the middle of the eighth century, and the victory of the Pippinid family, that expanded royal convocation rights were asserted again. At the Council of Ver, held in the year 755 on the orders of King Pippin I, it was decreed that kingdom-wide synods were to be held on the *Kalends* of March every year "where the *domnus rex* orders, and in his presence."[11] This canon, however, in no way forbade the meeting of non-royally convoked councils.

Those councils not convoked on the order of the king or his secular *fideles* were convoked on episcopal authority. According to numerous canonical pronouncements issued during this period, it was the duty of all metropolitan bishops to convoke a synod in their provinces, either annually[12] or biannually.[13] Serious illness was the only legitimate reason for failing to attend these mandatory assemblies.[14] Nevertheless, some scholars have seen an eclipse of provincial synods by royal or "national" councils during the course of the Merovingian

[10] E.g., *Vita Eligii Episcopi Noviomagensis* I.35; Jonas of Bobbio *Vitae Columbani Abbatis Discipulorumque Eius Libri Duo* II.9; *Annales Mettenses Priores*, entry for 692. Additionally, the Bavarian council of Ascheim (756) was convoked by Duke Tassilo. A further example of uncertain reliability is Constance (ca. 635/40), supposedly convoked by Duke Gunzo of Alamannia.

[11] Ver (755), c. 4.

[12] Orléans (533), c. 2; Orléans (538), c. 1; Orléans (541), c. 37; Orléans (549), c. 23; Chalon (647/53), Preface. Eauze (551), c. 7; Germania (742), c. 1; and Soissons (744), c. 2 require that a synod be held yearly, but do not indicate that it is the duty of the metropolitan to convoke it. This requirement is echoed by Boniface *S. Bonifatii et Lulli Epistolae*, no. 78. An earlier Gallic precedent for these decrees is Agde (506), c. 49.

[13] Tours (567), c. 1. Ver (755), c. 4, requires that synods be held biannually, but does not indicate that it is the duty of the metropolitan to convoke them. Earlier Gallic precedents for these decrees can be found in Riez (439), c. 7, and Orange (441), c. 28. Avitus of Vienne recalls this requirement, as well as the Gallic bishops' negligence in enforcing it, in his convocation letter for the Council of Epaone (517): De Clercq, ed., *Concilia Galliae: A.511–A.695*, 22–3. This requirement was likewise echoed by Pope Gregory III in a letter to the bishops of Allamania and Bavaria: Boniface *S. Bonifatii et Lulli Epistolae*, no. 44. For an even earlier precedent, see Nicaea (325), c. 5.

[14] Epaone (517), c. 1; Orléans (533), c. 1; Orléans (538), c. 1; Orléans (549), c. 18; Tours (567), c. 1. For general statements concerning the necessity of conciliar attendance, see also Eauze (551), c. 7; Mâcon (585), c. 20; St. Jean-de-Losne (673/75), c. 21; Pippin *Capitulary of 754/5*, in *Capitularia Regum Francorum*, no. 3.

period.[15] There are good reasons to accept this view: we can identify with some surety only eighteen provincial synods between the years of 511 and 768, fourteen of them in the sixth century, which could suggest that the practice of holding them was in a steady decline.[16] On the other hand, as provincial synods were less likely to issue original canons, we would expect our knowledge of their proceedings, as well as their very existence, to be limited in comparison with the royal or other interprovincial synods of the same period.[17] Moreover, the abundance of canonical pronouncements requiring their assemblage suggests, at the very least, that this requirement was taken seriously by the Gallic bishops, even if they failed in their duty to hold provincial councils on a regular basis. There is also no evidence to suggest that the Frankish kings had an active policy of discouraging provincial meetings. Finally, the growing importance of national borders in determining conciliar attendance did not necessarily require the cessation of the holding of councils on the provincial, or, for that matter, diocesan level, especially if the monarchy never succeeded entirely in appropriating the responsibility for convoking local synods.[18]

---

[15] Emile Lesne, *La hiérarchie épiscopale: Provinces, métropolitains, primats en Gaule et Germanie* (Lille: Facultes Catholiques, 1905), 16–7; Hinschius, *Kirchenrecht*, III.476–7; Loening, *Geschichte des deutschen Kirchenrechts*, II.208–9; Barion, *Das fränkisch-deutsche Synodalrecht*, 19, 25–6; Ewig, *Merowinger und das Frankenreich*, 105. In contrast to this view, see De Clercq, *La législation religieuse franque*, 73; Basdevant-Gaudemet, "Les évêques, les papes, et les princes," 4. Wallace-Hadrill, *The Frankish Church*, 263, notes that even during the reign of Charlemagne, which arguably saw the most radical centralization of conciliar activity under royal supervision, provincial councils continued to be held.

[16] I.e., Arles (524), Carpentras (527), Orange (529), Vaison (529), Marseilles (533), Eauze (551), Brittany (552), Arles (554), Saintes (ca. 558–61), Saintes (561/7), Saintes (579), Auvergne (584/91), Sorcy (589), Auvergne (590), Bourges (ca. 630/43), Bourges (ca. 643), Arles (648/50), Autun (ca. 662/76). The provincial status of several of these councils, e.g. Autun (ca. 662/76), cannot be proven definitively. Those councils whose authenticity or conciliar status is questionable have not been included in this tally, e.g., Tours (ca. 580).

[17] Champagne and Szramkiewicz, "Recherches sur les conciles des temps mérovingiens," 19. Because very often provincial councils had a judicial component to their agenda, it rightly has been suggested that their interest was more in applying than composing canons: Hermann Schmitz, "Die Tendenz der Provinzialsynoden in Gallien seit dem 5: Jahrhundert und die römischen Bussbücher," *Archiv für katholisches Kirchenrecht* 65 (1894): 29.

[18] Wallace-Hadrill, *The Frankish Church*, 107. Diocesan synods were held in Auxerre around the years 585/605 and 692/6. Boniface *S. Bonifatii et Lulli Epistolae*, no. 78, observes that it is the duty of metropolitans to compel their suffragans to hold diocesan synods in order to convey the decisions made at larger councils.

In a number of instances, it is clear that the individual who convoked a synod, whether king or bishop, had intentions for its agenda at the time of convocation. When a council had a judicial component to its agenda, for example, the individuals to be examined were identified and notified in advance. Such conciliar trials were common during this period, and canonical regulations are explicit about the fact that one of the primary functions of ecclesiastical synods is to serve as tribunals and courts of appeal for members of the clergy.[19] Additionally, advance planning can be assumed for those councils that met with the aim of confirming the appointment or election of new bishops or abbots,[20] as well as those that issued or confirmed monastic or other ecclesiastical privileges.[21] As for the legislation of the Frankish councils, most of the time it is impossible to ascertain from the surviving *acta* when specific items were added to the agenda. Those cases where the authors of a canonical document are explicit about the specific events and concerns that prompted their legislation are relatively sparse, and most involve judicial cases.[22] For example, the Council of Lyons (518/9), which discussed charges of incest laid against a powerful Burgundian royal official, acknowledged in its *acta,* "In the name of the Trinity, having congregated again in the *urbs* of Lyons for the reason of Stephanus, polluted by the crime of incest, we declare that we shall preserve untouched our earlier decision, which we agreed to unanimously, for the condemnation of both himself and the one joined with him in illicit union."[23] The few surviving letters of convocation are relatively vague about the legislative agendas of the proposed councils.[24] This, in itself, could be problematic, for a bishop not eager to make the trek to

---

[19] I.e., Orléans (538), c. 22; Orléans (538), c. 23; Orléans (538), c. 24; Orléans (549), c. 17; Arles (554), c. 1; Tours (567), c. 2; Tours (567), c. 7; Tours (567), c. 8; Tours (567), c. 9; Mâcon (585), c. 9; Paris (614), c. 4; Clichy (626/7), c. 6; Ver (755), c. 5; Ver (755), c. 13. This judicial function is reiterated in a number of other sources, e.g., *Epistolae aevi Merowingici Collectae*, no. 3; Boniface, *S. Bonifatii et Lulli Epistolae*, nos. 44, 51, 60, 80.

[20] E.g., Metz (550/5), Bordeaux (584/5), Mâcon (585), Clichy (636), and Soissons (744). Additional examples of questionable authenticity are Cologne (ca. 626), Constance (ca. 635/40), and Compiègne (665).

[21] On these privileges, see the introduction.

[22] E.g., Lyons (518/9), c. 1; Carpentras (527), Epistle; Orléans (549), c. 15; Mâcon (581/3), c. 20; Chalon (647/53), c. 20. Also, the use of the verb *cognovimus* is sometimes an indicator that the legislators are responding to a real-world situation: e.g., Epaone (517), c. 2; Tours (567), c. 23; Mâcon (585), cc. 14, 19; Chalon (639/53), c. 20.

[23] Lyons (518/9), c. 1.

[24] E.g., De Clercq, ed., *Concilia Galliae: A.511–A.695*, 23–4. Avitus of Vienne's convocation letter for the same council (Epaone) is silent about its goals: ibid., 22–3.

a council whose agenda was a mystery could take this silence as an excuse to stay home.[25]

Nevertheless, there is evidence that the conveners of at least some Frankish councils had an agenda of specific issues they wished to be addressed prior to meeting.[26] An example of a preconceived agenda can be noted as early as the year 511, when the bishops meeting at Orléans wrote in a letter to Clovis that "it is in accordance with your *consultatio* and with the articles (*tituli*) communicated by you that we respond with the decisions that seemed proper."[27] Although we do not possess the text of Clovis' *tituli*, their content can be inferred from the council's address of issues of royal concern, particularly in the first ten canons of the canonical record.[28] In another case of royal participation, Gregory of Tours offers a fascinating account of King Guntram enumerating for Gregory himself the topics that he wished to be addressed at a future synod (ca. 588), including a discussion of misdeeds that had recently been committed, the mysterious murder of Bishop Praetextatus in his own church, and the sin of *luxuria*.[29] Guntram also, prior to the Council of Valence of 585, sent his referendarius, Asclepiodotus, to deliver *epistolae* to the synod to communicate his intentions for its agenda.[30]

A few councils of this period explicitly relate their decision to meet and legislate with regard to lax discipline among the clergy.[31] It also was relatively common to justify the meeting of a synod by pointing to the needs of the poor.[32] Although one might be tempted to dismiss these claims of charitable intent as mere *formulae*, the Frankish councils did devote a considerable amount of legislation to poor-relief, as befitted the episcopal attendees' roles as lovers and governors of the

---

[25] *Epistolae Austrasicae*, no. 11 (Mappinus of Rheims to Nicetius of Trier).

[26] Barion, *Das fränkisch-deutsche Synodalrecht*, 91–6.

[27] Orléans (511), Letter to Clovis.

[28] J. M. Wallace-Hadrill, *The Long-Haired Kings* (London: Methuen, 1962), 177; Daly, "Clovis: How Barbarian, How Pagan," 659.

[29] Gregory of Tours *Decem Libri Historiarum* IX.20.

[30] Valence (583/5), Conciliar Acts.

[31] De Clercq, ed., *Concilia Galliae: A.511–A.695*, 23–4 (re. Epaone); Bordeaux (662/76), Preface; Boniface *S. Bonifatii et Lulli Epistolae*, no. 50 (re. Germania 742; see also Pope Zachary's response in epistle no. 51).

[32] Mâcon (581/3), Preface; Valence (583/5), Conciliar Acts; *Annales Mettenses Priores*, entries for 692 and 748. An additional example can be found in the unreliable *Vita Dagoberti III Regis Francorum*, ch. 8, whose language is derived from the *Annales Mettenses Priores* entry for 692.

poor.[33] Moreover, the church's ability to provide charity was tied intrinsically to its financial well-being and the preservation of its property, which were also legislative topics regularly addressed during this period.[34] It therefore seems safe to assume that many Frankish councils, especially those in which the monarchy played a substantial role, met with at least some of their agenda established in advance.

But before letters of convocation could be sent out, a time and location for the meeting had to be chosen. A number of factors influenced the selection of a date. Seasonal temperatures needed to be considered, for extreme heat and cold could make the journey unbearable for the attendees. In general, the relatively temperate months of September, October, and November, as well as May and June, were the most popular for holding councils.[35] Virtually no meetings were held between December and February, because of frigid temperatures, and August was equally unpopular due to its oppressive heat.[36] Bishop Ruricius of Limoges (ca. 485–510), in his correspondence, probably spoke for many of his episcopal brethren in stating his own preference for autumn as an ideal travel time.[37] At the Council of Mâcon (585) too, the attending bishops pleaded with the presiding metropolitans to speed along the proceedings, lest winter storms prevent them from returning home.[38] Still, the coincidence of the harvest could make the autumn a difficult

---

[33] Ullmann, "Public Welfare and Social Legislation in the Early Medieval Councils," 1–39; Edward James, "Beati Pacifici: Bishops and the Law in Sixth-Century Gaul," in *Disputes and Settlements: Law and Human Relations in the West*, ed. John Bossy (Cambridge: Cambridge University Press, 1983), 45; Pontal, *Histoire des conciles mérovingiens*, 292. On bishops as lovers and governors of the poor, see Peter Brown, *Poverty and Leadership in the Later Roman Empire* (Hanover, NH: University Press of New England, 2001).

[34] Michel Rouche, "La matricule des pauvres: Evolution d'une institution de charité du Bas Empire jusqu'à la fin du Haut Moyen Age," in *Études sur l'histoire de la pauvreté*, vol. 1, ed. Michel Mollat (Paris: Publications de la Sorbonne, 1974), 84–9. An individual who threatened church property was frequently labeled a *necator pauperum*, an expression that dates back to the Council of Vaison (442), c. 4. On this expression, see Michael Edward Moore, "A Sacred Kingdom: Royal and Episcopal Power in the Frankish Realms" (Ph.D. diss., University of Michigan, 1993), 132; Rouche, "La Matricule des Pauvres," 84–5.

[35] See attached Calendar of Councils. Late autumn had also been the most popular meeting time for fifth-century councils: Ralph Mathisen, ed., *Ruricius of Limoges and Friends: A Collection of Letters from Visigothic Gaul* (Liverpool: Liverpool University Press, 1999), 42; 195, note 12.

[36] Only one council, Eauze (551), is known to have been held in February.

[37] Ruricius of Limoges, *Epistulae*, MGH AA VIII, ed. Bruno Krusch (Berlin: Weidmann, 1887), II.10.

[38] Mâcon (585), Preface.

time for some bishops to leave their sees, a difficulty occasionally acknowledged by convokers.[39] When it came to choosing a specific day for the opening of the council, easily remembered dates such as the *Kalends* were popular choices.[40] Sometimes, too, councils were scheduled in order to coincide with other events of episcopal interest, such as the dedication of churches.[41] Beginning in the reign of Chlothar II, it became progressively more common for councils to meet in conjunction with royal assemblies, the so-called *concilia mixta*.

Choosing a location for a council similarly necessitated taking into consideration a number of relevant factors. Although the difficulty of travel for the individual attendees had to be considered, and a centralized location was to be preferred, ultimately the decision lay with the individual who convoked the council.[42] If he was the king, naturally he found it convenient to convene the council in or near one of his palaces or villas.[43] Such locations would not have been inconvenient in theory for the conciliar attendees, because royal residences tended to be situated in locations easily accessible by river and the Roman road system.[44] Nevertheless, it was the king's convenience that was being given priority.

---

[39] De Clercq, ed., *Concilia Galliae: A.511–A.695*, 22–3.

[40] Ten councils are known to have been convoked for the *Kalends* of the month; see attached Calendar of Councils.

[41] E.g., the Council of Arles (524), which was held in conjunction with the dedication of the basilica of St. Mary in Arles; Orange (529), which was held in conjunction with the dedication of a basilica by the *patricius* Liberius; Valence (583/5), which confirmed the foundation of the monastery of St. Marcellus; and Nantes (655/8), which met to discuss the rebuilding of the monastery of Hautvillier.

[42] E.g., as Avitus of Vienne states in his convocation letter for the Council of Epaone (517), in De Clercq, ed., *Concilia Galliae: A.511–A.695*, 22–3, "Therefore, brothers, we request that you agree to come, God willing, on the eighth day of the Ides of September to the parish of Epaone, which was selected as a central and opportune location for the meeting when we considered the fatigue of everyone." Similarly, Auvergne (590) met "in confinio vero termini Arverni, Gabalitani atque Ruteni." For the right of the convoker to choose the council's location, see Tours (567), c. 1.

[43] The Councils of Berny (580), Mâlay-le-Roi (677), Unknown (ca. 680), Les Estinnes (743), Düren (748), Ver (755), Verberie (756), Ascheim (756), Compiègne (757), Attigny (762), and Gentilly (767) all met in royal or ducal palaces. An even greater number of councils met in proximity to the capitals of the Frankish kings, if not in the residences themselves. On royal residences in Francia, see Eugen Ewig, "Résidence et capitale pendant le Haut Moyen Age," *Revue historique* 230 (1963): 47–70; Alain Dierkens and Patrick Périn, "Les sedes regiae mérovingiennes entre Seine et Rhin," in *Sedes Regiae (ann. 400–800)*, ed. Gisela Ripoll and Josep M. Gurt (Barcelona: Reial Academia de Bones Lletres, 2000), 267–304.

[44] Stéphane Lebecq, "Entre antique tardive et très Haut Moyen Age: Permanence et mutations des systèmes de communications dans la Gaule et ses marges," *Settimane di Studio del Centro Italiano di Studi Sull'Alto Medioevo* 45.1 (1997): 489.

Besides royal villas, councils were regularly scheduled to meet in ecclesiastical basilicas.[45] The selected building needed to be able to accommodate comfortably a large number of men, as well as offer some degree of privacy for the deliberations. In some cases, the individual who convoked a council had preexisting ties with the chosen location, such as the Merovingian royal family with the Basilica of St. Peter in Paris, located on the left bank of the Seine, where three separate councils assembled in the sixth and seventh centuries. Clovis I and his wife, Chlothild, had ordered the construction of this building, and it was the primary burial place of the Merovingian family during the first half of the sixth century.[46] In order to deliberate in relative seclusion, the bishops who attended the Council of Paris (577) gathered in the audience hall (*secretarium*) of the Basilica of St. Peter, the same location where episcopal court customarily was held.[47] The *secretarium* also was a regular assembly place for councils held throughout the late Roman and early medieval West.[48] The roughly equal number of attendees of the Council of Clichy (626/7) sat in the *atrium* of St. Denis, which provided a relatively spacious, if somewhat less private, forum for their deliberations.[49] Although these are our only two definite references to council locations within larger ecclesiastical structures, both *secretaria* and *atria* were customary choices for ecclesiastical meetings in Late Antiquity, and there is every reason to suppose that Gallic assemblies congregated in them frequently.

Convocation

A date and location having been chosen, the attendees could be officially invited to the council. The easiest way to publicize this decision

[45] The Council of Tours (567) met in the Basilica of St. Martin, Paris (573) in the Basilica of St. Peter, Paris (577) in the same basilica, Paris (614) also in the same basilica, Poitiers (589/90) in the Cathedral of Poitiers, Clichy (626/7) in the Basilica of St. Mary, Chalon (647/53) in the Cathedral of St. Vincent, Bordeaux (662/76) in the Basilica of St. Peter, and Auxerre (692/6) in the Church of St. Stephan. On ecclesiastical architecture in early medieval Gaul, see Jean Hubert, *L'architecture religieuse du Haut Moyen Âge en France* (Paris: Imprimerie Nationale, 1952).

[46] Jean-Charles Picard et al., *Province ecclésiastique de Sens (Lugdunensis Senonia)*, Topographie chrétienne des cites de la Gaule VIII (Paris: De Boccard, 1992), 116–9.

[47] Gregory of Tours *Decem Libri Historiarum* V.18.

[48] Jean-Charles Picard, "La fonction des salles de réception dans le groupe épiscopal de Genève," *Rivista di archeologia cristiana* 65, nos. 1–2 (1989): 87–104; MacMullen, *Voting About God in Early Church Councils*, 78–9.

[49] Clichy (626/7), Preface.

was for a council already in session to schedule a future meeting.[50] In general, however, this method does not seem to have been favored among the larger royally convoked synods. For these, kings took advantage of the metropolitan provincial system to announce their decisions to all of the invitees. Rather than write to all of the bishops of his kingdom personally, a king sent letters to the metropolitan bishops, so that they, in turn, could inform the suffragans under their supervision about the scheduled council.[51] In a surviving letter written by the metropolitan bishop Mappinus of Rheims in 550, for example, the bishop notes that he learned of a synod scheduled to be held in Toul from a letter written in the name of King Theudebald himself.[52] This was the most efficient means of communication, although it is certainly possible that kings occasionally chose to communicate their will via a single metropolitan.

For non-royally convoked interprovincial councils, too, it was the duty of the metropolitans to inform their respective suffragan bishops of the council's convocation. Two different letters of convocation survive from the Burgundian Council of Epaone (517), for example. One was written by Avitus, the metropolitan bishop of Vienne (ca. 494–518), and the other by Viventiolus, the metropolitan of Lyons (ca. 513/4–524). Each letter was addressed to the bishops of their respective ecclesiastical provinces.[53] In the case of provincial councils, a metropolitan similarly had the responsibility of contacting his suffragans directly.[54] Finally, all bishops had the right to convene the clerics under their supervision in diocesan synods.

Despite the often-stated claim that the partitioning of the Frankish kingdoms with new "national borders" caused an irreparable deterioration of the metropolitan provincial system, its use as a basis for council convocation can be taken as a sign of its continuing vitality, at least

[50] Carpentras (527), Epistle; Auxerre (585/605), c. 7; Mâcon (585), c. 20; Chalon (647/53), Epistle to Theudorius of Arles; St. Jean-de-Losne (673/75), c. 11. The Gallic Council of Orange (441) had ordered that no council should disband before another was scheduled (c. 28), but this rule seems not to have been regularly observed in the post-Roman period.

[51] Barion, *Das fränkisch-deutsche Synodalrecht*, 52–3.

[52] *Epistolae Austrasicae*, no. 11.

[53] De Clercq, ed., *Concilia Galliae: A.511–A.695*, 22–4.

[54] For the rules regarding the convocation of provincial councils by metropolitan bishops, see Epaone (517), c. 1; Orléans (533) c. 1; Orléans (533) c. 2; Orléans (538), c. 1; Orléans (541), c. 37; Orléans (549), c. 18; Orléans (549), c. 23; Tours (567), c. 1; Chalon (647/53), Preface.

through the late seventh century.[55] Take, for example, the Council of Mâcon of 581/3, a royally convoked interprovincial synod whose attendance was discussed in the preceding chapter. The twenty-one bishops who attended the council all came from *civitates* that lay within the territorial domain of King Guntram, which stretched from south-eastern to central Gaul.[56] These *civitates* also lay within six ecclesiastical provinces—Lyons, Vienne, Sens, Bourges, Arles, and Besançon—all of which, with the lone exception of Arles, were represented at the council by their metropolitan bishop. The metropolitans, in turn, were all from *civitates* within Guntram's *regnum*. Their leadership role at the council is reflected in the location of their signatures at the top of the conciliar subscription list. However, not every bishop from each of the represented provinces attended the council, and, in some cases, their absence can be explained by conflicting political borders. For example, Paris, Cahors, and Limoges, all of which lay within the represented ecclesiastical territories, were controlled at the time by Guntram's brother Chilperic, and their bishops did not attend.[57]

Similarly, at the Council of Bordeaux (662/76), the last seventh-century council with signed canonical *acta*, three provinces—Bourges, Bordeaux, and Eauze—were represented by their metropolitans, along with a substantial number of their respective suffragans. All of the attending bishops resided within the territory controlled by the Aquitanian *dux*, Lupus, in the name of King Childeric II, and the council clearly was intended to be an Aquitanian affair.[58] Like the Council of Jean-de-Losne (673/75), the meeting at Bordeaux seems to reflect Childeric's efforts to confirm his authority in a region of tenuous loyalty.[59]

---

[55] This claim is made to varying degrees by, among others, Lesne, *La hiérarchie épiscopale*, 8–29; Ewig, *Merowinger und das Frankenreich*, 105; Kaiser, "Les évêques et leurs pouvoirs," 99; James, *The Origins of France*, 197; Harries, "Church and State in the Notitia Galliarum," 28; Suntrup, *Studien zur politischen Theologie im frühmittelalterlichen Okzident*, 78, 131–2, 184–7; and Jean Heuclin, *Hommes de Dieu et fonctionnaires du roi* (Villeneuve d'Ascq: Septentrion, 1998), 73.

[56] Guntram had gained control over the valleys of the Rhône and Saône, and portions of Provence upon the death of his father, Chlothar I (561). He did not acquire the province of Arles until 567, upon the death of his brother Charibert. For a summary of the Merovingian *Teilreiche*, see Ian Wood, *The Merovingian Kingdoms*, 55–8.

[57] Paris, strictly speaking, was a shared city, although it lay within Chilperic's *regnum*.

[58] Pontal, *Histoire des conciles mérovingiens*, 229–31.

[59] Ibid., 222–3, 229–31. Not surprisingly, the two councils shared some common legislative concerns.

As these two examples illustrate, neither political nor ecclesiastical borders alone determined synodal attendance, even at royally convoked interprovincial councils. However, despite canonical prescriptions explicitly forbidding bishops from excusing their absences by claiming that shifting regnal territorial divisions prevented their attendance, the subscription lists demonstrate that, at the very least, these divisions were considered in determining which bishops would be invited to an interprovincial council.[60] As for the metropolitan provincial system, Gregory of Tours' *Historiae* confirm that it was still active in the 590s, although the power of individual metropolitans varied, and some, including Gregory himself, found it increasingly difficult to control their independent-minded suffragans.[61] Evidence that the system, even if in a diluted state, survived up until the eighth century can be found in the late-seventh-century episcopal privileges. Not only is it possible to discern hints of a rank order among the subscribing metropolitans, several of the charters are addressed to the episcopal authors' comprovincials.[62] This attention to hierarchy and order suggests the maintenance of a provincial organization that facilitated the convocation of ecclesiastical councils. This being said, there are only thirteen known instances in the Merovingian period of an ecclesiastical province being represented at a council by all of its dioceses.[63]

Avitus of Vienne's invitation to the Council of Epaone (517) suggests the form that a metropolitan convocation letter to an interprovincial synod might take. The epistle opens with a reminder of the necessity of holding regular councils, and the failure of the Gallic bishops to do so. Therefore, as the metropolitan representative of his province, Avitus proposes that they meet to raise their concerns, and take this opportunity to discuss old and new matters alike. He then requests his suffragans' presence on the eighth day of the Ides of September (September 6)

[60] Champagne and Szramkiewicz, "Recherches sur les conciles des temps mérovingiens," 7–15. For the canonical prohibition of the excuse of allowing national borders to interfere with conciliar attendance, see Orléans (538), c. 1.

[61] E.g., Gregory of Tours *Decem Libri Historiarum* VI.38, IX.20, IX.41. On the province of Tours in the later sixth century, see Luce Pietri, *La ville de Tours du IVe au Vie siècle: Naissance d'une cite chrétienne* (Paris: École Française de Rome, 1983), 293–302.

[62] Ewig, "Beobachtungen zu den Bischofslisten," 437–46. As Ewig notes, in several cases, the addressees include bishops who do not reside in the same province as the bishop granting the privilege. For example, the addressees of Emmo of Sens' privilege for St. Pierre-le-Vif include Audoenus of Rouen and Eligius of Noyon.

[63] Champagne and Szramkiewicz, "Recherches sur les conciles des temps mérovingiens," 19.

at Epaone. Avitus does not name a specific meeting place in the parish, which likely means that there was only one major church in the district. He begs that no one offer any excuse save illness to avoid attending, and that anyone who is unable to travel send two priests as delegates on his behalf. Finally, Avitus requests that these decisions be conveyed to all of the churches of the province, i.e., Vienne.[64]

It is informative to compare Avitus' letter with that written by his co-metropolitan, Viventiolus of Lyons, who, unlike Avitus, expresses the wish that both *clerici* and *laici* will attend the *conventus episcoporum*.[65] Viventiolus seems to have assumed that it was the prerogative of bishops to decide whether laymen ought to be invited.[66] The nun Baudonivia confirms this prerogative in her *Vita Sanctae Radegundis*, where she writes that the metropolitan bishop Leontius of Bordeaux invited a *Vir Inlustris* named Leo to attend a council in the *civitas* of Saintes ca. 558/61.[67] In other cases, however, it appears that the lay attendees were royal representatives, for example, Duke Lupus, who attended the Council of Bordeaux (662/76) on behalf of King Childeric II.[68] Regardless, it also is interesting to note that Viventiolus' letter was composed *sub die IIII idus mensis IIII* (April 10), almost a full five months before the September 6 convocation date, which Viventiolus neglects to give.[69]

This may seem to be an excessive amount of time, considering that the Council of Epaone's attendance was confined to the dioceses within the borders of the Burgundian kingdom. But when one takes into account the time it took for the metropolitans' letters to be delivered, travel preparations to be made, and the journey itself to be undertaken, five months is not an excessive amount of time. For example, Viventiolus' suffragan at Langres, Gregorius, lived approximately 165 miles north of Lyons.[70] It would have taken probably between seven and nine days for a messenger traveling by land just to make the journey to deliver the

---

[64] De Clercq, ed., *Concilia Galliae: A.511–A.695*, 22–3.

[65] Ibid., 23–4.

[66] Because the lay attendees of the Epaone (517) did not sign the canonical acts, their identities remain unknown.

[67] Baudonivia *Vita Sanctae Radegundis Liber II*, ch. 15.

[68] Bordeaux (662/76), Subscriptions.

[69] He states only that the council will be held "around the beginning of the month of September."

[70] According to *Die Peutingersche Tafel*, ed. Konrad Miller (Stuttgart: F. A. Brockhaus, 1962), Langres is located 121 *leugae* from Lyons, a distance equal to about 165 miles.

convocation letter, and even longer if he chose to go by boat via the Saône River.[71] However, travel time was not the only good reason to inform conciliar participants of the meeting date well in advance. Sometimes unforeseen circumstances forced the rescheduling of a synod, as was the case with a council convoked by Bishop Sulpicus of Bourges in the middle of the seventh century.[72] Moreover, the length of time that it took letters to go back and forth could provide those bishops reluctant to attend a council with an excuse for their absence. Bishop Mappinus of Rheims, for example, claimed that he did not attend a synod at Toul (550) because he learned too late the purpose of its convocation.[73] Mappinus had also failed to attend the Council of Orléans a year earlier, although he did send an archdeacon in his stead.[74]

Although conciliar attendance was determined by a combination of political and ecclesiastical borders, on many occasions bishops who, in theory, should have participated in a council failed to attend, or were not even invited.[75] The reasons for a bishop choosing not to attend a council naturally varied on a case-by-case basis. Sometimes the legitimate excuse of illness kept a prelate from attending. This was the reason Ruricius of Limoges gave to Caesarius of Arles for not being present at the Visigothic Council of Agde (506).[76] Caesarius, who rebuked Ruricius for failing even to send a representative,[77] would use the same excuse around twenty years later to justify his own absence from the Council of Valence (ca. 528).[78] As Caesarius' letter articulates, it was the

---

[71] Travelers in this period could cover, on average, between 30 and 40 km a day: Pierre Riché, *Daily Life in the World of Charlemagne*, trans. Jo Ann McNamara (Philadelphia: University of Pennsylvania Press, 1978), 22–3. Similarly, Raymond Chevallier, *Roman Roads*, trans. N. H. Field (Berkeley: University of California Press, 1976), 194, has argued that most travelers in the Roman world could not have expected to exceed 45 kilometers a day (basing his calculations on the *Itinerarium Burdigalense*).

[72] Desiderius of Cahors *Epistulae S. Desiderii Cadurcensis* II.16.

[73] *Epistolae Austrasicae*, no. 11. Hefele and Leclercq, *Histoire des conciles d'après les documents originaux*, III.1.164–5, rightly rejected Mappinus' excuses for not attending the council.

[74] Orléans (549), Subscriptions.

[75] See Champagne and Szramkiewicz, "Recherches sur les conciles des temps mérovingiens," 16–23, for some statistical generalizations on conciliar attendance.

[76] Ruricius of Limoges *Epistulae* II.33.

[77] *Fausti Aliorumque Epistulae ad Ruricium Aliosque*, MGH AA VIII, ed. Bruno Krusch (Berlin: Weidmann, 1887), no. 12.

[78] Caesarius, however, did send representatives in his place: *Vita Caesari Episcopi Arelatensis* I.60.

obligation of an absent bishop to send a representative delegate in his place. As already noted, in his convocation letter for the Council of Epaone (517), Avitus of Vienne, too, had specifically stipulated that those clerics legitimately unable to attend the council were to send two presbyters as delegates on their behalf. These delegates were to be well educated and of high status, and invested with the right to agree to any and all decisions made at the council.[79] Interestingly, the one bishop to take Avitus up on his offer, Salutaris of Avignon, sent a single delegate, the presbyter Peladius. As the subscription lists of the period indicate, sending a single representative was definitely the norm, despite Avitus' request for two.

Between the years 511 and 696, during which period subscription lists were regularly attached to conciliar *acta*, 101 delegates (representing 102 bishops) attended church councils in the *regnum Francorum*.[80] Of these delegates, the plurality (48) were presbyters, while the remainder were deacons (7), archdeacons (9), or "secular" abbots (12).[81] The rank of 25 of these men cannot be identified. The majority are known only through their conciliar attendance. A collation of subscription lists, however, does reveal some interesting details. For example, it appears that 4 of these delegates—the presbyters Baudardus (or Baudastes) of Avranches, Benenatus of Glandeve, and Vincentius of Die, and the deacon Claudianus of Riez—served as representatives on more than one occasion.[82] Additionally, certain dioceses sent delegates multiple times over the years. Five—Antibes, Die, Fréjus, Limoges, and Tours—sent 3 delegates each to councils between the sixth and seventh centuries. Tellingly, the first three of these *civitates* lay in the southeast

---

[79] De Clercq, ed., *Concilia Galliae: A.511–A.695*, 22–3.

[80] This tally is based on the subscription lists contained in De Clercq, ed., *Concilia Galliae: A.511–A.695*. It differs somewhat from that offered by Robert Godding, *Prêtres en Gaule mérovingienne* (Bruxelles: Societe des Bollandistes, 2001), 459. The primary reason for disparities is that Godding is concerned with tallying all clerical attendance at Merovingian synods; I am concerned only with those clerics who represented bishops. As for why 101 delegates were representing 102 bishops, the presbyter Catafronius represented two bishops at the Council of Arles (524): Agricius of Antibes and Severus, the bishop of an unknown diocese.

[81] On "secular" or basilica abbots, see Godding, *Prêtres en Gaule mérovingienne*, 229–39 (especially note 76).

[82] Baudardus attended the Councils of Orléans of 538 and 541; Benenatus attended the Councils of Orléans (541) and Arles (554); Vincentius attended the Councils of Orléans (549) and Lyons (567/70); and Claudianus attended the Councils of Orléans (549) and Arles (554). Benenatus and Claudianus represented different bishops at each council.

corner of Gaul, far away from the center of Merovingian conciliar activity.[83] If one also takes into account that 6 of the 9 bishops who sent delegates to multiple councils during this period resided in peripheral regions of Frankish Gaul, it becomes clear the extent to which geography played a role in determining actual episcopal attendance at church councils, a point to which I will return.[84] Among interprovincial synods, those with the greatest participation by representative clerics during the Merovingian era were the Council of Orléans in 549 with 18 in attendance, and the Councils of Orléans (541), Lyons (583), and Mâcon (585), all with 12 in attendance. Councils of a more local scope had a greater ratio of lower-ranking church personnel among their subscribers, although most of these were not attending as representatives. For example, 44 clerics attended the diocesan synod of Auxerre (585/605).

Despite the availability of the excuse of ill health, some bishops offered more dubious rationales for their conciliar absences. The bishops of the ecclesiastical province of Arles had a particularly problematic record in this regard. Despite canonical rules to the contrary, Caesarius of Arles himself apparently used the confusion of shifting political borders as an excuse not to attend the Councils of Orléans (538) and (541), probably because of a presumed slight to his status as papal vicar of Gaul.[85] His age, however, may also have been a factor in his decision. Sabaudus of Arles (ca. 552–86) failed to attend the Councils of Mâcon (581/3) and (585), both of which drew a number of their participants from his province, for reasons that are not entirely clear. Possibly King Guntram was still bitter over the bishop's ostensibly supportive behavior toward King Sigibert I (r. 561–75) during the latter's siege of Arles in 566.[86] We know from Gregory of Tours that when Sabaudus died a few years after the council, King Guntram, hoping to ensure the loyalty of Arles' episcopate, saw to it that his former *referendarius,* Licerius, took Sabaudus' place.[87] However, Sabaudus was present at Guntram's council at Valence this same decade, suggesting that perhaps the bishop had other reasons for failing to attend the

[83] Champagne and Szramkiewicz, "Recherches sur les conciles des temps mérovingiens," 20–22.

[84] I.e., Avolus of Sisternon, Gallicanus of Embrun, Leucadius of Bayeux, Lucretius of Die, Pappolus of Geneva, and Perpetuus of Avranches. Felix of Limoges, Gallus of Clermont, and Sustracius of Cahors also were represented at multiple councils.

[85] Klingshirn, *Caesarius of Arles: The Making of a Christian Community*, 258–9.

[86] Gregory of Tours *Decem Libri Historiarum* IV.30.

[87] Ibid., VIII.39.

Councils of Mâcon. Additionally, Agricius of Antibes (ca. 506–27) and Theudorius of Arles (ca. 632–53) stayed away from the Councils of Carpentras (527) and Chalon-sur-Saône (647/53), respectively, having learned that charges were to be laid against them at these meetings.[88] The bishops of the province of Arles were not the only churchmen to employ dubious reasons for avoiding councils. Columbanus, as noted in the previous chapter, chose to stay away from a synod convoked in response to his own activities and preaching in order to avoid what was certain to be a hostile environment. Additionally, in an extreme case of neglect of duty, the bishops of Childebert II's kingdom collectively refused to attend a council convoked by the king and his uncle, King Guntram, at Troyes (585). This refusal was allegedly because of Guntram's intention to prosecute Bishop Theodore of Marseilles (fl. 575–94), against his nephew's wishes.[89] Contemporary conciliar legislation confirms that some bishops indeed called upon royal authority to excuse their absence from synods, a practice unacceptable to their more diligent colleagues.[90]

Ecclesiastical penalties were frequently threatened by Frankish councils against those invitees who were reluctant to attend provincial synods and particularly against those invitees who outright refused to attend provincial synods. The general rule imposed by the Frankish councils had its origins in the conciliar prescriptions of Visigothic Southern Gaul. Both the "Second Council of Arles" and the Council of Agde (506) threatened suspension from duties against absent bishops until the next meeting of a provincial synod.[91] Because the Council of Agde declared that these meetings should be annual, it is clear that these suspensions were meant to last only a single year.

The first Frankish council to specify similar penalties was the Council of Orléans of 538. The attendees there declared that a bishop absent from a provincial council for a reason other than illness should be forbidden from holding mass for a year, as should a metropolitan who neglected summoning a council for two years.[92] A decade later, the Council of Orleans of 549 elaborated upon this decision, threatening a suspension from celebrating mass against those bishops who either

[88] De Clercq, ed., *Concilia Galliae: A.511–A.695*, 50, 309–10.
[89] Gregory of Tours *Decem Libri Historiarum* VIII.13.
[90] According to Tours (567), c. 1, "One may not keep oneself from a council by royal decree or for personal reasons."
[91] Second Council of Arles (ca. 442/506), c. 19; Agde (506), c. 35.
[92] Orléans (538), c. 1.

neglected to attend a synod or departed from one without permission before its business was complete. This council also added the stipulation that a bishop delayed from attending a council on account of some necessity ("quaecumque necessitas") could be recalled to the celebration of the mass after having requested the permission of his metropolitan.[93] Two years later, the provincial Council of Eauze (551) repeated the language of the Council of Agde in stating that a bishop who failed to attend a mandatory meeting should be kept "a caritate fratrum" until the next (presumably provincial) synod.[94] The Council of Tours of 567 made some slight alterations upon this basic principle, declaring that bishops absent from provincial synods should be suspended until the next great synod ("usque ad maiorem sinodum"), probably referring to a royal or interprovincial council. Moreover, these bishops were not to communicate with their brethren from other provinces until this great council met.[95] This principle of waiting for a major council to restore suspended prelates was repeated in 585 by the Council of Mâcon, which ordered these bishops to remain separated from their episcopal brothers "usque ad consilium universale."[96] The final Merovingian council to threaten ecclesiastical penalties against neglectful bishops was the Council of Jean-de-Losne (673/75), which vaguely promised the enforcement of penalties established by existing canons.[97] In the Pippinid era, when royal interests were more closely intertwined with conciliar business, King Pippin I issued a capitulary (754/5), which declared that it was the duty of archdeacons (with secular assistance) to make certain that presbyters and clerics attended synods. The king added, "If one refuses, let the count detain him, and if he is a presbyter or defensor, let him pay sixty *solidi*, and attend the synod. And the bishop must judge his presbyter or cleric according to the canons. The sixty *solidi* should go to the *sacello regis*."[98] We do not know whether this penalty was ever enforced.

---

[93] Orléans (549), c. 18.

[94] Eauze (551), c. 7.

[95] Tours (567), c. 1. A similar principle is at work in Tours (567), c. 8, as well.

[96] Mâcon (585), c. 20. As to the question of what benefit there was to be had in bringing the case of an excommunicated bishop before a "general" or "universal" council, the presence of multiple metropolitans (along with their suffragans) infused such meetings with a representative authority not possessed by provincial or diocesan synods.

[97] St. Jean-de-Losne (673/75), c. 21.

[98] Pippin *Capitulary of 754/5*, in *Capitularia Regum Francorum*, no. 3.

The quantity of conciliar legislation dealing with the issue of episcopal absence is indicative of the genuineness of this problem. The Frankish bishops were not in the habit of legislating on irrelevant matters, and who knew better than they the perpetual difficulty of ensuring mandatory conciliar attendance. The significance of their awareness lies not so much in the fact that Frankish bishops did not always fulfill their conciliar obligations—although this was the case on many occasions—but rather that conciliar attendance in Francia was deeply influenced by forces and obligations outside the meeting hall. Additionally, we should read those modifications in ecclesiastical policy as reactions by the Frankish bishops to the difficulty of enforcing canonical standards. Changing conditions necessitated the constant reevaluation of old decisions, if not old principles. The Frankish bishops never rejected their early-sixth-century precedents, but they were conscious that if allowed to remain static, these rules could lose their effectiveness.

The number of bishops who did attend a council after having been summoned could vary considerably, even among councils of similar types, such as two interprovincial councils. Nevertheless, some statistical generalizations can be made. The plurality (seven) of the twenty-two interprovincial councils held between the years 511 and 695 for which we possess subscription lists had between ten and twenty episcopal participants, and the majority of these meetings (twelve) were attended by two to five metropolitan bishops.[99] Additionally, the *civitates* of Bourges, Vienne, Lyons, and Autun were the most heavily represented bishoprics at these councils. In general, the more geographically peripheral a diocese (e.g., those of Brittany), the less often it was represented at interprovincial church councils. The most heavily represented *civitates* at Frankish synods, for the most part, were those located in the lands between the Seine and Loire valleys, stretching eastward toward the Saône-Rhône basin.[100]

---

[99] Champagne and Szramkiewicz, "Recherches sur les conciles des temps mérovingiens," 16–7. The Pippinid councils, by and large, do not possess subscription lists, a problem that is discussed in chapter 4.

[100] Champagne and Szramkiewicz, "Recherches sur les conciles des temps mérovingiens," 20–3; Gaudemet, *Les sources du droit de l'Eglise en Occident*, 109. On the limited Austrasian participation in Merovingian conciliar life, see Cardot, *L'espace et le pouvoir*, 145–7. On Neustrian attendance, see Wilfried Hartmann, "Conciles et synodes," in *La Neustrie: Les pays au nord de la Loire de Dagobert à Charles le Chauve (VIIe–IXe siècles)*, ed. Patrick Périn, and Laure-Charlotte Feffer (Rouen: Musées et Monuments Départementaux de Seine-Maritime, 1985), 115. The region in question generally corresponded with the center of intellectual life in Gaul: Pierre Riché,

Nevertheless, conciliar subscription lists are not complete tallies of all conciliar attendees, for they list only the names of those prelates and clerical representatives who sat in assembly as participants and witnesses to the deliberations and decision making. The lists rarely record the names of lay attendees,[101] nor do they make any mention of the members of the entourages that the episcopal participants typically brought along with them. It is only through secondary accounts of conciliar proceedings that we even know that these two groups were present. An example would be Gregory of Tours' description of a fight that broke out at the Council of Mâcon (585) between the servants (*famuli*) of Bishop Priscus of Lyons and the *dux* Leudegisel.[102] The subscription list attached to the canonical record of Mâcon (585) naturally makes no mention of any servants, nor does it reveal the presence of Duke Leudegisel.[103] Similarly, Duke Lupus, who attended the Council of Bordeaux (662/76), never signed its canonical *acta*, nor did the lay attendees of the Councils of Epaone (517) or Marseilles (533). Additional examples of lay attendance at councils without subscription lists, as well as the growing popularity of *concilia mixta* in the middle of the eighth century, confirm the acceptability of laymen attending synods during the Frankish period.[104] As already noted, in some cases

Education and Culture in the Barbarian West: Sixth Through Eighth Centuries, trans. John J. Contreni (Columbia, SC: University of South Carolina Press, 1976), 267–8, map 269. Similarly, Hen, *Culture and Religion in Merovingian Gaul*, 8, suggests that conciliar representation is indicative of this region's level of Christianization. The number of Germanic names in conciliar lists remains relatively insignificant until the seventh century, suggesting the maintenance of Roman identity in the Gallic heartland: Helene Wieruszowski, "Die Zusammensetzung des gallischen und fränkischen Episkopats bis zum Vertrag von Verdun (843) mit besonderer Berücksichtigung der Nationalität und des Standes," *Bonner Jahrbücher* 127 (1922): 28–9.

101 Exceptions include Orange (529) and Clichy (654).

102 Gregory of Tours *Decem Libri Historiarum* VIII.20.

103 On Leudegisel, see Martindale, ed., *The Prosopography of the Later Roman Empire*, IIIB.788–9.

104 Excluding the early-Pippinid *concilia mixta*, which are discussed in chapter 6, and those councils for which only the monarch's presence is recorded, the Councils of Orange (529), Marseilles (533), Saintes (ca. 558/61), Saintes (579), Valence (585), Mâcon (585), Auvergne (590), Paris (614), Clichy (626/7), Clichy (654), Council of Bordeaux (662/76), (probably) Mâlay-le-Roi (677), and Unknown (689) had lay attendees. Other examples of uncertain reliability or conciliar status are Lyons (572/3), Constance (635/40) and Strasbourg (728). Additional examples of doubtful reliability are Agaune (515/23), Le Mans (516/26), Paris (632), and Rouen (711/5). On the issue of lay attendance in general, see Hartmann, "Laien auf Synoden der Karolingerzeit," 249–69. Hartmann notes that the Visigothic-derived conciliar *ordo* found in the Pseudo-Isidorian corpus assumes the attendance of laymen (251–2). He also rightly dismisses

it seems to have been the prerogative of the presiding metropolitans to determine which laymen would be invited to a given council. In other cases, particularly when the council met on the order of, or in the presence of, the king, it is clear that laymen attended on the invitation of the monarch.

Along with the lay nobility, the Frankish kings themselves sometimes favored councils with their presence. Although during the Merovingian period the frequency of royal attendance depended largely on the interest of individual kings,[105] the practice became expected under the Pippinids, and was even made a canonical requirement, at first in the *regnum* of Carloman. At the German Council of 742, it was ordered that councils be held each year "in our [i.e., Carloman's] presence."[106] This rule was echoed thirteen years later in the fourth canon of the Council of Ver.[107] It probably is not coincidental that this development in conciliar attendance coincided with the newfound popularity of the *concilia mixta* model. Although, as we shall see, even non-attending kings had the means of influencing conciliar deliberations and decisions, making royal presence an expectation was a major step toward the integration of the Frankish church into the body of the state.[108]

Travel

Having been informed of a council's convocation, an invitee likely spent the intervening months making preparations for his journey. Such preparations included everything from the settling of affairs at home prior to departure to packing the necessary provisions for the journey. The quantity and quality of provisions, which often included gifts for friends, depended on a number of factors, including the length of the journey, the wealth of the attendee, and the size of his traveling

the suggestion made by Voigt, *Staat und Kirche*, 313 ff., that the practice of lay attendance was based on an Anglo-Saxon model brought to the Continent by Boniface (257–8).

[105] E.g., Chilperic at Paris (577) and Berny (580), Guntram at Lyons (581) and Unknown 2 (589), Clovis II at Clichy (654), and Childeric II at Saint-Jean-de-Losne (673/5).

[106] Germania (742), c. 1.

[107] Ver (755), c. 4.

[108] Ganshof, "The Church and the Royal Power in the Frankish Monarchy under Pippin III and Charlemagne," 205–39.

party.[109] These bishops were men of wealth and stature, accustomed to relying on the assistance of servants. The appearance of a staff of clerics or even fellow bishops surrounding them when they entered the city where the council was to be held served as an important visual symbol of both their social prestige and pastoral role.[110] Sidonius Apollinaris (ca. 432–85), for example, in a letter to his friend Domnulus, describes Bishop Patiens of Lyons' dramatic *adventus* into the *civitas* of Chalon-sur-Saône, where the holy man was escorted by his provincial *sacerdotes*.[111] Traveling parties need not have included only servants; accompanying friends and family could provide both companionship and support on the journey.[112]

At this stage in the travel preparations, letters in the care of messengers might also be sent ahead to friends who lived along the travel route, so that the journey might be interspersed with visits. Such visits also provided the weary traveler with a place to rest his head after a long day in transit. Sidonius Apollinaris was of the opinion that to ensure a comfortable respite, it generally was preferable to lodge with friends than to try one's luck at an inn.[113] Later travelers appear to have shared Sidonius' preference. When Bishop Eligius of Noyon was traveling in Provence in the seventh century, he made it a point to visit

[109] On provisions, see Lionel Casson, *Travel in the Ancient World* (Baltimore: Johns Hopkins University Press, 1994), 154–5, 176–8; Samuel Dill, *Roman Society in Gaul in the Merovingian Age* (London: Macmillan and Co.,1926), 238.

[110] Both episcopal and secular attendees would have been accompanied by servants to councils. See, e.g., Gregory of Tours *Decem Libri Historiarum* VIII.20; Baudonivia *Vita Sanctae Radegundis Liber II*, ch. 15. Other references to traveling with servants (not necessarily to councils) include Gregory of Tours, *Liber in Gloria Confessorum*, MGH SRM I.2, ed. Bruno Krusch (Hanover: Hahn, 1885), ch. 65; Gregory of Tours, *Libri de Virtutibus Sancti Martini Episcopi*, MGH SRM I.2, ed. Bruno Krusch (Hanover: Hahn, 1885), III.43; Sidonius Apollinaris, *Poems and Letters*, ed. W. B. Anderson (Cambridge, MA: Harvard University Press, 1936–65), IV.8.2; *Vita Eligii Episcopi Noviomagensis*, MGH SRM IV, ed. Bruno Krusch (Hanover: Hahn, 1902), II.13, 22.

[111] Sidonius Apollinaris *Poems and Letters* IV.25.1.

[112] Gregory of Tours seems to have preferred to travel in such company: Gregory of Tours, *Liber in Gloria Martyrum*, MGH SRM I.2, ed. Bruno Krusch (Hanover: Hahn, 1885), ch. 83; Gregory of Tours *Libri de Virtutibus Sancti Martini Episcopi* I.33, III.60; Gregory of Tours, *Liber de Passione et Virtutibus Sancti Iuliani Martyris*, MGH SRM I.2, ed. Bruno Krusch (Hanover: Hahn, 1885), ch. 24. See also *Vita Eligii Episcopi Noviomagensis* II.11.

[113] Sidonius Apollinaris *Poems and Letters* VIII.11.3. On the hospitality of friends, see ibid., I.5.2; Venantius Fortunatus *Opera Poetica* XI.25; and Rutilius Namatianus, *De Reditu Suo*, in *Minor Latin Poets II*, ed. J. Wight Duff and A. M. Duff (Cambridge, MA: Harvard University Press, 1934), I.465–74, I.491–510, I.541–58. On inns, see ibid., I.377–86.

and seek lodging in the villas of friends, including both lay aristocrats and bishops.[114] Time spent socializing could easily lengthen the duration of the trip, so conciliar attendees had to plan their itineraries wisely.[115] However, if the bishop did not have any acquaintances in a given *civitas,* he did have the recourse of requesting the hospitality of the local prelate, who was obligated to supply travelers with lodging in the *domus episcopi* or in another ecclesiastical building set aside for travelers.[116] When Gregory of Tours journeyed to Paris in 580 in order to attend a council, he sought lodging at a basilica attached to the Church of St. Julian.[117]

When friendly accommodations were not available, a traveling bishop might have to settle for potentially less comfortable lodgings, ranging from monasteries to inns to hostels. Gregory, on a return trip to Tours in 585, stayed at a monastery near Carignan.[118] In his descriptions of his own journeys, as well as those of other ecclesiastics, Gregory also frequently mentions *metati,* a somewhat vague term, by which he usually appears to be referring to lodgings located in the larger settlements and near important religious shrines, such as those of Saint Martin and Saint Julian.[119] Clerics and monks, aristocratic families, and poorer travelers all took advantage of such places of rest when they were available. They naturally varied in quality and comfort, but at least provided a weary traveler with a place to spend the night if friendlier lodgings were otherwise lacking.

However, when a traveler of any social standing found himself on the road as the sun was setting, with no substantial settlements within sight, sometimes his only recourse was to make camp and to pitch a tent. Tents could keep out the rain, but they provided minimal comfort and even less safety. When Abbot Lupentius of Javols was traveling home from the Austrasian royal court around the year 584, he pitched his tent along the River Aisne. Unluckily for Lupentius, this unprotected

---

[114] *Vita Eligii Episcopi Noviomagensis* II.11–13.

[115] Sidonius Apollinaris *Poems and Letters* I.5.2.

[116] Gregory of Tours *Decem Libri Historiarum* IX.6 and IX.25. On the obligation of hospitality, see Thomas Sternberg, *Orientalium More Secutus* (Münster: Aschendorff, 1991), 86–92.

[117] Gregory of Tours *Decem Libri Historiarum* IX.6

[118] Ibid., VIII.15.

[119] Ibid., VI.6 and VIII.2. Gregory of Tours *Libri de Virtutibus Sancti Martini Episcopi* I.33; Gregory of Tours *Liber de Passione et Virtutibus Sancti Iuliani Martyris,* chs. 24 and 28. On inns and lodgings, see Dill, *Roman Society,* 238–9. Gregory of Tours *Libri de Virtutibus Sancti Martini Episcopi* II.12 mentions that Bishop Germanus of Paris stayed at a villa in Tours in order to attend a festival.

location left him vulnerable to attack by his nemesis, the count of Javols, and the head of the unfortunate abbot ended up in the river.[120] Sometimes, when comfortable lodging was available, a wealthy traveler would take advantage of the roof, while his servants slept outside. In a letter to a friend, Sidonius Apollinaris describes a journey he took in which he sent his servants on eighteen miles ahead, so that a camp might be arranged prior to his arrival. The servants made camp at a predetermined location, which was situated near a spring and abundant grassland, and was in close proximity to the house of one of their master's friends. The servants, however, were expected to spend the night under the stars.[121]

Many dangers and oppressive conditions could lengthen the journey. Unpredictable bad weather of the sort experienced by the Austrasian bishops on their way to Verdun and Metz in 590 certainly affected travel time, and there are many other reports of weather tormenting travelers in Merovingian Gaul.[122] Excessive cold, oppressive heat, dust storms, flooding, snow, and muddy roads, as well as many other natural phenomena, were potential hazards. Unfortunately for travelers, weather was only one of the many dangers possibly awaiting them. There was also fear of bandits,[123] illness,[124] the closing of roads by royal authorities,[125] and the absence of permanent bridges at water crossings.[126] Despite such obstacles, the population of early medieval Gaul could and did take to the roads and rivers toward sometimes-distant destinations.[127] And it was not only the elites who traveled. Quantitative studies of pilgrimages to the shrine of Saint Martin at Tours have

---

[120] Gregory of Tours *Decem Libri Historiarum* VI.37.

[121] Sidonius Apollinaris *Poems and Letters* IV.8.2–3.

[122] E.g., Gregory of Tours *Decem Libri Historiarum* IX.39; Gregory of Tours *Liber in Gloria Confessorum*, ch. 18; Gregory of Tours *Liber in Gloria Martyrum*, ch. 83; Venantius Fortunatus *Opera Poetica* XI.25; Sidonius Apollinaris *Poems and Letters* IV.8 and VIII.12.

[123] E.g., Gregory of Tours *Decem Libri Historiarum* X.21; Gregory of Tours *Libri de Virtutibus Sancti Martini Episcopi* I.36. On the danger of bandits, see Michael McCormick, *The Origins of the European Economy* (Cambridge: Cambridge University Press, 2001), 74; Dill, *Roman Society in Gaul in the Merovingian Age*, 240–1.

[124] E.g., Gregory of Tours *Libri de Virtutibus Sancti Martini Episcopi* I.33. See also Dill, *Roman Society*, 241.

[125] E.g., Gregory of Tours *Decem Libri Historiarum* VI.11, IX.32.

[126] E.g., see ibid., III.15, IV.30; Gregory of Tours *Libri de Virtutibus Sancti Martini Episcopi* II.16–7. On water-crossing methods, see Albert C. Leighton, *Transport and Communication in Early Medieval Europe, AD 500–1100* (Newton Abbot: David and Charles, 1972), 93–4.

[127] Dill, *Roman Society*, 238–42. On the factors determining the movement of populations, see McCormick, *The Origins of the European Economy*, 65.

demonstrated the willingness of those who were not elite to travel, even when such journeys interfered with the constraints of the agricultural calendar.[128] Still, aristocratic bishops could afford luxuries that eased the rigors of the road.

Traveling bishops also were fortunate that a network of *viae publicae* crisscrossing Gaul made direct travel a great deal easier than it otherwise would have been.[129] Roman roads were designed to minimize the length of journeys, and, when properly maintained, had readable mileage markers indicating the distance between towns.[130] Archaeologists have uncovered hundreds of Gallic *miliarii,* and references to them in Merovingian-era sources suggest that many continued to be visible to travelers in the sixth and seventh centuries.[131] Gregory of Tours mentions them on several occasions, such at the site of the battle of Vouillé, fought between Clovis and Alaric II in 507, ten *miliarii* from Poitiers.[132] Gregory assumed that such a description would be meaningful to his readers, implying the continued use of milestones by his contemporaries as geographic markers. This is not to say, of course, that all of the original markers erected by the Roman imperial authorities still stood, pristine and unmoved, but only that enough seem to have remained standing to be of use to travelers.[133]

The use of public roads by conciliar attendees already had a lengthy history by the Merovingian period. Constantine I had permitted Bishop Chrestus of Syracuse to make use of the Roman post system, the *cursus publicus,* on his journey to attend the first Gallic synod in Arles in the year 314.[134] This allowance was multiplied to such a degree over the

---

[128] Pietri, *La ville de Tours du IVe au VIe siècle*, 546–75.

[129] On the Gallic road network, see Chevallier, *Roman Roads*, 160–73.

[130] Casson, *Travel in the Ancient World*, 166, 173.

[131] These milestones have been edited by Gerold Walser in *Miliaria Imperii Romani*, Corpus Inscriptionum Latinarum XVII.2 (Berlin: Walter de Gruyter, 1986).

[132] Gregory of Tours *Decem Libri Historiarum* II.38. Additional references: II.1, VI.45, IX.7.

[133] Bernard Bachrach, "Carolingian Military Operations: An Introduction to Technological Perspectives," in *The Art, Science, and Technology of Medieval Travel*, ed. Robert Bork and Andrea Kann (Aldershot: Ashgate, 2008), 21–2.

[134] Eusebius, *Ecclesiastical History*, ed. H. J. Lawlor, trans. Kirsopp Lake and J. E. L. Oulton (London: W. Heinemann, 1926–32), X.5.23. On the *cursus publicus,* see Erik Holmberg, *Zur Geschichte des Cursus Publicus* (Uppsala: A. B. Lundequistska Bokhandeln, 1933); A. H. M. Jones, *The Later Roman Empire* (Norman, OK: University of Oklahoma Press, 1964), II.830–4; Chevallier, *Roman Roads*, 181–95; Anne Kolb, "Transport and Communication in the Roman State: The Cursus Publicus," in *Travel and Geography in the Roman Empire*, ed. Colin Adams and Ray Laurence (London: Routledge, 2001), 95–105.

following decades that the historian Ammianus Marcellinus (ca. 330–95) complained that the Emperor Constantius II (r. 337–61) was clogging up the *cursus publicus* with all of the bishops rushing to attend church councils.[135] The Merovingians, who inherited the network of Roman *viae publicae,* similarly made heavy use of it for diplomatic and military operations.[136] Although conciliar attendees arguably were serving in such an official capacity when attending synods convoked by the Frankish monarchy, there is no evidence that they were given official requisition privileges for use on their journey, i.e., *tractoria* grants.[137] Such grants were probably unnecessary, considering the right of hospitality these episcopal travelers enjoyed in the *civitates* they visited.

The means of transport employed by these bishops determined the length of their journeys. Transport technology remained relatively consistent with the Roman past, with wealthy travelers employing such devices as the four-wheeled *raedae* and *carrucae,* as well as the two-wheeled *plaustra* and *cisia,* to move themselves or their property.[138] Carts and wagons, however, could slow down a traveler, who might prefer simply to ride on the back of a *caballus* (a riding horse) or even an ass if the rider was feeling particularly ascetic.[139] Mounted travelers could cover between thirty and forty kilometers per day. To ensure the health of the mount, the traveler needed to provide it with a steady supply of rations and water.[140] Some conciliar attendees walked the

[135] Ammianus Marcellinus, *Ammianus Marcellinus [Rerum Gestarum Libri],* trans. John C. Rolfe (Cambridge, MA: Harvard University Press, 1935–9), 21.16.18. On the continued use of the *cursus publicus* in the post-Roman kingdoms, see Holmberg, *Zur Geschichte des Cursus Publicus,* 148.

[136] Lebecq, "Entre antique tardive et très Haut Moyen Age: Permanence et mutations des systèmes de communications dans la Gaule et ses marges," 472–3.

[137] François Ganshof, "La tractoria: Contribution à l'étude des origines du droit de gîte," *Tijdschrift voor Rechtsgeschiedenis* 8 (1928): 69–91.

[138] See, e.g., Gregory of Tours *Liber in Gloria Confessorum,* chs. 5 and 19. On models of chariots and wagons, see Casson, *Travel in the Ancient World,* 179–80; Lebecq, "Entre antique tardive et très Haut Moyen Age," 473–5; Gérard Coulon, *Les Voies Romaines en Gaule* (Paris: Errance, 2007), 203–6.

[139] E.g., Gregory of Tours *Decem Libri Historiarum* X.8. The word *equus* is generally used to refer to horses, although Gregory of Tours *Liber in Gloria Confessorum,* ch. 19, does specify that Bishop Eufronius of Tours planned to make use of a *caballus* (i.e., riding horse). McCormick, *The Origins of the European Economy,* 76, suggests that pack animals were increasingly favored over wagon transport in this period, perhaps because of poor road conditions.

[140] On the logistics of food rations and animal transport in the ancient world, see Donald Engels, *Alexander the Great and the Logistics of the Macedonian Army* (Berkeley: University of California Press, 1978), 123–30.

route, but more often than not it was their servants who were obliged to travel by foot.[141]

Although roads provided a speedy route for bishops running late for a council, if time was not pressing, water transport could be both cheaper and safer, and it has even been suggested that water increasingly became the preferred means of transport during this period.[142] There certainly is no shortage of contemporary references to river travel by *navis, puppis,* or *linter*.[143] River transport was as old as the settlements these waterways connected. Commerce along the river systems of Gaul had encouraged early urbanization and the creation of markets that stimulated additional travel and trade.[144] By the sixth century, travelers were well accustomed to navigating their way among the *civitates* of Gaul through a crisscrossing network of waterways. As councils convoked on royal authority tended to be held in locales in close proximity to royal residences, nautical travel could be the most direct route, as these residences were often situated along navigable rivers.[145] Certainly, water transport had its dangers. Bad weather was even more dangerous for seafaring travelers than for those who journeyed by land. Venantius Fortunatus, for example, recalls in one of his poems a storm that arose while he was traveling by boat in northwest Gaul. The poet's craft was knocked about by the winds, and lifted aloft on waves as tall as mountains. Fortunatus describes the water as a deadly enemy, intent on doing harm to him and his traveling party.[146] Sometimes even a saint was powerless against the forces of evil that used severe weather to attack a holy man. Bishop Nicetius of Trier, for example, once found himself trapped beneath a bridge while sailing along the Moselle. The saint was saved from drowning only through the

---

[141] E.g., Baudonivia *Vita Radegundi* II.15. On servants traveling by foot, see Casson, *Travel in the Ancient World*, 181.

[142] Dill, *Roman Society*, 239; Lebecq, "Entre antique tardive et très Haut Moyen Age," 485–500; Bernard Bachrach, *Early Carolingian Warfare* (Philadelphia: University of Pennsylvania Press, 2001), 137.

[143] E.g., Gregory of Tours *Decem Libri Historiarum* I.48, II.40, IV.48, VI.6, VII.46; Venantius Fortunatus *Opera Poetica* VI.5, VI.8, X.9, XI.25; Sidonius Apollinaris *Poems and Letters* VIII.12; Rutilius Namatianus *De Reditu Suo* I.37–42.

[144] Joelle Burnouf, "Towns and Rivers, River Towns: Environmental Archaeology and the Archaeological Evaluation of Urban Activities and Trade," in *Post-Roman Towns, Trade and Settlement in Europe and Byzantium*, ed. Joachim Henning (Berlin: Walter de Gruyter, 2007), I.176–7 (on the Loire specifically); Chris Wickham, *Framing the Early Middle Ages* (Oxford: Oxford University Press, 2005), 794–805.

[145] Lebecq, "Entre antique tardive et très Haut Moyen Age," 489.

[146] Venantius Fortunatus *Opera Poetica* XI.25.

intervention of bystanders.[147] In some cases, travelers combined water and land routes to minimize the length of a trip. When the Visigothic princess Galswinth traveled from Spain to Francia in order to marry King Chilperic I, she traveled by carriage to the Loire Valley, and then by watercraft along the Vienne, Loire, and Seine toward Rouen.[148]

Because conciliar attendees, particularly of larger interprovincial councils, traveled a variety of different routes of varying distances, they arrived at their destination over the course of a number of days. Where they were lodged is not certain, but respect for episcopal status and office probably precluded hostels and the cheaper inns. More likely, they would have been put up in the city's *domus episcopi,* or perhaps in a local monastery, or maybe even in the royal villa itself, as was the case at the Council of Berny (580).[149] Although in the later Carolingian era, it would become increasingly common for those who convoked councils to inform attendees in their convocation letters to expect to provide board for themselves, it is not clear in this earlier period what degree of hospitality could be expected from hosts.[150]

Conciliar Protocol

When all of the invitees or their representatives arrived, the council itself could begin. For all of the documentary evidence we have for the decisions of these meetings, we have very little concerning how these decisions were made.[151] Those descriptions of synodal proceedings that we do possess largely concern the judicial agendas of larger councils. Moreover, the most detailed contemporary liturgical guidelines for conciliar procedures are of questionable evidentiary value. The earliest of these was composed by the Visigothic Fourth Council of Toledo in 633, which was chaired by Bishop Isidore of Seville.[152] This *ordo,* which

[147] Gregory of Tours *Liber Vitae Patrum* XVII.3.

[148] Venantius Fortunatus *Opera Poetica* VI.5

[149] Gregory of Tours *Decem Libri Historiarum* V.49. When Gregory himself sat with "convenientibus episcopis" in Paris in 580, he stayed at a *metatus* associated with the Church of St. Julian (IX.6).

[150] Barion, *Das fränkisch-deutsche Synodalrecht,* 51–2.

[151] Lippert, "Die Verfasserschaft der Canon gallischer Concilien des V. und VI. Jahrhunderts," 12–3; Barion, *Das fränkisch-deutsche Synodalrecht,* 56–7; Wilfried Hartmann, "Konzilsprotokolle aus karolingischer Zeit," *Annuarium Historiae Conciliorum* 15, no. 2 (1983): 260–1.

[152] *Die Konzilordines des Früh- und Hochmittelalters,* ed. Herbert Schneider (Hanover: Hahn, 1996), 125–41. This *ordo* shows a few signs of Roman procedural

provides instructions for conducting provincial councils, became the basic model for subsequent liturgical texts. The variation that enjoyed the most popularity in the Frankish kingdoms was written at the very end of the seventh century, probably in Toledo, and was disseminated north of the Pyrenees through its inclusion in the *Collectio Hispana Gallica* and the Pseudo-Isidorian corpus.[153] The oldest surviving manuscript of the former dates to ca. 787/8, and the collection itself cannot predate the late seventh century.[154] Moreover, there is no evidence to suggest that its liturgical directions were adopted by any Frankish synods.[155] The combination of its foreign origins, late composition, and uncertain usage makes the *ordo* a dubious source for Frankish conciliar procedures during the period under discussion.[156]

Still, there are several observations that can be made in regard to conciliar protocol. Our best source for the opening of conciliar proceedings is found in the *praefatio* to the canonical *acta* of the Council of Mâcon (585). Although it would be imprudent to assume that the procedures that the preface describes were universally followed by Frankish councils, it still provides us with a fairly detailed account of how one particular interprovincial council commenced its proceedings. According to the *praefatio,* when the metropolitans and their suffragans had taken their seats, Priscus of Lyons, the metropolitan bishop of the province in which the council was being held, offered a prayer of thanks to God on behalf of the assembled body. The other metropolitans, Evantius of Vienne, Praetextatus of Rouen, Bertram of Bordeaux, Artemius of Sens, and Sulpicius of Bourges, responded in unison with a prayer of their own for the health of the king and for divine aid in their deliberations. Then the rest of the bishops gave thanks for being allowed to assemble after so long a time, and requested that the issues raised by the metropolitans be settled quickly, so that they did not need

influence (see notes 7 and 11). Sieben, *Die Konzilsidee in der Alten Kirche*, 510, however, strangly claims that "Das Konzil des *ordo* ist das *Ding* der Landeskirche."

[153] *Die Konzilordines des Früh- und Hochmittelalters*, 142–86.

[154] Kéry, ed., *Canonical Collections of the Early Middle Ages*, 67–8.

[155] Hartmann, "Zu einigen Problemen der karolingischen Konzilsgeschichte," 16, note 36. C.f. Barion, *Das fränkisch-deutsche Synodalrecht*, 57; Charles Munier, "L'ordo de celebrando concilio wisigothique," *Revue des sciences religieuses* 37 (1963): 263–4; Moore, "A Sacred Kingdom," 50–1.

[156] The Franks did compose their own *ordo* around the year 800 (based on an earlier Visigothic model), which was primarily disseminated through liturgical books. On this *ordo*, see *Die Konzilordines des Früh- und Hochmittelalters*, 296–315; Martin Klöckener, "Eine liturgische Ordnung für Provinzialkonzilien aus der Karolingerzeit," *Annuarium Historiae Conciliorum* 12 (1980): 109–82.

to be absent from their sees for too long. The metropolitans agreed to decide essential questions by common deliberation ("communi deliberatione"), and urged all of the attendees to disseminate the decisions reached by the council.[157]

We have already concluded that most councils probably had worked out a portion of their agenda prior to meeting. Those new issues that were raised during the course of proceedings stemmed from discussions of the various problems and anxieties faced by the attending bishops.[158] However, as the prelates at the Council of Clermont (535) declared, "no bishop should dare to raise an issue which does not pertain to the improvement of life, the severity of the *regulae,* or the remedy of the spirit."[159] As to the discussions themselves, there is nothing in the Council of Mâcon's *acta* that fundamentally contradicts the senatorially derived procedures employed by pre-Frankish councils for the debating of individual issues. According to this protocol, following an exposition of a question or concern (*relatio*) by the presiding bishop, the conciliar attendees would express their own opinions (*sententiae*). A vote would follow, after which the approved resolution would be recorded.[160] Although there is no conclusive evidence from the Frankish period that definitively proves the use of this precise protocol, the Frankish bishops' employment of associated senatorially derived *formulae* can be read as indirect evidence of its influence.

The Frankish canonical *acta* themselves reveal little in the way of debate, however, as their very style and composition were intended to communicate unanimity of opinion. In theory, the consensus of the episcopal attendees was a mark of their adherence to orthodox tradition.[161] To this end, canonical collections, patristic works, and sometimes even collections of secular law were consulted during the course of deliberations.[162] These written sources likely were provided for the

[157] Mâcon (585), Preface. The phrase "communi deliberatione" appears also in *ordo* no. 1 (*Die Konzilordines des Früh- und Hochmittelalters*, 141).

[158] E.g., Mâcon (585), c. 7, which explicitly identifies Bishops Praetextatus of Rouen and Pappolus of Chartres as raising the issue of *iudices* harassing freedmen. See also Barion, *Das fränkisch-deutsche Synodalrecht*, 91–6.

[159] Council of Clermont (535), c. 1

[160] Sieben, *Die Konzilsidee in der Alten Kirche*, 476–82. On the possible use of this procedure in Anglo-Saxon England, see Cubitt, *Anglo-Saxon Church Councils*, 87–90.

[161] Morrison, *Tradition and Authority in the Western Church: 300–1140*, 4–5 (following Vincent of Lerins).

[162] On the use of canonical collections by councils, see Barion, *Das fränkisch-deutsche Synodalrecht*, 93; Mordek, *Kirchenrecht und Reform im Frankenreich*, 66–70; Mordek, "Bischofsabsetzung in spätmerowingischer Zeit: Justelliana, Bernensis,

conciliar participants either by the episcopal see of the city hosting the council, or perhaps by the metropolitan of the province.[163] By basing their own legislation on the language and precedents of earlier decisions, the Frankish bishops gave legitimacy to their resolutions. Additionally, a consultation of written sources offered guidance in determining the basis for a consensus of opinion, and it was common for councils during this period to justify their rulings through a *viva voce* reading of the canons.[164] The prelates trying Bishop Egidius of Rheims at Metz in 590, for example, read aloud the relevant *sanctiones canonum* prior to condemning him.[165]

Nevertheless, despite the conciliar attendees' willingness to draw upon earlier precedents, we can be sure that behind the semblance of consensus lay intense "negotiation and compromise."[166] Sources, however, are relatively silent about disputes among the bishops. There is Gregory of Tours' well-known account of a bishop at the Council of Mâcon (585) attempting to convince his colleagues that *mulier* was not included in the word *homo*. However, according to Gregory, the man humbly abandoned his position when shown the error of his logic by his fellow bishops.[167] If the debate were really this one-sided and easily settled, it is surprising that Gregory chose to mention it at all, except to ridicule the fool. A better explanation for its inclusion in the *Historiae* is its idealized depiction of episcopal consensus in action. In other words, this anecdote is less an accurate account of the events at Mâcon, and more an *exemplum* of episcopal harmony. On some occasions, ill

und das Konzil von Mâlay (677)," 31–53; Rosamond McKitterick, *The Frankish Church and the Carolingian Reforms, 789–895* (London: Royal Historical Society, 1977), 23. On the use of Roman legal sources by councils, see Gaudemet, "Survivances romaines," 164–8. For examples of citations of Frankish royal edicts by councils, see Tours (567), c. 21, and Mâcon (581/3), c. 14. On the use of the Bible, see Basdevant-Gaudemet, "Le Bible dans les canons des conciles mérovingiens," 51–67. For an index of the written sources for Frankish canonical decisions, see De Clercq, ed., *Concilia Galliae: A.511–A.695*, 331–6.

[163] Mordek, "Bischofsabsetzung in spätmerowingischer Zeit," 39, has suggested that Bishop Genesius of Lyons may have brought canonical materials with him to the Council of Mâlay-le-Roi (677), which he presided over.

[164] On the consultation and reading of canons, see, e.g., Mâcon (585), c. 7; Gregory of Tours *Decem Libri Historiarum* V.18, X.16, X.19; Boniface *S. Bonifatii et Lulli Epistolae*, nos. 77–8. The oral reading of old canons (by a deacon) is prescribed in the Visigothic conciliar ordos as well: *Die Konzilordines des Früh- und Hochmittelalters*, no.1 (c. 4) and no. 2 (c. 5).

[165] Gregory of Tours *Decem Libri Historiarum* X.19.

[166] Klingshirn, *Caesarius of Arles: The Making of a Christian Community*, 103.

[167] Gregory of Tours *Decem Libri Historiarum* VIII.20.

will and violence shattered this harmony, but our sources, not surprisingly, are relatively silent about these instances. Moreover, those few that are mentioned all involve laymen.[168] Although it is unlikely that serious fights were a frequent occurrence at Frankish councils, we must be ever wary of taking our sources' emphasis on easy episcopal consensus at face value.

Although our sources are not overly forthcoming about the deliberations underlying the bishops' legislation, they do offer a wealth of information about the judicial component of their agenda. A primary function of ecclesiastical councils was to serve as courts of appeal for bishops, clerics, and monks who believed themselves to have been treated unfairly by their superiors.[169] Councils also could restore to office those clerics who had been excommunicated in earlier hearings,[170] and punish those who refused to change their ways.[171] All three of these functions were predicated on the principle that conciliar authority supersedes that of individual bishops or an *episcopalis audentia*, i.e., episcopal court.[172] Moreover, following the Constantinian legal tradition, this authority could extend over clerics and laypeople alike.[173] Contemporary sources describe a few instances of conciliar trials of laypeople, all of which vary considerably in the legal issues under examination. These range from

[168] E.g., see ibid. Violence also flared up at a royal assembly at Clichy in 627, which can perhaps be associated with the council held there ca. 626/7: Fredegar *Chronica* IV.55. An additional fictionalized example of a conciliar dispute can be found in *Vita Dagoberti III Regis Francorum*, ch. 8.

[169] Orléans (538), c. 22; Orléans (538), c. 23; Orléans (549), c. 17; Paris (614), c. 4; Clichy (626/7), c. 6. Earlier Gallic precedents for this function can be found in Vaison (442), c. 5, and Arles II (442/506), c. 48.

[170] Arles (554), c. 1; Tours (567), c. 8–9; Mâcon (585), c. 9; Ver (755), c. 13.

[171] Orléans (538), c. 24 (re rebellious clerics); Tours (567), c. 2.

[172] On the superior authority of the conciliar tribunals, see Tours (567), c. 7; Mâcon (585), c. 9; Ver (755), c. 5. On the jurisdiction and administration of the *episcopalis audentia* in Late Antiquity, see James, "Beati Pacifici: Bishops and the Law in Sixth-Century Gaul," 25–46; Peter Brown, *Power and Persuasion in Late Antiquity: Towards a Christian Empire* (Madison: University of Wisconsin Press, 1992), 100; Wilfried Hartmann, "Der Bischof als Richter nach den kirchenrechtlichen Quellen des 4. bis 7. Jahrhunderts," *Settimane di Studio del Centro Italiano di Studi Sull'Alto Medioevo* 42, no. 2 (1994): 805–37; Jill Harries, *Law and Empire in Late Antiquity* (Cambridge: Cambridge University Press, 1999), 191–211.

[173] James, "Beati Pacifici," 29, identifies "marriage, sexual misdemeanors, religious belief…the property and other rights of the church, and also disputes involving certain categories of people—widows, orphans, freedmen, and the *pauperes*" as areas in which lay practice would come under episcopal jurisdiction. On Constantine's allowance of lay parties to bring their cases before ecclesiastical courts, and its relevance to the Anglo-Saxon conciliar context, see Cubitt, *Anglo-Saxon Church Councils*, 73–4.

incest,[174] to the renouncement of ecclesiastical vows,[175] to hostilities between laypeople and clerics.[176] In some cases, the issues at hand were not directly, but rather implicitly, concerned with spiritual matters. For example, a council of bishops convened in the Auvergne in the year 590 to judge the lawsuit brought against a noblewoman named Tetradia by her former husband, the *comes* Eulalius, for the restitution of his property. Eulalius had been a womanizer and cruelly abusive toward his wife. Having suffered enough, Tetradia escaped to the home of the *dux* Desiderius, carrying with her some of her husband's wealth. Eventually, she and the duke wed. When the case was pled before the council, the attending bishops ordered Tetradia to pay back Eulalius fourfold ("ut quadrupla satisfactione ablata restitueret"), and declared her children with Desiderius to be illegitimate.[177]

The majority of synodal trials and dispute settlements about which we are informed, however, involve churchmen, primarily bishops. We do not know if bishops were brought before conciliar hearings more often than lower clerics; certainly our sources are more inclined to mention cases involving the former. Furthermore, cases in which non-bishops were the defendants most likely were heard first by diocesan tribunals. Still, in light of the respective population and status of both groups, it is possible that lower clerics were more frequently the defendants in conciliar trials. The cases we know of against churchmen involve a number of criminal charges, including adultery,[178] murder,[179] treason,[180] illegitimate election,[181] the usurpation or alienation of ecclesiastical property,[182] heresy and improper religious observation,[183] and improper clerical

[174] Lyons (518/9), c. 1; *Vita Aviti Episcopi Viennensis*, ch. 2; Venantius Fortunatus *Vita Albini Episcopi Andegavensis*, ch. 18.

[175] Mâcon (581/3), c. 20; Gregory of Tours *Decem Libri Historiarum* IV.4.

[176] Gregory of Tours *Decem Libri Historiarum* V.36. A further example of dubious authenticity can be found in *Vita Dagoberti III*, ch. 8.

[177] Gregory of Tours *Decem Libri Historiarum* X.8.

[178] Marseilles (533), Conciliar Acts; Gregory of Tours *Decem Libri Historiarum* V.27; Sisebut *Vita Vel Passio Sancti Desiderii Episcopi Viennensis*, ch. 4 (see also Fredegar *Chronica* IV.24; *Passio Sancti Desiderii Episcopi Viennensis II*, chs. 7–8).

[179] Gregory of Tours *Decem Libri Historiarum* V.27, IX.20.

[180] Gregory of Tours *Decem Libri Historiarum* V.18, V.27, V.49, VIII.12, VIII.20, X.19; *Passio Leudegarii Episcopi I*, ch. 33 (see also *Passio Leudegarii Episcopi* II.16–7).

[181] De Clercq, ed., *Concilia Galliae: A.511–A.695*, 50, 212–5; Gregory of Tours *Decem Libri Historiarum* IV.26, VII.17, VIII.20; *Die Urkunden der Merowinger*, no. 122.

[182] Marseilles (533), Conciliar Acts; Gregory of Tours *Decem Libri Historiarum* VI.38.

[183] Jonas of Bobbio *Vitae Columbani Abbatis Discipulorumque Eius Libri Duo Auctore Iona* II.9; Soissons (744), c. 2. An additional example of unlikely reliability can be found in *Vita Faronis Episcopi Meldensis*, ch. 110.

behavior.[184] Although penance, excommunication, and deposition were the three most common penalties imposed by the councils, more serious crimes, particularly those against the crown, could merit harsher punishments, including imprisonment,[185] exile,[186] and even death.[187] As in the proceedings of secular courts, these conciliar hearings entailed the calling of witnesses (*testes*),[188] the examination of written evidence,[189] and the arguments and questioning of judicial advocates.[190] At Egidius of Rheims' trial at Metz, a former *dux* named Ennodius questioned the defendant on behalf of King Childebert II. Ennodius accused Egidius of improperly receiving *villae* as gifts from Childebert's uncle, Chilperic I. Protesting his innocence, Egidius produced *chartae* in his defense. These *chartae* were examined in court by the *referendarius* supposed to have composed them, a certain Otto, who denied that the writing was his. Egidius' personal correspondence was also brought forward as evidence, as were damning letters from Chilperic to the bishop. The conciliar attendees heard additional witnesses and testimony, which strengthened the case against the defendant. Faced with such overwhelming opposition, Egidius declared his guilt, whereupon he was deposed from office and sent into exile.[191] The trial procedures employed by the Frankish synods share close parallels with those followed by Anglo-Saxon councils. Conciliar trials in both regions were similar in their "adversarial" rather than "inquisitorial" approach, the attendees acting more as jurors than prosecutors.[192]

In those instances where the case in question impinged upon royal interests, such as the Egidius affair, the king was permitted to play a role in the proceedings so long as he acted according to canonical rule.[193]

---

184 Chalon (647/53), c. 20; Gregory of Tours *Decem Libri Historiarum* IX.20, IX.37; De Clercq, ed., *Concilia Galliae: A.511–A.695*, 309–10.

185 Gregory of Tours *Decem Libri Historiarum* V.18, V.27.

186 Ibid., V.18, X.19; Sisebut *Vita Desiderii*, ch. 4 (see also Fredegar *Chronica* IV.24).

187 *Passio Leudegarii* I.33.

188 Paris (552), Conciliar Acts; Marseilles (533), Conciliar Acts; Sisebut *Vita Desiderii*, ch. 4; Gregory of Tours *Decem Libri Historiarum* V.18, V.49, X.19.

189 Paris (552), Conciliar Acts; De Clercq, ed., *Concilia Galliae: A.511–A.695*, 309–10; Gregory of Tours *Decem Libri Historiarum* X.19.

190 Ibid., V.49, X.19.

191 Ibid., X.19.

192 Cubitt, *Anglo-Saxon Church Councils*, 92–6.

193 For the necessity of kings (and dukes) to follow canonical precedent in judicial proceedings against prelates, see *Leges Baiwariorum*, ed. Ernst Maria Augustin Schwind, MGH Leges V.2 (Hanover: Hahn, 1926), I.10: "And if a bishop seems guilty of a crime, one should not dare to kill him, because he is the *summus pontifex*, but rather bring

However, this obligation was not always met. King Chilperic's prosecution of Bishop Praetextatus of Rouen for treason in 577, for example, was an extreme case of royal exploitation of conciliar procedures. Chilperic not only questioned Praetextatus personally, and presented physical evidence to support his case, he also intimidated and attempted to bribe the attending bishops, had a dubious collection of canon law especially compiled for their use, tricked the defendant into confessing, and made sure that his punishment exceeded canonical standards.[194]

Although Chilperic's behavior at Praetextatus' trial may have been an extreme case of royal interference, if we are to believe Gregory of Tours' highly partisan account, it was by no means a lone one. Royal pressure could be strong enough to compel conciliar attendees to render their judgment according to the king's wishes, even if this meant committing an injustice.[195] Additionally, some kings did not hesitate to veto conciliar verdicts, such as Charibert (r. 561–7), who rejected the decision of the Council of Saintes (561/7) to expel Bishop Emerius of Saintes, because the king saw this decision as an insult to the authority of his own father, Chlothar (r. 511–61). Chlothar had ordered the appointment of Emerius without the approval of the latter's metropolitan. King Charibert went so far as to fine the presiding bishops at the council.[196] Sigibert I likewise ignored the decision of the Council of Paris (573) to depose Promotus as bishop of Châteaudun. Sigibert had conferred this position on Promotus as part of Sigibert's effort to control territory that rightfully belonged to the diocese of Chartres.[197] The Burgundian King Sigismund (r. 516–23) is even said to have harassed the distinguished Avitus of Vienne and his brother Apollinaris for their condemnation of one of his officials, the aforementioned Stephanus, for incest.[198] Even in those cases where council and crown were basically in agreement, such as the mutual condemnation of the revolt of the nuns of Poitiers in 589/90, royal involvement was sometimes

---

him before the king, *dux*, or his *plebs*. And if he is convicted of a crime, and cannot deny it, he should be judged according to the canons, and if found guilty, deposed or exiled."

[194] Gregory of Tours *Decem Libri Historiarum* V.18.

[195] E.g., Chalon's (602/4) deposition of Desiderius of Vienne, Mâlay-le-Roi's (677) deposition of Chramlinus of Embrun, and Unknown's (ca. 677/9) conviction of Leudegar of Autun. On the other hand, Chilperic was unsuccessful in his prosecution of Gregory of Tours at Berny (580).

[196] Gregory of Tours *Decem Libri Historiarum* IV.26.

[197] Ibid., VII.17.

[198] *Vita Aviti Episcopi Viennensis*, ch. 2.

deemed necessary to enforce the council's decision. The bishops who met to condemn this revolt requested in an epistle addressed to Kings Guntram and Childebert II that the monarchs use their *potestas* and *auctoritas* to see to the restitution of the nunnery's property stolen during the uprising.[199] That the Frankish kings were able to influence the course of synodal proceedings seems inarguable.

What is more, this was the case not only in judicial matters. Even when a king was not in attendance himself, he could still influence the content of a council's legislative agenda, both before and during the meeting. Already noted were the efforts of Clovis I and Guntram to determine in advance the topics to be discussed at synods convoked in their names. The conciliar records themselves offer additional examples of royal influence. For example, those synods that elected bishops probably in many instances were nudged toward their choice by royal pressure. This was the case at the Council of Metz (550/5), where King Theudebald ensured that the archdeacon Cautinus was consecrated bishop of Clermont over the protests of the already-elected Cato.[200] Cato refused to accept the council's decision, however, and continued to lobby the monarchy for reinstatement after Theudebald's death in 555.[201] Royal pretenders, too, took advantage of conciliar authority to appoint their favored candidates, as Gundovald did when he attempted to have Faustianus made bishop of Dax ca. 584/5.[202] But Faustianus made a poor choice in backing Gundovald: when his patron lost his life, the bishop lost his office.

Kings also convoked councils for specifically dogmatic or missionary[203] purposes. The Council of Orléans (549), convoked by Childebert I, weighed in on the "Three Chapters" controversy, which stemmed from the Emperor Justinian's condemnation of the writings of three theologians rejected by the Monophysites. The controversy spread to the West when Justinian forced Pope Vigilius in 548 to accept the condemnations, a move that provoked widespread anger and even schism. The

---

199 Gregory of Tours *Decem Libri Historiarum* X.16.

200 Ibid., IV.7. For additional examples, see Soissons (744), c. 3, and the late-ninth-century (or later) *Vita Cuniberti*, which relates that Cunibertus was chosen bishop of Cologne by means of a synod and a "praecepto regis" (Coens, ed., "Les vies de Saint Cunibert et la tradition manuscrite," ch. 3).

201 Gregory of Tours *Decem Libri Historiarum* IV.15.

202 Ibid., VII.31.

203 E.g., *Vita Agili Abbatis Resbacensis*, III.12. On the council described in this eighth- or ninth-century *vita*, see Ian Wood, *The Missionary Life: Saints and the Evangelization of Europe, 400–1050* (London: Longman, 2001), 37–8.

Council of Orléans, held one year later, supported the Council of Chalcedon (451)—and, by extension, the beleaguered papacy—by condemning the heresies of both Nestorianism and Monophysitism.[204] The council's ruling, however, did not succeed in settling the debate in Gaul over the papacy's actions.[205] The Three Chapters controversy was not the only trans-Mediterranean doctrinal dispute in which the Frankish councils had their say. Although Frankish theologians and legislators addressed Byzantine iconoclasm more thoroughly during the reign of Charlemagne, the *Annales Regni Francorum* records that King Pippin I convoked a synod at Gentilly in 767 "on account of a dispute between the Romans and Greeks concerning the Holy Trinity and the images of saints."[206] The representatives of Emperor Constantine V, however, appear to have failed to convince the attendees of the merits of the iconoclast position.[207]

Preservation of Decisions

Once a council had completed its business—legislative, judicial, or otherwise—it was time to record its decisions. The author of the conciliar acts was perhaps the presiding metropolitan himself, but more likely it was someone to whom he delegated the task.[208] Whoever he was, he based his composition on shorthand transcriptions taken

---

[204] Orléans (549), c. 1. On this canon, and the Frankish response to the Three Chapters controversy, see Ian Wood, "The Franks and Papal Theology, 550–660," in *The Crisis of the Oikoumene*, ed. Celia Chazelle and Catherine Cubitt (Turnhout: Brepols, 2007), 223–41. Bishop Aurelian of Arles, who attended the Council of Orléans, wrote to Vigilius for an explanation of his actions; he received a response in 550: *Epistolae Arelatenses Genuinae*, MGH Epistolae III, ed. Wilhelm Gundlach (Berlin: Weidmann, 1892), no. 45.

[205] Jonas of Bobbio *Vitae Columbani Abbatis Discipulorumque Eius Libri Duo Auctore Iona* II.9, accuses the monk Agrestius of supporting the Aquileian line against the papacy, a position that was supported moderately by Columbanus himself; see Wood, *The Merovingian Kingdoms*, 196–7, 244.

[206] *Annales Regni Francorum*, entry for 767 (see also *Annales Mettenses Priores*, entry for 767).

[207] Judith Herrin, *The Formation of Christendom* (Princeton: Princeton University Press, 1989), 384–5.

[208] Bretholz, "Die Unterschriften den gallischen Concilien des 6. und 7. Jahrhunderts," 532. Lippert has shown that *adnotati* in the canonical manuscripts identifying an author are unreliable: "Die Verfasserschaft der Canon gallischer Concilien des V. und VI. Jahrhunderts," 9–58. Moreover, he observes, those very rare instances where another source identifies the author of a council's records, e.g., the *Vita Melanii*'s naming of its protagonist as the author of Orléans' (511) canons, are no more believable.

during the course of deliberations.[209] Also, either simultaneous with the initial transcription, or perhaps following its signing by the conciliar attendees, additional copies were made for all of the bishops present.[210] The signing of the conciliar acts was a solemn moment, for it was through this act that the attending bishops acknowledged the consensus underlying their decisions.[211] Although the order of the subscriptions of the same council varies somewhat from manuscript to manuscript, it is clear that the bishops subscribed to the conciliar acts in rank order.[212] Thus, the metropolitan signatures come first, followed by those of their suffragans, and finally by those of the clerical representatives. The purpose of making multiple copies for each of the attendees was, of course, to ensure the dissemination of the council's decisions. Each bishop was expected to return home to his diocese and relay the council's decisions to his clerics, monks, and parishioners.[213]

---

[209] The Frankish canonical records, as we possess them, are formal documents that show no signs of having been written piecemeal over the course of multiple sessions. Nevertheless, this does not preclude the taking of notes during the course of deliberations, which, in turn, would have been used to compose the formal *acta*. Shorthand was used frequently by scribes in the Merovingian and Carolingian periods, and it had a history of being employed in a conciliar setting. On the use of shorthand in this era, see David Ganz, "Bureaucratic Shorthand and Merovingian Learning," in *Ideal and Reality in Frankish and Anglo-Saxon Society*, ed. Patrick Wormald, Donald Bullough, and Roger Collins (Oxford: Blackwell, 1983), 58–75; David Ganz, "On the History of Tironian Notes," in *Tironische Noten*, ed. Peter Ganz (Wiesbaden: Otto Harrassowitz, 1990), 35–51; Bernhard Bischoff, *Latin Paleography*, trans. Dáibhí O. Cróinín and David Ganz (Cambridge: Cambridge University Press, 1990), 80–2. Ganz notes that a number of contemporary canonical collection manuscripts—e.g., Cologne Dombibliothek 212 and Paris BN lat. 12097—contain Tironian annotations, and suggests that shorthand was used at councils ("On the History of Tironian Notes," 41). On the use of shorthand by stenographers (*exceptores* and *notarii*) at the earlier Council of Carthage (411), see Emin Tengström, *Die Protokollierung der Collatio Carthaginensis* (Göteborg: Göteborg University, 1962), 7–49. Tengström describes how scribes took notes on wax tablets (*tabulae*), which subsequently were collated as a *scheda*, to which subscriptions were attached. A final *editio* or *authentica* was then produced and signed.

[210] Bretholz, "Die Unterschriften den gallischen Concilien des 6. und 7. Jahrhunderts," 533, has argued that the copies were made at the same time as the "master copy." Thus, the subscription order in the chronological canonical collections derives not from the original transcript, but from the copies.

[211] Orléans (541), Preface.

[212] Mathisen has argued that episcopal status was measured in this period by time in office: Ralph Mathisen, "A Reconstruction of the List of Subscriptions to the Council of Orange," *Annuarium Historiae Conciliorum* 19, no. 1 (1987): 1–12; Mathisen, "Episcopal Hierarchy and Tenure in Office in Late Roman Gaul," 125–40.

[213] Macon (585), Preface.

The Council of Paris (556/73), relying on the Roman legal principle of "that which affects all must have the consent of all," went so far as to send copies of its decisions to bishops who did not attend, demanding that they subscribe to them as well.[214] The Council of Berny (580) did the same.[215] The canonical transcripts were stored in the archives of episcopal churches in order to preserve them for future reference. The *Definitio Fidei* of the Council of Orange (529) notes explicitly that "Bishop Caesarius [of Arles], in Christ's name, produced an *exemplar* of our *constitutiones* and retained an original copy (*authentica*) in the church archives (*arcivo ecclesiae*)."[216] Some of the copies that had been distributed to the various dioceses would eventually become the sources for compilers of canonical collections.

The council's business now complete, the attendees could return home to their dioceses. In all, they had probably spent the better part of a month (or more) in transit and in deliberation. Although councils varied in their duration, the Council of Epaone (517), which was convoked on September 6, and whose subscriptions are dated September 15, suggests how long a council during this period may have lasted.[217] Naturally, travel time varied, but we need only consider the geographic diversity represented at the larger national councils to appreciate the distances some bishops had to go in order to attend. The Council of Paris (614) had attendees from as far away as England.[218] Even those bishops from within Gaul had to make considerable journeys in order to attend Chlothar II's synod. One of the council's attendees, Florianus of Arles, had an approximately 460-mile journey each way to travel. If we assume that the episcopal entourage could cover between 18 and 25 miles a day with fresh horses, it would have taken at least nineteen to twenty-six days to travel to and from the council. The time investment alone should convince us that the Frankish bishops took their conciliar duties seriously. Moreover, as we shall see, those issues

[214] Paris (556/73), c. 9. On the unusual nature of this canon, see Gaudemet and Basdevant-Gaudemet, eds., *Les canons des conciles mérovingiens*, 422–3, note 3.

[215] Gregory of Tours *Decem Libri Historiarum* V.49.

[216] Orange (529), Definition of Faith. The vocabulary here is similar to that employed at the Council of Carthage (411). See note 209.

[217] According to Walahfrid Strabo, *Vita Galli Confessoris*, ch. 24, the Council of Constance (ca. 635/40) was scheduled to last three days.

[218] Paris (614), Subscriptions.

discussed and debated within a synod were of genuine concern to the episcopal attendees. They were real problems that had to be dealt with in a face-to-face meeting. The discussions of these problems reveal, too, the institutional importance of the ecclesiastical council to both the Frankish church and the Frankish royal government.

CHAPTER 3

THE REFLECTION OF REALITY IN CONCILIAR LEGISLATION

Although we know little about the formal and private discussions that went on among the participants in Frankish church councils, we know a great deal about the decisions that resulted from these discussions. Some of these decisions were considered essential enough to preserve in contemporary and later legal compilations, and were thereby disseminated across chronological and geographic space. In this way, legislation promulgated by councils with very different configurations, participants, and agendas became the source for medieval canon law. However, if we look at the decisions of the Frankish councils solely through the lens of canon law, we lose sight of the unique historical circumstances that led to their original composition.[1] The canons of the Frankish councils, no less than their judicial decisions, were reactions to events and circumstances outside the assembly hall. They were preventive measures certainly, but preventive measures that were informed by the very real concerns of the conciliar attendees. Certainly, these attendees were members of the social elite, and their perspectives were necessarily influenced by their elite status. Their concerns, in other words, were not necessarily those of their parishioners. Even in those instances where a concern affected individuals other than those at the top of the ecclesiastical hierarchy, it is the latter's perspective that is articulated in the canons of the Frankish councils. In the previous chapter, particular attention was given to the concrete physical realities of conciliar convocation and assembly. Similarly, political, social, and cultural conditions also informed the agendas of councils. Such conditions were rarely static; an infinite variety of fluctuating circumstances, including a meeting's location, the personalities of its attendees, and the interest or influence of the reigning monarch on the council's business, all played a role. In order to understand conciliar legislation, therefore, we are obliged to contextualize it. By doing so, we will be in a better position to judge its practical value.

[1] Barbara Rosenwein, *Negotiating Space: Power, Restraint, and Privileges of Immunity in Early Medieval Europe* (Ithaca, NY: Cornell University Press, 1999), 32.

Repetition of Concerns

Still, it can be difficult—and sometimes impossible—to identify the historical context underlying any given canon. This is due, in part, to the silence of the canons themselves—with a few exceptions—regarding the motivations behind their promulgation. It is also because these canons often appear to be extraordinarily repetitive in their rulings. This apparent repetition is usually interpreted by scholars in one of two ways: either as a sign of their ineffectiveness,[2] or as an indication of their detachment from real-world conditions, political, social, or cultural.[3] Both positions, however, underestimate the diversity that could exist within a body of canons all addressing the same issue. Additionally, both positions ignore the value of repetition for the canonical authors. By repeating, in part, the rulings, and sometimes language, of previous councils, bishops could invest their own decisions, however dissimilar in motivation and original in principle, with the authority of tradition.[4] The conciliar participants customarily described their use of older canons as an act of "renewing" (*renovanda*).[5] We need not take their claims at face value; the participants' professed desire to "renew" or "restore" tradition often serves to obscure a real willingness to innovate. This willingness is innately tied to the canons' applicability to real-world conditions.[6] When circumstances arose that revealed the ineffectualness

---

[2] See, e.g., Brian Brennan, "Episcopae: Bishops' Wives Viewed in Sixth-Century Gaul," *Church History* 54, no. 3 (1985): 314; Nancy Gauthier, "Le réseau de pouvoirs de l'évêque dans la Gaule du Haut Moyen-Âge," in *Towns and their Territories Between Late Antiquity and the Early Middle Ages*, ed. Gian Pietro Broglio, Nancy Gauthier, and Neil Christie (Leiden: Brill, 2000), 178; Godding, *Prêtres en Gaule mérovingienne*, viii.

[3] See, e.g., Hen, *Culture and Religion in Merovingian Gaul*, 176–7; Geisel, *Die Juden im Frankenreich*, 228–30; Bruno Dumézil, *Les racines chrétiennes de l'Europe* (Paris: Fayard, 2005), 23–4.

[4] Morrison, *Tradition and Authority in the Western Church*, 353; Walter Pakter, *Medieval Canon Law and the Jews* (Ebelsbach: Verlag Rolf Gremer, 1988), 90; Klingshirn, *Caesarius of Arles*, 98; Mathisen, "The Second Council of Arles and the Spirit of Compilation and Codification in Late Roman Gaul," 525, 544–5. Harries, *Law and Empire in Late Antiquity*, 86, has argued similarly in regards to Roman law that repetition provided "reassurance" by "advertising and sanctioning precedents, [and] confirming the validity of past laws while also affirming their continued validity in the present."

[5] See, e.g., Orléans (511), c. 14; Epaone (517), Preface; Orléans (533), Preface; Clermont (535), Preface; Epistle of Clermont (535) to Theudebert; Orléans (538), Preface; Orléans (541), Preface; Orléans (549), Preface; Eauze (551), Preface; Arles (554), Preface; Lyons (567/70), Preface; Mâcon (581/3), Preface; Lyons (583), c. 1; Paris (614), Preface (quotes Lyons [567/70]).

[6] The idea that real-world concerns underlay conciliar legislation is expressed by, among others, Dill, *Roman Society in Gaul in the Merovingian Age*, 460; Ullmann,

of earlier legislation, or demanded the promulgation of new measures, conciliar attendees could take this opportunity to craft original legislation.

In some rare instances, the Frankish bishops explicitly identify the inspiration for their legislation. Besides those canons that merely confirm the royal grant of privileges or property to the church,[7] these cases reveal the bishops' desire both to enforce existing canonical standards, as well as to guard against the repetition of unapproved behavior.[8] Take, for example, the reaction of the Council of Mâcon (581/3) to the news that a nun named Agnes had abandoned the monastic life. No information is provided as to the name or location of Agnes' monastery, her ancestry, or the names of those powerful individuals who assisted in her plan. Presumably, the monastery was located in one of the dioceses represented at the council. Additionally, it is likely that Agnes was from a prominent social background, as the authors of the canon felt it unnecessary to identify her beyond her name, and, moreover, explicitly mention her wealth, which she attempted to use to bribe those *potentes* whose influence was such to obstruct her return to the monastery. Although their identities are obscure, clearly their power rivaled that of the local abbess and bishop. The assembled prelates at the council not only condemned Agnes herself for her actions, but went on to exclude from communion all those who attempted to buy their way out of a habit:

> We declare by this *constitutio* that she or any other nun who has attempted by such efforts to free herself from the religious habit in order to pursue secular delights, or who has offered her property (*res*) to certain people for so unjust a plan, lest the rule of religion appear to be befouled by the prodding of ambition, God forbid, let both she who desired to give these things and those who received them be excluded from the grace of communion until restored by a satisfactory penance, and the wealth in question is restored to those from whom it was received.[9]

By generalizing their ruling, the conciliar attendees were hoping to prevent similar cases from occurring at other monasteries. In essence,

"Public Welfare and Social Legislation in the Early Medieval Councils," 2–3; Pontal, *Histoire des conciles mérovingiens*, 305; Basdevant-Gaudemet, "Le Bible dans les canons des conciles mérovingiens," 56–7.

[7] E.g., Orléans (549), c. 15; Valence (583/5), Conciliar Acts.

[8] E.g., Lyons (518/23), c. 1; Tours (567), c. 20; Mâcon (581/3), c. 20; Chalon (647/53), c. 20.

[9] Mâcon (581/3), c. 20.

all canons are generalized prescriptive declarations, but this does not preclude the inspiration of individual cases. What makes Agnes' situation unique is not the nature of her crime, nor the willingness of a synod to address it; rather, it is the decision by the authors of the Council of Mâcon's canonical *acta* to mention her by name. Their choice may have stemmed from their desire to prosecute Agnes herself during the course of the proceedings.

In other instances, it may not have been a single case that prompted the composition of a canon, but rather multiple manifestations of a common problem. Conciliar attendees occasionally introduce their rulings with the verb *cognovimus*, which implies that they are reacting to an existing situation, even though they do not provide the details of specific cases.[10] Still, we cannot assume that the promulgation of any given canon reflects anything other than a single or a handful of instances. Agnes had the wealth and connections to make her escape from her convent. And although other nuns of wealthy backgrounds used their worldly influence and wealth to express their displeasure with the monastic life—most famously, Chlotild and Basina in their revolt in Poitiers a decade later—we have no way of quantifying these events. Moreover, the cases that prompted canons with similar content may have occurred in entirely different local contexts. It is because of this that even the most seemingly repetitive of canonical pronouncements demonstrate variation over time and space.

Sometimes these changes are blatant, such as the reworking by the Council of Mâcon (581/3) of Clermont (535), c. 9, which had declared, "No Jews should be appointed *iudices* over a Christian populace." The latter council added the phrase "or toll collectors" ("aut tolonarii").[11] This was no trivial addendum. Presumably, at the time of the Council of Mâcon, Jews in the kingdom of Guntram were still serving in this important public office, which provided lucrative remunerations to the

[10] E.g., Epaone (517), c. 2; Tours (567), c. 23; Mâcon (585), cc. 4, 14, and 19; Chalon (639/53), c. 20. In this same vein, see also, e.g., Mâcon (585), c. 3 ("comperimus"). See Hess, *The Early Development of Canon Law*, 69–70, on the "contemporary" nature of canons introduced by such "personalized phrases" as *placuit nobis, statuimus, decrevimus, constituimus,* and *censuimus.*

[11] Mâcon (581/3), c. 13. On the collection of tolls in the Merovingian kingdoms, see François Ganshof, "A propos du tonlieu sous les Merovingiens," in *Studi in onore di Amintore Fanfani*, ed. Gino Barbieri (Milan: Giuffrè, 1962), I.291–315; Reinhold Kaiser, "Steuer und Zoll in der Merowingerzeit," *Francia* 7 (1979): 1–17.

Frankish monarchy.[12] The earlier proscription against Jews serving as *iudices* apparently had not, in the minds of the conciliar attendees, gone far enough in its efforts to constrict Jewish socio-political influence. Additionally, it may never even have been enforced in those *civitates* of Guntram's realm that had not participated in the earlier council. The bishops at Mâcon would be disappointed, however, as Jews continued to serve the Frankish royal government as *telonarii* well into the Carolingian era, despite continued efforts to bar Jews from holding public office.[13]

Ecclesiastical policy toward the Jews offers an important lesson in the relevance of canonical prescriptions to real-world situations. In the Frankish period, established Jewish communities could be found in Narbonne, Arles, Marseilles, Orléans, Bourges, and Clermont, among other *civitates*.[14] Although the vocations practiced by these Jews extended beyond the mercantile, contemporary sources do pay particular attention to their participation in commercial and banking ventures.[15] Some historians have questioned the value of our (mainly Christian) sources, which purport to describe the activities of Jews

[12] For various interpretations of this proscription, see Solomon Katz, *The Jews in the Visigothic and Frankish Kingdoms of Spain and Gaul* (Cambridge, MA: Medieval Academy of America, 1937), 121–2; Bachrach, *Early Medieval Jewish Policy*, 54; Geisel, *Die Juden im Frankenreich*, 175–7.

[13] On Jewish toll collectors in the Carolingian era, see Bachrach, *Early Medieval Jewish Policy*, 87 (citing Amulo *Liber contra Judaeos*, ch. 42), and 187, note 81. Under Chlothar II, efforts were made to bar Jews from all public offices: Paris (614), c. 17; Chlothar II *Edictum*, in *Capitularia Regum Francorum*, no. 10; and Clichy (626/7), c. 13.

[14] Jean-Pierre Devroey and Christian Brouwer, "La participation des Juifs au commerce dans le monde franc (VIe–Xe siècles)," in *Voyages et voyageurs à Byzance et en Occident du VIe au XIe siècle*, ed. Alain Dierkens, Jean-Marie Sansterre, and Jean-Louis Kupper (Geneva: Droz, 2000), 339–50 (see p. 345, note 26, and pp. 347–8, notes 33–37 for references). It is possible that the Jewish population of Southern Gaul increased as the result of immigration from Visigothic Spain, where Jews faced heavier persecution beginning in the late sixth century. David Noy, *Jewish Inscriptions of Western Europe*, paperback ed. (Cambridge: Cambridge University Press, 2005), I.267–70, has posited this explanation of an inscription found in the city of Auch (seventh to eighth century), in which a Jew named Jona welcomes travelers.

[15] On the commercial activities of Jews, see Jean-Pierre Devroey, "Juifs et Syriens à propos de la géographie économique de la Gaule au Haut Moyen Age," in *Peasants and Townsmen in Medieval Europe: Studia in Honorem Adriaan Verhulst*, ed. Jean-Marie Duvosquel and Erik Thoen (Ghent: Snoeck-Ducaju and Zoon, 1995), 51–72; Devroey and Brouwer, "La participation des Juifs au commerce dans le monde franc," 354–72.

living in the *regnum Francorum*.[16] It is true that many of these texts are polemical in nature. In the case of the conciliar canons, they are also normative, in the sense that they prescribe ideal circumstances and behavior. Additionally, the Frankish canons that dictate Jewish policy do echo formulaic concerns. But they also contain a great variety of specific policy proposals, and they differ considerably from near-contemporary Visigothic canons on similar themes. One need only compare the harsh legislation produced by the provincial Council of Narbonne (589) with any issued by Frankish councils of the same century to note the wide gulf that existed between these two legislative cultures within Gaul alone.[17]

Certainly, conciliar evidence alone does not tell the whole story of Gallic Jewish history. It is both prejudicial and composed from a position of power. But it does reflect attempts by the Frankish episcopate to engage with real communities, however small and scattered. Still, we can never take for granted the enforcement of ecclesiastical Jewish policy, particularly in the absence of evidence. Indeed, there are instances in which we know that canons were not enforced.[18] But these policies, nevertheless, were aimed at communities whose members engaged in activities, vocations, and behavior abhorred by the Frankish episcopate. And although the repetition of similar prescriptions over time has convinced some scholars that the prescriptions were detached

---

[16] E.g., Geisel, *Die Juden im Frankenreich*, 98–100, 228–30; Michael Toch, "The Jews in Europe, 500–1050," in *The New Cambridge Medieval History*, vol. 1, ed. Paul Fouracre (Cambridge: Cambridge University Press, 2005), 552–3; Michael Toch, "Mehr Licht: Eine Entgegnung zu Friedrich Lotter," *Aschkenas* 11 (2001): 465–87; Michael Toch, *"Dunkle Jahrhunderte": Gab es ein jüdisches Frühmittelalter?* (Trier: Arye-Maimon-Institut für Geschichte der Juden, 2001). Toch's arguments have been countered by Friedrich Lotter in a series of articles: "Totale Finsternis über 'Dunklen Jahrhunderten.' Zum Methodenverständnis von Michael Toch und seinen Folgen," *Aschkenas* 11 (2001): 215–32; Friedrich Lotter, "Sind christliche Quellen zur Erforschung der Geschichte der Juden im Frühmittelalter weitgehend unbrauchbar?" *Historische Zeitschrift* 278, no. 2 (2004): 311–27. See also on this question, David Malkiel, "Jewish–Christian Relations in Europe, 840–1096," *Journal of Medieval History* 29 (2003): 57–9, on the Council of Meaux–Paris (846).

[17] Narbonne (589), cc. 4, 9, and 14. On this council, see Orlandis and Ramos-Lissón, *Die Synoden auf der Iberischen Halbinsel biz zum Einbruch des Islam (711)*, 120–2. See also the comments of Stocking, *Bishops, Councils, and Consensus in the Visigothic Kingdom*, 114, on the influence of the anti-Jewish measures promoted at Narbonne.

[18] See, e.g., Gregory I *Registrum Epistularum* IX.214 and IX.216 on the issue of Jewish-owned slaves. Charles the Bald's rejection of the anti-Jewish legislation promulgated at the Council of Meaux–Paris (846) is a later example, on which see Bachrach, *Early Medieval Jewish Policy*, 110–1.

from the realities of the day, there is strong evidence that the opposite was the case.

The Frankish church's efforts to end the Jewish ownership of Christian slaves offer compelling evidence in this regard.[19] Although these efforts had their origins in Roman imperial legislation,[20] it was not until the Council of Orléans (538) that Gallic bishops directly addressed the issue. Why then? Orléans (538) was the first major synod to be held since the Frankish conquest of Burgundy in 534 and the annexation of Provence in 537. These acquisitions had brought territories with more substantial Jewish populations into the *regnum* of Childebert I, who may have been partly responsible for the council's convocation.[21] Although no Provençal bishops attended Orléans (538), its legislation seems suggestive of an effort to address an issue raised by the introduction of these new constituencies.[22] The council, presided over by Bishop Lupus of Lyons, ruled that Christian slaves who either had been forced to act in a way contrary to their religion, or were otherwise mistreated by their Jewish masters, could seek asylum in a church. The canon states that they should not be returned unless a *praecium* "is offered and bestowed, as pronounced by an *iusta taxacio*, for the slaves' value."[23]

---

19 Even Geisel, normally skeptical, admits that those canons dealing with the issue of Jewish slave ownership "do not, in every case, reflect quixotic declarations of intent that simply were not adhered to in everyday life" (*Die Juden im Frankenreich*, 228–9). Similarly, in his discussion of the asylum rights of Jewish-owned Christian slaves, Friedrich Lotter, "Zur sozialen Hierarchie der Judenheit in Spätantike und Frühmittelalter," *Aschkenas* 13 (2003): 344, asks rhetorically why the Merovingian bishops "should stress their own powerlessness in relation to the rights of Jewish *domini* and Frankish legal custom if this whole discussion was not about real Jews."

20 See, e.g., *Codex Theodosianus*, ed. Theodore Mommsen and Paul M. Meyer (Berlin: Weidmann, 1905), 3:1:5, 16:8:22, 16:9:1–5. On the Jewish policies of the later Roman Empire, see Bernard Bachrach, "The Jewish Community of the Later Roman Empire as Seen in the Codex Theodosianus," in *To See Ourselves as Others See Us*, ed. Jacob Neusner and Ernest Frerichs (Chico, CA: Scholars Press, 1985), 399–421; Amnon Linder, *The Jews in Roman Imperial Legislation* (Detroit: Wayne State University Press, 1987). On the issue of Jewish ownership of Christian slaves, see Geisel, *Die Juden im Frankenreich*, 98–230; Pakter, *Medieval Canon Law and the Jews*, 88–91; Bachrach, *Early Medieval Jewish Policy*, 46, 55, 58, 64; Linder, *The Jews in Roman Imperial Legislation*, 82–5, 138–51; Mikat, *Die Judengesetzgebung der merowingisch-fränkischen Konzilien*, 43–98.

21 Pontal, *Histoire des conciles mérovingiens*, 108. The council's attendance consisted of bishops from the kingdoms of Childebert and Theudebert I.

22 On efforts by this council to address issues of concern to the Provençal bishops, Caesarius of Arles especially, see Klingshirn, *Caesarius of Arles*, 258–9.

23 Orléans (538), c. 14. On this canon, see Walter Pakter, "Les esclaves chrétiens des juifs: Troisième Concile d'Orléans (538)," *Archives Juives* 21, nos. 1–2 (1985): 3–4. The Council of Orléans (511), c. 3, had stated that a slave who sought asylum had to return to his master if the latter promised to pardon him. But if the master was found to have broken the oath by punishing his slave, he was to be excommunicated.

The Council of Orléans (541), the first Frankish council to be attended by Provençal bishops, clarified this decree, which was problematically vague regarding the fate of the repurchased Christian slaves. The language of the earlier canon, in fact, could be read as implying that these slaves would be returned to bondage. The new decree states that slaves who have fled their masters' homes could be liberated ("liberentur") by an *iustum pretium*, estimated and paid for by the faithful.[24] Significantly, unlike its predecessor, the canon produced by Orléans (541) does not single out only those slaves who had been mistreated. So, in principle, all Christian slaves could flee to a church with the promise of their liberation. This same council also threatened Jewish slave owners who attempted to convert their slaves with the latter's confiscation (although precisely who would do the confiscating is not explicitly stated):

> We declare that it also must be observed that if a Jew attempts to convert a proselyte, who is called an *advena*, to Judaism, or to lead one who has become a Christian to the Jewish superstition, or if he allows his Christian slave woman to marry a Jew, or if he converts to Judaism one born of Christian parents in return for his freedom, let him be punished by the seizure of his slaves.[25]

This was a much milder penalty than the capital punishment threatened by Roman law for the same offense.[26] Additionally, unlike Roman imperial constitutions, these early Gallic canons do not strictly forbid Jews from purchasing Christian slaves. Also, by placing the burden on the slave himself for escaping from his captivity, they implicitly minimize the severity of the crime, and the likelihood that the Jewish master would ever lose his slave.

No further changes were made to this policy until forty years later, when the Council of Mâcon (581/3) met to take up the issue. The primarily Burgundian and Provençal attendees were forced to admit that previous legislation had been ineffective at addressing the problem: "[Even] now complaints have arisen that certain Jews in the *civitates* and *municipia* persist in their great insolence and utter brashness, so that objecting Christians are unable to be freed from servitude to them

[24] Orléans (541), c. 30.

[25] Ibid., c. 31. On the bishops' fear of Jewish masters converting their Christian slaves, see Lotter, "La crainte du prosélytisme et la peur du contact: Les juifs dans les actes des synodes mérovingiens," 849–79.

[26] *Codex Theodosianus* 16:9:2.

even by purchase."[27] There seems little reason to doubt the sincerity of this admission, although there is no reason to assume that it describes the situation beyond the kingdom of Guntrum, who convoked the council. The bishops at Mâcon resorted to more stringent measures. From then on, according to the sixteenth canon of their *acta*, Jews were not permitted to possess Christian slaves at all, and any Christian would be allowed to purchase an enslaved Christian from a Jewish owner for the fixed price of twelve *solidi,* which was a relatively low price for slaves.[28] The Jewish owners, however, presumably would have no choice but to accept this assessment. Additionally, the conciliar attendees decreed that if a slave owner was found to "have persuaded a Christian slave to unite himself with the Jewish error, he [the Jew] is to lose his slave, and be punished by legal condemnation."[29] Although, to a certain degree, these canons echo the severity of Roman statutes, they were composed in response to the failure of earlier *Frankish* legislation to end the hated practice. They would also prove as ineffective as their predecessors. The correspondence of Pope Gregory the Great confirms that Gallic Jews continued to possess slaves more than a decade after the Council of Mâcon sat. In two separate letters to the reigning Merovingian monarchs, Gregory pleads with the crown to put an end to Jewish ownership of Christian slaves.[30] Additionally, Frankish church councils continued to issue canons promoting new approaches to the problem of Jewish ownership of slaves and trade in slaves for the next century, including the Councils of Clichy (626–7) and Chalon-sur-Saône (647/653).[31] This sustained effort may suggest the failure of the royal government to support this legislation, quite possibly because of the importance of slavery and the slave trade to the Frankish

[27] Mâcon (581/3), c. 16.

[28] On the matter of the twelve *solidi*, see Walter Pakter, *Medieval Canon Law and the Jews*, 98, 115, 128. According to Pakter, the value of slaves usually averaged between twelve and thirty-five *solidi,* so the twelve *solidi* fixed rate would have been low, but still preferable to the complete lack of recompense offered in those areas where Justinian's policies were in effect. In the Carolingian period, the Mâcon fixed rate would be raised to twenty to thirty *solidi:* Katz, *The Jews in the Visigothic and Frankish Kingdoms of Spain and Gaul*, 100–1. For general guides to Merovingian currency, see Maurice Prou, *Les monnaies mérovingiennes* (Graz: Akademische Druck-U, Verlagsanstalt, 1969); Philip Grierson, *The Coins of Medieval Europe* (London: Seaby, 1991), 16–7.

[29] Mâcon (581/3), c. 17.

[30] Gregory I *Registrum Epistularum* IX.214 and IX.216.

[31] Clichy (626/7), c. 13; Chalon-sur-Saône (647/653), c. 9.

economy.[32] Although the extent of Jewish involvement in this slave trade continues to be a matter of considerable debate, at least some Gallic Jews did own or trade in slaves in the Frankish era, probably with the tacit approval of the monarchy.[33] Thus, when religious principles clashed with economic interests, the royal government, although respectful of the former, could not ignore the latter.

Protecting Church Property: A Case Study

A similar situation informed the development of a canonical tradition concerning the proper management and protection of church property. This issue was surpassed only by clerical discipline as the foremost concern in the minds of Frankish conciliar attendees.[34] This concern did not stem from a fear of financial destitution, at least in the sixth and seventh centuries. Indeed, there were those laymen who believed that the church in these centuries enjoyed far too much affluence. In a famous outburst recorded, or perhaps invented, for posterity by Gregory of Tours, King Chilperic miserably exclaimed, "Look at how our treasury has diminished! Look at how all of our wealth has fallen into the hands of the Church! No one has any power except the bishops!"[35] It is quite likely, as J. M. Wallace-Hadrill noted, that in bemoaning his loss, "the poor fellow exaggerated."[36] Still, there was still some

---

[32] On Frankish slavery, the classic study long has been that of Charles Verlinden, *L'esclavage dans l'Europe médiévale*, vol. 1 (Brugge: De Tempel, 1955), 633–728. But more recently, McCormick, *The Origins of the European Economy*, 733–7, has demonstrated the fundamental importance of the slave trade to the Frankish economy. He observes that in the Carolingian period, "the slave trade fueled the expansion of commerce between Europe and the Muslim world" (p. 776).

[33] Michael Toch, "Jews and Commerce: Modern Fancies and Medieval Realities," in *Il Ruolo Economico delle Minoranze in Europa Secc. XIII–XVIII*, ed. Simonetta Cavaciocchi (Florence: Le Monnier, 2000), 43–58, points out the weakness of much of the evidence, but pushes the argument a little too far. See also on this question Devroey and Brouwer, "La participation des Juifs au commerce dans le monde franc," 357–8. McCormick, *The Origins of the European Economy*, 645, notes the presence of Jewish slave traders in Lyons in the early ninth century (see also pp. 774–5). Adriaan Verhulst, *The Carolingian Economy* (Cambridge: Cambridge University Press, 2002), 98–9, observes that the tenth-century *Inquisitio de Teloneis Raffelstettensis* (ch. 9) confirms that Jewish traders of salt, slaves, and other goods, by long-standing custom, paid a toll on their cargo, but otherwise were not harassed.

[34] Pontal, *Histoire des conciles mérovingiens*, 277–8; Basdevant-Gaudemet, "L'évêque, d'après la législation de quelques conciles mérovingiens," 485–7.

[35] Gregory of Tours *Decem Libri Historiarum* VI.46.

[36] Wallace-Hadrill, *The Frankish Church*, 124.

truth to Chilperic's charge. Through the donations and bequests of the faithful, the Gallic church, by the late sixth century, had managed to acquire a patrimony of substantial size and value.[37] If Chilperic was looking for someone to blame for the church's affluence, he need have looked no further than his own family. The chroniclers of Merovingian history record numerous examples of royal generosity toward the church,[38] as do the surviving charters of the period, which record donations of both gifts and privileges,[39] along with the formularies, which offer documentary templates for these transactions.[40] The remainder of the faithful, at least those who could afford it, did their part as well to see that the holy church remained well funded.[41]

Despite the wealth flowing in, ecclesiastical authorities did not necessarily feel financially secure, as they were conscious of the many lay magnates eager to slice off portions of the church's patrimony for themselves. By means of canons, judicial decisions, and the grant of privileges, the Frankish bishops made a concerted effort to protect the church's property from greedy kings, nobles, and even fellow prelates.[42] Certainly, this effort predated the foundation of the Frankish kingdoms in Gaul; more than a few of the Merovingian-era canons cite earlier

---

[37] A. H. M. Jones, "Church Finance in the Fifth and Sixth Centuries," *Journal of Theological Studies* XI (New Series,), no. 1 (1960): 84–5; Emile Lesne, *Histoire de la propriété ecclésiastique en France* (Lille: Rene Giard, 1910–43), I.153.

[38] See, e.g., Gregory of Tours *Decem Libri Historiarum* IV.21, VII.7, X.7, X.11; Fredegar *Chronica* IV.1, IV.22, IV.79; *Liber Historiae Francorum*, ch. 42. On the importance of royal generosity toward the church, see Mayeux, "Les biens de l'Eglise considérés comme patrimoine des pauvres à travers les conciles occidentaux du VIe siècle," 151 ff. In contrast, Durliat, *Les finances publiques de Dioclétien aux Carolingiens*, 146, has suggested that "Clovis was a generous benefactor. His descendants were thriftier."

[39] The Merovingian royal diplomas have been reedited by the MGH, rendering the older Pertz edition superfluous: *Die Urkunden der Merowinger*, ed. Carlrichard Brühl, Theo Kölzer, Martina Hartmann, and Andrea Stieldorf (Hanover: Hahn, 2001). Several examples are discussed below.

[40] E.g., *Marculfi Formularum* I.14–16.

[41] See, e.g., J. M. Pardessus, ed. *Diplomata, Chartae, Epistolae, Leges Aliaque Instrumenta ad Res Gallo-Francicas Spectantia* (Aalen: Scientia Verlag, 1843–9), nos. 243 (*ChLa*, K1, no. 4), 331 (*ChLa*, K2, no. 6), 412 (*ChLa*, K3, no. 2.2) 413 (*ChLa*, K3, no. 1), 452 (*ChLa*, K4, no. 1), 456 (*ChLa*, K3, no. 13), and 547 (*ChLa*, K4, no. 5). See the relevant formulae for lay grants in, e.g., *Formulae Andecavenses*, in *Formulae Merowingici et Karolini Aevi*, MGH Leges V, ed. Karl Zeumer (Hanover: Hahn, 1886), no. 46; *Marculfi Formularum* II.1–6.

[42] In the *Decem Libri Historiarum*, Gregory of Tours provides many examples of church property being threatened by greedy dukes (III.16, VIII.12), counts (V.36), royal treasurers (VII.21), kings (IV.2, V.14, VI.46), and bishops (IV.12). An additional example of episcopal greed can be found in VII.31.

conciliar precedents for their decisions.[43] However, with the establishment of Frankish power, the Romano-Gallic church gained a new ally, albeit a sometimes fair-weather one, in its struggle to protect its property from usurpation. For this reason, it would be an oversimplification to read the Merovingian-era conciliar canons as the church's attempt to shield itself from the power of the Frankish royal government. A survey of royal legislation dealing with the protection of church property reveals that, for the most part, the monarchy did not operate in opposition to canonical principles.

As with much ancient legislation, we are largely ignorant as to the efforts made to enforce these conciliar canons. That they seem to have conformed to contemporary secular edicts suggests that there was some effort to implement them as official royal policy. Although we will include the issue of enforcement of conciliar canons regarding protection of church property in the following discussion, two other issues will receive more attention: the nature of the contemporary concerns addressed by the councils, and the ways in which these concerns and the legislative responses to them changed over time. Contemporary secular *leges, formulae,* charters, and wills possess comparative value, and so will provide a context for the councils' legislation.

The Frankish church's efforts to protect its patrimony date back to Clovis' convocation of the First Council of Orléans (511). The council's *acta* contributed to a definition of the relationship between the unified Gallic church and its new protector.[44] This is not to say that all of its pronouncements were entirely original. A number of the same issues, as well as bishops, were also present at the earlier Council of Agde (506), convoked under the auspices of the Visigothic king Alaric II.[45] Still, there are also indications that the bishops at Orléans were responding to immediate concerns in their legislating. Canon no. 5, for example, is concerned with those "donations (*oblationes*) and lands (*agri*) that our lord king has conferred as gifts to the Church."[46] Although it is

---

[43] See, e.g., Orléans (538), cc. 13, 22, 25, all of which are based on conciliar legislation issued at the Visigothic Council of Agde (506). Canon 25 also relies upon *Statuta Ecclesiae Antiqua*, c. 86, and the Council of Vaison (442), c. 4.

[44] Duchesne, *L'Eglise au VI siècle*, 502; Heuclin, "Le Concile d'Orléans de 511, un premier concordat," 435–50.

[45] On the relationship between the Councils of Arles and Orleans, see chapter 6. C.f. Daly, "Clovis: How Barbarian, How Pagan," 657. On Agde's legislative agenda, see Klingshirn, *Caesarius of Arles*, 97–104.

[46] Orléans (511), c. 5.

unclear whether the lands in question were those recently seized by the Franks from the Arian Visigoths,[47] there is no question that an attempt was being made to work out a standard policy regarding Clovis' gifts of property to the church. Indeed, a substantial portion of the canonical acts of Orléans (511) is devoted to formulating procedures for dealing with donations and the management of property, some based on earlier canons, others more original.[48]

The guiding principle underpinning these canons is that diocesan property is under the authority of the bishop. It is he who oversees and administers it and distributes it to his dependents. He possesses the right to bestow vineyards (*vineolae*) and land (*terrulae*) on clerics and monks in *usufructus*,[49] as well as to approve all other grants of benefices (*beneficiae*) to clerics or abbots by secular officials.[50] He maintains authority over all the basilicas (*basilicae*) within his diocese.[51] He retains half of all offerings left on the cathedral altar by the faithful, parcels out the rest to his clerics according to rank, and oversees all ecclesiastical estates (*praedia*) within his jurisdiction.[52] Even those donations granted to *parochiae* by the faithful—e.g. land, vineyards, and slaves—are under episcopal authority, and the bishop may keep for his own use one third of the donations placed on the parish altars.[53] Whether the bishop ever received his share, of course, was another matter altogether, and it appears that sometimes he did not.[54] Finally, the bishop is charged with using the revenues from gifted property for alms, building repairs, and purchasing the freedom of prisoners.[55]

This complex system of revenue collection and distribution has its origins in a relatively simple Roman rule, i.e., that all church income is

[47] De Clercq makes this assumption: *Concilia Galliae*, 6, note canon 5. In contrast, see Daly, "Clovis: How Barbarian, How Pagan," 658.

[48] I.e., canon nos. 5, 6, 7, 14, 15, 17, and 23.

[49] Orléans (511), c. 23.

[50] Ibid., c. 7.

[51] Ibid., c. 17.

[52] Ibid., c. 14.

[53] Ibid., c. 15. Rouche, "La matricule des pauvres: Évolution d'une institution de charité du Bas Empire jusqu'à la fin du Haut Moyen Age," 86, has suggested that the other two thirds went to local clerics and the poor. Although the meaning of the word *parochia* varied in this period, with the term often being used to refer to episcopal jurisdictional units (i.e., dioceses), in this case it is clearly referring to a *vicus*-based parish church. On the term *parochia*, see Susan Wood, *The Proprietary Church in the Medieval West* (Oxford: Oxford University Press, 2006), 66–7.

[54] Wood, *The Proprietary Church in the Medieval West*, 11.

[55] Orléans (511), c. 5.

to be divided into four parts, and distributed evenly among the bishop, the poor, lower clerics, and a building fund.[56] The complexity of the Frankish system was necessitated by a number of factors. First, there was the Frankish episcopate's struggle to cement its authority over country parishes, monasteries, and local diocesan hierarchies. Secondly, the Gallic system reflects the importance of donations to the church's financial stability.[57] Ecclesiastical institutions were not the only beneficiaries in such transactions. From the perspective of royal or local aristocratic patrons, their generosity invited not only spiritual rewards, but also a means by which to forge and maintain long-lasting relationships with powerful institutions.[58]

Considering the emphasis placed by the Frankish episcopate on the maintenance and administration of ecclesiastical property, a surprising feature of the canonical program of the Council of Orléans (511) is its lone direct statement on the issue of property alienation. According to the sixth canon of the council's acts, "If someone believes he can justly reclaim from a bishop either church property or property rightfully his own, so long as he does not speak abusively or makes criminal charges, he should not be excommunicated for this act alone."[59] This prescription legitimizes claims against the church for the recovery of property by forbidding the bishop the use of his most powerful weapon. Why would the bishops at Orléans have agreed to such a measure? Were they pressured by Clovis, or was this a show of generosity and evenhandedness? This act perhaps is best understood as a gesture of compromise. The Frankish church never completely abandoned its position on the inalienability of its property. However, it learned to cope with the reality that such property could be, and regularly was, lost to lay claimants. By legitimizing certain claims, while still espousing the traditional position that alienation of ecclesiastical property was forbidden, the bishops at Orléans were providing themselves and their successors with room to maneuver in future disputes. At the same time, they were offering a concession to the royal authorities.

---

[56] Jones, "Church Finance in the Fifth and Sixth Centuries," 92; Gaudemet, *L'Église dans l'Empire Romain*, 309–10; Lesne, *Histoire de la propriété*, 60–9; c.f., Rouche, "La matricule des pauvres," 86–7.

[57] Lesne, *Histoire de la propriété*, I.153. On this same point, see Jones, "Church Finance in the Fifth and Sixth Centuries," 84–5.

[58] Mathew Innes, *State and Society in the Early Middle Ages: The Middle Rhine Valley, 400–1000* (Cambridge: Cambridge University Press, 2000), 13–50.

[59] Orléans (511), c. 6.

Although the canons of the Council of Orléans (511) set the tone for all future conciliar legislation concerning church property in the Frankish kingdoms, they would be clarified and modified by subsequent councils. This observation is best demonstrated by looking topically at some of the major issues addressed at Orléans, beginning with donations. These gifts, as already noted, provided a critical source of income for the Gallic church, and a great number of councils dealt with the administrative issues surrounding the collection and use of donations by the faithful. The Council of Carpentras (527), a non-Frankish provincial synod convoked by Caesarius of Arles, and the Frankish Council of Orléans (538), for instance, added further complications to an increasingly complex collection and disbursement system. At Carpentras, Caesarius and his provincial suffragans established a policy whereby donations in wealthy *civitates* would be divided among the bishop, clergy, and a repairs fund, while in dioceses with great expenses and few resources, funds for clerics and maintenance had to be reserved, and any surplus revenue would be given to the bishop.[60] A decade later, at the Council of Orléans, the attending bishops declared that offerings made to urban basilicas were under the authority of the bishop, who could decide how much was to be allotted for maintenance and the subsistence of the religious. As for ecclesiastical institutions in the surrounding countryside, the council declared, "Concerning the resources (*facultates*) of the parishes and basilicas in the rural districts (*pagae*) of the cities (*civitates*), they should be maintained according to the traditional customs of the individual places."[61]

What was the significance of these policy innovations? Caesarius' legislation—which would have been in effect only in the province of Arles—made an important distinction between wealthy and financially modest dioceses. Caesarius was not interested so much in overturning existing policies concerning the beneficiaries of donations[62] as in assuring that bishops would not monopolize this income, particularly in the poorer dioceses.[63] As for the bishops at the Council of Orléans (538), they similarly were making distinctions among different recipients of the donations of the faithful. Their ruling seems to have been an

[60] Carpentras (527), Canonical Acts.

[61] Orléans (538), c. 5.

[62] His decisions do not necessarily conflict, for example, with Orléans (511), cc. 5 and 15.

[63] Klingshirn, *Caesarius of Arles*, 139–40, 230.

acknowledgment of the relative financial independence of rural parishes in relation to the episcopal seat. The local parish priest would know better than his bishop the needs of his congregation, and, therefore, could be trusted to parcel out his church's income in an appropriate way. More generally, the canon suggests that the administrative policies established by the Gallic bishops for their urban seats did not always carry over into the countryside.

Bishops also had to be ever watchful that donations to the church were not misused by their ecclesiastical recipients. The Council of Orléans (541), for example, warns abbots and parish priests against treating donations to the church as their own property, and forbids them from alienating gifts without episcopal permission.[64] The Councils of Eauze (551) and Paris (614) both stipulate that donations must be employed according to the wishes of the donor.[65] These later two canons remind us that we ought not to think of donations as merely a few coins tossed into an offering plate at the end of mass. As the canons make clear, and as the surviving wills and charters of the Merovingian period attest, wealthy patrons of the church often granted valuable landed resources to the churches and monasteries of Francia in transactions that necessitated the drawing up of legal contracts.[66] Although it has been suggested that such charters were not prevalent until the seventh century,[67] the legislation issued at Eauze seems to belie this. According to the council's acts, "If anyone, for the health of his soul, arranges to give slaves (*mancipia*) or land (*loca*) to a holy church or monastery, the contract (*conditio*) written by the donor must be observed in its entirety."[68] Copies of these charters would have been preserved both by the

---

[64] Orléans (541), c. 11.

[65] Eauze (551), c. 6; Paris (614), c. 8.

[66] There are twelve authentic wills that survive from the Merovingian period. On these, see Ulrich Nonn, "Merowingische Testamente: Studien zum Fortleben einer römischen Urkundenform im Frankenreich," *Archiv für Diplomatik* 18 (1972): 1–129.

[67] Innes, *State and Society in the Early Middle Ages*, 73. Innes argues from the charter evidence, which, indeed, is sparse for the sixth century. However, he neglects sixth-century conciliar legislation. Written grants and wills are also referred to in Orléans (541), c. 19; Lyons (567/70), c. 2; and Paris (614), c. 12. Orléans (541), c. 19, does indicate, however, that major grants of land were made without the use of a written contract: "It has been decided that if anyone, out of devotion, and desiring to make an offering, donates land or vineyards to the Church without a written grant ("absque scriptura")...." Later, the *Leges Alamannorum* I.1 would require donations by freemen to the church to be confirmed through charters. The same requirement is also repeated in the *Leges Baiwariorum* I.1.

[68] Eauze (551), c. 6.

recipient of the donation, and perhaps also in the local municipal archive, the *gesta municipalia*.[69] Preservation was necessary in case subsequent legal claims threatened the gift.

Despite these precautions, the substantial number of conciliar canons dealing with withheld donations implies that this process did not always run smoothly. Heirs of benefactors are frequently identified in canonical *acta* as potential obstructions to the transfer of donated land or wealth.[70] This is not surprising, as it was their inheritance being given away. Imagine the reaction of the child of a wealthy landowner upon learning that his inheritance, or a substantial portion thereof, would be going instead to the local monastery or hospice. Sometimes these heirs, or their spouses, refused to allow the transfer of land to occur. This was the case when Hector, the *patricius* of Marseilles, challenged a bequest by his concubine's mother, Claudia, to the church of Clermont ca. 673–5. Hector presented his case to King Childeric II (r. 662–75), who ordered the matter to be judged at the royal court (*aula regis*). Bishop Praejectus of Clermont traveled to Childeric's court to argue the position of his church. The case eventually was decided in favor of Praejectus, not on account of his legal arguments (he possessed some knowledge of both Roman and canon law), but rather because the king turned against his judicial opponent, Hector, who was put to death.[71] Royal interests similarly played no small role one hundred years later in a dispute (772) between Abbot Guntland of Lorsch and the *comes* Heimerich, whose father, Cancor, had founded the monastery. Charlemagne was able to use the case as means by which to take possession of Lorsch himself.[72] The church's recourse to royal courts thus was no guarantee of victory.

---

[69] On this institution, see Peter Classen, "Fortleben und Wandel spätrömischen Urkundenwesens im frühen Mittelalter," in *Recht und Schrift im Mittelalter*, ed. Peter Classen (Sigmaringen: Thorbecke, 1977), 42–7; Wood, *The Merovingian Kingdoms*, 204. But see also the comments of Alice Rio, *Formularies of Angers and Marculf: Two Merovingian Legal Handbooks* (Liverpool: Liverpool University Press, 2008), 255–8, on the problematic use of the formularies as evidence for the continued existence of the *gesta municipalia* in its traditional Roman form.

[70] E.g., Orléans (541), c. 14; Orléans (541), c. 19; Orléans (549), c. 16; Clichy (626/7), c. 12. See, on this long-standing issue, Stephen White's discussion of the *laudatio parentum* of the eleventh and twelfth centuries: *Custom, Kinship, and Gifts to Saints: The Laudatio Parentum in Western France, 1050–1150* (Chapel Hill: University of North Carolina Press, 1988), especially pages 130–76.

[71] *Passio Praeiecti Episcopi et Martyris Arverneni*, MGH SRM V, ed. Bruno Krusch (Hanover: Hahn, 1910), chs. 23–7.

[72] Innes, *State and Society in the Early Middle Ages*, 180–3.

Beyond legal arguments, the church did enjoy additional means of pressuring heirs to respect the inviolability of donations. The conciliar canons primarily threaten excommunication as a deterrent. However, by the later Merovingian period, secular law codes were adding additional proscriptions, which may indicate the difficultly faced by the church in enforcing its own pronouncements. According to the *Leges Alamannorum*, for example, an heir who attempts to reclaim property donated to the church will suffer not only excommunication, but must also pay a fine (*fredus*), stipulated in the original contract.[73] As already suggested, the endorsement of church claims by the lay government may indicate a general agreement on basic canonical principles. The extent to which secular pressure was used to enforce these principles probably fluctuated, based on the context of a specific dispute.

Another aspect of the conciliar policy regarding donations that developed far beyond anything envisioned by the bishops at the Council of Orléans (511) was the tithe. At the time of Clovis' council, the tithe was merely a voluntary offering made by the faithful, generally employed for charitable purposes.[74] A little more than fifty years later, several of the bishops assembled at the Council of Tours (567), convoked by King Charibert, composed a letter *ad plebem* of this province, urging them most vehemently (*instantissime*) to donate to the church a tenth of their wealth and slaves.[75] There is no reason to assume that this request was intended to reach an audience beyond the province of Tours. But, several years later, the Council of Mâcon (585), held in the *regnum* of Charibert's brother, Guntram, took a more stringent approach to the problem of the apparent frugality of the faithful. Claiming the authority of tradition, the council declared the tithe to be a spiritual and legal obligation, and warned that failure to pay it would result in excommunication:

> We state and decree that ancient custom must be renewed for the faithful, and that everyone who attends Church service must pay the tithe: priests, paying for the needs of the poor or for the redemption of prisoners, obtain peace and health for the people by their prayers. If anyone, however, is hostile towards this beneficial arrangement, he is to be separated from other members of the Church at all times.[76]

---

[73] *Leges Alamannorum* I.2. See also *Leges Baiwariorum* I.2.

[74] Lesne, *Histoire de la propriété*, I.186–90; Jones, "Church Finance in the Fifth and Sixth Centuries," 85; Ullmann, "Public Welfare and Social Legislation in the Early Medieval Councils," 7–9.

[75] Tours (567), Synodal Letter.

[76] Mâcon (585), c. 5.

Subsequently, the matter of the tithe went unaddressed elsewhere in the Frankish kingdoms for well over a century, and there is no reason to assume that it was systematically collected on a mass scale. Additional penalties were threatened only in 756, at the Bavarian Council of Aschheim, whose decrees were not enforceable beyond Duke Tassilo's realm. The council declared that those who withheld the tithe had to pay a double *censum*.[77] In the Frankish *regnum* proper, King Pippin I wrote in a letter to Boniface's successor, Archbishop Lull of Mainz (754–86), that all Christians were obligated to pay the tithe "whether they wished to or not."[78] In 779, Pippin's son, Charlemagne, confirmed that the Frankish royal government supported the compulsory nature of the fee: "Concerning tithes, everyone must pay them, and they must be distributed on the order of the bishop."[79] Thus, it was only through cooperation with secular authorities that the councils were able to impose their will on the tithe-paying masses, a legislative reality that took hundreds of years to achieve.

As challenging as it could be for the church to ensure the smooth transmission of voluntary and involuntary donations to its coffers, managing the property once it came into ecclesiastical hands was no less difficult a task. This issue necessitated considerable conciliar attention in the decades following the First Council of Orléans (511). One concern that was reiterated time and again by the councils of this period was the fear that the property of one diocese would fall into the hands of another bishop.[80] This was a very real concern, as constantly shifting political borders, as well as personal ambition, encouraged some bishops to seek to expand their territorial possessions at the expense of their neighboring brethren. The many Frankish canons that deal with this issue do not simply repeat the general principle that such theft is not to be tolerated. Most, in fact, seem to reflect attempts by the presiding bishops to expound on this legal standard in order to fashion an enforceable policy that could be applied to real-world disputes. The Fourth Council of Orléans (541), for example, ordered that disputes between bishops over property be settled, if possible, within a year. If

[77] Aschheim (756), c. 5. The same council warned priests against wrongfully appropriating the tithe (c. 7).

[78] Pippin I *Pippini ad Lullum Epistola*, in *Capitularia Regum Francorum*, 42.

[79] Charlemagne *Capitulare Haristallense (779)*, in *Capitularia Regum Francorum*, no. 7.

[80] Epaone (517), c. 14; Lyons (518/9), c. 2; Clermont (535), c. 10; Orléans (541), c. 12; Orléans (549), c. 8; Orléans (549), c. 14; Clichy (626/7), cc. 18 and 24; Chalon (647/53), c. 7.

one of the parties proved uncooperative, he was to be kept from communion until the dispute was settled.[81] At the next national council, the Council of Orléans (549), a massive meeting attended by bishops from all four corners of Gaul, the attendees elaborated upon this procedure for dealing with intra-ecclesiastical property disputes by allowing bishops whose claims were not satisfactorily addressed by the metropolitan bishop of their province to bring their case before a synod.[82] This policy appears to have been valid beyond the *regnum* of Childebert I, who convoked the council.

Such a case, in fact, was heard by a council convoked in the Auvergne between the years 584 and 591. Bishop Ursicinus of Cahors had been accused of illegally claiming parishes from the diocese of Rodez.[83] The charges had been leveled by the newly elected bishop of Rodez, Innocentius, who gained his office through the intervention of Queen Brunhild. In the course of the lengthy dispute for control of the bishopric, unscrupulous individuals took advantage of the situation, and stripped the church of Rodez of some valuable resources. A number of years had to pass before the dispute was finally brought before a council, presided over by the metropolitan bishop of Bourges. This lengthy delay suggests why the bishops at the Council of Orléans forty years earlier were so keen on ending such conflicts quickly. In this case, the provincial council found in favor of Ursicinus.

It is not surprising that the Gallic bishops would have wished to deal with such disputes within the church and, ideally, on the local (i.e., provincial) level. It is surprising that the lay authorities theoretically accepted this policy, and, on some occasions, went so far as to bring their own property disputes with bishops before ecclesiastical synods. As noted in the previous chapter, King Chilperic accused Bishop Praetextatus of Rouen of, among other crimes, stealing royal property. Chilperic pressured the bishops of his *regnum* to depose Praetextatus, but then had the disgraced prelate brought before an episcopal council meeting in the church of St. Peter the Apostle in Paris.[84] It is not difficult to imagine why Chilperic chose the judicial venue he did. By permitting Praetextatus' former comrades to try him, while at the same time making his royal presence felt, Chilperic was able to keep up some

[81] Orléans (541), c. 12.
[82] Orléans (549), c. 17.
[83] Gregory of Tours *Decem Libri Historiarum* VI.38.
[84] Ibid., V.18.

semblance of an impartial hearing even as he attained the verdict he desired through a variety of unscrupulous means.

It is probable, however, that many episcopal conflicts over property and dioceses were settled informally before they reached the conciliar level, as was often the case with judicial disputes in early medieval Europe.[85] Synods were seen as a last resort, and the conciliar canons make it clear that the Gallic bishops wanted such quarrels to be confined within the provinces where they occurred. However, the sheer number of canons devoted to the problem throughout the sixth and seventh centuries suggests that episcopal property disputes remained a regular occurrence. Bishoprics were sources of wealth and prestige, and thus were consistently fought over by aristocratic families.[86] Even when a seat had been won, an aristocratic bishop was not always satisfied with the wealth and prestige that came with his office, and looked for additional sources of revenue. Such sources could be found in parishes, monasteries, hostels, and private land plots, whose illegal annexation remained a pressing concern.[87] One bishop whose notorious reputation for greed earned him an unfavorable mention in Gregory of Tours' *Historiae* was Bishop Cautinus of Clermont. Cautinus, we are told, "was so avaricious that he considered it a personal defeat if he could not chip away at some of the property of those whose lands bordered his own. With arguments and temptations he stole from the powerful, and with violence he plundered from the powerless."[88]

The death of a bishop, in fact, could leave a diocese's holdings particularly vulnerable to pilfering by ecclesiastics and laymen alike. One strategy that the episcopate promoted at the Council of Orléans (533) to maintain the financial status quo was taking an inventory of church property at the death of a bishop: "A bishop who has come to the burial of a fellow prelate, having called together the presbyters, should take possession of the *domus ecclesiae*, and make an account (*descripta*) of that which was left behind, and place [these things] under the diligent guard of able men, so that the property of the church is not harmed."[89] A later ruling, issued at the Council of Paris (614), ordered that the

[85] Wendy Davies and Paul Fouracre, "Conclusion," in *The Settlement of Disputes in Early Medieval Europe* (Cambridge: Cambridge University Press, 1986), 226.

[86] Geary, *Before France and Germany*, 126; Van Dam, *Leadership and Community in Late Antique Gaul*, 206.

[87] Chalon (647/53), c. 7.

[88] Gregory of Tours *Decem Libri Historiarum* IV.12.

[89] Orléans (533), c. 6.

property of deceased churchmen be managed temporarily by an archdeacon or another cleric until the testament of its previous holder was read, and that the property was not to be disturbed on the order of any secular official prior to that.[90] The Council of Clichy (626/7) echoed the Council of Paris' threat of excommunication against anyone who attempted to seize the property of a deceased bishop before the reading of his will.[91]

There were, however, instances where the stipulations of an episcopal testament were ignored. Such a case was one involving the *dux* Sigivald, a relation of the Merovingian royal family. Sigivald had been stationed in Clermont to hold the city in the name of his kinsman Theuderic I (r. 511–34). He took advantage of the situation by laying his hands on as much wealth and property as he could. This included a *villa* that Bishop Tetradius of Bourges had left to the Church of St. Julian in his will.[92] In a similar case, at the death of Bishop Marachar of Angoulême, his nephew, the *comes* Nantinus, attempted to reclaim by force those properties that his uncle had bequeathed to the church.[93] He justified his actions by blaming Marachar's episcopal successor, Frontonius, for his murder (achieved by means of a poisoned fish head). Canonical proscriptions having proving insufficient, it took supernatural intervention for both Sigivald and Nantinus to recognize the error of their ways. Sigivald took ill several months after entering the stolen villa, and repented of his actions upon his recovery. Nantinus was not so lucky: he was burned to death by an invisible fire that turned his body pitch black in his final moments.

Most of the canons discussed thus far are concerned primarily with the actions of the highest echelons of the church hierarchy. But what of the priests, whose relation to this vast accumulation of land and wealth is not as obvious as with their episcopal supervisors? In regard to lower clerics, the conciliar canons reveal a complex system of land leasing whose origins are found in the Roman period, and which would have major repercussions for the exercise of royal power in the Carolingian era. Again, the conciliar canons make it clear that the ultimate responsibility for diocesan property lies with the bishop. Part of his supervisory

[90] Paris (614), c. 9.
[91] Clichy (626/7), c. 18.
[92] Gregory of Tours *Decem Libri Historiarum* III.16; Gregory of Tours *Liber de Passione et Virtutibus Sancti Iuliani Martyris*, ch. 14.
[93] Gregory of Tours *Decem Libri Historiarum* V.36.

role required him to provide his clerics (and monks, in some cases) with enough resources to support themselves. These resources were never considered the property of the clerics who held them. Rather, they were held in usufruct (*usu fructus*), meaning that the holder of the property was entitled to its profits, with the understanding that the property itself would return to its rightful owner upon his death. Such bequests were made through grants of *precaria*, a word roughly synonymous during this period with *usufruct*.[94] Precarial grants took a number of different forms during these centuries, e.g., *precaria data, precaria oblata, precaria remuneratoria,* and *precaria verbo regis,* although the conciliar canons are primarily concerned with grants in which the land being leased originated as church property.[95] As early as the First Council of Orléans (511), the Gallic bishops declared such grants to be acceptable, and not a form of property alienation.[96] Indeed, they were an ideal way to provide for the needs of the clergy. However, episcopal participants at future councils still found it necessary to remind the recipients of precarial grants that they did not own the land, suggesting that some recipients sought to keep the property within their own family.[97] Bishops initially left it up to the discretion of individual prelates whether or not to ratify or revoke grants made by their predecessors.[98] Realizing, perhaps, that this policy left clerics at

[94] Ernst Levy, *West Roman Vulgar Law: The Law of Property* (Philadelphia: American Philosophical Society, 1951), 162; Ian Wood accepts Levy's opinion: "Teutsind, Witlaic, and the History of Merovingian Precaria," in *Property and Power in the Early Middle Ages*, ed. Wendy Davies and Paul Fouracre (Cambridge: Cambridge University Press, 1995), 45–6. *Precaria* was considered a type of *beneficium* as well, and sometimes used synonymously with that term: Pontal, *Histoire des conciles mérovingiens*, 284; François Louis Ganshof, "Les liens de vassalité dans la monarchie franque," in *Les liens de vassalité et les immunités*, 2nd ed. (Bruxelles: Editions de la Libraire Encyclopédique, 1958), 156. For a general treatment of *precaria,* see Lesne, *Histoire de la propriété*, I.314–32.

[95] Pontal, *Histoire des conciles mérovingiens*, 284, note 1; Barbara Rosenwein, "Property Transfers and the Church, Eighth to Eleventh Centuries: An Overview," *Mélanges de l'Ecole française de Rome: Moyen Age* 111, no. 2 (1999): 572. The variety of precarial grants necessitated different contracts for different arrangements. Thus, we see various precarial *formulae* in the *Marculfi Formularum*, e.g., II.5, II.9, and II.39–40. Wood, "Teutsind," 44–5, notes that these formulae, as well as those in the *Cartae Senonenses* (nos. 16, 17, 33) concern either cases in which the leased land was originally owned by the holder of the precarial grant, or in which the holder's own land is somehow part of the transaction.

[96] Orléans (511), c. 23.

[97] E.g., Epaone (517), c. 18; Orléans (541), c. 18; Orléans (541), c. 34; Orléans (541), c. 36.

[98] Orléans (541), c. 35.

the mercy of bishops who could use their power to deprive their clerical charges of their livelihood, a later council, Lyons (567/70), voided the original rule in the kingdom of Guntram, and declared that church property held by a cleric could not be removed by the successor of the bishop who granted it.[99]

The language and quantity of conciliar canons legislating precarial grants reflect their frequency during this period. This observation is borne out by the frequency of references to *precaria* agreements in contemporary sources. Perhaps the most famous grant of this type was that made by Gregory of Tours to his friend the poet Venantius Fortunatus.[100] Gregory offered Fortunatus a villa located along the banks of the Vienne River as well as some land. The bishop's gifts were made through the type of lease we have been examining, i.e., *precaria data*. Precarial grants of various types also appear in the surviving Merovingian wills, including those of Bertram of Le Mans and the son of Idda,[101] as well as in royal diplomas[102] and private donation charters.[103] Collectively, they reveal the Gallic bishops attempting to find a way around their own canonical restrictions against the alienation of ecclesiastical property. By allowing church land to be leased to clerics and laymen alike, the bishops could still maintain ownership. But, just as important, they gained the possession of additional donated land through precarial agreements. Although such agreements potentially brought new financial burdens upon the church, rents (*census*) were charged to the leasers to recoup some of these losses.[104] The precarists,

[99] Lyons (567/70), c. 5.
[100] Venantius Fortunatus *Opera Poetica* VIII.19–20.
[101] Bertram of Le Mans, *Das Testament des Bischofs Berthramn von Le Mans vom 27. März 616*, ed. Margarete Weidemann (Mainz: Verlag des Römisch-Germanischen Zentralmuseums, 1986), 37, 49, 65. The text of the will of the son of Idda is available in Pardessus, ed., *Diplomata, Chartae, Epistolae*, no. 413 (also *ChLa* vol. 13, no. 569). The testament of Abbo also mentions ten units of property held as *beneficia:* Patrick J. Geary, *Aristocracy in Provence: The Rhône Basin at the Dawn of the Carolingian Age* (*Philadelphia:* University of Pennsylvania Press, 1985), nos. 11, 20, 24, 25, 32, 34, 35, 40, 48, 54 (see also p. 98).
[102] E.g., *Die Urkunden der Merowinger*, nos. 93, 135, 136.
[103] E.g., the charter of Vuademerus and his wife, Ercamberta, the manuscript of which dates to the eighth or ninth century: Pardessus, ed., *Diplomata, Chartae, Epistolae*, no. 547 (*ChLa*, vol. 14, no. 594). In this contract, the couple agrees to pay an annual rent of 30 *solidi* in return for holding the donated land in *precaria*.
[104] Durliat, *Les finances publiques de Dioclétien aux Carolingiens*, 144. At Heristal, in 779, Charlemagne adjusted the *census* policy by requiring the payment of the *nona* and *decima* for precarial lands: "Concerning the property of the Church for which now a *census* is charged, a *nona* and *decima* should be paid along with the *census*. And for

on the other hand, benefited from the "fruits" of the property. It proved to be an arrangement agreeable to all parties.

Although the sixth- and seventh-century councils concerned themselves primarily with precarial grants to clerics, an eighth-century development changed matters considerably. At Les Estinnes in 743, in a council convoked by Carloman, the son of Charles Martel, the decision was made that some church land would be held as *precaria* by those engaged in military service, and that this land would be subject to a *census* of one *solidus* per *casata* (household). Nevertheless, it was decided that only churches that could afford it would be subject to this imposition.[105] The significance of this decision cannot be overstated. First of all, it clarified the status of land loaned to, or seized by, laymen in the preceding decades.[106] The identity of this property as part of the ecclesiastical patrimony was reiterated, even though it effectively was now in the hands of lay owners. Also, the decision confirmed church property as a reward for military service. Finally, it made it clear that the royal government had the right to lease ecclesiastical property. This type of precarial agreement became known subsequently as *precaria verbo regis*.[107] It has not gone unnoticed that this legislative innovation followed closely on the heels of Carloman's decision to restore all property taken unjustly from the church during his father's lifetime.[108] It may have been Carloman's failure to keep this promise that led him to introduce the *precaria verbo regis* a year later.[109] Regardless, his policy

those properties for which [a *census*] did not exist before, a *nona* and *decima* likewise must be paid" (Charlemagne *Capitulare Haristallense*, in *Capitularia Regum Francorum*, no. 13). On the *nona* and *decima*, see Giles Constable, "Nona et Decima: An Aspect of Carolingian Economy," *Speculum* 35, no. 2 (1960): 224–250.

105 Les Estinnes (743), c. 2. Fouracre, *The Age of Charles Martel*, 139, has noted that any given estate would have contained dozens of *casatae*.

106 Fouracre, *The Age of Charles Martel*, 140.

107 For concise definitions of this term, see Emile Lesne, "Les diverses acceptions du terme 'beneficium' du VIIIe au XIe siècle," *Revue historique de droit français et etranger* Series 4, no. 3 (1924): 18–9; Brunner, *Deutsche Rechtsgeschichte*, II.340. A clear distinction between this type of precarial grant and those made willingly by the church was made by Charlemagne in his capitulary of 779: "Let there be a distinction between precarial grants of Church property made on our order and those which are made by free will" (Charlemagne *Capitulare Haristallense*, in *Capitularia Regum Francorum*, no. 13). Clermont (535), c. 5, which deals with the misuse of church property by those granted it by the king, suggests that the *precaria verbo regis* had antecedents. See also Paris (556/73), c. 1, which notes that Clovis I granted the use of ecclesiastical property to individuals in "times of discord."

108 Germania (742), c. 1.

109 Herwig Wolfram, "Karl Martell und das Fränkische Lehenswesen," in *Karl Martell in seiner Zeit*, ed. Jörg Jarnut, Ulrich Nonn, and Michael Richter (Sigmaringen:

did establish a means by which both the church and the royal government could profit from the same land.[110] It was logical that he chose to introduce it by means of synodal legislation, thereby showing the approval of the bishops. Approval, however, should not be confused with enthusiasm.[111] Pope Zacharias, in a letter written to Boniface in 745, thanked God that the bishop was able to get the Frankish princes to agree to an annual *census* of twelve *denarii* from each family unit of *servi,* but expressed his disappointment that the land in question was not being fully restored to the church.[112]

This justification of the use of church land by laymen necessitates revaluating prohibitions by the Frankish councils against its alienation, and their claims of its independence from secular jurisdiction. Legislative developments between the First Council of Orléans (511) and the early Pippinid councils reveal the ways in which these most basic of principles were elaborated, reworked, and manipulated, depending on the needs of the church and the royal government. As early as the First Council of Orléans (511), it was acknowledged by the church that legitimate claims on disputed property might arise, and that they deserved a fair hearing.[113] The necessity of bringing such disputes before a competent court was confirmed by the Council of Chalon-sur-Saône (647/53), which declared, "No one should dare to take possession of, or purloin, ecclesiastical property prior to the holding of a tribunal (*audentia*)."[114] Seventh-century *formulae* suggest the protocol for when these disputes caught the attention of the royal court. Kings could and did order bishops (or their *advocati*) to appear

Jan Thorbecke Verlag, 1994), 76. Fouracre, *The Age of Charles Martel*, 143, likewise posits "the turmoil of the mid-eighth century," as one of the primary causes for this development. It should be noted, however, that there has been some debate whether Carloman "invented" *precaria verbo regis,* or merely confirmed its use: see Constable, "Nona et Decima," 227, note 15.

[110] Susan Reynolds, *Fiefs and Vassals* (Oxford: Oxford University Press, 1994), 79, has similarly argued that we would be amiss to view the church's "loss of control of precarial lands as a loss of full and unambiguous property rights to unjust usurpers… [as] property rights are rights which are recognized and protected by the law of their relevant society," and, moreover, both renter and tenant were afforded some recognition of their rights.

[111] Hans Hummer, *Politics and Power in Early Medieval Europe: Alsace and the Frankish Realm, 600–1000* (Cambridge: Cambridge University Press, 2005), 105–129.

[112] Boniface *S. Bonifatii et Lulli Epistolae,* no. 60.

[113] Orléans (511), c. 6.

[114] Chalon (647/53), c. 6.

before royal *placita* to argue their claims for ownership of disputed property.[115]

For the most part, synods following the First Council of Orleans (511) focused on condemning the actions of the church's own members who failed to respect the inalienability of the property under their responsibility. Bishops, in particular, were warned against alienating ecclesiastical property.[116] The early sixth-century councils articulated the basic rules that prelates were expected to follow. The Burgundian Council of Epaone (517) forbade bishops from alienating property without permission from their metropolitan,[117] and ordered them to compensate their church for any lost property.[118] The same council, however, made an important concession: exchanges beneficial to all parties were permitted.[119] Later, the Frankish Council of Orléans (538), citing Roman legal principle, declared that in cases where the thirty-year rule was applicable, alienated properties could be reclaimed for the church.[120] According to this rule, which was never consistently enforced or respected during the Merovingian era, there was a thirty-year statute of limitations for bringing an action in legal disputes over property.[121] Following these initial formulations of policy, seventh-century councils added specific prohibitions against selling off diocesan slaves[122] and vases.[123] Bishops were permitted, however, to liberate ecclesiastical slaves so long as they continued their service to the church as freedmen.[124] The attendees of the Council of Paris (614), elaborating

115 *Marculfi Formularum* I.26. See also I.36. On these protocols in practice, see Paul Fouracre, "'Placita' and the Settlement of Disputes in Later Merovingian Francia," in *The Settlement of Disputes in Early Medieval Europe*, ed. Wendy Davies and Paul Fouracre (Cambridge: Cambridge University Press, 1986), 23–43.

116 E.g., Epaone (517), cc. 12 and 17; Orléans (538), c. 13; Orléans (541), c. 9; Clichy (626/7), cc. 15 and 25. For warnings specifically directed against priests and abbots, see, e.g., Epaone (517), c. 7; Orléans (538), c. 26; Orléans (541), cc. 11 and 25.

117 Epaone (517), c. 12.

118 Ibid., c. 17.

119 Ibid., c. 12.

120 Orléans (538), c. 13.

121 For the thirty-year rule, see *Codex Theodosianus* 4.14.1. Gaudemet and Basdevant-Gaudemet, eds., *Les Canons des conciles mérovingiens (VIe–VIIe siècles)*, 242, note 2, say that this legal principle was expressly rejected in Orléans (511), c. 23, and Orléans (541), c. 18. Conversely, it was upheld in the *Praeceptio* of Chlothar II (date unknown), in *Capitularia Regum Francorum*, no. 13.

122 Clichy (626/7), c. 15.

123 Ibid., c. 25.

124 Orléans (541), c. 9. Monks, on the other hand, were forbidden from selling their slaves, because it was considered unjust "that monks assume the burden of daily agricultural obligations while their slaves enjoy the leisure of freedom" (Epaone 517, c. 8).

on an earlier decision of the Council of Paris (556/73), forbade the seizure of a bishop's personal or ecclesiastical property under the pretext of new political or ecclesiastical territorial divisions:

> No bishop or laymen may dare to claim or seize the personal (*privatus*) or ecclesiastical property of a bishop on the grounds of [shifting] royal borders or the division of provinces. Nor should he dare to possess or retain anything by grant or by occupation. If anyone should attempt to do this, let him be deprived of the charity of all and denied the grace of communion until he makes satisfactory restitution of the property as well as its profit (*fructus*)."[125]

That the frequent civil wars of the Merovingian family, and the resulting territorial redistricting, threatened the security of church property goes without saying. Laymen and ecclesiastics alike took advantage of political disorder at the expense of the church. At the earlier Council of Tours (567), in a strongly worded canon, the attending bishops warned that the rivalries of the Frankish kings must not bring any harm to church property: "While our lords squabble amongst themselves, urged on by the counsel of evil men, and greedily invade the territory of one another, they should not dare to appropriate or spoil ecclesiastical property in the course of their futile operations against each other, and its sacrosanctity must be observed."[126] Additionally, the bishops declared, property confiscated during one of these disputes had to be returned under threat of excommunication. But when it came to the Frankish kings, the bishops' pleas to respect the legality of property ownership regardless of political boundaries sometimes fell upon deaf ears.[127]

This raises what is perhaps the fundamental question regarding church property: Did the Frankish kings respect its sanctity and inalienability? No simple yes or no answer can suffice, because we read numerous examples in contemporary narrative sources of kings both protecting and confiscating church land. Both practices had long histories in Gaul.[128] Still, underlying this seemingly contradictory behavior, we can perceive a general attitude, if not necessarily a policy. As

---

[125] Paris (614), c. 11. C.f. Council of Paris (556/73), c. 1.

[126] Tours (567), c. 25.

[127] Elisabeth Magnou-Nortier, "A propos des rapports entre l'Eglise et l'état franc," in *Societa, Istituzioni, Spiritualita: Studi in Onore di Cinzio Violante*, vol. 1 (Spoleto: Centro Italiano di Studi Sull'alto Medioevo, 1994), 519–34.

[128] Wallace-Hadrill, *The Frankish Church*, 134.

early as the First Council of Orléans (511), the Gallic bishops admitted that the rule of inalienability did not preclude challenges to ecclesiastical claims of ownership. Similarly, the existence of *precaria* demonstrates how reality and theory were not always in synch when it came to the ownership and use of ecclesiastical property. Nevertheless, there was a consistency in the Frankish kings' acknowledgment (if not active support) of the property rights of the church. Likewise, there was a consistency in the church's allowance that its property rights were subject to judicial review, and that its property could be held, if not owned, by lower clerics and monks, as well as laymen.[129] The willingness of the Frankish kings, in principle, to respect the patrimony of the church is readily apparent—in both their capitularies and their legal codes—as early as ca. 507/8, when Clovis wrote a letter to the bishops of Aquitaine. In this letter, Clovis reiterated orders given to his army at the outset of his campaign against Alaric II:

> In the first place, we declare regarding the governance of the Church that no one may attempt to steal its property, either from those women performing holy functions, or from widows who have devoted themselves to the religious life, or from clerics or the children of clerics and widows who live with their parents; likewise, concerning ecclesiastical slaves, who are proven by episcopal oaths to have been taken from the Church, they must not endure any violence or injury on our order.[130]

Damage and theft at the expense of church property were likewise expressly prohibited. The *Lex Salica*, probably compiled during Clovis' reign, required those who burned a church containing relics to pay a fine of 200 *solidi*, while the *Lex Ribuaria* ordered a threefold compensation for thefts from a church.[131] In a harsher decree, the *Leges Alamannorum* punished the illegal seizure of church property with a thrice ninefold reimbursement penalty ("tres novigildos"), and required those who murdered church-owned *servi* to compensate the church threefold, plus pay a forty-five *solidi* fine.[132] The *Leges Baiwariorum*, in turn, ordered a ninefold compensation for thefts from a church.[133] The latter two codes also threatened both spiritual and financial penalties

[129] See, e.g., Paris (556–73), c. 1; Les Estinnes (743), c. 2.

[130] Clovis I *Epistola ad Episcopos*, in *Capitularia Regum Francorum*, 1–2.

[131] *Pactus Legis Salicae*, ed. Karl August Eckhardt, MGH Leges IV.1 (Hanover: Hahn, 1962), 55.7; *Lex Ribuaria*, ed. Franz Beyerle and Rudolf Buchner, MGH Leges III.2 (Hanover: Hahn, 1954), 60.8.

[132] *Leges Alamannorum* VI–VII.

[133] *Leges Baiwariorum* I.3.

against those who attempted to confiscate property donated to a church.[134]

Further evidence of the crown's respect for the sanctity of church property can be seen in royal grants of privileges to monasteries and other ecclesiastical institutions. As early as the fifth canon of the First Council of Orléans (511), there is a reference to an immunity grant by Clovis to the Gallic church.[135] The Merovingian immunity is a much-studied and much-debated phenomenon, most of whose points of controversy do not concern us here.[136] In simple terms, the immunity was "an institution of Roman and Frankish public law that conferred exemption from various kinds of state obligations."[137] At one time, the immunity was thought to be indicative of a weakening of royal power, as it forbade the intrusion of royal officers into immune lands. More recently, however, the consensus has shifted, and it is now generally agreed that both donor and recipient alike benefited from the system.[138]

---

[134] *Leges Alamannorum* I.2; *Leges Baiwariorum* I.2. The same section of the *Leges Baiwariorum* also deals with the process of swearing innocence in response to such charges (I.3), the illegality of convincing a church slave to flee (I.4), the murder of a church slave (I.5), and the burning of church property (I.6).

[135] Orléans (511), c. 5.

[136] Studies of the Merovingian immunity include N. D. Fustel de Coulanges, "Étude sur l'immunité," *Revue historique* 22–3 (1883): 249–90, 1–27; Maurice Kroell, *L'immunité franque* (Paris: Librairie nouvelle de droit et de jurisprudence, 1910); Lesne, *Histoire de la propriété*, I.260–7; Léon Levillain, "Notes sur l'immunité mérovingienne," *Revue historique de droit français et etranger* series 4, no. 6 (1927): 38–67; François Louis Ganshof, "L'immunité dans la monarchie franque," in *Les liens de vassalité et les immunités*, 2nd ed. (Bruxelles: Editions de la Libraire Encyclopédique, 1958), 171–216; Walter Goffart, "Old and New in Merovingian Taxation," *Past and Present* 96 (1982): 3–21; Elisabeth Magnou-Nortier, "Étude sur le privilège d'immunité du IVe au IXe siècle," *Revue Mabillon* 60, no. 297–8 (1984): 465–512; Alexander Callander Murray, "Immunity, Nobility, and the Edict of Paris," *Speculum* 69, no. 1 (1994): 18–39; Paul Fouracre, "Eternal Light and Earthly Needs: Practical Aspects of the Development of Frankish Immunities," in *Property and Power in the Early Middle Ages*, ed. Wendy Davies and Paul Fouracre (Cambridge: Cambridge University Press, 1995), 53–81; Elisabeth Magnou-Nortier, "Remarques sur la genèse du *Pactus Legis Salicae* et sur le privilège d'immunité (IVe–VIIe siècles)," in *Clovis: Histoire et mémoire*, ed. Michel Rouche (Paris: Presses de l'Université de Paris–Sorbonne, 1997), 495–538; Rosenwein, *Negotiating Space*. A useful overview of much of this literature can be found in Rosenwein, pgs. 9–18. The major debates surrounding the Merovingian immunity have included the extent of its indebtedness to the Roman imperial immunities and its contribution to the origins of "feudalism."

[137] Murray, "Immunity, Nobility, and the Edict of Paris," 18.

[138] Fouracre, "Eternal Light and Earthly Needs," 80; Murray, "Immunity, Nobility, and the Edict of Paris," 30–5, etc.; Rosenwein, *Negotiating*, 6–7. Goffart, "Old and New in Merovingian Taxation," 11, has offered a useful analogy: "Depreciation and depletion allowances, grace periods and tax-free bonds, are variations on the same theme; where public burdens exist, forgiving them to special persons reflects as positive a

That the Merovingian kings themselves looked favorably upon the immunity, there can be no doubt: of the 196 surviving Merovingian royal diplomas, authentic and forged alike, 71 (36.2 percent) refer to immunities.[139] Among the genuine diplomas, 18 out of 78 or 79 refer to immunity grants (approximately 23 percent), and range in chronology from the 640s to 717/8. The number of genuine diplomas, taken in conjunction with their lengthy history, suggest the willingness of the Frankish kings to issue them, as well as other judicial and financial privileges, when it suited their interests.

However, when faced with financial or political stress, the generosity of the *principes* toward the church could suffer. One need not go so far as to suggest a fundamental legitimacy of royal claims to church wealth to see why the royal government might feel obligated and entitled to use, when needed, this tremendous source of wealth.[140] And use it the Merovingians and Pippinids did. Although Charles Martel, the classic villain in the traditional story of the purloining of Frankish church property, has received far too much credit for his role,[141] the church apparently did suffer a loss of wealth and property in the later seventh century and the eighth century.[142] Nevertheless, the royal government's claims on church property in this period were not new, nor were the confiscations the work of a single individual.[143] More importantly, these appropriations did not signal some sort of breakdown in relations between the Frankish church and secular authorities. Quite the contrary: it was in the middle of the eighth century that church councils began more commonly to take the form of mixed assemblies of clerics and laymen. Nor was this simply a matter of the Pippinids subsuming ecclesiastical power into their own authority. Carloman at least made some effort to assure the church of its property rights. The paradoxical early-Pippinid policy toward church property—protective

governmental decision as levying them upon ordinary ones." For the older view, see, e.g., Wallace-Hadrill, *Frankish Church*, 101.

[139] *Die Urkunden der Merowinger*, ed. Carlrichard Brühl et al.

[140] Durliat, *Les finances publiques de Dioclétien aux Carolingiens*, especially 148–9.

[141] Many of the contributors to Jarnut et al.'s *Karl Martell in seiner Zeit* reevaluate Charles Martel's relations vis-à-vis the church in a more positive light. See also Bernard Bachrach, "Charles Martel, Mounted Shock Combat, the Stirrup, and Feudalism," *Studies in Medieval and Renaissance History* 7 (1970): 66–75; Wallace-Hadrill, *Frankish Church*, 134; Wood, *Merovingian Kingdoms*, 287; Wood, "Teutsind," 35.

[142] Lesne, *Histoire de la propriété*, II.1–2; Walter Goffart, *The Le Mans Forgeries* (Cambridge, MA: Harvard University Press, 1966), 6–10; Wallace-Hadrill, *Frankish Church*, 134; Wood, *The Proprietary Church in the Medieval West*, 75.

[143] E.g., Wood, *The Proprietary Church in the Medieval West*, 75.

on the one hand, covetous on the other—was the ultimate expression of the royal government's longstanding attitude toward ecclesiastical property. Contemporary prelates were conscious that "the apostolic ideal was no longer applicable" to the reality of church landowning.[144] Although the ideal of inalienability had long since been compromised in Francia, eighth century conciliar legislation suggests that it still remained an important abstract principle. Moreover, although the Frankish church probably suffered depreciation in its landholdings during the eighth century, it has been estimated that in the following century it would double its holdings in German, Northern French, and Italian territories.[145] So in the long term, the church, in fact, benefited from its close relations with the secular ruling powers.

The situation discussed in this chapter is a complex one, and made even more so by a lack of real evidence that could corroborate the enforcement of the conciliar legislation. Nevertheless, it should be clear that conciliar evidence has an evidentiary value beyond simply its enactment or lack thereof. It not only allows us to distinguish the motivations and ideals of the ecclesiastical and secular policy makers of the Frankish kingdoms, but, more important, it provides insight into the contemporary contexts that necessitated this legislation. Even with a relatively straightforward issue such as the inalienability of church property, the councils did not simply repeat a proscription time and again without modification. On the contrary: over the course of 250 years, principles were elaborated, innovations were introduced, and ideals were compromised. These elaborations and subtle policy shifts were the result of an ongoing dialogue between the church and the royal government about the obligations and duties each owed the other. The Frankish church was not a branch of the government per se, but all the same, its wealth, authority, and spiritual support were fundamental props of the Frankish royal regime. The councils themselves were instrumental in defining the relationship between church and royal government. It is not surprising that the perpetually fluctuating nature of this bond should be mirrored in the ever-changing content of contemporary conciliar canons.

---

[144] David Ganz, "The Ideology of Sharing: Apostolic Community and Ecclesiastical Property in the Early Middle Ages," in *Property and Power in the Early Middle Ages*, ed. Wendy Davies and Paul Fouracre (Cambridge: Cambridge University Press, 1995), 23.

[145] David Herlihy, "Church Property on the European Continent," *Speculum* 36, no. 1 (1961): 86–7.

CHAPTER 4

THE ENFORCEMENT OF CONCILIAR RULINGS

The year was 599, and the pope was getting impatient. For four years, Pope Gregory the Great had been sending letter after letter to the bishops and monarchs of the Frankish kingdoms, exhorting them to stamp out ecclesiastical abuses he had been informed were rampant throughout the Gallic church, in particular simony.[1] In comparison with the majority of his predecessors, Gregory was relatively well informed about events in Gaul. And he maintained a steady correspondence with prominent ecclesiastical and royal personages there, including his personal agent, the presbyter Candidus, who managed the papacy's estates in Provence.[2] Candidus was Gregory's most important source of information on ecclesiastical conditions in Francia, and most likely the source of the accusations that reached the ears of the pope back in Rome. Candidus' allegations were grounded in fact. As far back as the Council of Orléans (533), the Gallic prelates themselves had attempted to get the problem of simony under control.[3] Three additional synods condemned this same offense in the decades between the First Council of Orléans and Gregory's correspondence in the 590s, and at least an additional four councils would condemn it in the years that followed.[4] Gregory, who may never have even succeeded in getting his own council convoked, is an important witness to the difficulties faced by the Frankish church in attempting to enforce its own rules.[5] We can observe

---

[1] Gregory I *Registrum Epistularum* V.58–60, VIII.4, IX.214, IX.216, IX.219–20, IX.223.

[2] On Candidus and the papal estates in Gaul, see Gregory Halfond, "Patrimoniolum Ecclesiae Nostrae: The Papal Estates in Merovingian Provence," *Comitatus* 38 (2007): 1–18. On the volume of Gregory's correspondence with the Gallic church, see Thomas F. X. Noble, "Gregory of Tours and the Roman Church," in *The World of Gregory of Tours*, ed. Kathleen Mitchell and Ian Wood (Leiden: Brill, 2002), 156.

[3] Orléans (533), cc. 3 and 4.

[4] Clermont (535), c. 2; Orléans (549), c. 10; Tours (567), c. 28; Paris (614), c. 2; Unknown (c. 614), c. 11; Chalon (647/53), c. 16; Ver (755), c. 24.

[5] Hefele and Leclercq, *Histoire des conciles d'après les documents originaux*, III.1.245–6, suggest that Gregory's council may be identical with the Council of Sens (594/614), about which we know next to nothing. For the Council of Sens, see *Vita Betharii Episcopi Carnoteni*, ch. 11. Duchesne, *L'Eglise au VI siècle*, 539, argues that

this dilemma also in the two letters Gregory posted to the Frankish monarchs in July 599, in which he inadvertently divulges that the numerous attempts by Gallic synods to put an end to the Jewish ownership of Christian slaves have been unsuccessful.[6]

The Promulgation of Conciliar Decisions

Historians have been rightly skeptical of the ability of the Frankish synods to implement their own rulings.[7] The repetition of conciliar pronouncements is often cited as evidence for this view. However, as argued in the previous chapter, this repetition was not due merely to a lack of success in enforcing canonical standards, but also to an effort to make the canons correspond more closely to changing conditions. Skeptics also have noted that we can rarely identify instances where efforts were made to enforce a specific canon. One rare example can be found in the written judgment of the Council of Paris (552) against Bishop Saffaracus of Paris, in which the episcopal attendees state that they have rendered judgment according to the precedent of the Council of Orléans (549):

> Following the canonical sentence that the Council of Orleans recently decreed in regards to this same type of transgression (c. 12), this written decision is to be maintained and prosecuted by the metropolitan in the aforementioned *urbs,* with whom lies the power of overseeing and ordaining the conprovincials of his church.[8]

However, as the correspondence of Pope Gregory the Great attests, there were many cases when canonical principles were blatantly rejected or ignored, despite the fact that they addressed real concerns. For example, despite several canonical pronouncements that churchmen should not own dogs, some ignored these decrees in order to use these animals as guards or for hunting.[9] We are told in the *Passio*

Gregory's proposed council was "unrealizable," as it conflicted with the interests of the Merovingian kings.

[6] Gregory I *Registrum Epistularum* IX.214 and IX.216.

[7] E.g., Duchesne, *L'Eglise au VI siècle*, 525; Wallace-Hadrill, *The Frankish Church*, 107–8; Gaudemet, *Les sources du droit de l'Eglise en Occident*, 110.

[8] Paris (552), Conciliar Record (re c. 12). Similarly, the relevant *sanctiones canonum* were recited at the trial of Bishop Egidius of Rheims at Metz in 590: Gregory of Tours *Decem Libri Historiarum* X.19.

[9] Epaone (517), c. 4; Mâcon (585), c. 13; Germania (742), c. 2.

Praejecti that when Praejectus of Clermont was still a boy, only divine intervention saved him from a pack of frothing guard dogs kept by a deacon named Babo.[10] Ignoring the miraculous elements of the story, it seems to reflect the ordinariness of dog-ownership by the Frankish clergy in the later seventh century. Hunting continued to be a favorite pastime of "Milo et eiusmodi similes" in the eighth century. Milo even was said to have lost his life to a wild boar while on the hunt.[11] In a similar example of the disregard of conciliar principles, despite the concerns of the attendees of the Council of Bordeaux (662/76) that churchmen were involving themselves in too many judicial disputes as litigants and advocates, near-contemporary *placita* suggest that the council's warnings had little effect.[12] Finally, many examples suggest that the canonical requirements for proper episcopal elections in Frankish Gaul were regularly ignored or manipulated by interested parties.[13] Improper royal involvement, bishops selecting their own successors, the appointment of laymen to high ecclesiastical office, and simony were all unfortunate realities of elections in this period. When Gregory of Tours wrote the biography of his great-uncle, Nicetius of Lyons, he made no effort to obscure the fact that Nicetius had received his office through an agreement between Nicetius' uncle, the previous occupier of the seat, and King Childebert I.[14] The gulf between legal norms and actual practice relating to this issue of fundamental importance to the Gallic church was wide.

Notwithstanding such examples, the question of whether the Frankish councils were able to implement their legislation is methodologically problematic, as it assumes that a proscribed action will cease to occur when a law or canon is passed. To use a simple analogy, virtually every society, ancient and modern alike, has outlawed murder, and has gone to various lengths to prevent and penalize its occurrence. Yet even the most autocratic regimes have been unsuccessful in eliminating

[10] *Passio Praeiecti Episcopi et Martyris Arverneni*, ch. 3.

[11] Boniface S. *Bonifatii et Lulli Epistolae*, nos. 50, 87; *Gesta Treverorum*, MGH SS VIII, ed. George Pertz (Hanover: Hahn, 1848), ch. 25.

[12] Council of Bordeaux (662/76), Preface and c. 2. On this discrepancy between theory and practice, see Fouracre, "'Placita' and the Settlement of Disputes in Later Merovingian Francia," 32. According to the *Passio Leudegarii Episcopi I*, ch. 1, when Leudegar, the future bishop of Autun, was serving as an archdeacon in Poitiers, he became an experienced *iudex* of secular law.

[13] Wood, *The Merovingian Kingdoms*, 77–9 (with references).

[14] Gregory of Tours *Liber Vitae Patrum* VIII.3.

the crime completely. Why, then, should we expect to see activities and behaviors prohibited by the Frankish councils disappear from the historical record following the termination of their proceedings? In the following discussion, no attempt will be made to provide a general answer to the question of whether conciliar legislation was enforced *en masse* in the Frankish kingdoms, because enforcement certainly varied on a case-by-case basis, with particular offenses more prevalent in some places and times than others. Instead, the focus will be on the problem of whether canonical pronouncements were common knowledge among clerics and laymen, and whether their status was equivalent to that of secular law (*lex*). This discussion will lead into a reevaluation of the role of the Frankish monarchy in the canons' promulgation and implementation.

When conciliar participants returned home to their respective *civitates* following the closing of proceedings, they carried with them copies of the council's decisions. There was a concern, however, that the bishops would file the documents away in the cathedral archives, where they would lie, forgotten. For this reason, the episcopal authors of the Council of Orléans' (541) canonical *acta* required parish clerics to "receive from their bishops the canons necessary for them to read lest either they or their *populi* claim ignorance of those things decreed for their health."[15] The attendees of the Council of Mâcon in 581/3 similarly ordered that, from the feast of St. Martin until Christmas Day, the canons were to be read aloud in churches, "so that no one can claim to have committed an offense on account of ignorance."[16] Presumably, the audience for these recitations would consist of both clerics and laymen. Another council held in Mâcon several years later, in 585, also ordered its participants to "make known to all the churches that which has been dictated by the Holy Spirit through all our mouths, so that everyone may learn without any excuses that which must be observed."[17] Although the canon does not specify how exactly this is to be done, we might speculate that additional copies of the council's canonical record were made for individual parishes and monasteries, or perhaps the record's contents were recited at local diocesan or provincial synods. Councils of all sizes, in fact, contributed to the preservation of former

[15] Orléans (541), c. 6.
[16] Mâcon (581/3), c. 9.
[17] Mâcon (585), Preface.

synodal decisions through the consultation and *renovanda* of old canons, which served as important memory aids.[18]

But were efforts such as these successful in increasing the awareness of conciliar decisions? The internalization of canons by individual prelates, clerics, and laymen obviously varied by person, and probably also by clerical rank.[19] Bishop Gregory of Tours, for example, in his writings regularly judges behavior as either canonical or non-canonical, immodestly implying his own substantial knowledge of ecclesiastical *regulae* and, by extension, his subjects' lack thereof.[20] In Book Eight of his *Historiae*, for example, Gregory relates the story of a certain Abbot Dagulf, who, among his other crimes, was a habitual adulterer. Unfortunately for Dagulf, his mistress' husband learned of the affair, and surprised the two drunken lovers in bed with an axe. Gregory, ever the moralist, advises his clerical readers to take this story as a warning against transgressing canonical standards regarding proper relationships with women.[21]

But even a general knowledge of conciliar precedent like Gregory's did not necessarily entail the memorization of specific decrees. And, on some occasions, a cleric may simply have not had access to canonical decisions relating to a particular topic of interest. In the middle seventh century, for example, Bishop Chrodebert of Tours composed a detailed epistle to an abbess Bobba, in response to the latter's request for a brief response in which the bishop would "locate the canonical regulations concerning women who have committed adultery after having been consecrated and sworn a vow of chastity."[22] Similarly, Pippin III contacted Pope Zacharias around the year 746 to request a canonical collection containing prescriptions dealing with the priestly *ordo* and illicit *copula*, which was to be read aloud to an assembled body of priests.[23] Presumably, Pippin believed that the clerics of his kingdom were deficient in their knowledge of proper canonical behavior. So rather than inquire in general terms how much canon law an

[18] See p. 100.

[19] Knowledge of canonical precedent can be perceived in the letter collection of Desiderius of Cahors: Sandrine Linger, "L'écrit à l'époque mérovingienne d'après la correspondance de Didier, évêque de Cahors (630–655)," *Studi Medievali* series 3, 33.2 (1992): 813–23.

[20] E.g., Gregory of Tours *Decem Libri Historiarum* V.49, VIII.19, IX.20, and IX.39.

[21] Ibid., VIII.19.

[22] *Epistolae aevi Merowingici Collectae* no. 16.

[23] Boniface *S. Bonifatii et Lulli Epistolae* no. 77.

individual prelate, monk, cleric, or layman knew, it was better to ask what access a cleric had to this knowledge.

Despite the experiences of the Abbess Bobba and of Pippin, extensive access was available, especially to those operating on the higher levels of church hierarchy. Even if no effort was made to enforce the canons already cited that dealt with the dissemination and publication of conciliar decisions, the substantial number of canonical collections produced in sixth- to eighth-century Francia—more than twenty original collections, not including recensions—speaks to a high level of local awareness of canon law.[24] Even in the "darkest days" of the early eighth century, despite Boniface's claims to the contrary, prelates of the Frankish church were still pursuing the project of collecting and compiling anthologies of canons to be used for practical purposes.[25] Moreover, unlike elsewhere in the former Roman West, local Gallic compilers made sure that their collections were up to date, and that they contained the decisions of recent and local councils.[26] Like later Carolingian reformers, their goal was not so much ensuring uniformity as providing "the essential authorities for the maintenance and promotion of ecclesiastical discipline and law."[27] When, in the later eighth century and the ninth century, Carolingian reformers took up the project of educating clerics in the fine points of canon law, they made sure to extend their efforts to include rural priests.[28] In this era, bishops

---

[24] Rosamond McKitterick, "Knowledge of Canon Law in the Frankish Kingdoms Before 789: The Manuscript Evidence," in *Books, Scribes, and Learning in the Frankish Kingdoms, Sixth–Ninth Centuries* (Brookfield, VT: Variorum, 1994), 97–117. See Rob Meens, "Reforming the Clergy: A Context for the Use of the Bobbio Penitential," in *The Bobbio Missal: Liturgy and Religious Culture in Merovingian Gaul*, ed. Yitzhak Hen and Rob Meens (Cambridge: Cambridge University Press, 2004), 154–67, on the fusion of Gallic conciliar canons with Columbanian materials in penitential texts aimed at clerical audiences. The tally of Gallic canonical collections is derived from Kéry, ed., *Canonical Collections of the Early Middle Ages*, 1–86.

[25] Hubert Mordek, "Kanonistische Activität in Gallien in der Ersten Hälfte des 8. Jahrunderts," *Francia* 2 (1974): 19–25.

[26] Gaudemet, *Les sources du droit de l'Eglise en Occident*, 142.

[27] McKitterick, "Knowledge of Canon Law in the Frankish Kingdoms," 99.

[28] Carine van Rhijn, *Shepherds of the Lord: Priests and Episcopal Statutes in the Carolingian Period* (Turnhout: Brepols, 2007); Yitzhak Hen, "Knowledge of Canon Law Among Rural Priests: The Evidence of Two Carolingian Manuscripts from Around 800," *Journal of Theological Studies* 50, no. 1 (1999): 117–34; Yitzhak Hen, "Educating the Clergy: Canon Law and Liturgy in a Carolingian Handbook from the Time of Charles the Bald," in *De Sion Exhibit Lex et Verbum Domini de Hierusalem: Essays on Medieval Law, Liturgy, and Literature in Honor of Amnon Linder*, ed. Yitzak Hen (Turnhout: Brepols, 2001), 43–58. For a late-ninth-century example of one of these

frequently issued *capitula* to instruct their clerics in proper canonical behavior.[29] Thus, the project of familiarizing the clergy with past conciliar decisions was an ongoing project in the Frankish kingdoms. Every generation of clerics needed to be taught anew the *regulae* of past councils, local or otherwise, a task most easily accomplished by the steady production of canonical collections. An aware clergy could then instruct the laity in those areas of canonical law that directly affected them, thus ensuring an informed Christian community.

Conciliar "Law"

Assuming that there was a serious effort by the Frankish prelates to promote knowledge of canonical principles, we can now turn to the problem of reception. In other words, would a cleric—or even a layman—in this period have considered such pronouncements to be compulsory? This problem is tied to the question of whether the *regulae* promulgated by the Frankish councils were received as *leges,* in the sense of authoritative statutory decrees.[30] Most of the time, Merovingian sources, including the canonical records themselves, distinguish explicitly between *canones* and *leges*, and the two terms are frequently placed in conjunction with each other, suggesting different meanings, but also an implicit relationship. On the other hand, there are contemporary references to *ius canonum* and *lex canonica,* which imply the legal force

priestly handbooks, see Frederick Paxton, "Bonus Liber: A Late Carolingian Clerical Manual from Lorsch," in *The Two Laws: Studies in Medieval Legal History Dedicated to Stephan Kuttner*, ed. Laurent Mayali and Stephanie A. J. Tibbetts (Washington, DC: Catholic University of America Press, 1990), 1–30. On the legal knowledge of Carolingian-era prelates, as well as the didactic aim of councils, see also McKitterick, *The Frankish Church and the Carolingian Reforms*, 23–5.

[29] Hen, "Knowledge of Canon Law Among Rural Priests," 121, has argued that the contents of *capitula episcoporum* assume that "the priests…possessed not only a considerable knowledge of canon law, but also decent copies of canonical texts and sufficient literacy to use them."

[30] Isidore of Seville *Etymologiae* V.3.2. In his study of the history of *regulae* in Roman law, Peter Stein, *Regulae Iuris* (Edinburgh: Edinburgh University Press, 1966), 72–3, notes that *regula* was originally "a term…introduced [by jurists] to describe certain *definitiones* which were regarded as having a general application." There was disagreement among the jurists, however, as to whether a *regula* had an "independent normative force" (73). By the later imperial period, the term came to denote legal maxims as well. Late Roman lawyers drew upon these rules in court, where their authority was recognized. Stein is incorrect, however, when he argues that the word *regula* was rarely used to denote a legal rule during the Early Middle Ages, and instead was used only in the sense of a monastic rule (127).

of conciliar pronouncements.[31] Additionally, the meaning of the term *lex* itself was somewhat elastic in this period, and was used in reference to both written law (*lex scripta*) and legal tradition, but also even in the sense of classical *regulae*.[32] Nevertheless, the frequent divisions drawn between *canones* and *leges* make it clear that a distinction was made, at least in theory, between ecclesiastical and secular legislation.

However, this distinction does not negate the fact that canonical *regulae* were intended by their authors to be compulsory prescriptive decrees even though they were not considered identical in nature to the codes and legislation issued by the Roman emperors or the Frankish kings. Since Constantine the Great, Roman emperors had acknowledged the compulsory nature of ecclesiastical *canones*.[33] The Frankish kings, too, explicitly recognized their *auctoritas*. Chlothar II, for instance, famously declared in his *Edictum* of 614, "It is our ruling that canonical statutes must be observed in their entirety, and that those that have been overlooked for some time be observed from now on."[34] Additionally, the legal force of conciliar canons becomes apparent through their citation as authoritative statements by subsequent councils, kings, and canonists. Following Friedrich Kratochwil's pragmatic definition of *law*, which holds that "the legal character of rules and norms can be established when we are able to show that these norms are used in a distinct fashion in making decisions and in communicating the basis for those choices to a wider audience," Frankish conciliar legislation most certainly had the value of law.[35] Of course, theoretical distinctions did not always carry over into practice. The Merovingian monarchs were not interested in delegating all legislative authority

[31] Orléans (541), c. 10; Epistle of Clermont (535) to Theudebert I; Germania (742), c. 1; Soissons (744), cc. 1 and 4; Gregory of Tours *Decem Libri Historiarum* V.2 and VIII.19.

[32] Patrick Wormald, *The Making of English Law: King Alfred to the Twelfth Century* (Oxford: Blackwell, 1999), 29–70; Maurizio Lupoi, *The Origins of the European Legal Order*, trans. Adrian Belton (Cambridge: Cambridge University Press, 2000), 414–20.

[33] Barnes, *Athanasius and Constantius*, 172 (citing Eusebius of Caesarea *Vita Constantini* 4.27.2). Similarly, Emperor Justinian in the sixth century ordered the *regulae* of the ecumenical councils to be maintained "sicut leges": *Novellae*, Corpus Iuris Civilis III, ed. Rudolf Schöll and Wilhelm Kroll (Berlin: Weidmann, 1990–5), Nov. cxxxi.1.

[34] Chlothar II *Edictum*, in *Capitularia Regum Francorum*, no. 1. See also Guntram *Edictum*, in *Capitularia Regum Francorum*, 11 (quoted below); Soissons (744), c. 1.

[35] Friedrich Kratochwil, *Rules, Norms, and Decisions* (Cambridge: Cambridge University Press, 1989), 42.

over the spiritual well-being of their subjects to the bishops, and theoretical distinctions between secular and canon law blurred in practice.[36] This culminated in the Pippinid councils of the middle eighth century, at which no differentiation was made between ecclesiastical and social legislation.

The Frankish episcopate's jurisdictional claims were one of the reasons for this blurring of distinction between secular and canon law. In theory, canons were concerned with the well-being of the Frankish church. Therefore, the vast majority of them regulate the behavior of bishops, priests, and monks. However, as early as the Council of Orléans in 511, synods were issuing canons reflecting a much broader interpretation of conciliar jurisdiction, and regulating the rights and behavior of everyone from slaves and freedmen[37] to lay nobles[38] to even non-Christians.[39] Although the majority of canons dealing with issues concerning non-Christians are aimed, in truth, at Christians, a number of them, particularly those prescribing Jewish policy, do restrict the rights of the non-Christians in question. Therefore, they can be said to assume the council's legal authority over these communities. For example, the fourteenth canon of the Council of Mâcon (581/3) declares this:

> Jews, following the *edictum* of lord King Childebert of good memory, are to be forbidden from strolling through the main streets and the marketplace from the *Cena Domini* up through the first day of Easter for the purpose of mockery; furthermore, they [the Jews] are to be respectful towards all priests and clerics of the Lord; and they must not dare to sit directly in front of priests unless ordered to do so. Anyone who has dared to do these things is to be punished by the *iudices* of that place in accordance with his status.[40]

[36] Wood, "Incest, Law, and the Bible," 293.

[37] E.g., Orléans (511), cc. 2, 3, and 8; Epaone (517), cc. 8, 34, and 39; Orléans (538), cc. 14 and 29; Orléans (541), cc. 9, 24, 30, 31, and 32; Orléans (549), cc. 6, 7, and 22; Eauze (551), c. 6; Paris (556/73), c. 9; Lyons (567/70), c. 3; Mâcon (581/3), cc. 16 and 17; Mâcon (585), c. 7; Paris (614), c. 7; Unknown (c. 614), c. 14; Clichy (626/7), cc. 9, 13, 15, and 19; Chalon (647/53), c. 9; Les Estinnes (743), c. 3; Verberie (756), cc. 6, 7, 8, 13, 19, and 20; Compiègne (757), cc. 7 and 8.

[38] E.g., those canons forbidding the mistreatment of the poor by the powerful: Tours (567), c. 27; Mâcon (585), c. 14; Ver (755), c. 23; Aschheim (756), cc. 10 and 11.

[39] C.f. James Brundage, *Medieval Canon Law* (New York: Longman, 1995), 20. In the Merovingian kingdoms, at least seventeen canons were issued dealing with the status and rights of Jews: Epaone (517), c. 15; Orléans (533), c. 19; Clermont (535), cc. 6 and 9; Orléans (538), cc. 14 and 33; Orléans (541), cc. 30–1; Mâcon (581/3), cc. 2, 13–7; Paris (614), c. 17; Clichy (626/7), c. 13; Chalon (647/53), c. 9.

[40] Council of Mâcon (581/3), c. 14. See also Orléans (538), c. 33.

References to royal legislative precedent and secular judicial officials suggest that the bishops at Mâcon were aware of the need for lay support in asserting their jurisdiction over the Jewish communities of Francia. Still, this authority is assumed in the canon's prescriptions.

In short, the conciliar legislators did not limit themselves merely to the regulation of ecclesiastical administration; they were concerned with the religious life of the Frankish *regnum* in its entirety. Moreover, they recognized that the social responsibilities of the church, including care for the poor, orphans, and widows, the redemption of captives, and the treatment of slaves, entailed canonical definition. In this sense, the councils were able to extend their sphere of influence, in theory at least, to include all of Frankish society. The second canon of the Council of Chalon-sur-Saône (647/53) explicitly states, in fact, that "canonical statutes must be observed virtuously by all."[41]

If the bishops of the Frankish kingdoms claimed jurisdiction over non-clerics, did they actually make any efforts to enforce this claim? The standard inducement that the Frankish canons offered to the laity to encourage obedience during the Merovingian period was the threat of excommunication.[42] The frequency of this action, combined with the fact that it would have been prelates like themselves who would be imposing it, suggests that the Frankish bishops were confident of their ability to enforce spiritual sanctions. There certainly is no shortage of references to actual excommunications in this era.[43] However, excommunication was not even applicable to non-Christians, and further distinctions even had to be drawn between those forms inflicted on clerics and Christian laymen in order to make the punishment effective.[44] Public penance as a prerequisite for readmittance into the fold, for example, was a penalty reserved for non-clerics.[45]

---

[41] Chalon (647/53), c. 2.

[42] Cyrille Vogel, "Les sanctions infligées aux laïcs et aux clercs par les conciles gallo-romains et mérovingiens," *Revue de droit canonique* 2, nos. 1–3 (1952): I.8–20.

[43] E.g., Gregory of Tours *Decem Libri Historiarum* IV.4, IV.26, V.18, VIII.20, IX.41, X.14, X.16–7.

[44] Vogel, "Les sanctions infligées aux laïcs et aux clercs par les conciles gallo-romains et mérovingiens," III.311–28; Cyrille Vogel, "Pénitence et excommunication dans l'Eglise ancienne et durant le Haut Moyen Age: Perspective historique," *Concilium* 107 (1975): 11–22. Jean Imbert, "Disciplina et communio à l'époque carolingienne," in *Comunione Interecclesiale Collegialita'—Primato Ecumenismo*, ed. Giuseppe d'Ercole and Alphonso M. Stickler (Rome: LAS, 1972), II. 534–5, does not note the same complexity in Carolingian-era canons and capitularies.

[45] Vogel, "Les sanctions infligées aux laïcs et aux clercs par les conciles gallo-romains et mérovingiens," III.325–7.

But how seriously would an excommunicate have taken his sentence? This partly depended on the individual, although we should never underestimate the coercive power of social exclusion.[46] Occasionally, temporal penalties also were added to the sentence. King Childebert II ruled in a capitulary that those excommunicated on charges of incest were to be barred from the royal palace. If these individuals refused to repent, their property would be seized and redistributed among their kin.[47] As this example shows, excommunication could be threatened as a penalty in royal edicts, indicating a belief on the part of the crown of its effectiveness as a judicial penalty.[48] Finally, excommunication promised not simply worldly detachment from friends and neighbors, but an eternal severance from these people—and from God. A person's spirituality in no small way determined whether the penalty was harsh. Still, for some excommunicates, even clerics, the severity of the sentence simply failed to resonate with them. One such individual was a Parisian deacon named Theudulf, who moved to Angers without the permission of his bishop, in order to live closer to his old friend Bishop Audioveus. When he refused to return to Paris, he was excommunicated. Unfortunately, this failed to resonate with Theudulf, and the sentence was repeated on multiple occasions, but to no effect. Spiritual sanctions having proved insufficient, it took divine intervention, combined with an excess of alcohol, to teach the unfortunate deacon the lesson of obedience.[49]

Excommunication, as effective as it could be in certain cases, was not necessarily applicable in all situations. Reclusion in a monastery, for example, was threatened against the wife of a subdeacon, exorcist, or acolyte who remarried after the death of her husband, as well as against the priest living alone who had broken his vow of chastity.[50] Women caught in adulterous relationships with clerics could be expelled from their *civitates*.[51] And *humiliores* and *servi* caught practicing magic were subject to capital punishment.[52] Later, a

[46] Gaudemet, *Les sources du droit de l'Eglise en Occident*, 110.

[47] Childebert II *Decretio*, in *Capitularia Regum Francorum*, no. 2.

[48] E.g., Chlothar II *Edictum*, in *Capitularia Regum Francorum*, no. 3. Similarly, secular law codes could also threaten excommunication as a penalty: e.g., *Leges Alamannorum* I.2.

[49] Gregory of Tours *Decem Libri Historiarum* X.14.

[50] Mâcon (585), c. 16; St. Jean-de-Losne (673/5), c. 13.

[51] Orléans (541), c. 29.

[52] Eauze (551), c. 3. Corporal punishment was actually a rarity among Gallic conciliar penalties, although the Visigothic councils of Agde (506) and Narbonne (589)

fifteen-*solidi* fine would be imposed on all individuals caught engaging in pagan rites.[53]

Royal Enforcement

These last two canons are particularly interesting, as they probably would have required secular assistance for their enforcement. Yet they are not unique in this regard. There are a large number of Frankish canons, the implementation of which would be unthinkable without royal aid.[54] The exclusion of Jews from public office is a good example of such a canon, as is the Council of Chalon-sur-Saône's (647/53) declaration that slaves (*mancipia*) could not be sold beyond the borders of Clovis II's kingdom.[55] The Frankish bishops were not naïve about their ability to enforce such canons without secular assistance, nor were they reticent about requesting a king's aid. In 511, the bishops at the Council of Orléans sent a letter to Clovis in which they acknowledged that "the consensus of so great a king and lord" strengthened (*firmet*) their resolutions.[56] Similarly, at the Council of Clichy in 626/7, the assembled bishops begged Chlothar II to help promulgate and maintain previously agreed-upon canons:

> We beg as supplicants that you preserve for us in their entirety the principles of those decisions (*constitutiones*) that you ordered to be rendered at that great and universal synod held in Paris in your presence [i.e., the Council of Paris of 614] according to canonical tradition. We would be most grateful if that which was promulgated generally by your authority (*imperium*), and decreed and disseminated by so many bishops, be maintained for everyone.[57]

The bishops' request is all the more interesting for the reason that Chlothar, as we shall see, did not preserve the decisions enacted at the Council of Paris in their entirety, but, in fact, rewrote them to suit his own interests.

---

threatened it a total of six times, suggesting an assumption on the part of the participating bishops of the Visigothic state's willingness to impose their rulings.

[53] Les Estinnes (743), c. 4.

[54] Ullmann, "Public Welfare and Social Legislation in the Early Medieval Councils," 39.

[55] Clermont (535), c. 9; Mâcon (581/3), c. 13; Chalon (647/53), c. 9.

[56] De Clercq, ed., *Concilia Galliae: A.511–A.695*, 4.

[57] Clichy (626/7), Preface.

The Frankish kings were eager for the opportunity to legislate on ecclesiastical matters. During the Merovingian period, royal edicts frequently used the decisions of earlier church councils as the basis for new secular decrees. When Chlothar I made a *pactum* with his brother Childebert I, sometime between 511 and 558, he elaborated on the decision of the Council of Orléans (511) that confirmed the church's right to grant asylum by clarifying the area that would be considered impenetrable in those churches without enclosed *atria*.[58] King Guntram's *Edictum* of November 585, which was issued following the conclusion of the Second Council of Mâcon the same year, similarly elaborated on that council's order to "observe the Lord's day" by discarding the bishops' rationale that Sunday memorialized God's day of rest, and declaring it, instead, to be a memorial to Christ's resurrection.[59] The significance of Sunday was further elaborated upon by Guntram's nephew, Childebert II, in a decree issued in 596, in which the king threatened a monetary fine of fifteen *solidi* against Franks, and a seven-and-a-half *solidi* fine against Romans, who dared to work on Sundays. Slaves had to pay either three *solidi*, or substitute labor for payment.[60]

Chlothar II's *Edictum* of 614 similarly reveals a willingness to rework conciliar decisions in accordance with royal interests.[61] Article one of the *Edict*, for example, takes up the Council of Paris' (614) declaration that new bishops must be selected by the provincial metropolitan in conjunction with his suffragans, the clergy, and the *populus civitatis*. Chlothar, however, provided an *addendum*: "If [the chosen individual] is worthy, he shall be ordained on the order of the king; certainly, if he is chosen from among the palace staff, he ought to be selected on account of his personal merit and learning."[62] Although Chlothar's postscript undercuts the fundamental principles of the original conciliar ruling, he shows no hesitancy in using the canon as the basis for his own declaration. In another example from the same edict, Chlothar adds a number of conditions to the Council of Paris' ruling that no

---

[58] Orléans (511), c. 1; Chlothar I *Decretio*, in *Capitularia Regum Francorum*, no. 14.

[59] Mâcon (585), c. 1; Guntram *Edictum*, in *Capitularia Regum Francorum*, 11. Heinzelmann, *Gregory of Tours: History and Society in the Sixth Century*, 186–8.

[60] Childebert II *Decretio*, in *Capitularia Regum Francorum*, no. 14.

[61] On Chlothar's use of the Paris canons, see De Clercq, *La législation religieuse franque*, 58–61, who notes additional variations between the synodal canons and Chlothar's edict.

[62] Paris (614), c. 2; Chlothar II *Edictum*, in *Capitularia Regum Francorum*, no. 1.

cleric should be tried by an *iudex* without the knowledge and approval of his bishop. Chlothar, in his own ruling, not only makes distinctions among priests and deacons and minor clerics, but also between civil suits ("civilibus causis") and criminal cases ("criminale negucia").[63] He also modifies the Council of Paris' warning that freedmen are under the protection of the bishops, and, therefore, not subject to the jurisdiction of the courts of the *iudices*, by clarifying that the bishop's protection is subject to the terms of the emancipation charter, and by forbidding the trials of freedmen only in those cases when they are not accompanied by their bishop.[64] Additionally, Chlothar amends the fifth canon of the Council of Paris to give himself the right to compel bishops to pardon disobedient clerics.[65]

The modification of conciliar precedents by Chlothar and his predecessors did not negate the original canons, however; they merely clarified the circumstances in which the monarchy would enforce them. In this way, the Merovingians avoided the embarrassment and potential political risk of trying to declare legitimately enacted canons invalid, while still manipulating the form in which they would be disseminated. However, by the middle eighth century, when it became standard practice for conciliar decisions to be disseminated through royal capitularies, there was no longer any need for the mayors of the palace or kings to re-write canonical rulings to their liking.[66]

The irony of this situation is that despite the Frankish kings' willingness to modify conciliar decisions, the very fact that they cited the councils as precedents speaks to their recognition of conciliar authority. Guntram, in his *Edictum* of 585, explicitly acknowledges his decree's reliance on the *auctoritas* of those present at the Council of Mâcon earlier that year: "All that we have decreed in this *edictum*, we wish to be observed in perpetuity, because all these things that we publish, we endeavored, as you know, to define at the holy synod of Mâcon by the

[63] Paris (614), c. 6; Chlothar II *Edictum*, in *Capitularia Regum Francorum*, no. 4.
[64] Paris (614), c. 7; Chlothar II *Edictum*, in *Capitularia Regum Francorum*, no. 7.
[65] Paris (614), c. 5; Chlothar II *Edictum*, in *Capitularia Regum Francorum*, no. 3.
[66] Hartmann, "Zu einigen Problemen der karolingischen Konzilsgeschichte," 18–9. This is not to imply, however, that the capitularies are *exact* transcriptions of conciliar or assembly proceedings; their contents may still reflect a process of "selection and redaction." For this observation, see Christina Pössel, "Authors and Recipients of Carolingian Capitularies," in *Texts and Identities in the Early Middle Ages*, ed. Richard Corradini, Rob Meens, Christina Pössel, and Philip Shaw (Vienna: Verlag der Österreichischen Akademie der Wissenschaften, 2006), 255–9.

auctoritas of those present."[67] But this raises an additional problem. If the original conciliar canons possessed *auctoritas,* was this compulsory power in any way transformed or magnified by royal adoption? Some have argued that although canons did not require royal confirmation for their validity in the ecclesiastical context, the adoption and confirmation of conciliar decrees by the Frankish kings invested these pronouncements with the full status of secular legal pronouncements.[68] Other have gone further, and maintained that the Frankish kings were not "confirming" the canons at all—because they required no such confirmation for their validity—but rather were adopting them as precedents for their own independent legislation.[69] There is something to be said for this latter position, as it does explain the willingness of the Frankish kings to manipulate the language and content of canonical precedents. Yet it neglects the fact that the conciliar attendees truly seem to have coveted royal assistance in the implementation of their decisions. We need to make a distinction between the enforcement and the adoption of canons by the monarchy. In the former case, the bishops requested royal aid in the implementation of their rulings; in the latter, the king, by his own volition, used conciliar decisions as the basis of his own legislation. Thus, the edicts of Chlothar I, Guntram, and Chlothar II already described are not confirmations of conciliar decisions, but rather independent royal statements that draw upon ecclesiastical canons as precedents. This explains not only their manipulation

[67] Guntram *Edictum*, in *Capitularia Regum Francorum*, 11. Guntram's edict only addresses a single canon issued by this council (c. 1). Voigt, *Staat und Kirche*, 252, has suggested that this reference may be to a royal assembly held at Mâcon, rather than an ecclesiastical synod, but there is no evidence to support such a theory.

[68] E.g., Loening, *Geschichte des deutschen Kirchenrechts*, II.150–6; Hinschius, *Kirchenrecht*, III.542–3; Hauck, *Kirchengeschichte Deutschlands*, I.155–6; Voigt, *Staat und Kirche*, 250–4; Barion, *Das fränkisch-deutsche Synodalrecht*, 233–52; Ewig, *Die Merowinger und das Frankenreich*, 104–5. Both Hauck and Hinschius argue that the king could strip a canon of its ecclesiastical authority if it conflicted with state law. Gaudemet argues vis-à-vis the Roman imperial government that an emperor's adoption of a conciliar canon did not affect the original pronouncement's authority: *La formation du droit séculier et du droit de l'Eglise*, 143. C.f. Weyl, *Das fränkische Staatskirchenrecht*, 21–5, who argues that royal confirmation was required for canons to have authority in the ecclesiastical context.

[69] Voigt, *Staat und Kirche*, 250–4; Thomas Martin Buck, *Admonitio und Praedicatio: Zur religiös-pastoralen Dimension von Kapitularien und kapitulariennahen Texten (507–814)* (Frankfurt am Main: Peter Lang, 1997), 269–73. Nevertheless, the word *confirmentur* is used by the bishops at Clichy (626/7) in their request to Chlothar II that he aid in the enforcement of their decisions.

of conciliar pronouncements, but also their selectivity regarding those canons they adopted.[70]

Conciliar attendees recognized both the value, and, in some cases, the necessity of royal assistance in enforcing their decisions. However, this does not mean that they harbored any illusions about the implications of enlarging the king's role in the legislative process.[71] The Frankish kings' right to convoke and participate in defining a council's legislative program had been conceded as early as the Council of Orléans in 511. It was at this meeting that the precedent for associating royal power with the enforcement of conciliar decisions was also established. This partnership between crown and council assumed the mutual recognition of their respective powers, while still acknowledging their limitations. The bishops were granted a broad jurisdiction over the spiritual and social realms of the Frankish kingdoms, while the king's executive role was similarly confirmed. There also was an implicit recognition that the breadth of the bishops' legislative interests necessitated royal assistance, while the kings' desire to oversee ecclesiastical affairs required legitimization by the church itself. The consensus of bishops offered this legitimacy, and even "bad" kings, such as Chilperic, who did not hesitate to persecute individual prelates, recognized the value of employing synods as the agents of their persecution, e.g., the Councils of Paris (577) and Berny (580). *Boni regi,* too, used councils to further their spiritual and political agendas. Chilperic's brother Guntram, for example, convoked at least a dozen councils during his reign, attended a number of them, and used them to punish his enemies within the church.[72] Like Constantine and his successors, the Frankish kings sought to unite political and spiritual rule in their own persons, and their executive function in the synods allowed them to assume the paternal role of defenders of the church.

But how far did this influence extend? Royal power rested on symbolism, but also upon institutions and personal charisma. Underage and weak-willed kings naturally were much less able to exert their authority in the court, let alone beyond it. This would seem to imply

[70] Voigt, *Staat und Kirche*, 252; Buck, *Admonitio und Praedicatio*, 271–2.

[71] Elisabeth Magnou-Nortier, "Existe-t-il une géographie gaulois des courants de pensée dans le clergé de Gaule au VIe siècle," in *Grégoire de Tours et l'espace gaulois*, ed. Nancy Gauthier and Henry Galinié (Tours: Revue Archéologique du Centre de la France, 1997), 148–9.

[72] Gregory of Tours *Decem Libri Historiarum* VIII.20.

that the so-called *Rois Fainéants* of the late seventh century and the eighth century were incapable of supporting conciliar legislation. But there is a difference between the person of the king and the royal government that he represents. One paradox of Merovingian political history is the persistence of institutional stability in the face of increasingly frequent political instability.[73] Royal power in the *regnum Francorum* was underpinned by a variety of financial, military, and judicial resources, some of which were Roman in origin. Although scholars continue to debate the extent of continuity in tax policy between Roman and Merovingian Gaul, there is general agreement that even a gradual decline of royal tax privileges was not necessarily indicative of a decline of public power.[74] Besides tax revenues, the royal treasury also drew steady and substantial income from land, plunder, tribute, commercial levies, and court fines.[75] Portions of this wealth were used to reward the sometimes-tenuous loyalty of followers (*leudes*), who fought in the interest of the crown.[76] Up to at least the middle seventh century, the Frankish monarchy also could draw upon select local levies to field armies, among other military divisions. For the remainder of the Merovingian period, kings and mayors of the palace leaned increasingly on the followers of powerful magnates, who had to be rewarded in the traditional manner of *leudes*.[77] Even when these magnates, as individuals or in factions, challenged the personal authority of the kings of the latter seventh century or the eighth century, they continued to respect the centrality of the royal court as a political and judicial venue.[78] The court attracted powerful laymen and churchmen

---

[73] An observation made by Paul Fouracre, "The Nature of Frankish Political Institutions in the Seventh Century," in *Franks and Alamanni in the Merovingian Period: An Ethnographic Perspective*, ed. Ian Wood (Rochester: Boydell Press, 1998), 285.

[74] Compare, e.g., Wickham, *Framing the Early Middle Ages*, 107–15, with Durliat, *Les finances publiques de Dioclétien aux Carolingiens*, 95–187 (with associated bibliography).

[75] Wickham, *Framing the Early Middle Ages*, 106; Wood, *The Merovingian Kingdoms*, 64–6.

[76] On the *leudes*, see Bernard Bachrach, *Merovingian Military Organization, 481–751* (Minneapolis: University of Minnesota Press, 1972), 30–1 and 84–5. Bachrach (p. 73) observes that kings had to labor to maintain the loyalty of all components of the Frankish military, e.g., the *laeti, milites,* and *pueri regis*.

[77] Bachrach, *Merovingian Military Organization*, 65–73 and 124–6.

[78] Fouracre, "'Placita' and the Settlement of Disputes in Later Merovingian Francia," 23–43; Fouracre, "The Nature of Frankish Political Institutions in the Seventh Century," 285–316.

alike, eager to legitimize claims to property, find resolution for disputes, and obtain justice. Although, by the early eighth century, the Merovingians had gradually ceded their monopoly on lawmaking, they retained their role as arbiters of justice.[79]

Although the institutional stability of the *regnum Francorum* in no way ensured political stability, it did offer the machinery of governance, by which ecclesiastical concerns could be heard, debated, and, perhaps, enforced. But regardless of whether the court was dominated by a king, a mayor, or a faction, if such concerns conflicted with the interests or agenda of the ruling party, their enforcement could not be assumed. Still, when conciliar concerns did not clash with political agendas, and when personal politics did not intrude, it was in the best interest of the ruler, at least ostensibly, to support the legislative activity of his bishops. Bishops were no less powerful politicians in the eighth century than they were in the sixth, and perhaps even more so. Their agendas demanded attention, if not active enforcement.

The conciliar *acta* suggest the means by which the assembled bishops expected the royal government to enforce their decrees. Essentially, it was assumed that the crown would rely upon secular *iudices* to enforce canonical decisions on the local level of the *civitas*. We can see this assumption in the acts of the Council of Orléans (538), which declare that it is the duty of the *iudex civitates* to aid the church in its fight against heresy.[80] At the Council of Tours (567), too, the bishops requested that *iudices* separate forcibly from their wives those monks who had left their monasteries in order to marry.[81] The Council of Clichy (626/7) went so far as to threaten excommunication of those *iudices* who failed to implement policies established at the preceding Council of Paris (614), suggesting the difficulty of enforcing legislation on the local level, even when royal support was forthcoming.[82] Still, this support, at least in theory, put secular officials at the disposal of the church.

Additionally, as noted above, the bishops' legislative relationship with the monarchy allowed them to legislate on *causae publicae* that might otherwise be the sole prerogative of the royal government, such

[79] Wood, *The Merovingian Kingdoms*, 118–9.
[80] Orléans (538), c. 34.
[81] Tours (567), c. 16.
[82] Clichy (626/7), c. 27. The bishops justify their threat by crediting the canons in question to the *auctoritas* of Chlothar II.

as the regulation of the slave trade.[83] A further benefit of encouraging royal involvement in conciliar processes was that it confirmed, in theory, the necessity of obeying canonical restrictions. The consensus of the episcopal participants gave the canons their spiritual authority; the king's role in enforcement gave them a secular authority as well. Certainly, this does not mean that the Frankish monarchs enforced every canonical decree with equal vigor; on the contrary, there were any number of issues, such as the inalienability of ecclesiastical property, for which their assistance was often halfhearted, or at least not in line with the hopes of the conciliar attendees. It does mean that the canonical *regulae,* although not *leges,* strictly speaking, were authoritative legislative acts, and a major component of the pluralistic legal system of the Frankish state.[84]

There was no solitary source of law in the *regnum Francorum.* Ecclesiastical legislation, royal edicts, compilations of Roman imperial law, and territorial law codes all possessed recognized legal value, and were composed or compiled with reference to one another. Canons recalled Roman and royal legislation, royal edicts drew upon canonical and imperial precedents, and territorial law codes, such as the *Pactus Legis Salicae* and *Lex Ribuaria*, not only included royal decrees among their contents, but were compiled with the aid of lawyers trained in Roman law.[85] So, despite the diversity of legal sources, they were by no

[83] Heinzelmann, "Bischof und Herrschaft vom spätantiken Gallien bis zu den karolingischen Hausmeiern," 68–70. The *Vita Sanctae Balthildis* credits the widow of Clovis II with helping to limit the sale of Christian slaves within Francia: *Vita Sanctae Balthildis*, MGH SRM II, ed. Bruno Krusch (Hanover: Hahn, 1888), 9. On the relationship between this passage and canon 9 of Chalon (647/53), see Mordek, *Bibliotheca Capitularium Regum Francorum Manuscripta*, 971–2.

[84] For the expression "legal pluralism," see Guillot, "La justice dans le royaume franc à l'époque mérovingienne," 653–731; Antti Arjava, "The Survival of Roman Family Law After the Barbarian Settlements," in *Law, Society, and Authority in Late Antiquity*, ed. Ralph Mathisen (Oxford: Oxford University Press, 2001), 38, prefers "mixed legal culture." The idea, however, is the same. Legal pluralism should not be confused with the principle of "personality of law." On this principle, see Simeon Guterman, *The Principle of the Personality of Law in the Germanic Kingdoms of Western Europe from the Fifth to the Eleventh Century* (New York: Peter Lang, 1990). Increasingly, scholars have rightly questioned the extent to which ethnicity served as a basis for legal status. See, e.g., Patrick Amory, "Meaning and Purpose of Ethnic Terminology in the Burgundian Laws," *Early Medieval Europe* 2, no. 1 (1993): 1–28.

[85] Gaudemet, "Survivances romaines," 163–206; Ian Wood, "The Code in Merovingian Gaul," in *The Theodosian Code*, ed. Jill Harries and Ian Wood (Ithaca, NY: Cornell University Press, 1993), 161–77; Wood, *The Merovingian Kingdoms*, 102–19; P. S. Barnswell, "Emperors, Jurists and Kings: Law and Custom in the Late Roman and Early Medieval West," *Past and Present* 168 (2000): 6–29; Alexander C. Murray, "'Pax

means incompatible, derived as they were from a common legal heritage.[86] However, the extent to which written law was consulted in the multiplicity of judicial venues available to Frankish litigants remains an issue of debate, despite a general agreement regarding ecclesiastical devotion to *lex scripta*.[87] Certainly, in the case of conciliar canons, their authors often experienced great difficulty imposing their vision of normative reality on the greater population. It is also true that disputing parties, when advantageous, sought out extrajudicial means of settlement.[88] Even within the context of a court (royal or comital) or a council, extrajudicial maneuvering could irrevocably affect the outcome of a hearing, as was certainly the case in the trials of Gregory of Tours, Praetextatus of Rouen, Desiderius of Vienne, and Leudegar of Autun. Although such maneuvering was always a danger, particularly for high-profile cases, it was tempered by the heavy emphasis placed on tradition and consensus in Frankish judicial culture.[89] Both of these played no small part in instilling conciliar legislation with their legal *auctoritas*.

Legal pluralism persisted under the Carolingians, despite their often-assumed proclivity for uniformity.[90] In the Merovingian era, ecclesiastical

---

et Disciplina': Roman Public Law and the Merovingian State," in *Proceedings of the Tenth International Congress of Medieval Canon Law*, ed. Kenneth Pennington, Stanley Chodorow, and Keith H. Kendall (Vatican City: Biblioteca Apostolica Vaticana, 2001), 269–85.

86 Ian Wood, "Disputes in Late Fifth- and Sixth-Century Gaul: Some Problems," in *The Settlement of Disputes in Early Medieval Europe*, ed. Wendy Davis and Paul Fouracre (Cambridge: Cambridge University Press, 1986), 21. Lupoi, *The Origins of the European Legal Order*, 368–436, on a much grander scale, proposes the existence of an early medieval "common law."

87 The skeptical position is brilliantly articulated by Patrick Wormald, "*Lex Scripta* and *Verbum Regis*: Legislation and Germanic Kingship from Euric to Cnut," in *Early Medieval Kingship*, ed. Peter Sawyer and Ian Wood (Leeds: University of Leeds, 1977), 105–38; Wormald, *The Making of English Law*, 70–92. In contrast, see McKitterick, *The Carolingians and the Written Word*, 23–75. See also the important discussions of Ian Wood, "Administration, Law, and Culture in Merovingian Gaul," in *The Uses of Literacy in Early Medieval Europe*, ed. Rosamond McKitterick (Cambridge: Cambridge University Press, 1990), 63–81; Janet Nelson, "Literacy in Carolingian Government," in *The Uses of Literacy in Early Mediaeval Europe*, ed. Rosamond McKitterick (Cambridge: Cambridge University Press, 1990), 258–96.

88 Patrick Geary, "Extra-Judicial Means of Conflict Resolution," *Settimane di studio del Centro Italiano di studi sull'alto Medioevo* 42, no. 1 (1995): 569–605. See also the individual contributions to Wendy Davis and Paul Fouracre, eds., *The Settlement of Disputes in Early Medieval Europe* (Cambridge: Cambridge University Press, 1986).

89 Fouracre, "'Placita' and the Settlement of Disputes in Later Merovingian Francia," 42–3.

90 See, e.g., the observation of Patrick Wormald, "The *Leges Barborum*: Law and Ethnicity in the Post-Roman West," in *Regna and Gentes*, ed. Hans-Werner Goetz, Jörg Jarnut, and Walter Pohl (Leiden: Brill, 2003), 46.

and secular law intermingled frequently, with conciliar canons drawing upon the precedents of royal edicts (and vice versa).[91] This continued to be the case with the Pippinid councils of the middle eighth century, but with some important differences. The Councils of Germania (742) and Les Estinnes (743) were, with regard to the issues addressed in their legislative programs, not radically divergent from their Merovingian predecessors.[92] Similarly, the subsequent Councils of Soissons (744) and Ver (755) largely concerned themselves with traditional matters of ecclesiastical interest. There were two major innovations, however, that did distinguish these four councils from their Merovingian antecedents: first, their decisions were promulgated in royal capitularies;[93] and second, these capitularies lacked the subscriptions of the conciliar participants. The royal adoption of conciliar canons was, as we have seen, nothing new. Chlothar II's *Edictum* of 614 drew directly upon fourteen of the canons issued a week earlier by a council of bishops that the king had convoked in Paris. Nevertheless, Chlothar did not adopt all of the Council of Paris' decrees *en masse*, and, moreover, did not hesitate to revise those that he did accept. When Carloman issued his capitulary of 742, he included, as far as we can tell, the entire legislative agenda of the Council of Germania, which, in any case, was articulated in the voice of the mayor.[94] There was no need for revisions, because it was Carloman's version of the canons that was officially promulgated throughout the kingdom. Moreover, there was no doubt as to the legal status of the council's decisions, because the method of dissemination allowed no distinction to be drawn between secular and ecclesiastical law.[95] Conciliar legislation became even more focused on the secular after

---

[91] E.g. Paris (556/73), c. 1; Tours (567), c. 21; Mâcon (581/3), c. 14.

[92] Hartmann, *Die Synoden der Karolingerzeit*, 52–3; Reuter, "Kirchenreform und Kirchenpolitik im Zeitalter Karl Martells," 37; Le Roy, "Les conciles gaulois et le Décret de Gratien," 569.

[93] Hartmann, "Zu einigen Problemen der karolingischen Konzilsgeschichte," 18–9. François Ganshof, *Recherches sur les capitulaires* (Paris: Sirey, 1958), 3, defines *capitularies* broadly as "acts of power whose texts were generally divided into articles, and which several Carolingian sovereigns used to publish measures of a legislative or administrative nature."

[94] See, for example, c. 1, in which Carloman states that he has "appointed bishops… with the advice of my bishops and magnates."

[95] François Louis Ganshof, "The Church and the Royal Power in the Frankish Monarchy under Pippin III and Charlemagne," in *The Carolingians and the Frankish Monarchy: Studies in Carolingian History*, trans. Janet Sondheimer (Ithaca, NY: Cornell University Press, 1971), 214; Imbert, "Le pouvoir législatif dans l'Église carolingienne," 593–4; Imbert, *Les temps carolingiens: L'Église: Les institutions*, 127–30; Hartmann,

Pippin III's usurpation of the Frankish throne. His councils at Verberie (756) and Compiègne (757), to a far greater extent than any preceding Frankish councils, devoted their attention to issues of socio-religious, as opposed to purely ecclesiastical, interest, such as marriage, incest, and the status of slaves.[96] Ironically, Pippin's Capitulary of 754/5, the possible synodal origins of which are debatable, shows just as much interest in church matters as the ecclesiastical capitularies.[97] It was, of course, during these same decades that councils frequently were held in conjunction with royal assemblies, and their legislative programs conformed to the broader agenda of the monarchy.[98]

By the reign of Charlemagne, the Carolingian monarchy had effectively co-opted much of the responsibility of legislating for the church, with royal capitularies addressing ecclesiastical and secular affairs alike.[99] Charlemagne's Merovingian predecessors had addressed ecclesiastical business in their edicts, privileges, and judicial decisions, but they had never taken the step of removing nearly entirely the distinction between the secular and the spiritual components of their pluralistic legal system. Under the early Carolingians, conciliar canons did not need to be adopted by kings in order to achieve the status of law; they already possessed it at the time of their initial publication as capitulary articles.[100] Therefore, we should not be surprised to see the

"La transmission et l'influence du droit synodal carolingien," 486; Brundage, *Medieval Canon Law*, 28; Roger Collins, *Charlemagne* (Toronto: University of Toronto Press, 1998), 104.

[96] I follow Hartmann, *Die Synoden der Karolingerzeit*, 73–4, who rejects De Clercq's theory that the Verberie capitulary was merely a draft for that of Compiègne (De Clercq, *La législation religieuse franque*, 142).

[97] Pippin III *Pippini Regis Capitulare*, in *Capitularia Regum Francorum* 31–2; Hartmann, *Die Synoden der Karolingerzeit*, 68.

[98] Ganshof, "The Church and the Royal Power in the Frankish Monarchy Under Pippin III and Charlemagne," 208.

[99] Imbert, *Les temps carolingiens: L'Église: Les institutions*, 130.

[100] I avoid here the issue of whether the legality of capitulary articles stems from their oral or their written origins; a discussion would require a lengthy digression. The debate about the legal status of capitularies (as opposed to the pronouncements they contain) is summarized by Rhijn, *Shepherds of the Lord*, 16–21. See Wormald, *The Making of English Law*, 49–53, on the technical distinction between *leges* and *capitula*. But see also Wood, *The Merovingian Kingdoms*, 108–14, who argues with regard to the *Lex Salica* that royal law was subsumed into the code over time, making distinctions difficult. McKitterick, *The Carolingians and the Written Word*, 34, has also noted that capitularies and national *leges* can often be found together in single legal collections.

indiscriminate intermingling of canons and capitulary articles in contemporary canonical collections.[101]

The lack of episcopal subscriptions on capitulary documents is another significant indicator of the changing perceptions of conciliar *auctoritas*. During the Merovingian period, these subscriptions had been proof of the group consensus that gave conciliar decisions their legislative authority. They were not a Frankish innovation; subscriptions had been a standard feature of canonical *acta* issued by Greek, African, Iberian, and Gallo-Roman councils alike.[102] It was, therefore, a critical change in procedure in the 740s when the Pippinid mayors chose not to include episcopal subscriptions in their conciliar capitularies.[103] This shift does not appear to be due merely to a change in the type of document, from canonical acts produced by churchmen to royal capitularies, particularly because subscriptions reappeared in the latter half of the ninth century.[104] Had episcopal consensus abruptly lost its authoritative value? The frequent references to *consensus* or *consilium* found in the mid-eighth-century capitularies suggest that the answer is no. Carloman, for example, prefaces his German Capitulary of 742 with this statement:

> In the name of our Lord Jesus Christ, I Carloman, *dux* and *princeps* of the Franks…with the *consilium* of the servants of God and of my *optimates*, have congregated, for fear of Christ, the bishops of my Kingdom, namely Archbishop Boniface, Burchard, Reginfred, Witta, Willibald, Dadanus, and Heddo along with their presbyters, in a *concilium* and *synodum*, so that they might give me their *consilium*, in order that the *lex* of God and ecclesiastical worship might be restored.[105]

Carloman similarly enacted decrees "cum consilio servorum Dei et populi christiani" in the Council of Les Estinnes a year later.[106] In the Capitulary of Soissons of 744, Carloman's brother, Pippin, makes a

[101] Brundage, *Medieval Canon Law*, 28.

[102] Hubert Mordek, "Karolingische Kapitularien," in *Überlieferung und Geltung normativer Texte des frühen und hohen Mittelalters*, ed. Hubert Mordek (Sigmaringen: Jan Thorbecke Verlag, 1986), 30–1. Mordek notes that the Visigothic conciliar *ordines* also required the signing of conciliar decisions by the attendees.

[103] Excluding Roman synods, the one council from this period whose protocol contains a subscription list is Attigny (762). Signatures were also attached to the privilege to Gorze issued by the Council of Compiègne (757).

[104] Mordek, "Karolingische Kapitularien," 30–1.

[105] Council of Germania (742), Preface.

[106] Council of Les Estinnes (743), c. 2.

distinction between the *consensus episcoporum* and the *consilium* of his *comites* and *optimates*, which suggests disparate value judgments of the two terms.[107] Additionally, canon 5 of the Council of Ver (755) orders a synodal act to be constituted through "the words and will of the lord king with the *consensus* of the servants of God."[108]

Although the eighth-century capitularies clearly recognize the authority of consensus, the word *consensus* is being employed in a very different way than it was in the Merovingian period. In each of these passages, the mayor or king is the primary legislator, although he is making his decisions with "the advice and agreement" (*consilium et consensus*) of the assembled body. The language reflects the legislation's origins in the royal council and assembly.[109] Therefore, the purpose of consensus here is not to invest the conciliar canons with religious authority, but rather to confirm that the *princeps* issued his decisions in accordance with the approval of his ecclesiastical and lay advisers alike.[110] Earlier, in the sixth and seventh centuries, *consensus* had been an indicator of universal agreement among the conciliar participants themselves; it had no direct association with royal authority. Now, it was irrevocably attached to the will of a secular legislator. It was this legislator who gave the canons their worldly *auctoritas*, and as long as he consulted his advisers before issuing his decrees, there simply was no need for episcopal signatures to be collected.[111]

Why did the Frankish bishops go along with a policy that was potentially damaging to ecclesiastical power and authority? A simple answer might be that they had no choice in the matter; pressure from the Pippinids forced their capitulation. However, it was not in either Pippin's or Carloman's style to run roughshod over the rights of the ecclesiastical aristocracy, and, in fact, one of their primary reforming goals was the strengthening of the Frankish church's episcopal hierarchy.[112] How,

---

[107] Council of Soissons (744), Preface, cc. 2 and 10. Hannig, *Consensus Fidelium*, 177.

[108] Ver (755), c. 5.

[109] On the relationship between capitularies and royal councils and assemblies, see Ganshof, *Recherches sur les capitulaires*, 22–9; Janet Nelson, "Legislation and Consensus Under Charles the Bald," in *Politics and Ritual in Early Medieval Europe* (London: Hambledon Press, 1986), 100.

[110] Hannig, *Consensus Fidelium*, 170–8.

[111] I do not accept McKitterick's argument that conciliar records lacking subscriptions do not possess "legal rigor." McKitterick, *The Frankish Church and the Carolingian Reforms*, 24.

[112] Claussen, *The Reform of the Frankish Church*, 49–50; Ganshof, "The Church and the Royal Power in the Frankish Monarchy Under Pippin III and Charlemagne," 210.

then, did the mayors enact this change in conciliar procedure? There is a strong possibility that the task had already been accomplished by the time the two brothers came of age. Around 600, an influential systematic canonical collection known today as the *Vetus Gallica* was compiled in the diocese of Lyons, perhaps on the order of the reigning bishop, Etherius (r. 586–602).[113] The *Vetus Gallica* and its successors are called systematic collections because they organize their canons topically, in the manner of a Roman law book, such as the *Codex Theodosianus*, instead of council by council, in chronological order. One notable thing about collections of this sort is the absence of subscription lists, which traditionally follow the canonical records of chronological collections. Over the course of the seventh century and early eighth century, copies, recensions, and imitations of the *Vetus Gallica* found their way into the hands of ecclesiastical reformers, who saw canon law as the solution to the Frankish church's woes.[114] By the time of the Pippinid councils of the 740s, the influence of the systematic collections had been felt deeply throughout the ecclesiastical community, which did not question the authority of the canons contained within the collections simply because of the absence of subscription lists.[115]

It is, therefore, possible that even before the Pippinid mayors chose a new manner of canonical dissemination, the Frankish episcopate had already begun to alter its thinking on canonical authority. Initially, it was perhaps the episcopate's familiarity with the contents of the systematic collections that made it willing to accept this new arrangement. Even so, it seems that a change in thinking did occur concerning the *auctoritas* of canons. The content of the decisions themselves, far more than the names of those who made them, was the necessary proof of orthodoxy. This shift, moreover, made it easier for the Frankish conciliar decisions to be subsumed into the greater body of canon law. Copied and recopied into a variety of local anthologies, they became

[113] Hubert Mordek, "Die Collectio Vetus Gallica, die älteste systematische Kanonensammlung des fränkischen Gallien," *Francia* 1 (1973): 45–61.

[114] Mordek, "Kanonistische Activität in Gallien in der Ersten Hälfte des 8. Jahrhunderts," 23.

[115] The uncertainty of authorship was one of the reasons given by Carolingian councils for their condemnation of penitential texts, on which, see Adriaan Gaastra, "Penitentials and Canonical Authority," in *Texts and Identities in the Early Middle Ages*, ed. Richard Corradini, Rob Meens, Christina Pössel, and Philip Shaw (Vienna: Verlag der Österreichischen Akademie der Wissenschaften, 2006), 195–6.

part of a vast nexus of ecclesiastical rules whose universality was assumed, if not necessarily enforced. Thus, although subscriptions continued to be obligatory for Frankish wills, charters, and other secular legal documents, a consensus seems to have emerged that they were not required for canonical pronouncements. This, in turn, allowed the Pippinids to begin to shift conciliar authority toward their own persons, which diminished even further any distinction between ecclesiastical and secular law.

This process that we have been examining, whereby the absolute legal status of conciliar canons were confirmed, had unforeseen consequences for those prelates and princes alike who struggled to enhance the royal role in the enforcement of ecclesiastical legislation. Although kings as far back as Clovis, who himself was following the model of the Christian Roman emperors, had believed it to be within their right to legislate on ecclesiastical matters, the Pippinids' success in redefining the source of conciliar authority temporarily weakened the very institution that they sought to control. Charlemagne, whose authority over the Frankish church was anticipated by, but surpassed that of, his father and uncle, saw councils as only one small part of his governance over spiritual matters.[116] His publication of the *Admonitio Generalis* in 789 demonstrated that he did not require councils in order to legislate for the church. And, from the time of his imperial coronation in December 800 until his reform councils of 813, Charlemagne oversaw only a handful of synods.[117] He did most of his important ecclesiastical legislating during this period through capitularies, and in the context of royal assemblies, which subsumed traditional synodal functions.[118]

It would be wrong, however, to credit Charlemagne's negligence of conciliar life to any sort of personal push for caesaropapal autocracy; the lessons and reforms of the past deeply informed his personal control over the church. The Frankish church was his church, and it was his duty to manage it both meticulously and justly.[119] It was also his

---

[116] Voigt, *Staat und Kirche*, 316.

[117] I.e., Aachen (801), Aachen (802), and Aachen (809). A handful of Bavarian synods were also held in these years.

[118] Imbert, *Les temps carolingiens: L'Église: Les institutions*, 130; Basdevant-Gaudemet, "Les évêques, les papes, et les princes," 8–9. During the reign of Louis the Pious, too, as Joel Rosenthal, "The Public Assembly in the Time of Louis the Pious," *Traditio* 20 (1964): 37, observes, assemblies produced legislation of both a secular and an ecclesiastical nature.

[119] Ganshof, "The Church and the Royal Power in the Frankish Monarchy Under Pippin III and Charlemagne," 205.

responsibility to ensure that its canonical regulations were enforced. To this end, Charlemagne largely subsumed them into his own legislative program, thus making certain that they would receive proportionate attention. There has long been disagreement among scholars as to how successful Charlemagne was in imposing his legislative agenda on the empire, a controversy that is likely to endure.[120] However, as already suggested, the question of successful enforcement is less important than that of intent. With regard to the latter, Charlemagne can scarcely be faulted, as François Ganshof once observed:

> Charlemagne very simply put his religious faith and his respect for the law above all other considerations; he fully realized his responsibilities as the head of an important state and later as emperor in the West; he did his best to make the realm's institutions achieve their maximum efficiency while still safeguarding the rights and property of his subjects.[121]

Even Ganshof acknowledges the probability that the decrees contained in Charlemagne's capitularies were not always universally enforced, but this makes him no different from any other legislator—ancient, medieval, or modern.[122] Where Charlemagne was unique was in the lengths that he was willing to go to assume responsibility for ecclesiastical affairs. His reign was the culmination of a lengthy process that may have begun with Clovis, but had its roots even deeper, in the Roman imperial period. For the churchmen of this Frankish era, who strove to perfect the *vita ecclesiastica* through the convocation of councils, the consistent presence of royal interest in their business was a mixed blessing. On the one hand, they gained an ally whose *auctoritas* and *potestas* as *rex* and *princeps* could help to ensure the enforcement of their decisions upon all of Frankish society. On the other hand, they sacrificed some of their legislative autonomy by initially inviting the king to contribute to their agenda, and by eventually surrendering to him the right to articulate and disseminate their decisions.

---

[120] A succinct statement of the problem can be found in Matthew Innes, "Charlemagne's Government," in *Charlemagne: Empire and Society*, ed. Joanna Story (Manchester: Manchester University Press, 2005), 76–9.

[121] François Ganshof, "The Impact of Charlemagne on the Institutions of the Frankish Realm," *Speculum* 40, no. 1 (1965): 62. C.f. Heinrich Fichtenau, *The Carolingian Empire*, trans. Peter Munz (Oxford: Blackwell, 1957), 130, who argues that Charlemagne ignored canonical precedent when it suited his interests.

[122] Ganshof, "The Impact of Charlemagne on the Institutions of the Frankish Realm," 51–2. Ganshof qualifies here his earlier characterization of the "failure of Charlemagne." C.f. Brown, *The Rise of Western Christendom*, 442.

But even during the reign of Charlemagne, the Frankish episcopate remained a force with which to be reckoned, and the bishops' personal authority and dignity were not in question. In fact, beginning with Charlemagne's reform councils of 813, the burden of responsibility for the holding of synods began to shift back to the episcopate.[123] By the end of the ninth century, Hincmar of Rheims could claim that although Carolingian royal justice took into account both secular and ecclesiastical law, it recognized the superiority of the latter.[124]

A final point is that whether or not one wishes to apply the terminology of "Landeskirche" or "Reichskirche" to the Frankish church—terms that are anachronistic in their implications, if not entirely devoid of truth, particularly for the reign of Charlemagne—modern U.S. notions about the separation of church and state certainly never applied to the Frankish kingdoms.[125] That said, the nature of the relationship between church and state was in constant flux, from Clovis to Charlemagne and beyond. Although there were no illusions in 511 that the Gallic church would be allowed complete independence to govern itself and to dictate the religious standards for the realm without royal oversight, the variety of ways in which the kings would interfere in conciliar business was as yet undefined. Some rulers, such as Guntram, would make it a point to regularly attend councils; others, such as Dagobert I and Charlemagne, preferred to oversee church business outside the context of synods.[126] In general, however, there was a growing realization that the interests of the church and the royal government were irrevocably intertwined, and that benefits were to be had for both in formalizing this relationship. Still, there were risks involved. One cannot help but wonder if the Frankish bishops of the later eighth century questioned whether it was their own decisions whose enforcement the kings were so generously assisting.

---

[123] McKitterick, *The Frankish Church and the Carolingian Reforms*, 12. C.f. Louis Halphen, *Charlemagne et l'empire carolingien* (Paris: Éditions Albin Michel, 1947), 217–8. See also Imbert, *Les temps carolingiens: L'Église: Les institutions*, I.132.

[124] Hincmar of Rheims, *De Ordine Palatii*, ed. Thomas Gross and Rudolf Schieffer (Hanover: Hahn, 1980), ch. 21.

[125] Karl Morrison, *The Two Kingdoms: Ecclesiology in Carolingian Political Thought* (Princeton: Princeton University Press, 1964), 26–36, has described Charlemagne's authority over the church as an incomplete "monism," in which the king "intervened in ecclesiastical affairs not on any principle of dominion over the Church…but rather on the premise that God had granted imperial power to him…most of all for the defense of the Church" (31).

[126] On the lack of evidence for church councils in Dagobert's kingdom, see Wallace-Hadrill, *The Frankish Church*, 106.

CHAPTER 5

FROM COUNCILS TO CANON LAW

During the course of their deliberations, the Frankish bishops assembled at Clichy in late September 626 or 627 found it useful to compile into "a single corpus" a number of the canons in the *diversi libri* that they had brought with them.[1] One of these *diversi libri* was none other than the *Vetus Gallica*.[2] The bishops at Clichy recognized the utility of canonical collections as reference tools. In the conciliar context especially, the ability to consult old legislation was necessary for crafting new decrees in accordance with canonical tradition. The relationship between church councils and canonical collections might seem self-evident because of the Frankish synods' habit of citing canonical precedent, as well as the inclusion of these same synods' rulings in subsequent anthologies. Nevertheless, a dichotomy has emerged in modern scholarship between studies of councils and those of canonical collections. Rarely is this divide breached. And when it is, it is mostly in superficial discussions of the source materials for individual collections. Hubert Mordek's work, therefore, is especially important in that it draws attention to the intrinsic relationship between Frankish councils and the compilations that contained their decisions.[3] His observations on the use of specific collections by councils reflect a larger trend: Frankish conciliar attendees not only consulted canonical collections as part of their protocol, they also had every reason to assume that their own decisions would eventually appear in similar compilations. They were conscious, in other words, that they were contributing to the

[1] Clichy (626/7), Preface.

[2] Mordek, *Kirchenrecht und Reform im Frankenreich*, 66–70.

[3] Along with his observations on the Council of Clichy, Mordek has demonstrated the use of the *Collectio Bernensis* by the Council of Mâlay-le-Roi (677) and Saint Boniface's consultation of the canonical *sententiae* copied in MS Würzburg, Universitätsbibliothek, M. p. th. q.31, foll. 52r–59r (late eighth century and ninth century) as *memoranda* at his eighth-century reform councils. See, respectively, Mordek, "Bischofsabsetzung in spätmerowingischer Zeit: Justelliana, Bernensis, und das Konzil von Mâlay (677)," 31–53, and Mordek, *Bibliotheca Capitularium Regum Francorum Manuscripta*, 960–4. For the Gallic conciliar sources of the *Vetus Gallica*, see Mordek, *Kirchenrecht und Reform im Frankenreich*, 43–51.

ever-growing, albeit amorphous, body of Western canon law. But the canon law of the Early Middle Ages was not the canon law of Gratian and his successors. Although some Frankish canons eventually would be absorbed into the medieval *Corpus Iuris Canonici*, their survival necessitated tearing them away from the original contexts of their enactment, even in cases where their language remained intact.

The Production of Canonical Collections

Like the convocation of councils, the compilation of canonical decisions long predated the establishment of the *regnum Francorum*. In Gaul, production of these anthologies was focused originally in the more heavily romanized south, where influential collections, such as the *Collectio Concilii Secundi Arelatensis* (ca. 442/506) and the *Statuta Ecclesiae Antiqua* (late fifth century), were originally compiled. The former compilation has long been the subject of much controversy, with scholars debating whether its canons reflect an actual council. Those who deny the collection's conciliar status point to the fact that most of its fifty-six canons are taken from the legislation of earlier synods, including the Councils of Arles (314), Nicaea (325), Orange (441), and Vaison (442).[4] In contrast, it also has been argued that an actual council met at Arles around the year 501, which drew heavily upon earlier conciliar canons, but altered and augmented its precedents to create something fundamentally new.[5] If so, it would have been engaging in a completely normal activity for Gallic councils of this time.

The *Statuta Ecclesiae Antiqua*, by contrast, although it has its points of dispute, has never engendered the same amount of controversy as the Second Council of Arles. The major questions surrounding this compilation of 102 canons and an episcopal profession of faith are about authorship and place of composition. The collection long circulated as the so-called Fourth Council of Carthage (398), and was labeled as such in both the *Hispana* (first recension, ca. 633) and the Pseudo-Isidorian corpus (middle ninth century). In the eighteenth century, the collection was proven to be Gallic in origin, and was

---

[4] Gaudemet, *Les sources du droit de l'Eglise en Occident*, 84; Kéry, ed., *Canonical Collections of the Early Middle Ages*, 6–7.

[5] Mathisen, "The Second Council of Arles," 511–54.

subsequently credited to the presbyter Gennadius of Marseilles (late fifth century).[6]

Despite the popularity of these two collections, neither was promulgated as an official compilation of canon law.[7] The Franks' subsequent monopolization of political power in Gaul, which culminated in the ceding of Alamannia and Provence to Merovingian rule in 536, did nothing to mitigate the localism that marked the Gallic production of canonical collections. The Merovingian kings and their bishops showed little interest in sponsoring the compilation of an official collection. Thus, the remainder of the sixth century saw the appearance of a plethora of regional compilations, including the *Collectio Corbeiensis*, the *Collectio Lugdunensis*, the *Collectio Coloniensis*, the *Collectio Sancti Mauri*, the *Collectio Albigensis*, the *Collectio Pithouensis*, the *Collectio Laureshamensis*, and the *Collectio Remensis*.[8] Although southern Gaul still dominated the production of collections in the early Merovingian period, the Rhône Valley and central Gaul began to emerge for the first time as centers of canon collecting.[9]

Over the next two centuries, the momentum continued to shift as the northern regions of Gaul witnessed the production of additional compilations, including the *Collectio Bernensis* (ca. 727), the *Collectio Burgundiana* (early eighth century), and the *Collectio 250 Capitulorum* (late eighth century).[10] Most of the new collections produced in the

[6] Gaudemet, *Les sources du droit de l'Eglise en Occident*, 84–6; Kéry, ed., *Canonical Collections of the Early Middle Ages*, 7.

[7] C.f. Ralph Mathisen, "Between Arles, Rome, and Toledo: Gallic Collections of Canon Law in Late Antiquity," *'Ilu: Revista de Ciencias de las Religiones* 2 (1999): 34–5, who argues that the *Collectio Concilii Secundi Arelatensis* was a failed attempt "to create a standard text of canon law" by the Gallic bishops of the Visigothic kingdom. Constant Van De Wiel, *History of Canon Law* (Louvain: Peeters Press, 1991), 49–50, who accepts that there was no officially promulgated collection, nevertheless points to the popularity of the *Statuta Ecclesiae Antiqua*.

[8] For the dating and geographic origins of these collections, see Kéry, ed., *Canonical Collections of the Early Middle Ages*, 43–50. Note that the name of an individual collection does not necessarily reflect its place of composition.

[9] The Rhône Valley was the probable place of origin of the *Collectio Lugdunensis* and the *Vetus Gallica*, although the *Collectio Pithouensis* was probably compiled at Sens or Auxerre. For the debates on places of production, see Kéry, ed., *Canonical Collections of the Early Middle Ages*, 43–4, 48–53. On the northward shift of canonical collection production, see Fournier and Le Bras, *Histoire des collections canoniques en Occident*, I.44; Mordek, *Kirchenrecht und Reform im Frankenreich*, 16, 74–5; Gaudemet, *Les sources du droit de l'Eglise en Occident*, 146–7.

[10] Kéry, ed., *Canonical Collections of the Early Middle Ages*, 53, 83–4, 86. Corbie has been suggested as the place of composition for the *Collectio Bernensis*.

late-Merovingian and early-Carolingian periods relied heavily on earlier anthologies for their contents. The Irish *Collectio Hibernensis* (early eighth century?), for example, influenced both the *Collectio 250 Capitulorum* and the *Collectio Sangermanensis* (both eighth century), while the *Vetus Gallica* was an important source for the *Collectio Bernensis*, the *Collectio Herovalliana* (late eighth century), and the *Collectio Frisigensis Secunda* (late eighth century).[11] The plethora of canonical collections produced in this era is all the more impressive because it took place amid the political turmoil of the late seventh century and the eighth century.[12] Still, no one collection was singled out by the monarchy or the episcopate in this period as official.

Traditionally, Charlemagne's promulgation of the *Dionysio-Hadriana* in 774, an expansion of Dionysius Exiguus' *Collectio Dionysiana* (ca. 500), has been seen as the important move toward canonical standardization in Francia.[13] However, without discounting the *Dionysio-Hadriana*'s influence, this compilation did not render others superfluous, and local collections continued to be read and copied at an impressive rate under the later Carolingians.[14] And homegrown collections were not the only ones to circulate in the Frankish kingdoms in the Merovingian and Carolingian eras. The *Collectio Hibernensis* and the Spanish *Hispana*, for example, both became quite well known outside their places of origin.[15] The latter not only circulated in a uniquely

[11] Northern Gaul and the Lake Constance region have been proposed as places of origin for the *Collectio 250 Capitulorum* and the *Collectio Frisingensis Secunda*, respectively. See Kéry, ed., *Canonical Collections of the Early Middle Ages*, 57, 83–4.

[12] Mordek, "Kanonistische Activität in Gallien in der Ersten Hälfte des 8. Jahrunderts," 19–25. On northern Gaul as the center of canonical collection production in the eighth century, see McKitterick, "Knowledge of Canon Law in the Frankish Kingdoms Before 789," 107.

[13] See, e.g., Wallace-Hadrill, *The Frankish Church*, 294.

[14] Roger E. Reynolds, "Unity and Diversity in Carolingian Canon Law Collections: The Case of the *Collectio Hibernensis* and Its Derivatives," in *Carolingian Essays: Andrew W. Mellon Lectures in Early Christian Studies*, ed. Uta-Renate Blumenthal (Washington, DC: The Catholic University of America Press, 1983), 103; Rosamond McKitterick, *History and Memory in the Carolingian World* (Cambridge: Cambridge University Press, 2004), 250; McKitterick, "Knowledge of Canon Law in the Frankish Kingdoms Before 789," 98.

[15] Roman canonical material, too, made its way to Gaul, on which, see Davis Ganz, "Roman Manuscripts in Francia and Anglo-Saxon England," *Settimane di Studio del Centro Italiano di Studi Sull'Alto Medioevo* 49, no. 1 (2002): 625–9. English attendance at the Council of Paris (614) may also indicate an exchange of legal ideas between the Franks and the Anglo-Saxons, on which, see Wormald, *The Making of English Law*, 100–1.

Frankish edition (the so-called *Collectio Hispana Gallica*, compiled ca. late seventh century), but also, along with the *Dionysio-Hadriana*, was an important source for the influential *Collectio Dacheriana*, compiled around 800.[16] Fournier and Le Bras go so far as to declare that "the history of [canonical] collections in the first half of the ninth century is, to a large degree, the history of the union between the *Hispana* and the *Hadriana*."[17] However, this international dialogue did not go only one way, and the Irish and Iberians adopted canonical materials from the Franks.[18] Amid this flurry of compiling, copying, and diffusion, synods continued to be held throughout the Frankish kingdoms. By what processes, then, did the decisions of these councils find their way into canonical collections?

From Council to Collectio

I have noted how, at the termination of conciliar proceedings, copies of a council's decisions were made for each of the attendees. It was expected that, upon returning home, the participating bishops would inform their parishioners of the council's business. This may have involved the production of additional copies of the canonical *acta* for local parishes. Once the council's decisions had been relayed, the original transcriptions of the canons were stored in cathedral archives or libraries. Presumably, these depositories already contained an array of

---

[16] The *Dacheriana*, fifty-two manuscript copies of which survive, was originally compiled in southern Gaul, possibly Lyons. For its complicated history and bibliography, see Abigail Firey, "Ghostly Recensions in Early Medieval Canon Law: The Problem of the *Collectio Dacheriana* and Its Shades," *The Legal History Review* 68, nos. 1–2 (2000): 63–82; Kéry, ed., *Canonical Collections of the Early Middle Ages*, 87–92. On the influence of the *Collectio Hibernensis*, see Reynolds, "Unity and Diversity in Carolingian Canon Law Collections," 99–135; Michael Edward Moore, "La monarchie carolingienne et les anciens modèles irlandais," *Annales* 51, no. 2 (1996): 307; Rob Meens, "The Oldest Manuscript Witness of the Collectio Canonum Hibernensis," *Peritia* 14 (2000): 1–19. On the *Collectio Hispana Gallica* and the influence of the *Collectio Hispana*, see Kéry, ed., *Canonical Collections of the Early Middle Ages*, 67–8; Fournier and Le Bras, *Histoire des collections canoniques en Occident*, I.103–7; Mathisen, "Between Arles, Rome, and Toledo," 42–43; Luis García Moreno, "Les relations entre l'Église des Gaules et l'Église d'Espagne du Ve au VIIe siècle: Entre suspicion et méfiance," *Revue d'histoire de l'Église de France* 90, no. 224 (2004): 52.

[17] Fournier and Le Bras, *Histoire des collections canoniques en Occident*, I.103.

[18] Mathisen, "Between Arles, Rome, and Toledo," 33–46; Luned Mair Davies, "Statuta Ecclesiae Antiqua and the Gallic Councils in the Hibernensis," *Peritia* 14 (2000): 85–110; Moreno, "Les relations entre l'Église des Gaules et l'Église d'Espagne du Ve au VIIe siècle," 39.

canonical materials in the form of both conciliar transcripts and compilations. The quantity of material would have varied, depending on the size, wealth, and prestige of the diocese, and it is unlikely that the smaller suffragan bishoprics possessed more than a single canonical collection. However, a metropolitan see, particularly one with a lengthy history of participation in Gallic conciliar life, such as Arles or Lyons, would have had considerably more material at its disposal. Such a *civitas* also was more likely to become a center of production of new canonical collections.

The essential role played by a compiler's own church archive or library was not adequately appreciated before the work of Fournier and Le Bras. These coauthors argued that earlier scholars, such as Friedrich Maassen and Louis Duchesne, overestimated the role of manuscript exchange and the influence of the diocese of Arles, in particular, in the production of new collections.[19] Mordek's work on the *Vetus Gallica* has validated Fournier and Le Bras' position, for he was able to demonstrate that the Lyonnaise compiler of this systematic anthology drew upon original transcriptions of the Council of Mâcon (581/3), housed in the episcopal archives of Lyons, and not upon those canonical collections that also included canons from that council, i.e., the *Collectio Lugdunensis*, the *Collectio Sancti Amandi*, the *Collectio Burgundiana* and the *Collectio Bellovacensis*.[20]

Mordek's observation makes the Council of Mâcon (581/3) a good case study for an examination of the processes by which conciliar canons made their way into a variety of collections of often considerably distant places of origin. It is clear that the episcopal attendees of this council had access to the written records of earlier councils. Canons 1 and 11, for example, quote directly from the Council of Clermont (535), cc. 16 and 13.[21] Similarly, canon 2 repeats the language of the

---

[19] Fournier and Le Bras, *Histoire des collections canoniques en Occident*, I.46–8.

[20] Mordek, *Kirchenrecht und Reform im Frankenreich*, 71–3.

[21] Mâcon (581/3), c. 1: "Ideoque definitum est, ut episcopi, presbyteri atque diaconi ita sanctae conscientiae luce resplendeant, ut effugiant in probitate actuum maledicorum obloquia et testimonium in se divinum implere contendant, quod Dominus ait: Sic luceat lumen vestrum coram hominibus, ut videant vestra bona opera et magnificent Patrem vestrem, qui est in coelis. Igitur auctoritate canonica atque mansura in aevum constitutione sancimus, ut fugiatur ab his extranearum mulierum culpanda libertas et tantum cum avia, matre, sorore, vel nepte, si necessitas tulerit, habitent." Clermont (535), c. 16: "Episcopus, presbyter atque diaconus ita sancte conscientiae luce resplendeant, ut effugiant probitate actuum maledicorum obloquia et testimonium in se divinum inplere contendant, quod Dominus ait: Sic luceat lumen vestrum

Council of Epaone (517), c. 38.[22] There were a number of canonical collection manuscripts available to the conciliar fathers at Mâcon that contained the relevant canons, i.e., the *Collectio Corbeinsis*, the *Collectio Lugdunensis*, the *Collectio Sancti Mauri*, the *Collectio Pithouensis*, and the *Collectio Laureshamensis*. The last of these is a particularly plausible option, because it also contains the canons of the Council of Orléans (541), of which the attendees at Mâcon seem also to have been aware.[23] Although we cannot say with absolute certainty whether the bishops were drawing upon a compilation or original canonical transcripts, the former option seems more likely, especially in light of the fact that

coram hominibus, ut videntes vestram bonam operam glorificent Patrem vestrum, qui est in caelis. Igitur auctoritate canonica adque mansura in aevum constitutione sancimus, ut fugiatur his extranearum mulierum culpanda libertas et tantum cum avia, matre, sorore, vel nepte, si necessitas tolerit, habitent." Mâcon (581/3), c. 11: "Episcopi, presbyteri vel universi honoratiores clerici cum sublime dignitatis apice sublimantur, actibus omnino renuntient saeculi et ad sacrum electi mysterium repudient carnale consortium ac permixtionis pristinae contubernium permutent germanitatis affectu; et, quisquis ille est, divino munere benedictione percepta uxori prius suae frater ilico efficiatur ex coniuge. Eos vero, quos repperimus ardore libidinis inflammatos abiecto religionis cingulo ad vomitum pristinum et inhibita rursus coniuga repetiisse atque incesti quodammodo crimine prodiderunt: quod quisquis fecisse cognoscitur, omni in perpetuo, quam admisso iam crimine perdidit, dignitate privabitur." Clermont (535), c. 13: "Cum presbyteri adque diaconi sublimi dignitatis apice prorogantur, actebus omnino renuntient saeculi et ad sacrum electi mysterium repudient carnale consortium ac permixtionis pristinae contubernium permutent germanitatis affectu; et, quisquis ille est, presbyter adque diaconi, divino munere benedictione percepta uxoris prius suae frater ilico efficiatur ex coniuge. Quosdam repperimus ardore lividinis inflammatus abiecto militiae cingulo vomitum pristinum et inhebeta rursus coniuga repetisse atque incesti quodammodo crimine clarum decus sacerdotii violasse, quod nati etiam filii proderunt. Quod quisque fecisse dignuscetur, omni in perpetuum, quam admisso iam crimine perdedit, dignitate privabitur."

[22] Mâcon (581/3), c. 2: "Ut nullus episcopus, presbyter, diaconus, clericus, vel quicumque secularis in monasteriis puellarum nisi probatae vitae et aetatis provectae praeter utelitatem aut quamcumque reparationem monasterii ad quascumque earum necessitates habitare aut secretas conlocutiones habere praesumant nec extra salutaturium aut oraturium ulterius ingredi permittatur. Praecipue iudaei non pro quorumcumque negotiorum occasiones puellis intra monasterium Deo dicitas aliquid secretius conloqui aut familiaritatem vel moras ibi habere praesumant." Epaone (517), c. 38: "In monasteria puellarum non nisi probatae vitae et aetatis provectae ad quascumque eorum necessetates vel ministrationis permittantur intrare."

[23] Mâcon (581/3), c. 17, echoes the Council of Orléans' threat to confiscate the Christian slaves of Jews whose masters attempted to convert them (c. 31). Textual parallels with the Council of Orléans (538) have also been noted: Mark Vessey, "The Origins of the *Collectio Sirmondiana*: A New Look at the Evidence," in *The Theodosian Code*, ed. Jill Harries and Ian Wood (Ithaca, NY: Cornell University Press, 1993), 196. Vessey suggests that it was the *Collectio Lugdunensis* that the bishops consulted. On the southern Gallic *Collectio Laureshamensis*, see Kéry, ed., *Canonical Collections of the Early Middle Ages*, 49–50.

the tenure of the Council of Mâcon's president, Bishop Priscus of Lyons, coincided with Lyons becoming a center of canonical collection production.[24]

Between 581 and 1140, Mâcon's canons were cited more than one hundred times in various collections. Some compilers included the council's entire record of twenty canons in their anthologies, while others were more selective, choosing only those decisions they considered the most important or relevant.[25] Among those collections that contain the council's complete acts, the *Collectio Lugdunensis* (sixth century), the *Collectio Sancti Amandi* (seventh/eighth century), and the *Collectio Bellovacensis* (late ninth century), it is clear that not all derived from a common source. The order of the subscription list contained in the *Collectio Lugdunensis*, for example, differs from that in the subscription lists found in the *Collectio Sancti Amandi* and the *Collectio Bellovacensis*. Indeed, the latter two collections share a number of textual similarities; it is clear that they have a common source.[26] As for the *Collectio Lugdunensis*, it went through a number of editions, and adopted the Mâcon canons only in its fifth edition, for which a Burgundian origin has been proposed (ca. 585).[27] Divergences in the order of subscriptions, as well as the absence of an *Explicit*-clause following the subscriptions, differentiate it from the other two collections.[28] Perhaps the subscription list of the Lyons collection is a condensed version of a more complete document, but this does not explain the divergences in the order of signatures from the *Collectio Sancti Amandi* and the *Collectio Bellovacensis*. It seems more likely that the two lists were based on two different original transcriptions of the council.[29] So we can infer with some confidence the existence of distinct manuscript traditions in the early stages of the canons' dissemination.

---

[24] Vessey, "The Origins of the *Collectio Sirmondiana*," 196–7.

[25] That churchmen considered some canons more important than others is confirmed in the *Gesta Episcoporum Autissiodorensium*, ch. 19, whose author singles out canons 8 and 10 of the Council of Mâcon (585) as the most essential.

[26] Friedrich Maassen, ed., *Concilia aevi Merovingici*, MGH Legum, Section III: Concilia, Tomus I (Hanover: Hahn, 1893), 155; Kéry, ed., *Canonical Collections of the Early Middle Ages*, 85.

[27] Vessey, "The Origins of the *Collectio Sirmondiana*," 192–3.

[28] Maassen, ed., *Concilia aevi Merovingici*, 155.

[29] Bretholz, "Die Unterschriften den gallischen Concilien des 6. und 7. Jahrhunderts," 533–5.

The vast majority of collections including canons from the Council of Mâcon do not contain the full acts of the council. This fact makes it easier to determine the relationships among different manuscripts, because content can indicate influence. The first collection to contain only selections from this synod was the *Vetus Gallica*, which included all but canons 1, 6, 8, 14, 17, and 20 (70 percent of the total). The influence of the *Vetus Gallica* on the canons from the Council of Mâcon ensured that those canons contained within it would be copied into such derivative collections as the *Collectio Herovalliana*, the *Collectio Frisingensis Secunda*, the *Collectio Bonaevallensis*, and the *Collectio in 22 Chapters* (ca. 860).[30] Nevertheless, canons not included in the Lyonnaise compilation continued to circulate as well, and were referenced in, among other sources, Florus of Lyons' *De Fugiendis Contagiis Iudeorum* (early to middle ninth century), which cited *en masse* Mâcon's plethora of canons formulating the Frankish church's Jewish policy.[31] Mâcon canon 8, which forbids clerics from bringing cases against their brethren before secular judges, also proved popular up through the eleventh and twelfth centuries.[32] Well into the Central

[30] Tables listing the inclusion of the Merovingian canons in conciliar collections can be found in Pontal, *Die Synoden im Merowingerreich*, 294–304, and Gaudemet and Basdevant-Gaudemet, eds., *Les canons des conciles mérovingiens*, 626–9. Similar data for the Pippinid era is provided by Hartmann, *Die Synoden der Karolingerzeit*, 482–92. These tables serve as the primary sources for the tallies that follow, unless stated otherwise. Omissions, such as both Merovingian tables' failure to cite the *Collectio Frisingensis Secunda*'s inclusion of canons from the Council of Mâcon (581/3), have been noted. I have also consulted Linda Fowler-Magerl's database of early medieval canonical collections: *Clavis Canonum: Selected Canon Law Collections Before 1140*. For a survey of those collections that derive their contents from the *Vetus Gallica*, see Jean Gaudemet, *Les sources du droit canonique VIIIe–XXe siècle* (Paris: Les Éditions du Cerf, 1993), 27–9.

[31] For the specific citations, see Amnon Linder, ed., *The Jews in the Legal Sources of the Early Middle Ages* (Detroit: Wayne State University Press, 1997), 606–7. Another collection that contains Mâcon canons not found in the *Vetus Gallica* is the *Collectio Burgundiana* (early eighth century), on which, see Kéry, ed., *Canonical Collections of the Early Middle Ages*, 86.

[32] It appears in the interrelated *Collectio XXXI Titulorum* (tenth/eleventh century), Burchard's *Decretum*, the *Collectio XII Partium* (early eleventh century), the *Collectio Canonum* in Paris BN Lat. 13368 (late eleventh century), the *Collectio VII Librorum*, Turin (late eleventh century), the *Collectio Canonum of St-Hilaire-le-Grand* (late eleventh century), the *Collectio IX Voluminorum Sangermanensis* (ca. 1100), the *Collectio Sancte Genoveve* (early twelfth century), and the *Collectio Canonum* in MS Paris, Bibliothèque de l'Arsenal 721 (twelfth century). On these collections, and their relationships with one another, see the relevant entries in Kéry and Fowler-Magerl.

Middle Ages, therefore, the Mâcon canons continued to circulate in a variety of collections and permutations.

Nevertheless, the number of canons from the Council of Mâcon that remained popular among collectors noticeably diminished as time progressed. When Burchard of Worms compiled his *Decretum* (ca. 1012–1022), he included only canons 8, 16, and 18.[33] Ivo of Chartres (ca. 1040–1115), who drew upon Burchard as one of his sources, included only canon 18 in his *Collectio Tripartita A*, and canons 13, 16, and 18 in his *Decretum*. The anonymous reformer who compiled the *Collectio Caesaraugustana* (ca. 1108–40) borrowed canons 13 and 18 directly from Ivo.[34] Similarly, Gratian's *Decretum* (in its augmented recension) included only those canons cited by either Burchard or Ivo: 8, 16, and 18.[35] These three canons would be all that would join the medieval *Corpus Iuris Canonici*. Still, the fact that manuscripts containing the remainder of the Council of Mâcon's legislative program survive today reveals that the seventeen canons not adopted by Gratian did not vanish; they continued to be preserved in the libraries of Europe until their "rediscovery" by Renaissance conciliar scholars.[36]

The fate of the conciliar canons of Mâcon (581/3) is emblematic of that endured by many of the councils of the period. Initially copied into a plethora of collections in a variety of forms, over time most of their decisions fell out of heavy circulation. Certainly, some councils fared better than others. The canons of the First Council of Orléans (511) had a quite successful afterlife, for example. All or most of these

[33] Hartmut Hoffmann and Rudolf Pokorny, eds., *Das Dekret des Bischofs Burchard von Worms* (Munich: Monumenta Germaniae Historica, 1991), IV.88 and XVI.21. The editors neglect XVI.8, which is an excerpt of canon 18. It is not certain what Burchard's sources were for these canons, although Mordek, *Kirchenrecht und Reform im Frankenreich*, 175–8, has suggested that Burchard may have used the *Collectio in 22 Chapters*.

[34] On Ivo of Chartres as a source for the *Collectio Caesaraugustana*, see Kéry, ed., *Canonical Collections of the Early Middle Ages*, 260; Fowler-Magerl, *Clavis Canonum: Selected Canon Law Collections Before 1140*, 239.

[35] These canons are cited as C.11.1.6, D.54.18, and C.22.5.7, respectively. C.11.1.6 and D.54.18 are both *paleae*, however, and, in fact, only the *dictum post canonem* of C.22.5.7 was present in the first recension. For the contents of the first recension, see Winroth, *The Making of Gratian's Decretum*, 197–227.

[36] Rare references to canons 2, 3, 5, 7, and 14 appear, respectively, in the *Collectio CCCXLII Capitulorum* (ninth–eleventh century) [using as its source the *Vetus Gallica*], the *Collectio Canonum* in MS Paris, Bibliothèque de l'Arsenal Paris 713 (twelfth century), the *Collectio XIII Librorum* (late eleventh century), the *Collectio XXXI Titulorum* (tenth–eleventh century), and the *Collectio XIII Librorum*. On these collections, see the relevant entries in Kéry and Fowler-Magerl.

were initially disseminated through the *Collectio Corbeinsis*, the *Collectio Lugdunensis*, the *Collectio Laureshamensis*, the *Collectio Coloniensis*, the *Collectio Sancti Mauri*, the *Collectio Remensis*, the *Collectio Pithouensis*, and the *Collectio Sancti Amandi*.[37] The *Vetus Gallica* likewise included twenty-two out of thirty-one canons (71 percent), and the council's pronouncements found their way in their entirety into the various editions of the *Collectio Hispana*, whose influence has been noted. Burchard, relying heavily on Regino of Prüm's *Libri Duo de Synodalibus Causis* (ca. 906), considered nine of Orléans' canons worth citing, while Ivo of Chartres included twenty-seven canons in his *Collectio Tripartita* and fourteen in his *Decretum*.[38] Finally, Gratian's *Decretum* cited twenty-five of its canons, a greater percentage of the whole (81 percent) than the selection contained in the *Vetus Gallica*. This is astonishing, considering that the latter collection was compiled only a hundred years after the First Council of Orléans met.

In contrast to the remarkable popularity enjoyed by the Council of Orléans (511), other councils did not fare nearly as well. The Council of St. Jean-de-Losne (673/5), for example, survives in only a single ninth-century manuscript, Albi Bibliothèque Municipale 2 (147), and contributed not a single canon to the *Corpus Iuris Canonici*. The Council of Lyons (567/70) did not fare much better. Four of its canons (2, 3, 5, and 6) showed up in the *Vetus Gallica*, and two appeared in the derivative *Collectio Frisingensis Secunda* (5 and 6), but the council's complete acts survived only into the early-modern period in one now-lost manuscript.[39] The important Council of Paris (614) had an only marginally more successful afterlife. Its full canonical record was preserved in the eighth-century manuscripts of two chronological collections, the *Collectio Remensis* and the *Collectio Diessensis*, and four of its canons (6, 11, 14, and 15) were included among the Pseudo-Isidorian false decretals (middle ninth century). Burchard adopted two of its canons (6 and 15) from Regino of Prüm, and Ivo of Chartres included only 15 in his *Decretum*. Gratian adopted the same canons as Burchard. Such figures are a further reminder of the precarious nature of canonical

[37] Canons 4, 5, and 7 are absent from the *Collectio Lugdunensis* (which is also missing canon 10), the *Collectio Coloniensis*, the *Collectio Sancti Mauri* (also missing canon 10), and the *Collectio Remensis*.

[38] Pontal, *Die Synoden im Merowingerreich*, 294–5. Burchard seems to have drawn on Regino of Prüm for canons 8, 17, 19, 25, and 26.

[39] Gaudemet and Basdevant-Gaudemet, eds., *Les canons des conciles mérovingiens*, 400. This manuscript was cited by Surius in his 1567 edition of the councils.

transmission. Many of the Frankish councils survive only by mere luck, and there is no way to know how many have been lost through the hazards of time.

Chance and Choice

Despite the incomplete nature of our source base, it is still possible to make some general observations about the transmission of conciliar decisions. Two major forces were at work in the determination of what canons would enjoy long afterlives, and, in a few select cases, inclusion in Gratian's *Decretum*: chance and choice. To a considerable degree, canonists were restrained in their selections by the availability of previous collections in their own, or nearby, libraries. This is one reason why conciliar decisions that were disseminated widely in the initial centuries after their composition were more likely to be cited in collections compiled later in the Middle Ages. It is also why canons that appeared in especially popular collections, such as the *Hispana* or the *Vetus Gallica*, were more likely to be preserved. The Council of Orléans (511), as already noted, had its entire canonical record preserved (occasionally minus a few canons) in more than a dozen compilations in the Merovingian and Carolingian periods, and selections of it appeared in many more. Its canons also appeared in great numbers in such important collections as the *Vetus Gallica*, the *Hispana*, the Pseudo-Isidorian Decretals, and Ivo of Chartres' various anthologies. Those other councils whose decisions eventually found their way into Gratian's *Decretum* generally had similar histories. Canons published by the Council of Epaone (517), for example, were copied into at least thirty-five collections prior to 1140.[40] The canons of the Councils of Arles (524), Clermont (535), Orléans (538), Orléans (549), Arles (554), Paris (556/73), Auxerre (585/605), and Mâcon (581/3) similarly had successful afterlives in terms of the quantity and influence of the collections they appeared in.[41] Those who argue that Gratian's selection of Gallic councils and canons was, to a considerable

[40] This tally is based on the data collected by Fowler-Magerl.
[41] For the inclusion of these canons in the major pre-Gratian collections, see Gaudemet and Basdevant-Gaudemet, eds., *Les canons des conciles mérovingiens*, 626–9.

degree, predetermined by the choices of his predecessors are therefore correct.[42]

However, there were those councils that enjoyed initial popularity that Gratian failed to include in his collection, such as the synods that Caesarius of Arles held at Carpentras (527), Orange (529), and Vaison (529), and the Council of Orléans (541).[43] This is where choice becomes relevant. For example, Gratian had access to canons 4, 8, and 9 of the Council of Mâcon (585), which appeared in the collections of both Burchard and Ivo, yet he chose not to include them in the *Decretum*. He also failed to include canons 2 or 4 from the Council of Vaison (529), or 6, 10, or 30 from the Council of Orléans (541), which Ivo also cited. Similarly, the compiler of the *Collectio Frisingensis Secunda* included fewer than half of the canons of the Council of Orléans (511) provided by his primary source, the *Vetus Gallica* (ten out of twenty-two).[44] The author of the *Collectio Bonaevallensis*, who also made use of the *Vetus Gallica*, chose to omit nine canons of the Council of Orléans (538) present in the latter collection, while still citing nineteen other of that council's decisions.[45]

A particularly revealing example of the selective inclusion of canons is the *Collectio Burgundiana*, an early-eighth-century anthology compiled in northern Gaul.[46] Little is known about the direct sources for this small, unstructured collection of canonical and penitential

[42] Le Roy, "Les conciles gaulois et le Décret de Gratien," 556–60. Le Roy notes that although Gratian relied heavily on the choices made by Ivo of Chartres, there was a preexisting "vulgate" of canonical texts that was transmitted from collection to collection. Schröder, "Zur Rezeption merowingischer Konzilskanones bei Gratian," 234, has observed that although Gratian included the canons of eleven Merovingian-era councils, half of the total canons he cites (twenty-five out of fifty-one) were originally issued by the Council of Orléans (511).

[43] Gaudemet and Basdevant-Gaudemet, eds., *Les canons des conciles mérovingiens*, 626–9.

[44] Those canons that the compiler does include are 1, 6, 11, 12, 15, 16, 19, 24, 27, and 30. The missing canons are 2, 3, 8, 9, 13, 14, 17, 20, 25, 26, 28, and 31. For an edition of the *Collectio Frisingensis Secunda*, see Mordek, *Kirchenrecht und Reform im Frankenreich*, 618–33.

[45] Those canons that the compiler chose not to include are 2, 3, 5, 6, 13, 16, 25, 27, and 33. For lists of the relevant canons, see Hubert Mordek, "Die Rechtssammlungen der Handschrift von Bonneval—ein Werk der karolingischen," *Deutsches Archiv für Erforschung des Mittelalters* 24, no. 2 (1968): 432; Mordek, *Kirchenrecht und Reform im Frankenreich*, 660.

[46] For the contents of this collection, see Maassen, *Geschichte der Quellen und der Literatur des canonischen Rechts*, 636–8. For dating and bibliography, see Kéry, ed., *Canonical Collections of the Early Middle Ages*, 86.

materials, although it seems certain that its compiler had access to a number of different manuscripts. The collection contains decisions from the Gallic Councils of Orléans (511), Epaone (517), Clermont (535), Tours (567), Mâcon (581/3), Lyons (583), and Auxerre (585/605). No known earlier anthology contains all of the canons and councils included in the *Collectio Burgundiana*. Additionally, the compiler's choice of individual canons is highly selective, with the represented Frankish councils contributing only a handful of canons each, with the exception of the Councils of Clermont and Auxerre, which are included in almost their entirety.[47] The compiler, by and large, favors canons regulating clerical and episcopal discipline,[48] as well as those that prescribe liturgical procedure and dress.[49] He also includes, as a group, the three canons of the Council of Orléans (511) regulating ecclesiastical asylum.[50] Along with the Frankish canons, the collection also contains the *Statuta Ecclesiae Antiqua*, the monastic rules of Macarius and Caesarius, cc. 1–39 of the *Paenitentiale Merseburgense*, as well as translated Greek canonical material. Although there does not seem to be a single "program" per se dictating the contents of the collection, it would be reasonable to assume that it was originally intended as a canonical handbook for bishops. It does not pretend to be a comprehensive anthology like the *Vetus Gallica*; rather, it provides a selection of some of the basic canonical material that a diocesan bishop might be expected to know.

Thus, it was not always mere luck that determined what canons made it into the compilations of the Frankish period and beyond. The compilers of canonical collections, especially in the case of systematic anthologies, selected their contents in accordance with their own interests, biases, and agendas.[51] Because these compilers are almost always

---

[47] The compiler excludes c. 14 and the conclusion of c. 16 of the Council of Clermont (535). There is nothing controversial about c. 14; it threatens with excommunication those believers who renege on written agreements to make offerings to the church. The compiler of the *Collectio Burgundiana* possibly left it out because it overlaps with c. 86 of the *Statuta Ecclesiae Antiqua*, which is also included in the collection. The compiler also excludes Mâcon (581/3), c. 4, which likewise harkens back to the *Statuta Ecclesiae Antiqua* decree.

[48] Orléans (511), cc. 8, 9, 29, and 30; Epaone (517), cc. 4, 12, 13, and 22; Tours (567), cc. 6 and 8; Mâcon (581/3), cc. 3 and 8.

[49] Orléans (511), cc. 25, 26, and 31; Tours (567), cc. 3, 4, and 10; Mâcon (581/3), cc. 5, 6, and 9; Lyons (583), c. 5.

[50] Orléans (511), cc. 1–3.

[51] Fournier and Le Bras, *Histoire des collections canoniques en Occident*, I.44–5, argue that even sixth-century compilers were governed by "certain preoccupations," if not defined programs.

anonymous, their collections must speak for them. Still, we can draw some general conclusions about the preferences of these early medieval compilers. Among the Gallic synods, compilers favored those canons issued by the initial "national" synods of the early sixth century, i.e., Agde (506), Orléans (511), and Epaone (517), over all subsequent Merovingian-era meetings.[52] Among the early-Pippinid synods, the Councils of Germania (742), Les Estinnes (743), Soissons (744), and Ver (755) had relatively unsuccessful afterlives with regard to their contributions to the *Corpus Iuris Canonici*. Only canon 2 from the German Council made its way into Gratian's *Decretum*. In contrast, Regino, Burchard, Ivo, and Gratian heavily favored the legislation issued by the Councils of Verberie (756) and Compiègne (757). Together, these two councils were cited a dozen times in the second recension of the *Concordia Discordantium Canonum*. This is telling, as these two councils broke from legislative tradition to a far greater extent than the initial Pippinid councils by their overwhelming focus on socio-religious (as opposed to merely ecclesiastical) issues. It seems that the conservative nature of the canons of the initial Pippinid councils made their inclusion superfluous for subsequent canonists.

Indeed, the repetition of conciliar concerns during the Frankish era (and beyond) permitted a compiler, in theory, to pick and choose those canons that best suited his own position on a given issue. It has been suggested that compilers largely favored the initial formulation of a given canonical rule, because later restatements would merely elaborate upon the original principle in order to make it relevant to contemporary situations.[53] If, in other words, subsequent councils revised a decision originally made by the Council of Orléans (511), for many compilers the inclusion of these subsequent canons would have been superfluous.[54] Nevertheless, sometimes it was a later elaboration that was preferred, despite Isidore of Seville's opinion that "whenever

[52] Schröder, "Zur Rezeption merowingischer Konzilskanones bei Gratian," 234. Conciliar attendance, she observes, does not seem to have played much of a role in selection, as the Council of Orléans (549), the best-attended council of the sixth century, is represented in Gratian by only two canons. Epaone, as Schröder acknowledges, may not have been a "national" council per se.

[53] Schröder, "Zur Rezeption merowingischer Konzilskanones bei Gratian," 234–5.

[54] For example, the Councils of Eauze (551), c. 3, and Auxerre (585/605), c. 4, restate the prohibition of Orléans (511) against divination and magic. Unlike the Orléans canon (30), the subsequent proscriptions had minimal representation in later canonical collections.

sententia in conciliar acts are found to be discordant, the *sententia* of that council which possesses either older or weightier *auctoritas* should be held the greater."[55] In the Frankish kingdoms, where canonists often demonstrated a preference for relatively recent (and local) canons, there was a willingness to favor relevance over tradition. In the preface to his *Libri Duo de Synodalibus Causis*, Regino of Prüm, for example, explains his preference for the decisions of Gallic and Germanic councils as an attempt "to include those decisions I believed more relevant to our dangerous age, and which seemed to pertain to matters of concern."[56] So, although certain canonical enactments were already favored centuries before Gratian began his own task of selection, the early medieval compilers of canonical collections still were able to pick and choose among a vast reservoir of legislative precedents.

Conciliar Decisions as Canon Law

This raises another question: Did the conciliar participants of the sixth–eighth centuries craft their rules as contributions to a recognized corpus of canon law? When put in these terms, the answer is no. The primary reason that the Frankish bishops issued canons was to address issues of immediate concern. Nevertheless, they obviously were aware of, and often contributors to, the steady production of up-to-date canonical collections throughout this period. They made use of these collections in the course of their deliberations, and sometimes even used the occasion of a council to compile a new anthology. In what sense, then—to rephrase the question—did conciliar participants recognize their decisions as part of a larger body of ecclesiastical law?

---

[55] Isidore of Seville, *Epistolae*, PL 83, ed. J. P. Migne (Paris: Garnier Brothers, 1862), no. 4. On Isidore's letter, whose authorship is questionable, see Roger Reynolds, "The Isidorian Epistola ad Massonam on Lapsed Clerics: Notes on Its Early Manuscript and Textual Transmission," in *Grundlagen des Rechts: Festschrift für Peter Landau zum 65. Geburtstag*, ed. Peter Landau and R. H. Helmholz (Paderborn: Ferdinand Schöningh, 2000), 77–92. Le Roy also cites the example of Orléans (511), c. 18, which was abandoned by some compilers in favor of Epaone (517), c. 30: "Les conciles gaulois et le Décret de Gratien," 559.

[56] Regino of Prüm, *Das Sendhandbuch des Regino von Prüm*, ed. and trans. Hermann Wasserschleben and Wilfried Hartmann (Darmstadt: Wissenschaftliche Buchgesellschaft, 2004), 20–3.

On a strictly terminological level, there was recognition of the existence of an *Ius Canonum* or *Lex Canonica* in this era.[57] But of what did this body of law consist? Did every canon issued by every council *pro forma* become part of the corpus? Or, on the other hand, were only those decisions enacted by, say, ecumenical councils included?[58] Admittedly, any answers to these questions are conjectural, because of the absence of any sustained theoretical discussion of the nature of church law from Merovingian Francia. Our best indicators for the legal thinking of the Frankish bishops are the canons themselves, as well as the contents of those collections that preserved and transmitted them for future use.

Much of the authority of conciliar canons derived from either their implicit or their explicit claims to reflect orthodox tradition. This, of course, did not inhibit conciliar participants from elaborating upon previous legislation to the extent of effectively enacting unprecedented decrees.[59] In the same way, canonists occasionally edited and rewrote earlier decisions to suit their interests.[60] This willingness to reshape or, in some cases, to ignore the past reflects the Frankish bishops' belief in the authority of their own pronouncements, even when not obviously consistent with the decisions of their predecessors.[61] The bishops certainly did not challenge their precursors' authority, nor did they dismiss their relevance. They did believe, however, that their own conciliar consensus ensured the orthodoxy of their decisions, thereby shrouding legislative enactments more applicable to contemporary concerns in the authoritative cloak of tradition. Conciliar procedures ensured that the judgment of the bishops was orthodox, even if it deviated from earlier precedent.[62]

The Frankish conciliar attendees were not involved in a conspiratorial effort to subvert traditional church law; on the contrary, their

---

[57] See pp. 137–8.

[58] Isidore of Seville *Etymologiae* VI.16.5–10 singles out Nicaea (325), Constantinople (381), Ephesus (431), and Chalcedon (451) as the most authoritative ecclesiastical synods.

[59] Klingshirn, *Caesarius of Arles: The Making of a Christian Community*, 98.

[60] Ralph Mathisen, "Syagrius of Autun, Virgilius of Arles, and Gregory of Rome: Factionalism, Forgery, and Local Authority at the End of the Sixth Century," in *L'Église et la mission au VIe siècle*, ed. Christophe de Dreuille (Paris: Éditions du Cerf, 2000), 270–6.

[61] Mathisen, "Between Arles, Rome, and Toledo," 38–40.

[62] Morrison, *Tradition and Authority in the Western Church*, 195–6.

frequent citation of conciliar precedents clearly demonstrates their deep belief in the authority of these precedents. Nevertheless, the bishops did not believe earlier conciliar precedents to be immune from useful elaboration. What is more, they had no doubt of the authority of their own pronouncements, which can be seen in the Merovingian-era preference for local and recent legislation in the compilation of canonical collections. Canon law, for the Frankish bishops, was a living body, in much the same way that the church itself was.[63] Just as apostolic succession ensured the continuity of episcopal authority, despite the ever-changing identities of the individual officeholders, so, too, did the regular convocation of councils ensure orthodox tradition, despite their explicit function of enacting original legislation. The work of councils, therefore, was never done. New circumstances constantly called for new decrees, and the task of *renovanda*—which did not preclude revision—was a perpetual one.

Although it is true that even after Gratian, the corpus of canon law continued to be augmented, there is an important disparity as compared with the Frankish situation. Post-Gratian, certain reference works were singled out as authoritative. In the Early Middle Ages, the absence of any standard collection of canonical decrees made this a non-issue. Certainly, there were particular councils whose decisions were considered especially authoritative, but one need only consider that the Merovingian-era synods referenced the decisions of the Councils of Epaone (517), Clermont (535), and Orléans (538) as often as those of Nicaea (325) to recognize the practical limitations of such distinctions.[64] Canon law in this period was defined by its reference to orthodox tradition, not by its inclusion in an authoritative corpus. This definition not only justified the compilation of canonical collections with sometimes broadly disparate contents, but also the selective citation of earlier decisions by the Frankish councils.[65] There certainly were disadvantages to this system: the sheer quantity of new canons "presented a maze of conflicts and inconsistencies, too numerous and

---

[63] The observations of Peter Brown, *The Rise of Western Christendom*, 439, are applicable to the Merovingian context.

[64] De Clercq, ed., *Concilia Galliae A.511–A.695*, 332–3.

[65] Firey, "Ghostly Recensions in Early Medieval Canon Law," 81, observes that in the Carolingian era, compilers were less interested in producing definitive collections of canon law than collections that could serve more immediate and idiosyncratic purposes. She concludes that canon law in this period was more a "conceptual corpus" than a fixed, codified body.

too difficult for most priests and bishops to master," and also contributed to the localization of Christian practice.[66] Such impediments were an impetus for the compilation of more "user-friendly," systematic canonical collections, which made up for in coherence what they lacked in comprehensiveness.

Thus, the Frankish bishops recognized both a preexisting body (if not a fixed corpus) of canon law, as well as their own authoritative right to add to it. But did the Frankish bishops consider all of their decisions to be contributions to canon law? On the one hand, it was ordinary for Gallic councils to conclude their canonical acts with a warning to the faithful to obey all that which was decided by the consensus of those present.[67] However, the selection of only some canons for inclusion in systematic canonical collections suggests that even if all canons were created equal, some came to be considered more equal than others. Does this mean that those canons that were never collected into systematic anthologies possessed less authority than those that were? The lack of any differentiation in the original conciliar acts themselves suggests that, in theory, the answer is no. Nevertheless, in practice, certain decisions obviously were given more preference than others, appearing with far greater frequency in subsequent compilations. This is not surprising. If the councils truly were addressing contemporary concerns in their legislation, then not all of their decisions would be worth copying into those systematic canonical collections intended for general long-term use.[68]

However, those who maintain that these frequently cited canons form a "vulgate" overstate the situation.[69] The line of tradition that included both the *Vetus Gallica* and the later compilations of Regino of Prüm, Burchard of Worms, Ivo of Chartres, and Gratian did not encompass all canonical collecting activity between 600 and 1200.[70] It did not even represent a closed tradition, because individual canons

[66] Brundage, *Medieval Canon Law*, 22–3.

[67] E.g., Epaone (517), c. 40; Orléans (533), c. 21; Orléans (538), c. 36; Orléans (541), c. 38; Orléans (549), c. 24; Paris (556/73), c. 9; Auxerre (585/605), c. 45.

[68] Le Roy, "Les Conciles Gaulois et le Décret de Gratien," 558–9.

[69] Ibid., 560. Schröder, "Zur Rezeption merowingischer Konzilskanones bei Gratian," 233, estimates that there were 174 canons circulating among the "important" canonical collections of the Early Middle Ages.

[70] On Burchard's use of Regino's collection, see Fournier and Le Bras, *Histoire des collections canoniques en Occident*, I.371. On Burchard's influence on Ivo of Chartres' collections, see Fournier and Le Bras, *Histoire des collections canoniques en Occident*, II.70. On Ivo as a source for Gratian, see Winroth, *The Making of Gratian's Decretum*, 16.

were being continuously added and abandoned at the discretion of individual compilers. Although those Frankish canons frequently adopted by the aforementioned canonists and their predecessors were more likely to have a lengthy afterlife, other canons were still cited by other compilers and other councils. Returning again to the example of the Council of Mâcon (581/3), we can observe this clearly. In the middle to late ninth century, no less than three church councils cited Mâcon's decisions on Jewish policy: Meaux-Paris (845–6), Metz (893), and Benevento (ca. 900).[71] Among the canons cited by these councils were 14, 15, and 17, which ultimately were absent from the anthologies of Regino, Burchard, Ivo, and Gratian. Canons 14 and 17 had not even appeared in the *Vetus Gallica*. A few decades later, Gerhard of Mainz quoted canon 14 in a letter to Bishop Frederick of Mainz (937).[72] As late as the last decade of the twelfth century, the Council of Rouen (1190) cited canon 17, proving that conciliar decisions beyond those preserved by the major collections continued to be accessible.[73] Thus, we cannot differentiate the legality of Frankish canons on the grounds of "popularity" alone. A canon's inclusion in particularly influential collections did not make it any more obligatory than a canon whose transmission was more limited. The further back we look, the more true this observation appears: in the Merovingian period, when popular chronological canonical collections preserved all (or most) of the decisions of certain councils, it was virtually impossible to make any differentiations.

But what of those councils whose acts never made their way into canonical collections? Were their decisions any less binding? From what we have observed so far, it would seem that as long as these decisions were enacted according to orthodox tradition and episcopal consensus, they were considered compulsory at the time of their enactment. Consider those councils that left no canons at all, such as the

---

On Gratian's use of Burchard, see Peter Landau, "Burchard of Worms et Gratian: Pour l'étude des sources directes du Décret de Gratien," *Revue de droit canonique* 48, no. 2 (1998): 233–45.

[71] Meaux-Paris (845–6), c. 73, cites canons 13–17. Amulo of Lyons' *Liber Contra Judaeos* is related textually to this citation: *Die Konzilien der Karolingischen Teilreiche 843–859*, 122, note 239. Metz (893), c. 7, relies on Mâcon (581/3), c. 15. Benevento (c. 900) cites canons 13, 15, and 16, possibly from the *Vetus Gallica* edition, on which, see Linder, ed., *The Jews in the Legal Sources of the Early Middle Ages*, 550, note 190.

[72] Linder, ed., *The Jews in the Legal Sources of the Early Middle Ages*, 622–33.

[73] On the Council of Rouen, see Odette Pontal, *Les conciles de la France capétienne jusqu'en 1215* (Paris: Cerf, 1995), 360–2.

Council of Valence (583/5), whose acts confirmed the royal family's gifts to the church. Although the seventeen episcopal participants left their decision in the form of a document composed in the style of a *placuit*-form canonical record (complete with subscriptions), the specificity of their agenda led to its near-absence from subsequent canonical collections. The council, in fact, survived in only a single manuscript into modern times, although it, too, is now lost.[74] Nevertheless, the bishops at Valence made it clear that their enactments were obligatory, threatening perpetual anathema against "the murderers of the poor" who coveted church property.[75] Although it is difficult to say whether the conciliar participants would have considered such a document part of the *Ius Canonum*, the similarities between it and traditional canonical acts (including even the use of a "cum…convenissemus" preface) suggest that such distinctions may not always have been clear-cut in the Frankish period. The Council of Valence's acts were as binding as those of any synod, even if their applicability was chronologically limited.

To review our conclusions thus far: 1) the Frankish conciliar participants recognized the existence of an *Ius Canonum* and their prerogative to contribute to it; 2) this body of ecclesiastical law was therefore "living," not fixed; and 3) the inclusion of canons in canonical collections did not, in theory, determine their legal value, merely their visibility. For the Frankish bishops, the orthodoxy of their decisions alone made them binding, although they rarely presumed to extend the authority of these decrees beyond the borders of Francia. These decisions were fundamentally local, but no less authoritative because of it.[76] For the very reason that they were connected to ecclesiastical tradition, the Frankish canons could be copied and disseminated to regions with no attachment to the original council. Canon law, for the Frankish bishops, was not a corpus, but a tradition, and one to which they were contributors.[77]

Frankish Canons in the Post-Frankish Era

How, then, did later generations of prelates and canonists view the Frankish conciliar decrees? Did they think of them as local decisions

[74] Pontal, *Histoire des conciles mérovingiens*, 172.
[75] Valence (583/5), Conciliar Acts.
[76] Gaudemet, *L'Église dans l'Empire Romain (IVe–Ve siècles)*, 37.
[77] McKitterick, *The Frankish Church and the Carolingian Reforms*, 17, has made the same observation vis-à-vis the late-ninth-century Frankish bishops.

made by men like themselves, or as anonymous components of a larger system of canon law? The ever-increasing popularity of systematic canonical collections must have contributed to the disassociation of particular conciliar decisions from the councils that had originally issued them. The farther away, both geographically and chronologically, one was from a council, the more likely that it was just a name, with the identities of its participants faded or forgotten. When the attendees of the Council of Metz of 893 cited the Council of Mâcon (581/3), c. 15, they credited the canon solely to Bishop Syagrius of Autun, who had not even been the president of the council.[78] No doubt Syagrius' frequent appearances in the *Registrum* of Gregory the Great helped his subsequent prestige surpass that of his metropolitan, Priscus of Lyons, who had actually presided over the meeting. Priscus was best remembered in subsequent centuries through Gregory of Tours' unflattering portrayal.[79] Therefore, it is not surprising that Syagrius, probably the best-known Mâcon attendee in the post-Merovingian period, was given full credit for the council's decisions. But his situation was an exceptional one permitted only by his unusually prominent stature. With the important exception of Caesarius of Arles, awareness of the identities of the vast majority of episcopal participants from the Merovingian period was limited. As we have seen, the necessity of providing subscription lists as proof of a council's *auctoritas* became increasingly less obligatory in the middle eighth century, further diminishing any knowledge of past conciliar participants.

With only tradition to indicate orthodoxy, it is no wonder that the Carolingian and post-Carolingian eras gave birth to a number of forgeries and pseudo-councils. The most famous is the Pseudo-Isidorian corpus, whose popularity among canonists is confirmed by the extraordinary quantity of surviving manuscripts (more than one hundred).[80] Consisting of the *Collectio Hispana Gallica Augustodunensis*, the *Capitula Angilramni*, the *Capitularia Benedicti Levitae*, and the Pseudo-Isidorian false decretals, these forgeries were aimed at bolstering

[78] Metz (893), c. 7.

[79] Gregory of Tours *Decem Libri Historiarum* IV.36, VIII.20; Gregory of Tours *Liber Vitae Patrum* VIII.5.

[80] For the manuscripts of the decretals alone, see Kéry, ed., *Canonical Collections of the Early Middle Ages*, 100–8. Abigail Firey, "Carolingian Ecclesiology and Heresy: A Southern Gallic Juridical Tract Against Adoptionism," *Sacris Erudiri* 39 (2000): 255, has noted that the number of surviving Pseudo-Isidorian manuscripts is greater even than that of the *Dacheriana* (52).

episcopal independence from metropolitical authority.[81] Yet canonical forgers were not the only ecclesiastics with agendas: the Gregorian Reform and its aftershocks similarly encouraged a wealth of new canon law compilations, including the works of Ivo of Chartres.[82] As genuine and forged materials alike found their way into a variety of collections, the gap between canonists and their sources grew ever wider. Canonists' knowledge of individual councils, in many cases, probably did not extend much beyond the information contained in those canonical sources they had at hand. When they decided to select a canon for use in their own work, they were affirming their faith in its authors' adherence to orthodox tradition, as well as these authors' legislative authority. This faith, along with the individual canonist's own social, religious, and political inclinations, ideology, and agenda, helped dictate the contents of his collection.

It was Gratian who put an end to the "assembling, in ever new selection and combination, the authorities of the past in all their bewildering variety."[83] It was Gratian who turned canonical studies into a "scientific" project, governed by both reason and faith.[84] What meaning did the Frankish councils have for him? Gratian's compilation had a very different premise than the canonical collections of the past: its first recension was written as a basic textbook for students of canon law that would iron out the perceived discrepancies among different canonical authorities. It was intended as a teaching text.[85]

Canon law, prior to Gratian, was not a university concern; rather, it was a practical affair. Collections were compiled to help clerics maintain discipline, settle disputes, and encourage ecclesiastical reform. None of these collections pretended to resolve discrepancies among various canons and papal decretals, and an inexperienced student of canon law would have found them difficult primers. Thus, Gratian's *Decretum* addressed an important need. Nevertheless, despite its stated

[81] Horst Fuhrmann, "The Pseudo-Isidorian Forgeries," in *Papal Letters in the Early Middle Ages*, ed. Detlev Jasper and Horst Fuhrmann (Washington, DC: Catholic University of America Press, 2001), 140–4; Reynolds, "The Organization, Law and Liturgy of the Western Church, 700–900," 616–7.

[82] Brundage, *Medieval Canon Law*, 34–43. For the individual collections, see Kéry, ed., *Canonical Collections of the Early Middle Ages*, 203–94.

[83] Stephan Kuttner, "The Scientific Investigation of Mediaeval Canon Law," *Speculum* 24, no. 4 (1949): 495.

[84] Ibid., 497.

[85] Winroth, *The Making of Gratian's Decretum*, 144–5.

purpose of bringing order to disorder, the first recension was not a particularly comprehensive collection. The rapid growth of both canonical and Roman legal studies in the decades following the publication of the first edition necessitated the compilation of a second recension, twice the size of the first.[86] The number of Frankish canons in the initial version of the *Decretum* was small: from the Merovingian period, Gratian cited ten canons from five councils, and from the Pippinid period, eight canons from two councils.[87] It was only with the second recension that the representation of these canons increased: fifty-one canons from eleven Merovingian councils, and fifteen canons from three Pippinid councils.[88]

What significance did these canons have for Gratian? Consider an example that appears in the original recension of the *Decretum*. In 517, the Council of Epaone declared that "if a bishop should die before giving absolution to someone who has been excommunicated (*damnati*), his successor may absolve that individual once he has been chastised and has repented."[89] This canon subsequently found its way into a variety of canonical collections, including the *Vetus Gallica*, Burchard of Worms' *Decretum*, and all three of Ivo of Chartres' anthologies.[90] Gratian, in turn, cited it in Causa 11, Questio 3, of his *Decretum*.[91] This particular Causa deals with a hypothetical case involving the episcopal punishment of clerics who have brought legal cases before lay judges. In Questio 3, Gratian asks "whether a cleric who dared to celebrate holy office contrary to the [theoretically unjust] prohibition of his bishop ought to be deposed."[92] On the surface, the Burgundian canon offers little guidance in answering Gratian's question. Anders Winroth, in his analysis of this Questio, calls particular attention to the *dictum post canonem* that immediately follows the Epaone canon (c. 40 in the

[86] Ibid.

[87] The councils cited are Orléans (511), Epaone (517), Orléans (538), Orléans (549), Paris (614), Verberie (756), and Compiègne (757). These tallies are based on the table of contents for the first recension, provided by Winroth, *The Making of Gratian's Decretum*, 197–227.

[88] See the tables in Le Roy, "Les Conciles Gaulois et le Décret de Gratien," 571–4; Hartmann, *Die Synoden der Karolingerzeit*, 482–92.

[89] Epaone (517), c. 28.

[90] Pontal, *Die Synoden im Merowingerreich*, 297.

[91] Winroth, *The Making of Gratian's Decretum*, 96, admits that textual variations do not offer any clues to Gratian's direct source for this canon.

[92] Gratian, *Decretum*, Corpus Iuris Canonici I, ed. Emil Friedberg (Leipzig: Bernhardi Tauchnitz, 1879), C.11.Q.3.

Decretum). He observes how it elucidates a clear program behind the original fifteen canons of the first recension, explaining the contradiction between those authorities who believe that a prelate's unjust sentence must be "feared" (*timendam*), and those who say such sentences can be appealed. Gratian, Winroth explains, removed this contradiction by arguing that one feared an unjust sentence by not disobeying it for reasons of pride. One could still ignore it, however. But if an individual was himself responsible for an unjust sentence, he had to obey it until his appeal was heard.[93]

So how does the Epaone canon assist in clarifying this analysis? In the first recension, canon 40 was originally preceded by cc. 34–7, all of which emphasized the right of appeal of unjust sentences.[94] Although the Epaone canon makes no reference to the fairness of the episcopal sentence, or even whether the excommunicate in question is a cleric or a layman, it does neatly answer in the affirmative the question of whether an appeal can be heard after the death of the original episcopal judge. Although Gratian does not explicitly change the meaning of the original canon, he contextualizes it in a way unimagined by its authors.

This is the fate of those Frankish canons that managed to survive long enough to be incorporated into the *Decretum*. The price of survival was the loss or radical change of original intent. Even those canons whose language remained virtually undisturbed over the course of centuries could not continuously reflect the original circumstances that warranted their composition. But it could not have happened any other way if topical collections were to be compiled. A canon irrevocably tied to a particular place and time simply had no meaning for subsequent generations of clerics and canonists. It was only those canons whose principles were broad and malleable enough to withstand changing conditions, both within and outside the church, that could have application centuries later.

As already noted, a fundamental principle of ecclesiastical law was its embodiment of an evolving tradition: it drew its authority from the past and its relevance from the present. For the Frankish conciliar fathers, their decisions were merely the transitory waves that formed out of the vast ocean of tradition; the waves crested, crashed, and were

93 Winroth, *The Making of Gratian's Decretum*, 78–9.
94 Ibid., 79.

then reabsorbed. Each wave was made of the same substance as its predecessors, although its shape and form were utterly unique to its moment in the sun. The relationship between conciliar canons and their immediate historical contexts was an elementary one. Although we should not dissociate our analyses of these canons from the framework of medieval canon law, to look back on them entirely from this perspective is to deemphasize their primary function as context-specific decrees.

CHAPTER 6

CONTINUITY AND CHANGE IN THE EIGHTH CENTURY

Conciliar Continuity: Alaric to Clovis

In September 506, thirty-four Gallo-Roman clerics met in the city of Agde "with the permission of our most glorious, magnificent, and pious lord king."[1] The honored *rex* was Alaric II, an Arian Christian, who hoped that by authorizing a council of Catholic prelates, he would be able to rely on their loyalty in the ongoing fight for political domination in Gaul.[2] Alaric's dream of a Visigothic-dominated Gaul would be crushed only a year later, when he was defeated and killed by Clovis at the Battle of Vouillé.[3] But in 506, the king was still vigorously attempting to hold together a unified Visigothic realm. The same year that he convoked the Council of Agde, he also issued the *Lex Romana Visigothorum* (or *Breviarium*), a compilation of Roman law whose influence would far outlive Alaric himself.[4] Following Clovis' victory, and the establishment of Merovingian dominance in Gaul, the *Lex Romana Visigothorum* continued to be copied and consulted frequently, even though manuscripts of the *Codex Theodosianus* were still in circulation.[5] For Alaric, however, the codification project had a more immediate aim: uniting the Roman subjects of his kingdom under a single code of laws issued in his own name. Alaric's unification efforts were

---

1 Agde (506), Preface.

2 Mathisen, "The Second Council of Arles," 543, has suggested that Arles II (442/506) was convoked for the same reasons already postulated for the Council of Agde (506).

3 The Visigoths continued to control Septimania in the south, and held a synod there in 589.

4 Herwig Wolfram, *The Roman Empire and Its Germanic Peoples*, trans. Thomas Dunlap (Berkeley: University of California Press, 1997), 156, emphasizes that we should not view Alaric's convocation of Agde and his issuing of the *Breviarium* as acts independent of each other.

5 On the use of the *Codex Theodosianus* in Merovingian Gaul, see Wood, "The Code in Merovingian Gaul," 161–77; Arjava, "The Survival of Roman Family Law After the Barbarian Settlements," 38. Janet Nelson, "The Merovingian Church in Carolingian Perspective," in *The World of Gregory of Tours*, ed. Kathleen Mitchell and Ian Wood (Leiden: Brill, 2002), 243, notes that the Carolingians followed the Merovingian clerics in their use of the *Code*.

paralleled by those of the president of the Council of Agde, Bishop Caesarius of Arles, whose interests were pastoral rather than political.[6] For Caesarius, the standardization of Gallic ecclesiastical administration was a project still to be accomplished, and the legislative program, whose composition he oversaw at Agde, was a motley mix of old standards, reworked canons, and new decrees. A recent biographer has observed that Caesarius' canons "drew attention to the continuity of the church with its Gallo-Roman past and to its solidarity with the universal church."[7] But Caesarius' hopes for ecclesiastical uniformity under the watchful eye of the episcopate of Arles would be dashed by the Frankish military victory, and he himself would be increasingly marginalized in the final decades of his life.[8]

The canons of the Council of Agde, however, did not share the fate of either their author or their royal sponsor. Along with those canons issued by the Councils of Orléans (511) and Epaone (517), they would prove to be among the most influential precedents for subsequent Frankish conciliar decrees. Although Alaric's name mysteriously disappeared from some manuscripts of Agde's canonical record, and Caesarius stopped attending royally convoked synods altogether, many of the broad issues debated and discussed at the council of 506 did not lose their relevance for the Gallic church.[9] And not simply legislation, but conciliar protocol, too, remained remarkably consistent in Gaul from the fifth through the eighth century. Certainly, important changes took place, but it is the continuities that are striking in the acts of the Frankish councils. But did these continuities extend to those synods held in the transitional decades linking the Merovingian era and the Carolingian era? Boniface's councils of the 740s, for example, are categorized almost universally in the scholarly literature as "Carolingian" councils.[10] This is surprising, considering the trend in early medieval scholarship to recognize continuities on either side of the year 751, when Pippin III had himself crowned king of the Franks. Richard Sullivan famously observed that "recent scholarship in a variety of areas involving both pre-Carolingian and Carolingian history forces

[6] On the pastoral focus of Agde's legislative program, see Klingshirn, *Caesarius of Arles*, 97–104.

[7] Ibid., 98.

[8] Ibid., 244–72.

[9] R. A. Markus, *Gregory the Great and His World* (Cambridge: Cambridge University Press, 1997), 169. On the disappearance of Alaric's name from some manuscripts of the council, see Mathisen, "Between Arles, Rome, and Toledo," 37.

[10] Godding, *Prêtres en gaule mérovingienne*, vi.

one to the conclusion that continuity rather than discontinuity was the essential characteristic of a long historical continuum reaching forward from late antiquity, a continuum in which the Carolingian age constituted a not so distinctive segment."[11] Sullivan's conclusion has been borne out by subsequent research, particularly with regard to the Frankish church, and fewer readers now are willing to take Boniface at his word when he describes its leaders as corrupt, worldly, and decadent.[12] Nevertheless, this skepticism has yet to be extended to Boniface's criticisms of the conciliar activities of the Franks, or, as the case may be, the lack thereof. So were the councils of the middle eighth century really that different from those that had preceded them? And, if so, in what ways were they innovative? The assumptions underlying the traditional "Merovingian" and "Carolingian" periodization of Frankish conciliar activity require reevaluation—with regard to both protocol and legislation—in order to determine whether a paradigm of continuity is more appropriate than one of change.

But first, let us return to the half decade following the convocation of the Council of Agde. This was a busy time for Clovis; he had extended his rule into Aquitaine (although Septimania and Provence remained under Gothic control), necessitating the consolidation of his rule. It was in this context that he convoked the first synod to be held under Frankish auspices. The Council of Orléans (511), however, was similar to the Gallo-Roman meetings that preceded it, the Council of Agde in particular. Clovis' convocation was certainly in *imitatio imperii*, but it also had as a more direct precedent Alaric's summoning of the Gallic bishops.[13] Alaric, who was an Arian, had shown that a barbarian king possessed the necessary *auctoritas* to convene an ecclesiastical assembly of Roman bishops, and Clovis was aware of this when he decided that a Frankish synod was necessary soon afterward.

Clovis' synod and the Council of Agde had a number of subscribers in common: eight of the thirty-two bishops present had either participated in, or been represented at, the earlier council.[14] Both meetings issued their decisions as *placuit*-form documents, prefaced by

---

[11] Richard Sullivan, "The Carolingian Age: Reflections on Its Place in the History of the Middle Ages," *Speculum* 64, no. 2 (1989): 281.

[12] E.g., Reuter, "Kirchenreform und Kirchenpolitik," 37; Claussen, *The Reform of the Frankish Church*, 37.

[13] Daly, "Clovis: How Barbaric, How Pagan," 657.

[14] I.e., Cyprianus of Bordeaux, Tetradius of Bourges, Cronopius of Périgueux, Quintianus of Rodez, Boetius of Cahors, and Nicetius of Auch. Eufrasius of Clermont and Sextilius of Bazas, who were represented at Agde, also attended Orléans.

statements addressed to the convoking monarch, and terminated by dates and subscriptions. The earlier council's actual legislative influence on Clovis' synod is less certain, because similarities in discussion topics do not necessarily imply direct influence.[15] Although this is true, a textual relationship between Agde's canonical record and that of the Council of Orléans is less significant than shared legislative concerns. Both councils forbade laymen from leaving church before the end of the mass,[16] both rebuked monks who abandoned their monasteries without permission,[17] both legislated the proper observance of Easter, Christmas, and Pentecost,[18] and both condemned the practice of divination.[19] The repetition by the Council of Orléans of the same issues discussed at Agde probably reflects an attempt to address some of the specific concerns of the Aquitainian prelates, newly integrated into the Frankish *regnum*.

The Council of Agde's influence, however, continued to be felt well after Clovis' death. Almost a quarter century after the Council of Orléans (511), a synod at Clermont (535) used the preface to Agde's acts as a model for its own. The Council of Clichy (626/7), too, quoted from three of Agde's canons: 4, 6, and 7.[20] These references—some direct, some implied—were joined in the canonical *acta* of the Merovingian councils by those from other Gallo-Roman synods, such as the Councils of Valence (374) and Orange (441), and the Second Council of Arles (ca. 442/506).[21] The prelates at Orléans (511) frankly acknowledged in their canonical record their consultation of *antiquae canones*.[22] As we have seen, the citation of earlier precedents did not prohibit innovation on the part of the Frankish bishops; these earlier canons were merely

[15] For negative assessments of the Council of Agde's influence on Orléans' legislative program, see De Clercq, *La législation religieuse franque*, 9; Daly, "Clovis: How Barbaric, How Pagan," 657. De Clercq, unlike Daly, does accept the influence of Agde (506), c. 47, on Orléans (511), c. 26.

[16] Agde (506), c. 47; Orléans (511), c. 26.

[17] Agde (506), c. 38; Orléans (511), c. 22.

[18] Agde (506), c. 21; Orléans (511), c. 25.

[19] Agde (506), c. 42; Orléans (511), c. 30.

[20] See Clichy (626/7), cc. 12, 22–3, 15, respectively.

[21] For these references, see Orléans (511), c. 1; Marseilles (533), Caesarius' Additions to the Epistle of Pope John II; Eauze (551), c. 4; Tours (567), c. 21. The canons of the non-Gallic synods of Elvira (ca. 306), Ancyra (314), Neocaesarea (314/25), Nicaea (325), Antioch (332), Carthage (416), and Chalcedon (451) also proved influential for the Frankish synods (for the complete list of references, see De Clercq, *Concilia Galliae: A.511–A.695*, 332.

[22] I.e., Orléans (511), cc. 14–5, and 17.

the bearers of tradition that invested the Frankish decisions with *auctoritas*. Legislative continuities thus lay not so much in verbatim repetitions of canonical standards, although this certainly happened,[23] but rather in the reiteration of certain broad principles and legal standards that informed the composition of new decrees.

The innovations of the first Frankish council were neither in its protocol, nor in the issues its participants discussed, but rather in the ways that it addressed these issues. The prelates there knew that they were entering upon a new political reality. Their legislation is both a recognition of this reality, and an attempt to conform their basic principles to it. Clovis, too, recognized the importance of the council, and, like his Roman imperial predecessors, played a role in defining its agenda.[24] The canons that resulted were a compromise between royal and episcopal expectations. On the one hand, the church's right of asylum was confirmed,[25] as was the authority of bishops over ecclesiastical property.[26] On the other hand, the council acknowledged the king's right to be consulted with regard to the ordination of clerics,[27] and permitted the church's ownership of its landed assets to be challenged in court.[28] The conciliar participants also agreed upon the proper use of revenues earned from those gifts and lands donated by Clovis to the church, and forbade lower clerics from receiving benefices from the king without

[23] See, for example, the frequent prohibitions on Christians dining with Jews in Late Antiquity: e.g., Elvira (306), c. 50; Laodicea (Date Unknown), c. 38; Vannes (465), c. 12; Agde (506), c. 40; Épaone (517), c.15; Orléans III (538), c. 14 (13); Mâcon (581/3), c. 15. Even these canons, however, developed over time. Looking just at the Gallic synods, the Council of Vannes, which forbade clerics from dining with Jews, made no explicit mention of Christian laymen nor threatened any specific penalties. The Council of Agde (506) did include lay Christians in its proscription, but still did not recommend specific punishments. This development came a few years later at the Council of Épaone (517), which laid out the consequences of ignoring this decree: "Anyone defiled by a banquet with Jews should not eat bread with any cleric of ours." However, excommunication was established as the penalty for dining with Jews a short time later by the Frankish council of Orléans (538), which failed to differentiate between clerics and laymen. It would be the Council of Mâcon (581/3) that would clarify this issue by stating that clergy and laity alike would face excommunication if they dined with Jews.

[24] The bishops at Orléans acknowledge as much in their letter to the king. For the historiographical tradition regarding Clovis' personal involvement in the composition of the canons of Orléans (511), see Daly, "Clovis: How Barbaric, How Pagan," 659, note 131.

[25] Orléans (511), cc. 1–3.

[26] Ibid., cc. 5, 7, 14, 15, 17, and 23.

[27] Ibid., c. 4.

[28] Ibid., c. 6.

episcopal approval.[29] Although it probably would be an exaggeration to consider the canonical record of the Council of Orléans a "concordat" between the Gallic church and the Frankish crown, one of the meeting's primary functions was to delineate the prerogatives of both.[30]

The First Council of Orléans became the model for future Frankish councils, with the bishops relying upon canonical tradition to justify their own agendas, and the kings participating to the extent that they could be sure their interests were being taken into consideration. Naturally, the extent of conciliar subservience to the royal will varied by council and by king. In those cases when the king himself attended the meeting, he probably had a substantial impact on the composition of conciliar canons. But rarely can we say with certainty whether an individual canon was written by royal command. What we can do is identify to whose interests it responded. And, as the legislation of the Council of Orléans (511) demonstrates, the canonical *acta* of the Merovingian era addressed the interests of both the royal government and the ecclesiastical elite.

Conciliar Continuity: The Pippinid Councils

The degree of royal involvement in conciliar activities may have varied from council to council and from canon to canon, but the royal presence was an accepted reality after Alaric and Clovis demonstrated that kings, like emperors, could convoke synods. When the Pippinid mayors became the real source of political power in the eighth century, they, too, assumed this right. They were acting partly out of necessity: in taking responsibility for the convocation of church councils, Carloman and Pippin could establish and strengthen ties with powerful bishops, whose support was necessary for the consolidation of their rule. The mayors' usurpation of royal prerogative was not without precedent, however. A century earlier, powerful mayors, acting in the names of kings, had overseen the convocation of synods. The Neustro-Burgundian Council of Chalon-sur-Saône (647/53), for example, claimed to have met "on the summons and order" of the teenaged Clovis II, but may have been convoked, in reality, by the mayor Erchinoald (641–58) in the name of

---

29 Ibid., cc. 5 and 7.

30 Duchesne, *L'Eglise au VI siècle*, 502; Heuclin, "Le Concile d'Orléans de 511, un premier concordat," 435–50.

the king.[31] Similarly, around 677/9, the Neustrian mayor Ebroin, acting in the name of Theuderic III, convoked a council of bishops at the palace to convict Bishop Leudegar of Autun on the charge of regicide, thus justifying his assassination.[32] Mayor Pippin II, according to the *Annales Mettenses Priores*, assembled bishops around 689 to discuss the well-being of churches, orphans, and widows.[33] We read also in the *Vita Eusthasii* of attempts by Mayor Warnacharius (613–626/7) to convince Chlothar II to hold a synod ca. 626/7 in opposition to Abbot Euthasius of Luxeuil.[34] Warnacharius died, however, before the council convened. Carloman and Pippin III were not in uncharted territory when they promoted a new series of councils in the middle eighth century.

Nevertheless, in the examples already noted—with the possible exception of Pippin II's council—the mayors acted in the names of the Merovingian kings.[35] Although there was a Merovingian on the throne from 743 to 751, Childeric III, this king is mentioned only once in the conciliar acts of the period. In the preface to the Capitulary of Soissons (744), the regnal year of the synod is recorded as "in anno secundo Childerici regis Francorum."[36] Nevertheless, Pippin credits himself, not Childeric, with the council's convocation.[37] Pippin and Carloman's status as "duces et principes," combined with their personal *auctoritas*, was sufficient to allow them to convoke synods personally without

---

[31] Chalon (647/53), Preface. On Erchinoald, see Horst Ebling, *Prosopographie der Amtsträger des Merowingerreiches: Von Chlothar II (613) bis Karl Martell (741)* (Munich: Fink, 1974), 137–8. On his convocation of the Council of Chalon, see Pontal, *Histoire des conciles mérovingiens*, 217. In the subscriptions to a diploma of Clovis II from 653, which was composed at a council held in Paris, the name of the Burgundian mayor Radobert is present (*Die Urkunden der Merowinger*, no. 85). It is possible that he dominated the council in Clovis' name. On Radobert, see Ebling, *Prosopographie der Amtsträger des Merowingerreiches*, 202–3.

[32] *Passiones Leudegarii Episcopi et Martyris Augustodunensis*, chs. I.33 and II.16–7. Mordek, "Bischofsabsetzung in spätmerowingischer Zeit," 31–53, suggests that this council is identical with that held at Mâlay-le-Roi (677).

[33] *Annales Mettenses Priores*, entry for 692. On the dating of this council, see editor's note, page 13, no. 8.

[34] Jonas of Bobbio *Vitae Columbani Abbatis Discipulorumque Eius Libri Duo Auctore Iona*, ch. II.9. On Warnacharius, see Ebling, *Prosopographie der Amtsträger des Merowingerreiches*, 235–8.

[35] Although the *Annales Mettenses Priores* does not say so, Pippin's hesitancy to rule without a Merovingian figurehead increases the probability that he did, in fact, convoke his synod under the name of Theuderic III. On Pippin's reign, see Fouracre, *The Age of Charles Martel*, 38–56.

[36] Council of Soissons (744), Preface.

[37] Ibid.: "Nos...apud Suessionis civitas synodum vel concilio facere decrevimus: quod ita in Dei nomine et fecimus."

royal approval.[38] So far as we can ascertain, the Frankish bishops did not dispute their claim. Boniface certainly did not, nor did his papal correspondents. Of course, despite the claims of King Sigibert III (or perhaps his mayor Grimoald), royal approval was never an absolute requirement for the convocation of synods in Merovingian Francia. Episcopal, specifically metropolitan, authority was sufficient to assemble a council greater than the diocesan level, and the two clerical guiding lights of the Pippinid synods, Boniface and Chrodegang of Metz, who were both invested with the pallium by the papacy, possessed it.[39] There was nothing heterodox, therefore, about the Pippinids' convocation of synods. Moreover, their quiet dismissal of the royal prerogative to approve of conciliar meetings was made possible by innovations introduced by their mayoral antecedents in the preceding century.

Nevertheless, the form that the Pippinids' councils took has also been interpreted as a radical departure from the past, as most of these gatherings were attended by both clerics and laymen. This has fueled much debate about whether a given meeting should be considered an ecclesiastical council with lay attendance or a royal assembly with clerical attendance.[40] This confusion is due, in part, to terminological inconsistency or imprecision on the part of contemporary writers, who used the words *synodus, placitum, concilia,* and *conventus* interchangeably. Therefore, some historians have tried to distinguish Carolingian synods from royal assemblies by their respective attendances, topics of discussion, and methods of disseminating decisions.[41] However, such distinctions ignore the fact that much of the confusion is the result of the merger of lay and ecclesiastical institutions during this period. Historians, in other words, are emphasizing a division that the early Carolingians were trying to eliminate.[42]

---

[38] If the *Vitae Gallii* can be believed, the Alamannian duke Gunzo convoked a synod in Constance ca. 635/40 without royal approval: Wettinus, *Vita Galli Confessoris*, chs. 24–5; Walahfrid Strabo, *Vita Galli Confessoris*, I.24–5.

[39] Boniface received his pallium from Pope Gregory II in 732; Chrodegang received his from Stephen III upon Boniface's death (754/5).

[40] See, for example, the comment of Ganshof, "The Church and the Royal Power in the Frankish Monarchy under Pippin III and Charlemagne," 207: "For all that it synchronized with a *diet*, the Council of Frankfurt of 794 was of such consequence that it can rank as an autonomous *council*." (Emphasis mine.)

[41] Hartmann, "Zu einigen Problemen der karolingischen Konzilsgeschichte," 13–4. These, as Hartmann observes, are the approaches of Hinschius, Barion, and De Clercq, respectively.

[42] De Jong, "Charlemagne's Church," 109–10.

The umbrella term *concilia mixta* is often used to describe the Pippinid councils as a group, because it acknowledges that dynasty's efforts to unite secular and ecclesiastical governance under its own authority. In these conglomerate meetings, the ecclesiastical attendees met either separately or alongside the secular magnates as part of the general assembly of the *regnum*.[43] The agenda of the assembly was set by the mayor or king, who legislated *cum consensu* of the participating *proceres* and *episcopi*, and who issued the meeting's decisions in the form of a capitulary.[44] The Frankish royal assembly was already a venerable institution by the middle eighth century, and its origins may stretch as far back as the fifth.[45] Were there precedents, therefore, for the subsuming of traditional synodal functions by this secular institution prior to the Pippinids' usurpation of power?

Before addressing this question, let us examine the evidence for the prevalence of the *concilia mixta* in the early Carolingian era. In some cases, our sources are explicit about the nature of meetings: according to the *Annales Mettenses Priores*, in 748, Pippin III "held his *placitum* in the *villa* called Düren, in which he ordered a *synodus* to gather."[46] Similarly, the same *Annales* tell us that Pippin, as king, held a *placitum* in the year 757, in the *villa publica* of Compiègne, which dealt with *causae publicae*.[47] According to Chrodegang's privilege for the monastery of Gorze (757), this *placitum* included a *synodus* attended by at least twenty-one bishops.[48]

In other cases, the nature of the meeting is more obscure. The capitulary containing the decisions of the first Pippinid council, the Council of Germania, which met in late April 742, begins with this statement: "In the name of our Lord Jesus Christ, I, Carloman, *dux* and *princeps* of the Franks…with the *consilium* of the servants of God and my

[43] Ganshof, *Recherches sur les Capitulaires*, 25; François Ganshof, *Frankish Institutions Under Charlemagne*, trans. Bryce and Mary Lyon (Providence: Brown University Press, 1968), 22–3; Janet Nelson, *Charles the Bald* (London: Longman, 1992), 46. Hincmar of Rheims *De Ordine Palatii*, ch. 7, describes the separate meetings of laymen and clerics.

[44] Ganshof, *Frankish Institutions Under Charlemagne*, 22–3.

[45] Fouracre, *The Age of Charles Martel*, 29. On Gregory of Tours' famous story of the vase and the *Campus Martius* (*Decem Libri Historiarum* II.27), see Bernard S. Bachrach, "Was the Marchfield Part of the Frankish Constitution?" *Medieval Studies* 36 (1974): 178–85.

[46] *Annales Mettenses Priores*, entry for 748.

[47] *Ibid.*, entry for 757. C.f. *Annales Regni Francorum*, entry for 757.

[48] The text of the privilege is found in Werminghoff, ed., *Concilia aevi Karolini*, 59–63.

optimates, have congregated for fear of Christ the *episcopi* of my realm with their *presbyteri* in a *concilium* and *synodus*."[49] Carloman then goes on to list the names of the episcopal attendees, with no mention of any of the *optimates*. However, in the first article, he writes, "With the *consilium* of my *sacerdotes* and *optimates*, I have ordained bishops in the *civitates*."[50] Did this advice come during the course of the synod itself, or at a preceding assembly? The similarity of the phrasing in the opening statement and the first article suggests that the advice was given at the same time that Carloman was advised to convoke his ecclesiastical council. Thus, although it appears that the *synodus* itself was attended by only prelates, it probably met in relation to the larger spring assembly.[51] The dating and publication of the canons' documentation seem to support this conclusion.

The same holds true for the next two Pippinid synods, the Councils of Les Estinnes (743) and Soissons (744). Carloman's *synodalis conventus* of 743, which issued its decisions in the form of a capitulary, was attended by *sacerdotes, comites*, and *praefecti* (i.e., military commanders).[52] The date of this council, the *Kalends* of March, increases the probability that it took place in conjunction with a royal assembly.[53] Pippin's first "synodum vel concilio," held in the *civitas* of Soissons in 744, also assembled in early March.[54] In his capitulary, Pippin refers separately to the *consensus* of his bishops and the *consilium* of his *comites* and *optimates*. This may be taken as evidence of separate sessions in a larger assembly.[55]

---

[49] Germany (742), Preface.

[50] Ibid., c. 1.

[51] This conclusion is reached also by Depreux, "L'expression statutum est a domno rege et sancta synodo annonçant certains dispositions du Capitulaire Francfort (794)," 87–8; Geary, *Before France and Germany*, 216–7.

[52] Les Estinnes (743), c. 1.

[53] De Clercq, *La législation religieuse franque de Clovis à Charlemagne*, 120; Hartmann, *Die Synoden der Karolingerzeit*, 54.

[54] Soissons (744), Preface. In 755, the holding of two yearly synods in the fall and the spring would be made official policy. Ver (755), c. 4: "Synods should be held twice a year: the first in the first month, that is the *Kalends* of March, at a location where the *domnus rex* orders, in his presence. The second synod should be held on the *Kalends* of October, either at Soissons or at the location where the bishops met on the *Kalends* of March; and the bishops should congregate there, those installed in the place of metropolitans, and those bishops and abbots and presbyters whom the metropolitans order to come with them should meet there in this second synod."

[55] The council's relation to an assembly is affirmed by De Clercq, *La législation religieuse franque de Clovis à Charlemagne*, 122; and Roger Collins, "Pippin III as Mayor

As for the Councils of Ver (755), Verberie (756), Attigny (762), and Gentilly (767), all met at royal *villae*, all appear to have been convoked on royal authority, and Ver and Verberie issued their decisions in the form of capitularies.[56] However, the presence of secular officials at all of these gatherings is not certain.[57] The subscriptions for the Council of Attigny—devoid of the names of lay officials, and not attached to any capitulary—may be evidence that the religious attendees sat separately, at least for part of the *placitum*.[58] Additionally, the Council of Gentilly, despite the possible presence of lay attendees, had a primarily theological agenda, i.e., the debate between the Byzantines and the Western church about the nature of the Trinity and the reverence of holy images.[59] A religious agenda, particularly one with diplomatic implications, does not preclude the possibility that the council took place in relation to Pippin's general assembly, but there is no compelling evidence to this effect. Thus, although the *concilia mixta* model seems to have been a predominant one during the Pippinid period, we cannot necessarily say that all ecclesiastical meetings took this precise form. Nevertheless, the fact that independent councils become increasingly difficult to identify in the middle eighth century is strong evidence of the Pippinids' efforts to absorb their functions into secular governing institutions.

Still, the early Carolingians' use of blended institutions seems less an innovation than a preference. Mixed gatherings of clerics and laymen were not unheard of in the Merovingian era, with the Council of Paris

of the Palace: The Evidence," in *Der Dynastiewechsel von 751*, ed. Matthias Becher and Jorg Jarnut (Münster: Scriptorium, 2004), 90–1.

[56] Claussen, *The Reform of the Frankish Church*, 47, assumes that "at most of the councils with which he [Chrodegang] is associated [i.e., Düren, Ver, Verberie, Compiègne, and Attigny], the bishops met in conjunction with a noble *placitum*." De Clercq, *La législation religieuse franque de Clovis à Charlemagne*, 133 and 143, assumes the same regarding the Councils of Ver and Attigny. The canonical record of Attigny does not explicitly credit Pippin with convoking the council, but the meeting's location suggests that this was the case.

[57] Hartmann, *Die Synoden der Karolingerzeit*, 69 and 82, argues that their presence was likely at the Council of Ver, and points to a reference in the third version of the *Vita Austremonii* (AASS, Nov. 1.1; from a twelfth-century manuscript) to *praesules clarissimi et comites* as evidence for their presence at Gentilly.

[58] The absence of lay signatures is not surprising, because the list reflects the establishment of a clerical *Totenbund*, which is, in the words of Wallace-Hadrill, *The Frankish Church*, 172, "a society of men bound to recite so many masses and psalms for the death of any one of them." On the Attigny *Totenbund*, see also Karl Schmid and Otto Oexle, "Voraussetzungen und Wirking des Gebetsbundes von Attigny," *Francia* 2 (1974): 71–122; Claussen, *The Reform of the Frankish Church*, 55–7.

[59] *Annales Regni Francorum/Revised Annales*, entry for 767; *Annales Mettenses Priores*, entry for 767; Ado of Vienne, *Chronica*, entry for 767.

(614), convoked by Chlothar II, perhaps the best-known example.[60] Following his unification of the Frankish kingdoms, Chlothar assembled twelve metropolitans, sixty suffragan bishops, and one abbot in the Basilica of St. Peter. The attendees came from all corners of Gaul. The council finished its business on October 10, when it produced its written acts. Eight days later, Chlothar issued an *edictum,* which contained variations of fourteen of the Paris canons. In the final chapter of his *edictum,* Chlothar ordered the observance of those decisions "which we drew up with our *pontifices,* our *optimates,* and our *fideles nostri* in a *synodalis concilium,*" thus revealing the mixed nature of the event.[61] However, the Paris assembly may not have been Chlothar's only use of combined assemblages of prelates and nobles. Two years later, he assembled the Burgundian *farones* and *pontifices* together at his *villa* at Bonneuil to hear their *petitiones.*[62] According to Fredegar, he agreed to all their requests, presumably to ensure the loyalty of these potentates to his newly established rule in Burgundy. Finally, the Council of Clichy (626/7), which Chlothar convoked near the end of his life, may have met in conjunction with a *conventus* of *nobilites.* According to Fredegar, in his forty-fourth regnal year (627), Chlothar met at Clichy "with all of the *episcopi* and *proceres* of his kingdom from both Neustria and Burgundy, for the good of the king and for the health of the country."[63] The similarities in date, geography (Chlothar's assembly the previous year had met at Troyes), and attendance make it likely that these two meetings are one and the same.[64]

For Chlothar, these mixed assemblies served as effective reminders of his sovereign *auctoritas* over the entirety of the Frankish polity, religious and secular spheres alike—an important lesson for his Carolingian successors.[65] Subsequent seventh-century kings also consulted their

---

[60] Heinzelmann, *Gregory of Tours: History and Society in the Sixth Century*, 185, n. 100, has suggested that Lyons (581) was an earlier *concilium mixtum*, but there is no strong evidence to support this conjecture.

[61] Chlothar II *Edictum*, in *Capitularia Regum Francorum*, no. 24.

[62] Fredegar *Chronica* IV.44. Hefele and Leclercq, *Histoire des conciles d'après les documents originaux*, III.1.254–6, have suggested that a fragmentary canonical record composed sometime after 614 was published following this assembly. C.f. Pontal, *Histoire des conciles mérovingiens*, 211–2.

[63] Fredegar *Chronica* IV.55.

[64] Ibid., IV.54. The council's acts state that the bishops congregated in September of Chlothar's thirty-third regnal year, but this might still refer to the year 627, depending on what month Chlothar's regnal year began. See Gaudemet and Basdevant-Gaudemet, eds., *Les canons des conciles mérovingiens*, 526, note 2.

[65] Fouracre, *The Age of Charles Martel*, 25.

prelates and magnates collectively. A diploma of Clovis II, issued in 654, states that the king confirmed the granting of privileges to St. Denis "with the council of our bishops, illustrious men, and nobles."[66] Similarly, a diploma of King Theuderic III, produced after a council held at the royal *villa* of Mâlay-le-Roi (677), states that the king ordered the bishops of Neustria and Burgundy to meet "for the state of the church and to encourage peace."[67] Further along in the diploma, however, Theuderic acknowledges that he reached his decision regarding the improper appointment of Bishop Chramlinus of Embrun "with the council of our subscribing bishops and nobles." It is not clear from the context if these *proceres* participated in the synod, or if the king consulted them in a separate meeting. In general, whether the later Merovingians regularly combined their annual assemblies with ecclesiastical synods (as *concilia mixta* proper), or whether they simply encouraged or required these synods to assemble in the presence of the king and his officials, is less important than the precedent they set in blending religious and secular governance.[68] Those who look abroad to Anglo-Saxon England for models for the early Carolingian councils are setting their sights too far afield.[69]

Directly related to the Pippinids' preference for mixed meetings was their favored use of the capitulary as the principal instrument of recording and transmitting conciliar decisions. This was a critical shift,

---

66 *Die Urkunden der Merowinger*, no. 85.

67 *Ibid.*, no. 122.

68 Ewig, "Beobachtungen zu den Bischofslisten der merowingischen Konzilien und Bischofsprivilegien," 451, has observed with regard to two *placita* from 693 and 697 (*Die Urkunden der Merowinger*, nos. 141 and 149), that their subscription lists reveal a transition from the purely ecclesiastical synods of the early Merovingian period to the Carolingian mixed assemblies.

69 Voigt, *Staat und Kirche*, 312 ff., for example, has suggested that the prevailing synodal model of the Pippinids, in which laymen participated, originated in Anglo-Saxon England and was carried over to the Continent by Boniface. C.f. Hartmann, "Laien auf Synoden der Karolingerzeit," 257–8. Theodor Schieffer, *Winfrid-Bonifatius und die christliche Grundlegung Europas* (Freiburg: Verlag Herder-Freiburg, 1954), 213, likewise has credited the Anglo-Saxons with introducing the practice of publishing conciliar decisions in capitularies. Against this theory, see Reuter, "Kirchenreform und Kirchenpolitik im Zeitalter Karl Martells," 49–50, note 69. Wilhelm Levison, *England and the Continent in the Eighth Century* (Oxford: Clarendon Press, 1946), 70–93, also overstates Anglo-Saxon influence on the reform councils of the 740s and 750s, although an English influence on the use of *anno domini* dating for capitularies is likely (pp. 83–4). Additionally, a number of the newly consecrated bishops who attended the Council of Germania (742), e.g., Burchard of Würzburg, Witta of Büraburg, and Willibald of Erfurt, were Anglo-Saxons.

but not an unprecedented one. As we have seen, the Frankish bishops' understanding of canonical *auctoritas* had begun to change back in the seventh century, and made possible their later acceptance of the *princeps* as the primary source of conciliar authority. The Pippinids thus were less innovators than shrewd manipulators of preexisting institutions and trends. They took the convention of royal involvement in synodal life to its logical conclusion by subsuming conciliar legislation into their own decrees. In doing so, they made it unnecessary for kings to "adopt" canons and rewrite them to suit their interests, because the canons themselves were now articulated in the royal voice.

Reform, Revolution, or Renewal?

Although the councils of the middle eighth century differed in some way from those that preceded them, their transformation was neither unprecedented nor sudden. Those who see a significant chronological division between Merovingian and Carolingian conciliar practices point to the letter of Boniface to Pope Zacharias of 742, in which the Anglo-Saxon missionary complained of the Franks' unwillingness to hold councils. According to Boniface, it had been eighty years since one had been convoked. Far too many scholars have been willing to take the great missionary at his word.[70] To begin with, Boniface, or his source, was mistaken by at least forty years. According to the *Gesta Episcoporum Autissiodorensium*, a council was held in Auxerre the year of Bishop Treticius' ordination, which occurred sometime between 692 and 696.[71] Additional councils are reported as well in the first half of the eighth century, although most of these admittedly are of dubious authenticity or questionable conciliar status.[72] Nevertheless, it is clear that ecclesiastical and theological discussions went on during these years, concerning, among other issues, clerical marriage and Easter observance, although we cannot be certain that they occurred in a conciliar context.[73]

---

[70] E.g., Wallace-Hadrill, *The Frankish Church*, 107; Pontal, *Histoire des conciles mérovingiens*, 15, 260; James, *The Origins of France*, 198; Fouracre and Gerberding, *Late Merovingian France*, 49; Fouracre, *The Age of Charles Martel*, 133; Rosamond McKitterick, *The Frankish Kingdoms under the Carolingians* (London: Longman, 1983), 55.

[71] *Gesta Episcoporum Autissiodorensium*, ch. 24.

[72] I.e., Liege (708/56), Tongres (708/56), Rouen (711/15), Utrecht (719), Strasbourg (728), Danube Valley/Augsburg (732/40). On these councils, see appendix B.

[73] Reuter, "Kirchenreform und Kirchenpolitik," 50.

The absence of uncontroversial conciliar references in this period, however, by no means precludes their existence. The first half of the eighth century, compared with the previous 150 years, is poorly served in the quality of contemporary sources that survive. There is certainly nothing with the detail and depth of, for example, Gregory of Tours' corpus of writings, which offers a wealth of information on otherwise-unknown councils. The absence of conciliar canons from this period certainly does not negate the existence of episcopal meetings. Moreover, despite Boniface's assertions to the contrary, we know that the Frankish episcopate of the early eighth century devoted considerable energy to preserving canonical standards of behavior through the composition and copying of canonical collections.[74] There is no reason to suppose that this project did not include the convocation of church councils, even if only on the provincial or diocesan level.

Did Boniface, then, merely concoct this story to justify his program of ecclesiastical reform to the pope? This seems unlikely, because Zacharias' predecessors had actively encouraged Boniface's conciliar program in Germania.[75] That Boniface was ignorant of current conditions in the Frankish church is similarly unlikely. His desire to bring ecclesiastical order to Eastern Francia meant that he had to be aware of current conditions within the church, and cultivate contacts with the mayoral courts that could be additional sources of information. As early as 723, Charles Martel sent a letter to the episcopal and secular *nobilites* of his realm to inform them that Boniface was under his protection.[76] And this relationship with the Pippinids and their circle of supporters only grew stronger after Charles' death, and the succession of his sons Pippin and Carloman. Boniface even tried strengthening his position by also making friendly gestures toward their half brother Grifo (fl. 726–53).[77] Thus, although he was an outsider by origin and temperament, Boniface did enjoy relations with the highest levels of the mayoral government.

There was, however, a limit to his Frankish experience. Boniface had spent his continental career up to this point in Germania. This was the part of the Frankish kingdom with which he was the most familiar, and

[74] Mordek, "Kanonistische Activität in Gallien in der Ersten Hälfte des 8. Jahrunderts," 19–25.

[75] Boniface *S. Bonifatii et Lulli Epistolae*, nos. 44–5.

[76] Ibid., no. 22.

[77] Ibid., no. 48. On Boniface's gestures toward Grifo, see Fouracre, *The Age of Charles Martel*, 167.

over which his episcopal influence officially extended.[78] Moreover, it was primarily in this region that he was interested in reforming the ecclesiastical infrastructure. The synod to which he refers in his letter to Zacharias was intended to represent only that part of the kingdom under Carloman's authority ("in parte regni Francorum quae in sua est potestate"), and the attendance and canons of the council clearly reflect this plan. The bishops who gathered on Carloman's orders included, besides Boniface himself, Burchard of Würzburg, Reginfred of Cologne, Witta of Büraburg, Willibald of Erfurt, Heddo of Strasbourg, and Dadanus of Utrecht (or Speyer).[79] The canons they composed, in turn, represented an effort to bring order and structure to the 'German' church.[80] In Carloman's name, bishoprics were established in the *civitates* under the oversight of Boniface, and the regular meeting of synods was instituted. The authority of the newly appointed bishops was confirmed, as were the standards for proper clerical behavior. Paganism was condemned, and the *episcopi* and *comites* were reminded of their duty to stamp out its vestiges.

Political geography thus largely dictated the legislative program of Carloman's first council. We ought to interpret Boniface's comments as a critique not of the Frankish church in its entirety, but specifically of its eastern branch, which was not nearly as entrenched as its Gallic counterpart. It is true certainly that the eastern part of the Frankish kingdom had never experienced as strong a conciliar tradition as Gaul. Indeed, most of the councils reported to have taken place east of the Rhine are of questionable authenticity, such as the Alamannian Council of Constance (ca. 635/40). Although the deficiency of contemporary evidence makes it impossible to know for certain what Boniface was implying in his criticisms of the Frankish church, the context in which he made them speaks strongly for his focus on Germania.[81]

In the same letter, however, Boniface lays another charge against the Frankish church: it has not elected an *archiepiscopus* for as long as it had failed to hold a council. We have seen how the metropolitan system

[78] Eugen Ewig, "Saint Chrodegang et la reforme de l'Eglise franque," in *Spätantikes und fränkisches Gallien*, ed. Hartmut Atsma (Munich: Artemis Verlag, 1979), II.239–40.

[79] Germany (742), Preface. I follow the identifications of Hartmann, *Die Synoden der Karolingerzeit im Frankenreich*, 51.

[80] Boniface *S. Bonifatii et Lulli Epistolae* no. 50.

[81] Eugen Ewig, "Milo et Eiusmodi Similes," in *Spätantikes und fränkisches Gallien*, Hartmut Atsma (Munich: Artemis Verlag, 1979), II.210, reaches the same conclusion.

was fundamental for the convocation of Merovingian-era synods. Had this system not survived the troubles of the early eighth century? Did Charles Martel, in particular, cause a severe disruption in provincial governance? Charles' reputation, once dreadfully poor, has only very recently begun to be redeemed. Previously caricatured as a scourge of bishops and a secularizer of church property, Charles now appears more a pursuer of realpolitik. He certainly was no innovator in his granting of church lands and offices as rewards for loyalty and service.[82] But even if Charles as an individual has been judged unfairly by history, his career may still have brought disorder to the church as much as to the political sphere. Additionally, until recently, most historians agreed that the secularization of church property coincided with a secularization of the church itself. Timothy Reuter has rightly questioned this assumption, noting that no dioceses, so far as we can tell, disappeared as the result of patrimonial secularization, and that there is no evidence that the church as a unified institution was unable to perform its normal sacral and charitable functions in this period.[83]

But contemporary and near-contemporary sources offer conflicting accounts of the fate of the metropolitan provinces during Charles' career. A privilege-charter granted by Bishop Ibbo of Tours to the monastery of St. Martin around 720 refers explicitly to "the metropolitans of Belgica and Aquitaine," although it has been suggested that the title "metropolitan," as used here, was merely a "vague souvenir of a ruined institution."[84] On the other hand, some near-contemporary chronicles and the lives of saints offer anecdotal evidence of possible disruption in metropolitan governance. Ado of Vienne, for example, recalls in his late-ninth-century chronicle that Vienne and Lyons, both metropolitan sees, were "devastated and laid to waste" by Charles Martel's army in the 730s, and were forced to go without bishops for several years ("aliquot annis").[85] The metropolitan bishop Rigobert of

---

[82] Hans-Werner Goetz, "Karl Martel und die Heiligen: Kirchenpolitik und Maiordomat im Spiegel der spätmerowingischen Hagiographie," in *Karl Martell in seiner Zeit*, ed. Jörg Jarnut, Ulrich Nonn, and Michael Richter (Sigmaringen: Jan Thorbecke Verlag, 1994), 103.

[83] Reuter, "Kirchenreform und Kirchenpolitik," 46–7.

[84] Pardessus, ed., *Diplomata, Chartae, Epistolae*, no. 512. Lesne, *La hiérarchie épiscopale*, 23–4.

[85] Ado of Vienne *Sancti Adonis Chronicon*, col. 122. Fouracre, *The Age of Charles Martel*, 92–3, suggests that Ado's account may have been influenced by the then-stereotypical view of Charles Martel as the scourge of church property. Nevertheless, bishop lists do not record another bishop in Vienne until the 760s. Unfortunately, we

Rheims, too, found himself on the wrong side of Charles, and was summarily exiled and replaced in his seat by the infamous Milo of Trier.[86] Non-metropolitan dioceses are also said to have suffered. The ninth-century *Gesta Episcoporum Verdunensium*, for example, reports that the episcopal throne of Verdun was vacant for "many days" in the late 720s or early 730s.[87] Additionally, an eighth-century *vita* records that Bishop Eucherius of Orléans was dispossessed and exiled by Charles around 732, and the ninth-century *Gesta Episcoporum Autissiodorensium* reports Charles' deposition of Bishop Hainmar around 737.[88] Although such anecdotes reveal how the early eighth century was a traumatic time for a number of individual prelates, there was nothing necessarily new about the tendency of politics, war, and factionalism to threaten personal security and status. Anecdotes are also no proof that this trauma was universal or grave enough to necessitate the rebuilding of a church hierarchy from scratch.

Do the fragmentary episcopal lists, as edited by Louis Duchesne, offer any more consistent a picture?[89] For the first half of the eighth century, there are numerous gaps in these lists, along with the names of dozens of otherwise unknown and unverifiable prelates. In order to sort through this haphazard set of data of uneven reliability, I have categorized the early-eighth-century information contained in the *fastes episcopaux* into four groups: (1) no obvious gaps in episcopal succession, (2) documented gaps in episcopal succession, (3) deposition and replacement of bishops, and (4) absences of named bishops, along with possible but otherwise undocumented gaps.

---

do not know the dates of Bishop Madalbertus of Lyons' term in office, which seem to have been sometime during the reign of Charles Martel or his sons: Duchesne, *Fastes épiscopaux de l'ancienne Gaule*, II.171. There is a reference, however, to Madalbertus' predecessor, Foaldus (fl. early eighth century), in the *Vita Boniti Episcopi Arverni*, MGH SRM VI, ed. Bruno Krusch (Hanover: Hahn, 1913), ch. 35.

[86] *Vita Rigoberti*, MGH SRM VII, ed. Wilhelm Levison (Hanover: Hahn, 1920), chs. 9–12. On Milo, see Ewig, "Milo et Eiusmodi Similes," II.189–99.

[87] *Gesta Episcoporum Virdunensium*, MGH SS IV, ed. George Pertz (Hanover: Hahn, 1841), ch. 12.

[88] *Vita Eucherii Episcopi Aurelianensis*, MGH SRM VII, ed. Wilhelm Levison (Hanover: Hahn, 1920), chs. 7–9; *Gesta Episcoporum Autissiodorensium*, ch. 27.

[89] Fouracre, *The Age of Charles Martel*, 136–7, suggests that the answer is no, and argues that the gaps in episcopal lists for this period are not strong evidence of breaks in episcopal succession, because they often simply reflect the ignorance of a later compiler. See also Jacques Dubois, "Les listes épiscopales témoins de l'organisation ecclésiastique et de la transmission des traditions," in *La christianisation des pays entre Loire et Rhin (IV–VII siècle)*, ed. Pierre Riché (Paris: Éditions du Cerf, 1993), 21.

Our knowledge of succession is largely determined by the survival of episcopal *fastes;* for those dioceses lacking formal episcopal lists, there is not enough information to say whether a break in succession occurred. For a period devoid of conciliar subscription lists, this problem becomes even more acute, because we lack our other major source for episcopal identification. This caveat aside, there are only 4 cases from the early eighth century, out of 113 dioceses, where it is possible to identify a documented gap in succession, and 4 additional instances in which a bishop is known to have been forced from office.[90] However, in the case of 77 dioceses, there are either no identifiable bishops for the first half of the eighth century or insufficient information to say whether a break in succession occurred. In contrast, 28 dioceses reveal no obvious gaps.[91] Those ecclesiastical provinces with the highest proportion of dioceses without documented gaps are Trier, Rheims, Sens, and Tours, the first 2 being under the control of Charles' loyal supporter Milo. Among the metropolitan dioceses, a little less than a quarter show documented gaps or depositions in the early eighth century, while approximately 35 percent reveal no signs of discontinuity in succession. For the plurality of metropolitan dioceses in this period, 41 percent, we cannot say whether their episcopal thrones sat vacant. In summary, the *fastes* evidence does not offer strong proof of discontinuity, but, in fact, suggests that there were many dioceses, metropolitan included, unaffected by the political and military tribulations of the early eighth century.

What, then, are we to make of the celebrated Carolingian *correctio* of the Frankish church? Presumably, if the descendants of Charles Martel, along with Boniface, made such an effort to reconstitute ecclesiastical order and discipline, these things must have fallen into severe decline. For example, we could interpret Boniface's attempts in the middle eighth century to establish archbishops in, among other sees, Rouen, Rheims, and Sens, as evidence of the need to rebuild a decimated metropolitan system.[92] In a letter to Boniface written in 744, Pope Zacharias

[90] I.e. Lyons, Vienne, Utrecht, and Verdun, and Auxerre, Orléans, Reims, and Mainz respectively. I have excluded the Septimanian dioceses from this tally, because they traditionally had been part of the Visigothic church, not the Frankish.

[91] I.e. Amiens, Angers, Arles, Beauvais, Bourges, Cambrai, Chalons, Clermont, Coutances, Laon, Le Mans, Limoges, Metz, Nantes, Nevers, Noyon, Paris, Poitiers, Rennes, Rouen, Sens, Strasbourg, Térouanne, Tongres/Liege/Maastricht, Toul, Tours, Trier, and Troyes.

[92] Boniface *S. Bonifatii et Lulli Epistolae*, nos. 57–8.

approved his legate's appointments of Grimo of Rouen, Abel of Rheims, and Hartbert of Sens to those metropolitan sees. Should we assume that the provincial organization of these three provinces had collapsed? There is no indication in the *fastes* that these three sees experienced substantial breaks (that is, a break for more than a year or two) in episcopal governance in the first half of the eighth century.[93] Indeed, Boniface's bête noire, Milo of Trier, was still holding office in Rheims when the future saint attempted to have him replaced with the Anglo-Saxon Abel.

There is a further problem with interpreting Boniface's new appointments as a sign of organizational disintegration: the archiepiscopal system that Boniface wished to establish in Francia was not identical to the metropolitan organization that had prevailed in the preceding centuries.[94] Archbishops, in Boniface's understanding, received their authority directly from the papacy, a relationship symbolized by the gift of the *pallium*. Although the Council of Soissons in March 744 agreed to establish the bishops of Rheims and Sens as *archiepiscopi,* many, it seems, were unhappy with the arrangement. Just a few months later, Boniface had informed the pope that only one *pallium* would be needed, and that was for Grimo of Rouen. It has been suggested that the Frankish bishops "vetoed" Boniface's plan because of their commitment to the "old metropolitical grouping."[95] The reluctance that the Frankish bishops felt about Boniface's episcopal reforms seems to have been shared by their *principes,* whose disinclination to establish and maintain archbishoprics Boniface was still complaining about to Pope Zacharias in 751.[96] In short, Boniface's reform program cannot be taken as evidence of the destruction of the traditional metropolitan system. Even during Charlemagne's reign, the Gallic dioceses designated as metropolitan sees were, for the most part, the same as those during the Merovingian era.[97]

---

[93] Duchesne, *Fastes épiscopaux de l'ancienne Gaule*, II.209, II.417–8, and III.85–6.

[94] Lesne, *La hiérarchie épiscopale*, 30–7; Levison, *England and the Continent in the Eighth Century*, 18–22; Wallace-Hadrill, *The Frankish Church*, 157; Fouracre, *The Age of Charles Martel*, 133.

[95] Wallace-Hadrill, *The Frankish Church*, 157. Wallace-Hadrill's conclusion seems to be supported by Ver (755), c. 2. On Boniface's failure, see also Lesne, *La hiérarchie épiscopale*, 50–2.

[96] Boniface *S. Bonifatii et Lulli Epistolae*, no. 86.

[97] Compare, for example, the Gallic dioceses listed by Einhard, *Vita Karoli Magni*, MGH SRG 25, ed. Oswald Holder-Egger (Hanover: Hahn, 1911), ch. 33, with the provinces enumerated in the *Notitia Galliarum*, MGH AA IX.1, ed. Theodore Mommsen

However, another possible hint of ecclesiastical disorder can be found in the second canon of the Council of Ver (755), which affirms the authority of those bishops appointed by King Pippin "in the place of the metropolitans…while we repair (*emendare*) fully that which was constituted in accordance with the canons."[98] This canon has been interpreted as a stopgap measure on Pippin's part, with the bishops in question not being full metropolitans.[99] But other canons issued at the Council of Ver affirm the traditional metropolitan rights of those "quos modo vicem metropolitanorum constituimus," both in the determination of conciliar attendance and in the oversight of monastic discipline.[100] In other words, we cannot distinguish these new appointees from traditional metropolitans with respect to their authority.

As to the second part of Pippin's statement, what had the canons established that needed repair? Pippin appears to be referring to the ordination of metropolitan bishops. Although we cannot say whether existing Frankish canonical precedent was rigorously enforced in the early eighth century or even before that time, clear rules delineated how this process was supposed to work. The Council of Orléans of 533 had decreed that an elected metropolitan had to be ordained amid the assembled body of his comprovincials, a command echoed by the Council of Orléans of 538, which added that the ordination should be carried out by another metropolitan.[101] It is possible, then, that the bishops Pippin refers to in the canons of the Council of Ver had not been ordained according to canonical (if not necessarily customary) procedure. This would explain the canons' unusual phrasing. There was nothing unusual about Pippin filling empty episcopal seats with his own candidates; Clovis I had done much the same thing in the final years of his reign in the early sixth century.[102] As for the possible implication that these newly appointed metropolitans were installed because of an earlier breakdown in episcopal governance, it seems more likely that Pippin, having decided not to support the total administrative

(Berlin: Weidmann, 1892), 552–612. Lesne, *La hiérarchie épiscopale*, 61–79, exaggerates the importance of the 'rediscovery' of canon law as the impetus for Charlemagne's efforts to organize the church.

[98] Ver (755), c. 2.

[99] Lesne, *La hiérarchie épiscopale*, 53–4.

[100] Ver (755), cc. 4–5.

[101] Orléans (533), c. 7; Orléans (538), c. 3.

[102] Heuclin, "Le Concile d'Orléans de 511," 439–40; Pontal, *Histoire des Conciles Mérovingiens*, 56.

overhaul proposed by Boniface, was attempting to integrate improperly ordained bishops of metropolitan sees into the now-reaffirmed traditional ecclesiastical hierarchy. It seems to have been Pippin's intention, however, that their successors should be ordained according to canonical standards. His legislation at Ver, therefore, seems to be addressing not so much the disruptions of his father's reign as the uncertainty caused by Boniface's proposed provincial reforms.

One final issue about provincial continuity needs to be addressed: the so-called *vocati episcope*, whose subscriptions appear in a handful of charters from the eighth century and in a few other sources.[103] Who were these men, and might those metropolitans Pippin refers to in his legislation of 755 be included among their number? Were they unconsecrated prelates, or perhaps choirbishops? We possess biographical information on only a few of these men. Bishops Agatheus and Amitto, for example, are explicitly titled *vocati episcopi* in the episcopal catalog of Nantes, and we know from a late-eighth-century saint's life that they combined the comital and episcopal offices of both Nantes and Rennes.[104] Hainmar of Auxerre is known from the *Gesta Episcoporum Autissiodorensium*, which identifies him as a *vocatus episcopus* (as well as a martyr and a saint) who wielded considerable secular power in Burgundy.[105] There are other men who are not explicitly labeled *vocati episcopi* in the sources, but who appear to share similar characteristics. Charivius of Le Mans, a *vir illuster*, is known from an immunity charter issued in 723, which refers to him having authority over the church of Le Mans.[106] Margarete Weidemann has identified Charivius as the son of Duke Rotgar, and an ally of Charles Martel. She has argued convincingly that he was not the bishop of Le Mans at all, but rather a political partisan of the actual bishop, Berarius, with whom he held dual control of the local church.[107] Finally, there are "Milo et eiusmodi similes," those infamous bishops Boniface found in Eastern Francia, and accused in his correspondence of being drunkards, hunters,

[103] For the first half of the century, see, e.g., Pardessus, ed., *Diplomata, Chartae, Epistolae*, nos. 543 and 596.

[104] Donatus, *Vita Ermenlandi*, MGH SRM V, ed. Wilhelm Levison (Hanover: Hahn, 1910), ch. 13.

[105] *Gesta Episcoporum Autissiodorensium*, ch. 27.

[106] Pardessus, ed., *Diplomata, Chartae, Epistolae*, no. 523.

[107] Margarete Weidemann, "Bischofsherrschaft und Königtum in Neustrien vom 7. bis zum 9. Jahrhundert am Beispiel des Bistums Le Mans," in *La Neustrie: Les pays au nord de la Loire de 650 à 850*, ed. Hartmut Atsma (Sigmaringen: Jan Thorbecke Verlag, 1989), 174–6.

warriors, and false bishops. Their dishonorable ranks included Milo of Trier (and Rheims) and Gewilib of Mainz.[108]

Recent scholars have challenged the traditional assumption that Milo and his ilk were not consecrated bishops, and also have noted that Boniface's accusations might have been inspired by personal disputes.[109] Thus, it seems that a number of the *vocati episcopi* were legitimate bishops, if not necessarily pious men ordained according to canonical standards. Furthermore, the expression *vocatus* appears to have been fairly malleable in this period. It was applied to men who held both ecclesiastical and secular office simultaneously, as well as to bishops and lower clerics as a self-descriptive statement of humility in both formularies and charters.[110]

It appears, then, that the Frankish church of the early-Pippinid era was not an institution teetering on the edge of destruction. Certainly, the reign of Charles Martel had witnessed disruptions in the administration of individual dioceses, and it is also true that it became more common in the eighth century for individual prelates to hold multiple sees and for laymen to possess bishoprics.[111] Additionally, thanks to Boniface, a new concept of superior archiepiscopal authority had been introduced to Francia, and new dioceses had been created in Germania, requiring a small degree of realignment in provincial organization.[112] Nevertheless, subsequent conciliar evidence does not support the idea of a complete breakdown in episcopal order in the

---

108 Boniface *S. Bonifatii et Lulli Epistolae*, nos. 50, 60, and 87.

109 For Milo, see Reuter, "Kirchenreform und Kirchenpolitik," 47; for Gewilib, see Wallace-Hadrill, *The Frankish Church*, 137. See also Fouracre, *The Age of Charles Martel*, 133–4.

110 See, e.g., *Formulae Bituricensis*, in *Formulae Merowingici et Karolini Aevi*, no. 19; *Formulae Senonenses Recentiores*, in *Formulae Merowingici et Karolini Aevi*, no. 10; *Formulae Salicae Merkelianae*, in *Formulae Merowingici et Karolini Aevi*, no. 55. See, on this issue, Johann Friedrich, "Die Vocati Episcopi Erchanfried und Otkar der Passauer und der Oadalhart episcopus der Freisinger Urkunden," *Sitzungsberichte der philosophisch-philologischen und historischen Classe* 1 (1882): 313–48.

111 Ewig, "Milo et Eiusmodi Similes," II.199–207; Heuclin, *Hommes de Dieu et fonctionnaires du roi*, 239; Fouracre, *The Age of Charles Martel*, 136. Of those bishops to possess multiple sees, besides Milo, the best known is Hugo, the bishop of Rouen, Bayeux, and Paris (as well as the abbot of St. Wandrille). On Hugo, see *Gesta Abbatum Fontanellensium*, ch. 4. It is worth noting that his dioceses lay in three different ecclesiastical provinces.

112 I accept the basic premise of Steffen Patzold, "Créer un grade ecclésiastique: Métropolitains et archevêques du royaume franc (VIIIe–IXe siècles)," Hiérarchie, ordre et mobilité dans l'Occident médiéval (400–1100) (conference, Auxerre, 2006), 1–26, that gradual change occurred in the Frankish provincial organization from the

first half of the eighth century. What is more, this evidence does show the Pippinids' willingness to allow the metropolitans to play a key role in conciliar business.

An additional problem with the notion of the Pippinid councils as the start of a new conciliar epoch is the fact that the canons attributed to Boniface's influence were not wholly original. Several scholars have noted the similarity between the early-Pippinid conciliar legislation and that of the preceding Merovingian era, and some have questioned whether we should consider Boniface's canons to be reforms at all.[113] Reuter, for example, observes that Boniface's concerns were not limited to his own place or time; they extended to numerous councils in the preceding centuries. Although Reuter underestimates the role that contemporary and local concerns played in the composition of the Pippinid canons, his basic point is sound: the matters with which the conciliar attendees of the middle eighth century concerned themselves were largely enduring problems inherited from the Merovingian period.

It has been observed about the German council of 742 that the only truly original elements of its canonical program were its harsh treatment of sinful clerics, and its mandate for the return of church property unjustly seized in the preceding decades.[114] However, the basic principles behind these canons were nothing new: clerical discipline and the protection of church resources were concerns that predated even Clovis' council at Orléans in 511. Similarly, at the Council of Les Estinnes (743), Carloman's introduction of the *precaria verbo regis* was an important innovation, but it was the result of a progression in legal thought that began in the Roman period. Carloman's efforts to find a way for both church and the royal government to benefit from the use of the same land also had more immediate roots in the attitudes of the Merovingians toward church property. The remainder of the council's canons show even less originality, most being restatements of previous conciliar legislation that addressed enduring problems for the church, such as incest and the ownership of Christian slaves

---

740s through the reign of Charlemagne. But I do not agree with his assessment that this organization required restructuring because of its decimation in the first half of the eighth century.

[113] Reuter, "Kirchenreform und Kirchenpolitik," 37; Hartmann, *Die Synoden der Karolingerzeit im Frankenreich*, 52–3; Hen, *Culture and Religion in Merovingian Gaul A.D. 481–751*, 201–3; Le Roy, "Les conciles gaulois et le Décret de Gratien," 569; Nelson, "The Merovingian Church in Carolingian Perspective," 243–4.

[114] Hartmann, *Die Synoden der Karolingerzeit im Frankenreich*, 53 (re cc. 1 and 6).

by non-Christians.[115] Similarly, the canons issued at the Council of Soissons under Pippin III the following year proceed logically from the program established by the two prior councils orchestrated by Carloman.[116]

That Carloman's and Pippin's initial forays into legislating by conciliar canons were conservative is not surprising. And, over time, the originality of their decrees did increase. This, however, did not negate a continued reliance on previously articulated standards and precedents. The attendees congregated at the Council of Ver in 755 had with them a canonical collection, which they drew upon for the formulation of several of their pronouncements, "adapting older norms to contemporary usages" in the same fashion as their Merovingian-era predecessors.[117] Additionally, the mass of rulings on marriage and incest found in the capitularies of Verberie (756) and Compiègne (757) had a lengthy history behind them, and have been interpreted by some as an attempt to make secular policy conform to pre-established religious standards.[118]

So, what then of the Carolingian *correctio*? Reuter argues that we risk anachronism if we assign to the eighth century the concept of church reform, which implies, in his words, "an institutionally-anchored clerical hierarchy under papal leadership which is brought by juridical-institutional measures once again into a normative state." But papal connections aside, Reuter devalues the structural complexity and vigor of the Frankish church.[119] Additionally, Carolingian attention to canonical tradition encouraged broad agreement concerning the sorts of standards that needed to be imposed (or reimposed).[120] To see the Carolingian governance of the church through the lens of reform does not preclude the recognition of antecedents for their efforts. Indeed,

[115] Les Estinnes (743), c. 3. The council also reaffirmed Charles Martel's monetary fine for the practice of pagan rituals (c. 4).

[116] Hefele and Leclercq, *Histoire des conciles d'après les documents originaux*, III.2.859.

[117] Claussen, *The Reform of the Frankish Church*, 50. See also Hartmann, *Die Synoden der Karolingerzeit im Frankenreich*, 73.

[118] Hartmann, *Die Synoden der Karolingerzeit im Frankenreich*, 73; Jo-Ann McNamara and Suzanne F. Wemple, "Marriage and Divorce in the Frankish Kingdom," in *Women in Medieval Society*, ed. Susan Mosher Stuard (Philadelphia: University of Pennsylvania Press, 1976), 101–2; Suzanne F. Wemple, *Women in Frankish Society* (Philadelphia: University of Pennsylvania Press, 1981), 76–8; Jean Fleury, *Recherches historiques sur les empêchements de parenté dans le mariage canonique* (Paris: Recueil Sirey, 1933), 183–96.

[119] Reuter, "Kirchenreform und Kirchenpolitik," 39.

[120] On the consensus of opinion, see Wallace-Hadrill, *Frankish Church*, 278.

the practice of constantly reviewing, revising, and reintroducing canonical standards, which the eighth- and ninth-century conciliar participants inherited from generations of ecclesiastical legislators, is itself emblematic of the perpetual state of reform that characterized the early church. Whether guided by a desire to restore "a normative state" or to bring Christian order to an area that previously did not enjoy it, the Gallo-Roman, Merovingian, and Carolingian legislators sought to recreate their world in an image informed by Christian tradition. In this sense, they were reformers all.[121] What distinguished the Carolingian reformers from their predecessors was the amount of assistance they received from the secular government—if it can be called assistance. One recent scholar has characterized the Carolingian regime as "theocratic," because of its proactive approach to ecclesiastical governance.[122] This is more true for the reign of Charlemagne than that of his father or uncle, although they, like their Merovingian predecessors, made this development possible. Without Clovis—or Constantine or Alaric—there would have been no Charlemagne.

Continuity: Clovis to Charlemagne

What would a Gallic bishop, present at both the Councils of Agde and Orléans, have thought if he somehow was able to observe the Pippinids' initial forays into ecclesiastical legislation? What would have seemed familiar to him? What would have seemed alien? He surely would not have been surprised to witness the convocation of the council by the secular authorities, nor by the latter's input into the composition of a legislative agenda. Clovis, after all, had sent *tituli* to the attendees of Orléans (511) to guide them in their proceedings, and the bishops acknowledged upon the completion of their business that they had acted in accordance with his will.[123] Similarly, our bishop would certainly have been pleased to see the willingness of the Pippinids to shoulder the

[121] I am not as confident as R. A. Markus, "From Caesarius to Boniface: Christianity and Paganism in Gaul," in *The Seventh Century: Change and Continuity*, ed. J. Fontaine and J. N. Hillgarth (London: The Warburg Institute, 1992), 154–72, that Boniface's reforms in particular initiated a "new start" to Frankish Christianity.

[122] Fouracre, *The Age of Charles Martel*, 25. Fouracre rightly recognizes the Merovingian precedents for the royal use of church councils as articulators of the king's "universal authority."

[123] Orléans (511), Epistle to Clovis.

burden of enforcement. He and his brethren had requested the same of Clovis back in 511.[124] Even the presence of laymen might have seemed familiar: only six years after Clovis' council, the presiding Burgundian metropolitans invited laymen to attend their meeting at Epaone.[125] He probably would have nodded in recognition upon hearing many of the topics of discussion at the synod, topics that reflected enduring problems. Some of the legislative responses to them might have seemed innovative to a bishop unaware of later Merovingian legislation.

In short, despite the changes that conciliar procedures underwent over the course of two and half centuries, continuities in practice prevailed. Carloman and Pippin's councils showed a natural progression from those of the previous century, and Charlemagne took their innovations to perhaps their logical conclusion. If scholars are to periodize Frankish synodal history, Charlemagne's reign is a better choice for the beginning of a 'Carolingian conciliar era' than Boniface's councils of the 740s. But as useful as chronological demarcations are for understanding the past, they are inherently misleading because of their emphasis on significant or noteworthy changes at the expense of the more obvious aspects of continuity. The Pippinids may have been political revolutionaries who displaced a ruling dynasty that had endured for almost three centuries, but they were not radicals who engineered drastic institutional changes in the relationship between the royal government and the church. Indeed, their adherence to tradition helped them to cloak their illegal usurpation of power in the guise of legitimacy. Like their Merovingian antecedents, they were the protectors and leaders of the church. It was their right and obligation to ensure its proper management in the manner of Frankish kings, Roman emperors, and biblical kings "like David, governing with prophetic aid."[126]

---

[124] Ibid.

[125] De Clercq, ed., *Concilia Galliae: A.511–A.695*, 23.

[126] Clichy (626/7), Preface. C.f. Gregory of Tours *Decem Libri Historiarum* IV.20, where Chlothar I is referred to as the "Novus David." On the Franks' use of Davidic imagery prior to Charlemagne, see Aryeh Graboïs, "Un mythe fondamental de l'histoire de France au Moyen Age: Le roi David, précurseur du roi très chrétien," *Revue historique* 287, no. 1 (1992): 15–9.

CONCLUSION

In the preceding pages, we examined Frankish church councils through the lens of institutional history. An institution, however, is only the sum of the human bodies that allow it to execute its mission.[1] The minimal biographical information we possess about individual prelates in the Frankish kingdoms makes it easy to forget the men behind the institution. Few survive as anything more than a name on a subscription list. However, even if we cannot associate every name on a list with an individual, with his own agenda, biases, and concerns, we must never forget that the canons of the Frankish councils were collaborative efforts. Certainly, larger-than-life personalities, such as Caesarius of Arles, Guntram, Chilperic I, and Boniface, could dominate proceedings. But at no point between 511 and 768 were the opinions of the collective body of attendees brushed aside as irrelevant. Even with changing ideas of conciliar consensus, cooperative decision making was a long-standing ideal. And even in the councils of the middle eighth century—whose agendas were often predetermined by the mayoral convoker—discussion and debate were considered requisite steps in the legislative process.

Most episcopal attendees took their conciliar obligations seriously, and were willing to risk the hazards of travel and the neglect of their own *civitates* to answer the summons of the convoker. Certainly, some tried to shirk their duties, but they could expect to be chastised for it by their brethren. Those who did attend councils saw them as an opportunity to address local problems by means of corporate pronouncements, whose authority exceeded that of individual prelates. Nevertheless, application of these decisions on the local level was always a challenge, and probably a failure in many instances. Sometimes this failure was due to a canon's unrealistic expectations, such as the requirement by the Council of Germania that all property unjustly seized from the church be returned.[2] In other cases, it was because of

[1] This point is often ignored in studies of councils. MacMullen, *Voting About God in Early Church Councils*, is a refreshing exception.

[2] Germania (742), c. 1.

an individual prelate's unwillingness to enforce a decree. For example, Bishop Priscus of Lyons' wife, Susanna, was in the habit of entering her husband's personal living quarters accompanied only by other women, despite a canonical prescription of the Council of Mâcon (581/3), a meeting chaired by Priscus himself, that a woman must not enter the bedroom of a bishop unless accompanied by two priests.[3]

In some cases, the episcopal agenda clashed with that of the monarchy, usually resulting in the disappointment of the prelates. The Gallic bishops' unrelenting efforts to ban the Jewish ownership and sale of Christian slaves, for example, found little support with the Frankish kings, who ignored any religious scruples because of the economic importance of slavery and the slave trade.[4] But individual failures to enforce canonical rulings should not be taken as evidence of a general lack of respect for the pronouncements of church councils. Certain issues, naturally, were more or less relevant to individual bishops. A prelate of a city with few Jewish residents, for example, would have been far less concerned with their activities than one whose *civitas* contained a thriving Jewish community. Moreover, despite the fact that a canon's authority was considered to be wide-reaching, the circumstances that led to its initial formulation were tied irrevocably to a particular place and time. Therefore, the canon's applicability, if not its authority, was effectively limited.

Changing circumstances also influenced the choices made by compilers of canonical collections. Certain issues lost their currency over time, while others remained pressing concerns. The more general the prescription, the more likely it was to be adopted, copied, and then recopied in subsequent centuries. In the same way, conciliar attendees looked back to earlier assemblies for inspiration and precedent, although they were highly selective in their choice of canons and in no way shunned innovation. The role played by the Frankish councils in the development of medieval canon law was a critical one, although observing them from that perspective alone is misleading.

The Frankish bishops were aware that they were contributing to a body known as "canon law," but their understanding of it was far different from that held by high medieval canon lawyers. Gratian's concordance of the canons, followed closely by glosses and scholarly

[3] Gregory of Tours *Decem Libri Historiarum* IV.36; Mâcon (581/3), c. 3.
[4] Bachrach, *Early Medieval Jewish Policy*, 64, 86–7.

commentaries, turned what had previously been a heterogeneous and amorphous morass of overlapping and sometimes conflicting decrees into a coherent and accessible legal system. Canon law in the Frankish era was no system. Rather, it was a tradition on which ecclesiastical legislators relied as the authoritative basis for their own proclamations. The Carolingian kings, Charlemagne in particular, made some effort to standardize canonical tradition, but were ultimately unsuccessful in their efforts to eliminate diversity and impose uniformity.[5]

Where the early Carolingians were successful was in their efforts to subsume ecclesiastical governance under the general oversight of the monarchy. To be sure, Clovis and his descendants exercised considerable power over the church, convoking councils, choosing bishops, and interfering in ecclesiastical trials. Their efforts to imitate Roman imperial prerogative in relation to the church led them to assume an almost paternal role, even in those cases where the king's own piety was questionable. But it was the Pippinids who made royal convocation of councils mandatory, who co-opted the right to issue ecclesiastical legislation, and who saw their personal *auctoritas* as sufficient to dictate church policy. It would be a mistake, however, to view these efforts as merely a coarse power grab. The descendants of Charles Martel took their responsibility to protect and care for the church very seriously indeed, an attitude some have credited to the "sacralization of kingship" that began with Pippin the Short's anointing.[6]

It seems more likely, however, that the Carolingians' assumed responsibility for the church was more a natural outgrowth of Merovingian—if not Roman imperial—precedent than an *ex nihilo* innovation. But we should not underestimate the personal piety of the Pippinid family, or their early recognition of the intrinsic relationship between religious authority and political power in Francia. By the time Charlemagne took the throne in 768, the Pippinids knew well the benefits of close ties with the church, its wealth, and its politically influential members.[7] Even

[5] Wallace-Hadrill, *Frankish Church*, 294; Reynolds, "The Organization, Law and Liturgy of the Western Church, 700–900," 615; McKitterick, "Knowledge of Canon Law in the Frankish Kingdoms Before 789," 99; Hen, "Knowledge of Canon Law Among Rural Priests," 118; Janet Nelson, "On the Limits of the Carolingian Renaissance," in *Politics and Ritual in Early Medieval Europe* (London: The Hambledon Press, 1986), 56.

[6] Imbert, "Le pouvoir législatif dans l'Eglise carolingienne," 590–1.

[7] See the discussion of the Pippinid *Klosterpolitik* by Fouracre, *The Age of Charles Martel*, 48–50.

though by the end of Charlemagne's reign the Frankish episcopate was beginning to reassert itself as a guiding force in conciliar business, royal participation remained a regular feature of ninth-century councils.[8]

Although the close governance of the church by the early Carolingians drained away some of the episcopate's legislative independence, the need to conform ecclesiastical policy and administration with the expectations of secular authorities was by no means an eighth-century innovation. As far back as the fourth century, imperial intrusion into the Arian and Donatist controversies was a very important factor in determining the course of these debates.[9] In the middle sixth century, Byzantine emperors similarly did not hesitate to pressure the papacy to accept the condemnation of the Three Chapters in an effort to bring the Monophysites back into the orthodox fold.[10] The Frankish kings largely avoided matters of dogma until the eighth century, and in their efforts to imitate imperial prerogative, were comparatively benign in their interventions. They were more interested in dictating policy in specific cases—having a particular ally elected bishop, for example, or having a synod address a certain issue—than in acting as executive administrators of the Frankish church. The popularity of immunity grants in the latter half of the Merovingian era reveals the extent to which the royal authorities were willing to trust the church with rights of governance.

The Frankish council as an institution epitomized the complex relationship between the monarchy and the church. The conciliar acts can be read as indicative of regal strength as well as a thriving episcopate, and both readings are accurate. The Frankish episcopate was an aristocracy, one with close ties—familial and otherwise—to secular power. We need only recall the normalcy of former lay officeholders acquiring the bishop's throne to appreciate this fact. Certainly, these men were accustomed to showing deference to the king. But deference is not subservience. In King Guntram's edict of 585, he explicitly recognized the *auctoritas* possessed by conciliar participants, specifically the attendees of the Second Council of Mâcon, held earlier that same year.[11] Guntram,

---

[8] Janet Nelson, "National Synods, Kingship as Office, and Royal Anointing," *Studies in Church History* 7 (1971): 47–8.

[9] On Constantine's intervention at Nicaea, see Timothy Barnes, *Constantine and Eusebius* (Cambridge, MA: Harvard University Press, 1981), 12–9.

[10] Markus, *Gregory the Great and His World*, 125–42.

[11] Guntram *Edictum*, in *Capitularia Regum Francorum*, 11.

perhaps more than any other Merovingian king, was conscious of the value of conciliar legislation, and encouraged the frequent meeting of councils, often in his own presence. Although he was no supporter of clerical independence, he recognized that a strong episcopate was beneficial for both the church and the *regnum*. Although his influence certainly was felt in those councils he convoked, the canons issued during these meetings do not reveal a weakening of episcopal power.

Guntram, like his relations, did not assume the role of a despotic master of the Frankish church. The Merovingians and the Carolingians, who had very different ideas about the public role of the bishops, both recognized the value of sharing administrative power with the ecclesiastical elite. Certainly, conflict arose between the church and the royal government because of the differing priorities of each; the confiscation of church property by the Frankish kings and their supporters is an obvious example. However, these conflicts themselves were indicative of the relative power of both bodies, or, more accurately, the individuals who governed them. The fact, too, that both the church and the royal government recognized the importance of the ecclesiastical council indicates the latter's essential role in governance.[12]

How does this observation impinge on our understanding of the Frankish council as an institution? To begin with, it clarifies the question of legislative authority. In the Merovingian period, this authority lay, in theory, with the episcopal attendees themselves, as manifested in their show of consensus. During the early Carolingian era, the bulk of legislative authority shifted to the mayors and kings, who, nevertheless, recognized the necessity of issuing their decrees *cum consensu* of the clerical (and lay) attendees. In the reign of Charlemagne, it became acceptable practice for the king to legislate for the church independent of a council.

Any reading of the surviving ecclesiastical legislation from the Frankish kingdoms must, therefore, take into account these changing concepts of conciliar *auctoritas*, as well as the varying degree of royal involvement in any given council. Even in the reign of Charlemagne, provincial and diocesan synods continued to meet independent of direct royal or imperial oversight.[13] As important as continuities in tradition were for the composition of conciliar canons, the immediate circumstances in which a council was held were of at least equal

[12] Barion, *Das fränkisch-deutsche Synodalrecht*, 251–2.
[13] Wallace-Hadrill, *The Frankish Church*, 263.

significance. Canons cannot easily be detached from the contexts that warranted their enactment without substantially changing their meaning, as we saw with regard to Gratian's co-opting of a canon originally published by the Burgundian Council of Epaone (517).

As context-specific decrees, the Frankish canons have often been used as windows into the socio-religious world of Gallia and Germania. However, as normative prescriptions, they are less reflections of reality than reactions to it. Their true evidentiary value is their ability to inform us of those things that prompted concern and apprehension among the conciliar attendees. Rarely can we deduce the precise context and frequency of the occurrences or practices that caught the attendees' attention, but their basis in reality seems beyond doubt. The seriousness with which the Frankish bishops took their conciliar duties suggests the relevance of the issues they discussed in their councils. Moreover, when bishops "renewed" an old canon, they were not only making a conscious choice from among a body of hundreds of precedents, they were also signaling their belief in the canons' applicability to their own situation. The chosen decree would often be adjusted textually so as to ensure this. There is much to be learned from the ways in which general principles were adapted over time into often very different pronouncements.

There is still a great deal that we do not know about conciliar practices in the Early Middle Ages. More comparative work, for example, needs to be done to situate the Frankish synods within the overall context of post-Roman conciliar developments. Why, for example, did the national councils of the Franks differ so considerably from the Visigothic councils of Toledo?[14] How deeply was Frankish influence felt in the Anglo-Saxon synods, and vice versa?[15] Did the circulation of canonical collections across national borders lead to consensus or difference among the churches of various regions? These questions are vital ones, and they warrant additional study. The question of how much the so-called *Landeskirchen* of the Roman successor kingdoms were truly isolated from one another has yet to be answered satisfactorily.

---

[14] The relevant *Konziliengeschichte* volume contains the most thorough analysis of these synods: Orlandis and Ramos-Lissón, *Die Synoden auf der Iberischen Halbinsel biz zum Einbruch des Islam (711)*.

[15] On which, see Hanna Vollrath, *Die Synoden Englands bis 1066* (Paderborn: Ferdinand Schöningh, 1985); Cubitt, *Anglo-Saxon Church Councils c. 650–c. 680*.

Still, we must first understand the internal procedures, protocol, and institutions of the individual regional churches. Our understanding of the history of the spiritual world of early medieval Europe has benefited immensely in the past thirty years from the penetrating work of many important scholars. But this spirituality was both defined and enforced by infrastructure, officeholders, and rules. When the Frankish bishops took their seats at an ecclesiastical council, they were conscious that the discussions and debates of the days to come would help to determine the religious standards they expected their church and their society to abide by. Their task was administrative as well as pious: they gathered together with their clerical brethren to ensure both the maintenance of the church and the spiritual health of the entire *populus christianus*.

APPENDICES

APPENDIX A

FRANKISH COUNCILS, 511–768

Both Appendix A and Appendix B have been collated from a variety of primary and secondary sources, references to which appear in the individual entries for each council. Both appendices are the most complete catalogs of Frankish councils that have been compiled to date. In identifying councils as either genuine or dubious I have erred on the side of following scholarly convention, although I cite dissenting opinions where relevant. For each council, I provide entries, when the information is available, for its location, date, attendence, regions or provinces represented, and evidence of royal or mayoral involvement.

Location	Orléans
Date	511
Size	32 bishops
Provinces Represented	Bordeaux (6), Bourges (4), Eauze (2), Tours (6), Rouen (5), Sens (5), Rheims (4)
Royal Involvement	Convoked by Clovis I
Sources	*Acta* (CCSL 148A, 3–19); Epistle of Chrodebert of Tours (*Epistolae aevi Merowingici*, no. 16); *Vita Melanii*, ch. 4 (MGH SRM III); Hincmar of Rheims, *Vita Sancti Remigii*, ch. 19 (MGH AA IV.2)
Bibliography	Hefele, *Histoire*, II.2.1005–15; De Clercq, *Legislation*, 8–13; Pontal, *Histoire*, 47–57

Location	Lyons
Date	ca. 516
Size	Unknown
Provinces Represented	Burgundian Kingdom (Lyons, Vienne, others?)
Sources	Avitus of Vienne, ep. 30 (MGH AA VI.2)
Bibliography	Hefele, *Histoire*, II.2.1025; Pontal, *Histoire*, 60–1

Location	Epaone
Date	517
Size	24 bishops, 1 presbyter
Provinces Represented	Lyons (5), Vienne (5), Besançon (2), Sens (1), Arles/ Vienne (12)

Sources	*Acta* (CCSL 148A, 20–37); Avitus of Vienne, Invitation Epistle (CCSL 148A, 22–3); Epistle of Viventiolus (CCSL 148A, 23–4)
Additional Notes	Some cities represented at this Burgundian council were claimed by both the metropolitans of Arles and Vienne. Also, Besançon did not have metropolitan status at this time. This status would be sporadically acknowledged in the centuries to come. In this catalog, the province of *Maxima Sequanorum* will be treated as a distinct unit.
Bibliography	Hefele, *Histoire*, II.2.1031–42; Pontal, *Histoire*, 58–71

Location	Lyons
Date	518/9
Size	11 bishops
Provinces Represented	Lyons (3), Vienne (7), Besançon (1)
Sources	*Acta* (CCSL 148A, 38–41); *Vita Aviti Episcopi Viennensis*, ch. 2 (MGH AA VI.2); *Vita Apollinaris Episcopi Valentinensis*, ch. 2 (MGH SRM III)
Additional Notes	This Burgundian council considered charges of incest laid against Stephanus, a royal official, which had been discussed at an earlier council. Pontal suggests that the latter might be identical with Lyons (ca. 516), but this is uncertain.
Bibliography	Hefele, *Histoire*, II.2.1042–46; Pontal, *Histoire*, 71–3

Location	Arles
Date	524
Size	14 bishops, 4 presbyters
Provinces Represented	Arles
Sources	*Acta* (CCSL 148A, 42–6)
Bibliography	Hefele, *Histoire*, II.2.1060–2; Pontal, *Histoire*, 77–80

Location	Carpentras
Date	527
Size	16 bishops
Provinces Represented	Arles
Sources	*Acta* (CCSL 148A, 47–50); Epistle of the Synod to Agricius (CCSL 148A, 50); Epistle of Felix IV to Caesarius of Arles (CCSL 148A, 51)
Bibliography	Hefele, *Histoire*, II.2.1074–6; Pontal, *Histoire*, 80–2

Location	Valence
Date	ca. 528
Size	Unknown (bishops, presbyters, and deacons attended)
Provinces Represented	Vienne, Lyons, others?
Sources	*Vita Caesari Episcopi Arelatensis*, I.60 (MGH SRM III)
Bibliography	Hefele, *Histoire*, II.2.1108–10; Pontal, *Histoire*, 94

Location	Orange
Date	529
Size	14 bishops, praetorian prefect, 7 *viri clarissimi*
Provinces Represented	Arles
Sources	*Acta* and Definition of Faith (CCSL 148A, 53–65); Epistle of Boniface II to Caesarius of Arles (CCSL 148A, 66–9); Capitula Sanctorum Patrum (CCSL 148A, 69–76)
Additional Notes	The council addressed the controversy regarding the Augustinian conception of Divine Grace.
Bibliography	Hefele, *Histoire*, II.2.1085–1108; Pontal, *Histoire*, 94–9

Location	Vaison
Date	529
Size	12 bishops
Provinces Represented	Arles
Sources	*Acta* (CCSL 148A, 77–81); Council of Carpentras (528)
Additional Notes	At the council of Carpentras (527), it was ordered that another council be held the following year, on November 22nd, at Vaison. For an unknown reason the council was put off another year.
Bibliography	Hefele, *Histoire*, II.2.1110–15; Pontal, *Histoire*, 82–4

Location	Marseilles
Date	533
Size	15 bishops, 1 abbot, unknown number of laymen
Provinces Represented	Arles
Sources	*Acta* (CCSL 148A, 85–86); Epistles of John II to Caesarius (CCSL 148A, 86–96); Epistle of Agapitus to Caesarius of Arles (CCSL 148A, 96–7)
Bibliography	Hefele, *Histoire*, II.2.1125–9; Pontal, *Histoire*, 84–7

Location	Orléans
Date	533
Size	26 bishops, 5 presbyters
Provinces Represented	Bourges (3), Bordeaux (4), Lyons (1), Eauze (4), Tours (3), Rouen (4), Vienne (1), Sens (5), Unknown (6)
Royal Involvement	The council was convoked by Childebert I, Chlothar I, and Theuderic I
Sources	*Acta* (CCSL 148A, 98–103)
Bibliography	Hefele, *Histoire*, II.2.1130–5; De Clercq, *Legislation*, 14–6; Pontal, *Histoire*, 101–4

Location	Clermont
Date	535
Size	15 bishops
Provinces Represented	Bourges (5), Lyons (1), Narbonne (1), Rheims (2), Cologne (1), Besançon (1), Vienne (1), Trier (3)
Royal Involvement	The council was convoked by Theudebert I
Sources	*Acta* (CCSL 148A, 104–111); Epistle of the Synod to King Theudebert I (CCSL 148A, 111–2)
Bibliography	Hefele, *Histoire*, II.2.1139–42; De Clercq, *Legislation*, 17–20; Pontal, *Histoire*, 104–7

Location	Orléans
Date	538
Size	19 bishops, 7 presbyters
Provinces Represented	Bourges (3), Lyons (7), Tours (2), Rouen (7), Vienne (1), Sens (6)
Sources	*Acta* (CCSL 148A, 113–30)
Bibliography	Hefele, *Histoire*, II.2.1155–62; De Clercq, *Legislation*, 20–6; Pontal, *Histoire*, 107–114

Location	Orléans
Date	541
Size	42 bishops, 1 abbot, 10 presbyters
Provinces Represented	Bourges (6), Eauze (4), Lyons (2), Tours (4), Rouen (7), Vienne (3), Sens (5), Arles (17), Bordeaux (4), Besançon (1)
Sources	Acta (CCSL 148A, 131–46); *Vita Dalmatii*, ch. 7 (MGH SRM III)
Bibliography	Hefele, *Histoire*, II.2.1164–74; De Clercq, *Legislation*, 27–31; Pontal, *Histoire*, 114–22

Location	Orléans
Date	549
Size	50 bishops, 6 archdeacons, 3 deacons, 10 presbyters, 2 abbots
Provinces Represented	Bourges (5), Eauze (7), Lyons (5), Tours (3), Rouen (6), Vienne (6), Sens (7), Arles (18), Bordeaux (4), Trier (3), Cologne (1), Rheims (4), Besançon (2)
Royal Involvement	The council was convoked by Childebert I
Sources	*Acta* (CCSL 148A, 147–61); Gregory of Tours, *Liber Vitae Patrum*, VI.5
Additional Notes	The council restored Bishop Marcus of Orléans to his see. See Sirmond I.289–91 for the pseudo-council at Clermont (on which, see Pontal, *Histoire*, 123).
Bibliography	Hefele, *Histoire*, III.1.157–64; De Clercq, *Legislation*, 31–4; Pontal, *Histoire*, 122–31

Location	Toul
Date	550
Size	Unknown
Provinces Represented	Rheims, Trier, others?
Royal Involvement	The council was convoked by Theudebald
Sources	Epistle of Mappinus of Rheims (*Epistolae Austrasicae*, no. 11)
Additional Notes	Hefele rejects Mappinus' excuses for not attending the council, arguing that he simply did not wish to attend.
Bibliography	Hefele, *Histoire*, III.1.164–5; Pontal, *Histoire*, 132–3

Location	Metz
Date	550/5
Size	Unknown
Provinces Represented	Bourges, Trier, others?
Royal Involvement	The council was convoked by Theudebald
Sources	Gregory of Tours, *D.L.H.*, IV.6–7
Additional Notes	The council ordained the archdeacon Cautinus as Bishop of Clermont
Bibliography	Hefele, *Histoire*, III.1.165; Pontal, *Histoire*, 132–3

Location	Eauze
Date	551
Size	8 bishops, 1 presbyter

Provinces Represented	Eauze
Sources	*Acta* (CCSL 148A, 162–5)
Bibliography	Hefele, *Histoire*, III.1.165–7; De Clercq, *Legislation*, 73–4; Pontal, *Histoire*, 136–7

Location	Paris
Date	551/2
Size	27 bishops
Provinces Represented	Arles (10), Vienne (2), Bourges (1), Sens (4), Bordeaux (1), Lyons, (3), Rheims (1), Besançon (2), Unknown (3)
Royal Involvement	The council was convoked by Childebert I
Sources	*Acta* (CCSL 148A, 166–9); Gregory of Tours, *D.L.H.*, IV.36
Additional Notes	The synod deposed Bishop Saffarac of Paris
Bibliography	Hefele, *Histoire*, III.1.167–8; De Clercq, *Legislation*, 34–5; Pontal, *Histoire*, 131–2

Location	Brittany
Date	ca. 552
Size	Unknown
Provinces Represented	Tours
Sources	Gregory of Tours, *D.L.H.*, IV.4
Additional Notes	Bishop Macliaw of Vannes was excommunicated for leaving the priesthood.
Bibliography	Hefele, *Histoire*, III.1.170–1; Pontal, *Histoire*, 133

Location	Arles
Date	554
Size	11 bishops, 4 presbyters, 2 archdeacons, 2 deacons
Provinces Represented	Arles
Sources	*Acta* (CCSL 148A, 170–3)
Bibliography	Hefele, *Histoire*, III.1.169–70; De Clercq, *Legislation*, 74–5; Pontal, *Histoire*, 137–9

Location	Paris
Date	556/73
Size	15 bishops
Provinces Represented	Bourges (1), Bordeaux (1), Rouen (5), Sens (2), Tours (4), Rheims (1), Unknown (1)
Sources	*Acta* (CCSL 148A, 204–10)
Bibliography	Hefele, *Histoire*, III.1.171–4; De Clercq, *Legislation*, 44–5; Pontal, *Histoire*, 151–55

Location	Saintes
Date	558/61
Size	Unknown number of clerics and laymen
Provinces Represented	Bordeaux
Sources	Baudonivia, *Vita Sanctae Radegundis Liber II*, ch. 15
Additional Notes	This council was attended by Leo, a *vir inlustris*. It is unlikely to be identical with Saintes (561/7), attended by Bishop Emerius of Saintes. Baudonivia mentions the attendance of a Bishop Eusebius, who is probably to be identified with Emerius' predecessor. This Eusebius died no later than 561, the year that Chlothar I, who appointed Emerius, died. Leo is said to have stopped at Radegund's monastery, which was founded ca. 558.

Location	Saintes
Date	561/7
Size	Unknown
Provinces Represented	Bordeaux
Sources	Gregory of Tours, *D.L.H.*, IV.26
Additional Notes	This provincial council, under Leontius of Bordeaux, removed Emerius of Saintes from his see.
Bibliography	Hefele, *Histoire*, III.1.181–2; Pontal, *Histoire*, 155–6

Location	Tours
Date	567
Size	9 bishops
Provinces Represented	Tours (5), Sens (2), Rouen (2)
Royal Involvement	The council was convoked by Charibert
Sources	*Acta* (CCSL 148A, 175–94); Epistle of the Synod to Radegund (CCSL 148A, 195–6); Epistle of the Synod to the People of Tours (CCSL 148A, 197–9); Gregory of Tours, *D.L.H.*, IX.39
Bibliography	Hefele, *Histoire*, III.1.184–92; De Clercq, *Legislation*, 40–4; Pontal, *Histoire*, 156–63

Location	Lyons
Date	567/70
Size	8 bishops, 5 presbyters, 1 deacon
Provinces Represented	Vienne (5), Lyons (5), Besançon (2), Sens (1), Arles (1)
Royal Involvement	The council was convoked by Guntram

Sources	*Acta* (CCSL 148A, 200–3); Gregory of Tours, *D.L.H.*, V.20
Bibliography	Hefele, *Histoire*, III.1.182–4; De Clercq, *Legislation*, 46–7; Pontal, *Histoire*, 166–9

Location	Paris
Date	573
Size	32 bishops, 1 presbyter
Provinces Represented	Vienne (4), Arles (13), Lyons (2), Sens (5), Eauze (2), Bourges (2), Bordeaux (2), Tours (1), Besançon (1), Rouen (1)
Royal Involvement	The council was convoked by Guntram
Sources	Epistle of Pappolus of Chartres to the Synod (CCSL 148A, 212); Epistle of the Synod to Egidius of Rheims (CCSL 148A, 212–5); Epistle of the Synod to King Sigibert (CCSL 148A, 215–7); Gregory of Tours, *D.L.H.*, IV.47
Additional Notes	This council was convoked to deal with the controversy surrounding Promotus' election as bishop of the new diocese of Châteaudun. The enactment of the council's decision that Promotus should be deposed was delayed until after Sigibert's death (575).
Bibliography	Hefele, *Histoire*, III.1.195–7; De Clercq, *Legislation*, 47–8; Pontal, *Histoire*, 169–70

Location	Paris
Date	577
Size	45 bishops
Provinces Represented	Tours, Bordeaux, Sens, others?
Royal Involvement	The council was convoked and addressed by Chilperic
Sources	Gregory of Tours, *D.L.H.*, V.18, VII.16
Additional Notes	The council deposed and jailed Praetextatus of Rouen. Guntram considered convoking a council ca. 584 to hear the bishop's appeal, but nothing came of it.
Bibliography	Hefele, *Histoire*, III.1.198–9; Pontal, *Histoire*, 173–4

Location	Saintes
Date	579
Size	Unknown
Provinces Represented	Bordeaux

Sources	Gregory of Tours, *D.L.H.*, V.36
Additional Notes	The council attempted to settle the dispute between Count Nantinus of Angoulême and Bishop Heraclius of Angoulême.
Bibliography	Hefele, *Histoire*, III.1.201; Pontal, *Histoire*, 178

Location	Chalon-sur-Saone
Date	579
Size	Unknown
Regions Represented	Kingdom of Guntram
Royal Involvement	The council was convoked by Guntram
Sources	Gregory of Tours, *D.L.H.*, V.27, Marius of Avenches, *Chronica*, entry for 579
Additional Notes	The council deposed and jailed Bishops Salonius of Embrun and Sagittarius of Gap. Gregory notes that there were many other matters on the agenda.
Bibliography	Hefele, *Histoire*, III.1.201; Pontal, *Histoire*, 171

Location	Berny
Date	580
Size	Unknown
Regions Represented	Kingdom of Chilperic
Royal Involvement	The council was convoked by Chilperic, and held at his villa. He attended the proceedings.
Sources	Gregory of Tours, *D.L.H.*, V.49; Venantius Fortunatus, *Carmina*, IX.1
Additional Notes	The council cleared Gregory of Tours of charges of treason, and excommunicated Count Leudast of Tours.
Bibliography	Hefele, *Histoire*, III.1.200–1; Pontal, *Histoire*, 175

Location	Lyons
Date	581
Size	Unknown
Provinces Represented	Lyons, others?
Royal Involvement	The council met with Guntram.
Sources	Gregory of Tours, *D.L.H.*, V1.1
Additional Notes	The council dealt with judicial issues and the treason of Mummolus. Heinzelmann has suggested that laymen were in attendance.
Bibliography	Hefele, *Histoire*, III.1.206; Pontal, *Histoire*, 171–2; Heinzelmann, *Gregory of Tours*, 185, n. 100

Location	Mâcon
Date	581/3
Size	21 bishops
Provinces Represented	Vienne (6), Lyons (5), Sens (5), Arles (4), Bourges (1)
Royal Involvement	The council was convoked by Guntram
Sources	*Acta* (CCSL 148A, 222–30); *Gestorum Episcoporum Autissiodorensium*, ch. 19
Bibliography	Hefele, *Histoire*, III.1.202–5; De Clercq, *Legislation*, 49–51; Pontal, *Histoire*, 181–5

Location	Lyons
Date	583
Size	8 bishops
Provinces Represented	Lyons (4), Vienne (3), Sens (1)
Sources	*Acta* (CCSL 148A, 231–3)
Bibliography	Hefele, *Histoire*, III.1.206–7; De Clercq, *Legislation*, 48–9; Pontal, *Histoire*, 185–6

Location	Valence
Date	583/5
Size	17 bishops
Provinces Represented	Arles (9), Lyons (3), Vienne (5)
Royal Involvement	The council was convoked by Guntram
Sources	*Acta* (CCSL 148A, 234–6); Fredegar, *Chronica*, IV.1 (disputed)
Additional Notes	Guntram, prior to the council, sent his referendarius, Asclepiodotus, to deliver *epistolae* to the synod. Fredegar writes that Guntram convoked a synod of 40 bishops in 584 to confirm the foundation of the monastery of St. Marcellus. C.f. De Clercq, who has argued that the founding occurred in conjunction with Mâcon (585) (p. 237).
Bibliography	Hefele, *Histoire*, III.1.207–8; De Clercq, *Legislation*, 51; Pontal, *Histoire*, 172

Location	Auvergne
Date	584/91
Size	Unknown
Provinces Represented	Bourges
Sources	Gregory of Tours, *D.L.H.*, VI.38–9
Additional Notes	This provincial council mediated a dispute between Bishops Ursicinus of Cahors and Innocentius of Rodez.
Bibliography	Hefele, *Histoire*, III.1.221; Pontal, *Histoire*, 178–9

Location	Troyes
Date	585
Size	Unknown
Provinces Represented	Sens, others?
Royal Involvement	The council was convoked by Guntram and Childebert II
Sources	Gregory of Tours, *D.L.H.*, VIII.13
Additional Notes	Guntram and Childebert II had planned to hold a council at Troyes, but the bishops of Childebert's kingdom refused to attend, probably because of Guntram's plans to prosecute Theodore of Marseilles against Childebert's wishes.

Location	Mâcon
Date	585
Size	54 bishops, 12 delegates of unknown rank
Provinces Represented	Vienne (8), Arles (21), Lyons (5), Sens (7), Eauze (8), Bourges (4), Bordeaux (5), Tours (1), Besançon (3), Rouen (1), without seats (3)
Royal Involvement	The council was convoked by Guntram
Sources	*Acta* (CCSL 148A, 237–50); Gregory of Tours, *D.L.H.*, VII.31, VIII.7, 12, 20; *Gestorum Episcoporum Autissiodorensium*, ch. 19
Additional Notes	The council, held in October, deposed Faustianus of Dax and excommunicated Ursicinus of Cahors; the bishops debated the meaning of the word *homo*; a fight broke out between the servants of Priscus of Lyons and those of Duke Leudegisel.
Bibliography	Hefele, *Histoire*, III.1.208–14; De Clercq, *Legislation*, 51–55; Pontal, *Histoire*, 186–91

Location	Auxerre
Date	585/605
Size	1 bishop, 34 presbyters, 3 deacons, 7 abbots
Regions Represented	Diocese of Auxerre
Sources	*Acta* (CCSL 148A, 264–72); *Gestorum Episcoporum Autissiodorensium*, ch. 19
Additional Notes	Canon 7 of the conciliar record orders "Ut medio Madio omnes presbyteri ad synodum in civitatem veniant et Kalends Novembris omnes abbates ad concilium conveniant." Whether these additional diocesan synods were ever held is unknown.
Bibliography	Hefele, *Histoire*, III.1.214–21; De Clercq, *Legislation*, 75–8; Pontal, *Histoire*, 192–3

Location	Unknown 1
Date	588
Size	Unknown
Regions Represented	Kingdom of Guntram
Royal Involvement	The council was to meet "cum dispositione magnifici principis nostri"
Sources	Mâcon (585), c. 20
Additional Notes	This council was ordered to meet by the Council of Mâcon (585); whether it did so is unknown.

Location	Unknown 2
Date	588
Size	Unknown
Regions Represented	Kingdoms of Guntram and Childebert II
Royal Involvement	The Council was convoked by Guntram (possibly with Childebert II)
Sources	Gregory of Tours, *D.L.H.*, IX.20
Additional Notes	The council was to discuss the murder of Praetextatus, and the crime of *luxuria*. It is not known whether it actually took place.
Bibliography	Hefele, *Histoire*, III.1.222; Pontal, *Histoire*, 173

Location	Sorcy
Date	589
Size	Unknown
Provinces Represented	Rheims, others?
Sources	Gregory of Tours, *D.L.H.*, IX.37
Additional Notes	The council reinstated Bishop Droctigisel of Soissons
Bibliography	Hefele, *Histoire*, III.1.230; Pontal, *Histoire*, 176

Location	Unknown 1
Date	589
Size	Unknown
Regions Represented	Kingdom of Guntram
Royal Involvement	The council was convoked by Guntram
Sources	Gregory of Tours, *D.L.H.*, IX.32
Additional Notes	The council was to deal with accusations against Brunhild, but when she swore her innocence, it was cancelled.
Bibliography	Pontal, *Histoire*, 173

Location	Unknown 2
Date	589

Size	10 bishops (or more)
Provinces Represented	Rouen (1), Lyons (1), Sens (2), Vienne (2), Arles (2), Rheims (1), Tours (1)
Royal Involvement	The council was attended by Guntram
Sources	Gregory of Tours, *D.L.H.*, IX.41
Additional Notes	The council sent a letter to Gundegisel of Bordeaux in response to the convent revolt in Poitiers.

Location	Poitiers
Date	589/90
Size	4 bishops (or more)
Provinces Represented	Cologne (1), Tours (1), Bordeaux (2+),
Royal Involvement	The council was convoked by Childebert II and Guntram
Sources	Gregory of Tours, *D.L.H.*, IX.39–43, X.15–7
Additional Notes	The council, attended by Gregory of Tours, excommunicated Chlothild and Basina for the revolt at the convent in Poitiers. An initial meeting had been scheduled for the Kalends of November (589). (A council already had been scheduled and cancelled for that same date (Gregory of Tours, *D.L.H.*, IX.32).
Bibliography	Hefele, *Histoire*, III.1.230–1; Pontal, *Histoire*, 176

Location	Auvergne
Date	590
Size	Unknown
Provinces Represented	Bourges
Sources	Gregory of Tours, *D.L.H.*, X.8
Additional Notes	The council listened to the suit brought against Tetradia by Count Eulalius. Laymen were in attendance.
Bibliography	Hefele, *Histoire*, III.1.233; Pontal, *Histoire*, 178–9

Location	Verdun/Metz
Date	590
Size	Unknown
Regions Represented	Kingdom of Childebert II
Royal Involvement	The council was convoked by Childebert II
Sources	Gregory of Tours, *D.L.H.*, X.19–20
Additional Notes	The council deposed Bishop Egidius of Rheims, and lifted the excommunication of Basina and Chlothild
Bibliography	Hefele, *Histoire*, III.1.232; Pontal, *Histoire*, 176–7

Location	Chalon-sur-Saone
Date	602/4
Size	Unknown
Provinces Represented	Lyons, Vienne, others?
Royal Involvement	Brunhild and Theuderic II were involved in the council's convocation and deposition of Desiderius of Vienne
Sources	Fredegar, *Chronica*, IV.24; Sisebut, *Vita Desiderii*, ch. 4 (MGH SRM III); *Passio Desiderii*, chs. 7–8 (MGH SRM III)
Additional Notes	The synod deposed Bishop Desiderius of Vienne. It is possibly identical to the council referred to in *Columbae Epistolae* no. 2, although it also is possible that this letter refers to the Council of Sens (594/614).
Bibliography	Hefele, *Histoire*, III.1.246–7; Pontal, *Histoire*, 177; Bullough, "Career of Columbanus," 10, 13–4

Location	Paris
Date	614
Size	76 bishops, 1 abbot
Provinces Represented	Vienne (5), Arles (11), Lyons (4), Sens (7), Eauze (7), Bourges (6), Bordeaux (6), Tours (5), Besançon (3), Rouen (6), Trier (3), Cologne (2), Rheims (7), Mayence (3), England (2)
Royal Involvement	The council was convoked by Chlothar II
Sources	*Acta* (CCSL 148A, 274–82); Edict of Chlothar II (CCSL 148A, 283–5)
Additional Notes	There is a reference in the *Vita Agilii* III.12 to a council held after Chlothar's unification of the Frankish kingdoms and around three years after Columbanus' exile (610), which sent Abbot Eustasius and St. Agilius to proselytize among neighboring peoples. Neither man's signature appears in the *acta* of Paris. On this otherwise-unknown council, see Wood, *The Missionary Life*, 37–8.
Bibliography	Hefele, *Histoire*, III.1.250–4; De Clercq, *Legislation*, 57–62; Pontal, *Histoire*, 205–11

Location	Unknown
Date	ca. 614 (or later)
Size	Unknown

Provinces Represented	Unknown
Sources	*Acta* (CCSL 148A, 286–9)
Additional Notes	Hefele and Leclercq suggest that this council may be identical with an assembly of Chlothar II held in 616 at the Villa Bonneuil.
Bibliography	Hefele, *Histoire*, III.1.254–6; De Clercq, *Legislation*, 66–7; Pontal, *Histoire*, 211–2

Location	Clichy
Date	626/7
Size	40 bishops, 1 deacon, 1 abbot
Provinces Represented	Vienne (1), Lyons (3), Sens (6), Eauze (2), Bourges (7), Bordeaux (5), Tours (4), Besançon (1), Rouen (2), Trier (3), Cologne (1), Rheims (7)
Royal Involvement	The council was convoked by Chlothar II.
Sources	*Acta* (CCSL 148A, 290–7); Fredegar, *Chronica*, IV.55
Additional Notes	Fredegar writes that Chlothar assembled the leading men and bishops of his kingdom in 627; the council may have been the ecclesiastical half of the assembly.
Bibliography	Hefele, *Histoire*, III.1.260–5; De Clercq, *Legislation*, 62–5; Pontal, *Histoire*, 212–6

Location	Mâcon
Date	626/7
Size	Unknown
Provinces Represented	Burgundian provinces
Royal Involvement	The council was convoked by Clothar II
Sources	*Vita Eusthasi Abbatis Luxouiensis*, ch. 9 (MGH SRM IV)
Additional Notes	At the council, Abbot Eusthasius of Luxeuil disputed with the monk Agrestius over the legacy of Columbanus.
Bibliography	Hefele, *Histoire*, III.1.259–60; Pontal, *Histoire*, 225; Charles-Edwards, *Early Christian Ireland*, 364–9; Lifshitz, *The Name of the Saint*, 16–19

Location	Bourges
Date	ca. 630/43
Size	Unknown
Provinces Represented	Bourges

Sources	*Desiderii Epistolae*, ep. II.16
Additional Notes	In a letter from Verus of Rodez to Desiderius of Cahors, Verus states that he has "received your directions with copies of letters from Bishop Sulpicius, in which the Bishop made it known that the *placitum* of this *synodo* was moved to another time...we learned of this by your grace through your servant the Deacon Bocolenus, and afterwards by your message." Whether the rescheduled council was actually held is unknown. Letter II.5 from Sulpicius of Bourges to Verus also refers to a *placitum* to be held on the Kalends of April to deal with the crimes of Verus' deacon Perricius of Aronnacus. Whether the two meetings are related is unknown, and whether the latter can even be identified as a synod is also questionable.

Location	Clichy
Date	636
Size	26 bishops
Provinces Represented	Sens (6), Lyons (4), Vienne (3), Besançon (1), Rheims (3), Trier (1), Arles (4), Bourges (1), Tours (1), Bordeaux (1), Flanders (1)
Royal Involvement	The council was convoked by Dagobert I
Sources	Fredegar, *Chronica*, IV.78; *Vita Agilii Abbatis Resbacensis*, ch. 5 (AASS Aug. VI); Privilege of Rebais (Pardessus, no. 275)
Additional Notes	*Vita Agilii:* "Proinde in episcopali synodo, quae calendis Maii in Clypiaco eo anno est habita b. Agilium praecellentissimus rex in memorato coenobio praefecit abbatem."
Bibliography	Hefele, *Histoire*, III.1.278–9; Pontal, *Histoire*, 226

Location	Orléans
Date	639/41
Size	Unknown
Provinces Represented	Sens, Lyons, others?
Royal Involvement	The council was convoked by Clovis II
Sources	*Vita Eligii Episcopis Noviomensis*, I.35 (MGH SRM IV)
Bibliography	Hefele, *Histoire*, III.1.397–8; Pontal, *Histoire*, 216

Location	Bourges
Date	ca. 643

Size	Unknown
Provinces Represented	Bourges
Sources	*Desiderii Epistolae*, ep. II.17
Additional Notes	Convoked by Wulfoleude of Bourges, this council was forbidden by Sigibert III on the grounds that he was not informed first. Whether a later approved meeting was held is unknown.

Location	Chalon-sur-Saone
Date	647/53
Size	39 bishops, 5 abbots, 1 archdeacon
Provinces Represented	Arles (9), Vienne (7), Lyons (5), Sens (7), Bourges (2), Tours (4), Besançon (3), Rouen (6), Rheims (2)
Royal Involvement	The council was convoked in the name of Clovis II by the Neustrian mayor Erchinoald
Sources	*Acta* (CCSL 148A, 302–9); Epistle of the Synod to Theodorius of Arles (CCSL 148A, 309–10)
Bibliography	Hefele, *Histoire*, III.1.281–5; De Clercq, *Legislation*, 67–70; Pontal, *Histoire*, 216–20

Location	Arles
Date	648/60
Size	Unknown
Provinces Represented	Arles, others?
Sources	Letter of the Council of Chalon (647/53) to Theudorius of Arles (CCSL 148A, 309–10)
Additional Notes	This (provincial?) council was scheduled to be held in Arles, probably in the year following the Council of Chalon. Theudorius of Arles was expected to attend and be judged.

Location	Paris
Date	653
Size	26 bishops
Provinces Represented	Sens (6), Lyons (3), Vienne (3), Bourges (1), Rheims (6), Bordeaux (1), Rouen (1), Eauze (1), Arles (1), Unknown (3)
Sources	*Die Urkunden der Merowinger*, no. 85 (Clovis II); Privilege of St. Denis (Pardessus, no. 320)
Bibliography	Hefele, *Histoire*, III.1.296; Pontal, *Histoire*, 226

Location	Clichy
Date	654

Size	15 bishops, 2 deacons, 8 *viri inlustri*, mayor of the palace, unidentified others
Provinces Represented	Sens (4), Lyons (3), Vienne (2), Bourges (1), Rheims (2), Arles (1), Tours (1), Unknown (1)
Royal Involvement	The council was convoked and attended by Clovis II
Sources	*Die Urkunden der Merowinger*, no. 85 (Clovis II)
Bibliography	Hefele, *Histoire*, III.1.296; Pontal, *Histoire*, 226

Location	Nantes
Date	655/8
Size	Unknown
Provinces Represented	Rheims, others?
Sources	Vienne ms. 2198; Paris Bibl. St. Genevieve ms. 166; *Vita Nivardi*, ch. 7 (MGH SRM V); Flodoard of Rheims, *Historia Ecclesiae Remensis*, II.7 (MGH SS 36)
Additional Notes	Bishop Nivard of Rheims assembled the bishops of Gaul under papal orders and royal approval to rebuild the monastery of Hautvillier. The acts associated with this council are highly contested.
Bibliography	Hefele, *Histoire*, III.1.296–8; Pontal, *Histoire*, 226–7, 235–41

Location	Bordeaux (St. Pierre de Granon)
Date	662/75
Size	16 bishops, 2 abbots, 1 *dux*
Provinces Represented	Bourges (4), Bordeaux (5), Eauze (9)
Royal Involvement	The council was convoked by Childeric II
Sources	*Acta* (CCSL 148A, 311–13)
Bibliography	Hefele, *Histoire*, III.1.298–300; De Clercq, *Legislation*, 70; Pontal, *Histoire*, 229–31

Location	Autun
Date	ca. 662/76
Size	Unknown
Provinces Represented	Lyons, others?
Sources	*Acta* (CCSL 148A, 318–20; Mordek and Reynolds 84–92)
Additional Notes	The dating above is based on the chronology of the career of Leudegar of Autun as posited by Fouracre and Gerberding, *Late Merovingian France*, 193–253. Mordek and Reynolds place the council around 670.

Bibliography	Hefele, *Histoire*, III.1.307–9; Pontal, *Histoire*, 220–2; Mordek and Reynolds, "Bischof Leodegar," 71–92

Location	Saint-Jean-de-Losne
Date	673/5
Size	Unknown
Regions Represented	Kingdom of Childeric II
Royal Involvement	The council was convoked and met in the presence of Childeric II
Sources	*Acta* (CCSL 148A, 314–7)
Bibliography	Hefele, *Histoire*, III.1.300–2; De Clercq, *Legislation*, 70–2; Pontal, *Histoire*, 222–3

Location	Unknown
Date	675
Size	Unknown
Regions Represented	Kingdom of Childeric II
Royal Involvement	The council was convoked by Childeric II
Sources	Saint-Jean-de-Losne, c. 11
Additional Notes	The 11th canon of the Council of Saint-Jean-de-Losne ordered another council to be held in mid-September, in the 14th regnal year of Childeric II. As Childeric died in 675, the council was probably never held.

Location	Mâlay-le-Roi
Date	677
Size	Unknown
Provinces Represented	Lyons, Vienne, Sens, Besançon, + 1 unknown
Royal Involvement	The council was convoked by (in the name of?) Theuderic III
Sources	*Die Urkunden der Merowinger*, no. 122 (Theuderic III)
Additional Notes	The date above is that proposed by Mordek. Concerning this meeting, Philippe Depreux has argued that it was a *concilia mixta*. The council deposed Bishop Chramlinus of Embrun.
Bibliography	Hefele, *Histoire*, III.1.309; Pontal, *Histoire*, 232–3; Mordek, "Bischofsabsetzung in spätmerowingischer Zeit," 31–53; Depreux, "L'expression," 86

Location	Unknown
Date	ca. 677/9
Size	Unknown

Regions Represented	Kingdom of Theuderic III
Royal Involvement	The council was convoked by Ebroin in the name of Theuderic III
Sources	*Vita Leudegarii Episcopus Augustodunensis*, I.33, II.16–7 (MGH SRM V)
Additional Notes	Mordek has argued that this council is identical with that of Mâlay-le-Roi. This council tried Leudegar of Autun for the murder of King Childeric II.
Bibliography	Hefele, *Histoire*, III.1.551–2; Pontal, *Histoire*, 233; Mordek, "Bischofsabsetzung in spätmerowingischer Zeit," 39–42

Location	Unknown
Date	689
Size	Unknown
Provinces Represented	Unknown
Royal/State Involvement	The council was convoked by Pippin II
Sources	*Annales Mettenses Priores*, entry for 692

Location	Auxerre
Date	692/6
Size	Unknown
Regions Represented	Diocese of Auxerre
Sources	*Gestorum Episcoporum Autissiodorensium*, ch. 24
Additional Notes	The council was held in the year of Treticius' ordination
Bibliography	Hefele, *Histoire*, III.1.590

Location	Germania
Date	742
Size	7 bishops (with presbyters)
Regions Represented	Germania
Royal/State Involvement	The council was convoked by Carloman
Sources	Capitulary of Carloman (MGH Concilia II.I.1–4); Boniface, ep. 50–1 (MGH Epistolae III)
Bibliography	Hefele, *Histoire*, III.2.815–25; De Clercq, *Legislation*, 117–120; Hartmann, *Die Synoden*, 50–3

Location	Les Estinnes
Date	743
Size	Unknown
Regions Represented	Kingdom of Carloman
Royal/State Involvement	The council was convoked by Carloman

Sources	Capitulary of Carloman (MGH Concilia II.I.5–7); Hincmar, ep. 37 (MGH Concilia II.I.5–6)
Additional Notes	Hartmann suggests that this council may have coincided with a royal assembly.
Bibliography	Hefele, *Histoire*, III.2.825–44; De Clercq, *Legislation*, 120–22; Hartmann, *Die Synoden*, 53–5

Location	Soissons
Date	744
Size	23 bishops, An unknown number of clerics and *optimates*
Regions Represented	Kingdom of Pippin III
Royal/State Involvement	The council was convoked by Pippin III
Sources	Capitulary of Pippin (MGH Concilia II.I.33–6)
Bibliography	Hefele, *Histoire*, III.2.854–61; De Clercq, *Legislation*, 122–5; Hartmann, *Die Synoden*, 56–9

Location	Düren
Date	748
Size	Unknown
Regions Represented	Kingdom of Pippin III
Royal/State Involvement	The council was convoked by Pippin III
Sources	*Annales Mettenses Priores*, entry for 748
Additional Notes	This council was held in conjunction with a *placitum*. Hartmann suggests that Ver (755), cc. 20–1 may be citations of decisions originally made at Düren.
Bibliography	Hefele, *Histoire*, III.2.911–2; Hartmann, *Die Synoden*, 66–7, 71 (note 22)

Location	Ver
Date	755
Size	Unknown
Regions Represented	Kingdom of Pippin
Royal/State Involvement	The council was convoked by King Pippin
Sources	Capitulary of Pippin (MGH Capitularia I, p. 32–7)
Bibliography	Hefele, *Histoire*, III.2.934–8; De Clercq, *Legislation*, 133–7; Hartmann, *Die Synoden*, 68–72

Location	Verberie
Date	756
Size	Unknown
Regions Represented	Kingdom of Pippin

Sources	Capitulary of Pippin (MGH Capitularia I, p. 39–41)
Bibliography	Hefele, *Histoire*, III.2.917–21; De Clercq, *Legislation*, 140–2; Hartmann, *Die Synoden*, 73–6

Location	Aschheim
Date	756
Size	Unknown
Regions Represented	Bavaria
Royal/State Involvement	The council was convoked by Duke Tassilo
Sources	*Acta* (MGH Concilia II.I.56–8)
Bibliography	Hefele, *Histoire*, III.2.945–50; Hartmann, *Die Synoden*, 90–2

Location	Compiègne
Date	757
Size	21 bishops, 1 abbot, 1 deacon, 16 of unknown rank
Regions Represented	Kingdom of Pippin
Royal/State Involvement	The council was convoked by King Pippin
Sources	Privilege of Gorze (MGH Concilia II.I.59–63); Decretum of Pippin (MGH Capitularia I, p. 37–9); *Annales Mettenses Priores*, entry for 757; *Annales Regni Francorum/Revised Annales*, entry for 757
Bibliography	Hefele, *Histoire*, III.2.941–3; De Clercq, *Legislation*, 137–40; Hartmann, *Die Synoden*, 76–9

Location	Attigny
Date	762
Size	27 bishops; 17 abbots
Regions Represented	Kingdom of Pippin
Sources	*Acta* (MGH Concilia II.I.72–3)
Bibliography	Hefele, *Histoire*, III.2.951–2; De Clercq, *Legislation*, 143; Hartmann, *Die Synoden*, 79–81

Location	Gentilly
Date	767
Size	Unknown
Regions Represented	Kingdom of Pippin
Royal/State Involvement	The council was convoked by King Pippin
Sources	*Annales Mettenses Priores*, entry for 767; *Annales Regni Francorum/Revised Annales*, entry for 767; *Vita Austremonii* (Mansi XII.662); Ado of Vienne, *Chronica*, entry for 767 (PL 123)

Additional Notes	Hartmann associates a reference to a synod in the *Vita Austremonii* with Gentilly, which Mansi interprets as a reference to another synod held in Volvic.
Bibliography	Hefele, *Histoire*, III.2.725–6; Hartmann, *Die Synoden*, 81–2

APPENDIX B

CONTESTED AND DUBIOUS COUNCILS, 511–768

Location	Rheims
Date	514
Size	Unknown
Provinces Represented	Rheims, "Episcopi demum Galliae ac Belgicae provinciarum"
Sources	Hincmar of Rheims, *Vita Sancti Remigii*, ch. 21 (MGH AA IV.2); Flodoard of Rheims, *Historia Ecclesiae Remensis*, I.16 (MGH SS 36)
Additional Notes	Remigius of Rheims convoked this synod known only through post-Merovingian sources, and there converted an Arian bishop
Bibliography	Pontal, *Histoire*, 135

Location	Agaune
Date	515/23
Size	60 bishops, *comites*
Provinces Represented	Lyons, Vienne, others?
Sources	Fredegar, *Chronica*, IV.1; Avitus of Vienne, *Hom.* 25 (MGH AA 6.2); Forged Foundation Charter (Reymond, "La Charte de Saint Sigismond," 3–6)
Additional Notes	This council is said to have been held at the completion of the monastery of St. Maurice and the installation of its abbot. Its date, acts, and status as a council have all been disputed.
Bibliography	Hefele, *Histoire*, II.2.1017–22; Pontal, *Histoire*, 60–3; Theurillat, "L'Abbaye de Saint-Maurice d'Agaune," 1–128; Wood, "Prelude to Columbanus," 15–18

Location	Le Mans
Date	516/26
Size	9 bishops, 4 *comites*, 1 abbot, 1 viscount, 8 of unknown rank
Provinces Represented	Tours, others?
Sources	Charter of Haregarius (Pardessus, no. 108)

Additional Notes	Haregius' charter confirms a donation for the founding of a monastery in honor of Mary and the martyrs Gervasius and Protasius in Le Mans. Pardessus notes: "Porro falsitate arguunt subscriptiones testium quae profecto supposititiae videntur. Cum enim octo legantur nomina subscribentium episcoporum, ne unum quidem nomen ex his apparet in indicibus episcoporum provinciae Turonicae, excepto nominee Innocentii, tunc episcopi Cenomanici. Aliam proferemus chartam sub anno 738, Carilepho adscriptam, exeodem fonte sumptam, et olim falsi damnatam, quae easdemad unam exhibit subscriptiones episcoporum ignororum his temporibus et locis" (Pardessus, I.72, note 7).
Bibliography	Pontal, *Histoire*, 135

Location	Tournai
Date	520
Size	Unknown
Provinces Represented	Rheims
Sources	Sermon of Eleutherius of Tournai on the Trinity (PL 65, col. 90–1)
Additional Notes	The authenticity of this sermon is doubtful. The council was supposedly convoked to combat heresy.
Bibliography	Hefele, *Histoire*, II.2.1054

Location	Unknown
Date	ca. 538
Size	Unknown
Provinces Represented	Tours, others?
Sources	Venantius Fortunatus, *Vita Albini*, ch. XVIII (MGH AA IV.2)
Additional Notes	This synod was said to have ordered Bishop Albinus of Angers to allow a man that he had excommunicated for incest to receive the blessed host (*eulogia*). In response, Albinus travelled to Arles to get the backing of Bishop Caesarius. The validity and location of the episode are uncertain.
Bibliography	Mikat, *Die Inzestverbote*, 13–4, 17–18; Klingshirn, *Caesarius of Arles*, 258

Location	Lyons
Date	572/3
Size	Unknown number of clerics and laymen
Provinces Represented	Lyons
Sources	Gregory of Tours, *D.L.H.*, V.5
Additional Notes	Heinzelmann argues that this provincial meeting, which Gregory calls a *placitum*, was actually a synod; Pontal, however, disagrees. The meeting acquitted Gregory of Tours' brother Peter of murdering Bishop Silvester of Langres.
Bibliography	Heinzelmann, *Gregory of Tours*, 185; Pontal, *Histoire*, 167

Location	Paris
Date	580
Size	Unknown
Provinces Represented	Sens, Tours, Eauze, others?
Sources	Gregory of Tours, *D.L.H.*, IX.6
Additional Notes	Gregory of Tours mentions "convenientibus episcopis" at Paris, which he joined, and informed of the activities of a runaway servant of Amelius of Bigorre. It is not clear from the context if this meeting was a formally-convoked council, although the terminology is suggestive of one.

Location	Tours
Date	ca. 580
Size	Unknown
Provinces Represented	Tours
Sources	Gregory of Tours, *D.L.H.*, V.49
Additional Notes	After his trial at Berny, Gregory of Tours "cum consilio provincialium" prosecuted the priest Riculf. This appears to have been a provincial synod.

Location	Bordeaux
Date	584/5
Size	Unknown
Provinces Represented	Bordeaux, Eauze, others?
Sources	Gregory of Tours, *D.L.H.*, VII.31
Additional Notes	The pretender Gundovald convoked a meeting of bishops to elect the priest Faustianus as bishop of Dax. Bachrach identifies the meeting as a synod.
Bibliography	Bachrach, *Anatomy of a Little War*, 99–100

Location	Orléans
Date	585
Size	Unknown
Provinces Represented	Sens, Tours, others?
Royal Involvement	Guntram appears to have attended.
Sources	Gregory of Tours, *D.L.H.*, VIII.5
Additional Notes	Guntram, at a meal with several bishops, declared that he would punish Bishop Theodore of Marseilles "si ad synodum veniret." Possibly this reference is directed towards those bishops present at the meal. More likely it is a reference to either the Council of Troyes or Mâcon (585), both of which met after the July Orléans sojourn and were scheduled to discuss Theodore's case. The interrogation of Bishops Palladius of Saintes and Bertram of Bordeaux, referenced in *D.L.H.*, VIII.2, may also have taken place in the context of a *concilia mixta*, although most certainly a different one.

Location	Sens
Date	594/614
Size	Unknown
Provinces Represented	Sens, others?
Sources	*Vita Betharii Episcopi Carnotensis*, ch. 11 (MGH SRM III)
Additional Notes	The council is attested only by a post-Merovingian-era *vita*.
Bibliography	Hefele, *Histoire*, III.1.245–6; Pontal, *Histoire*, 178; Gouyer, "Quelques Mots," 61–6

Location	Unknown
Date	Late 6th/Early 7th Century
Size	Unknown
Provinces Represented	Unknown
Sources	Pope Gregory I, *Registrum Epistularum*, V.58–60, VIII.4, IX.214, IX.216, IX.219–20, and IX.223
Additional Notes	It is not certain whether this council, which Pope Gregory I encouraged to deal with simony and other abuses, was ever officially convoked or held. It has been suggested that it was identical with Sens 594/614.
Bibliography	Hefele, *Histoire*, III.1.245–6

Location	Cologne
Date	ca. 626
Size	Unknown
Provinces Represented	Cologne
Royal Involvement	Dagobert I commands that Cunibert be appointed bishop.
Sources	*Vita Cuniberti*, ch. 3 (*Annalecta Bollandiana* vol. 47, pgs. 363–7)
Additional Notes	According to his *vita* (late 9th century +), by means of a synod and a "praecepto regis," Cunibert was chosen to assume the episcopate of the city of Cologne.
Bibliography	Müller, "Kunibert von Köln,"12–3

Location	Rheims
Date	626/7
Size	See Clichy (626/7) entry in appendix A
Provinces Represented	See Clichy (626/7) entry in appendix A
Sources	*Acta* in Flodoard of Rheims, *Historia Ecclesiae Remensis*, II.5 (MGH SS 36)
Additional Notes	This pseudo-council is to be identified with the Council of Clichy (626/7).
Bibliography	Hefele, *Histoire*, III.1.260–5; De Clercq, *Legislation*, 65–6; Pontal, *Histoire*, 215–6

Location	Paris
Date	632
Size	12 bishops, 1 *praefectus*, 4 *comites*
Provinces Represented	Unknown
Sources	*Die Urkunden der Merowinger*, no. 43 (Dagobert I, forgery)
Additional Notes	According to this forged royal diploma, in a synod in Paris Dagobert I confirmed a grant of immunity previously given to Saint-Denis in a general assembly held at Compiègne.

Location	Constance
Date	ca. 635/40?
Size	Unknown number of bishops, priests, deacons, clerics, and laymen
Regions Represented	Alamannia
Royal/State Involvement	The council was convoked and attended by Duke Gunzo (Cunzo)

Sources	Wettinus, *Vita Galli Confessoris*, chs. 24–5 (MGH SRM IV); Walahfrid Strabo, *Vita Galli Confessoris*, I.24–5 (MGH SRM IV).
Additional Notes	Convoked by the Alamannian Duke Gunzo, who also attended, this council appointed the deacon Johannes bishop of Constance after the death of Gaudentius. The reliability of the *Vita Galli* is contested.
Bibliography	Keller, "Fränkische Herrschaft und alemannisches Herzogtum im 6. und 7. Jahrhundert," 1–30; Geuenich, *Geschichte der Alemannen*, 98–9

Location	Unknown
Date	645
Size	12 bishops
Provinces Represented	Sens (6), Lyons (3), Besançon (1), Rheims (1), Unknown (1)
Sources	Privilege of Saint-Maur-des-Fosses (Auvray, *Mem. Soc.* 19, pgs. 12–17); *Vita Baboleni* (Bouquet III. 569); *Die Urkunden der Merowinger*, nos. 76 and 87 (Clovis II and Chlothar III, both forgeries)
Additional Notes	It is not certain whether the subscriptions attached to this privilege are indicative of a council.
Bibliography	Pontal, *Die Synoden*, 205

Location	Unknown
Date	657
Size	Unknown
Regions Represented	Kingdom of Clovis II
Royal Involvement	The council was convoked by Clovis II
Sources	Pseudo-Anastasius Bibliothecario (Peter the Deacon), *Epitome Chronica Casinensis* (Rerum Italicarum Scriptores II.1, p. 355)
Additional Notes	This council supposedly ordered the restitution of the relics of St. Benedict and St. Scholasticus to Pope Vitalian.
Bibliography	Hefele, *Histoire*, III.1.296; Pontal, *Histoire*, 243; Caspar, *Petrus Diaconus und die Monte Cassineser Fälschungen*, 111–21

Location	Unknown
Date	660
Size	26 bishops

Provinces Represented	Sens (6), Lyons (1), Vienne (1), Bourges (1), Rouen (6), Borderaux (1), Tours (1), Rheims (5), Unknown (4)
Sources	Privilege of Saint-Colombe (Pardessus, no. 333)
Additional Notes	It is not certain whether the subscriptions attached to this privilege are indicative of a council.
Bibliography	Pontal, *Die Synoden*, 206

Location	Mâlay-le-Roi
Date	660
Size	26 bishops
Provinces Represented	Lyons (3), Sens (6), Rheims (5), Vienne (1), Arles (3), Bourges (1), Bordeaux (1), Tours (2), Rouen (1), Unknown (3)
Sources	Privilege of Saint-Pierre-le-Vif (Pardessus, no. 335); Odorannus of Sens, *Chronicon* (PL 142)
Additional Notes	It is not certain whether the subscriptions attached to this privilege are indicative of a council.
Bibliography	Hefele, *Histoire*, III.1.296; Pontal, *Histoire*, 227

Location	Sithiu
Date	663
Size	9 bishops, 1 abbot, 1 monk
Provinces Represented	Rouen (1), Rheims (6), Unknown (2)
Sources	Privilege of Saint-Omer (Pardessus, no. 344)
Additional Notes	It is not certain whether the subscriptions attached to this privilege are indicative of a council.
Bibliography	Pontal, *Die Synoden*, 207–8

Location	Unknown
Date	663/75
Size	7 bishops, 1 archdeacon, 1 of unknown rank
Provinces Represented	Trier (1), Mayence (2), Unknown (4)
Sources	Privilege of Saint-Die (Pardessus, no. 360)
Additional Notes	It is not certain whether the subscriptions attached to this privilege are indicative of a council.
Bibliography	Pontal, *Histoire*, 227

Location	Chatou
Date	664
Size	16 bishops
Provinces Represented	Lyons (2), Sens (4), Rheims (5), Vienne (2), Bordeaux (1), Rouen (2)

Sources	Privilege of Corbie (Pardessus, no. 345)
Additional Notes	It is not certain whether the subscriptions attached to this privilege are indicative of a council.
Bibliography	Pontal, *Die Synoden*, 208

Location	Compiègne
Date	665
Size	12 bishops (or more)
Provinces Represented	Unknown
Sources	Bede, *Historia*, III.28; Eddius Stephanus, *Vita Wilfridi*, ch. 12 (MGH SRM VI)
Additional Notes	Although Eddius states that Wilfrid's consecration took place in a "conventus magnus," it is not certain whether this meeting can be considered a synod proper. No Frankish sources mention the meeting.

Location	Soissons
Date	667
Size	19 bishops
Provinces Represented	Rheims (3), Lyons (3), Rouen (3), Vienne (1), Sens (8), Unknown (1)
Sources	Privilege of Notre-Dame in Soissons (Pardessus, no. 355)
Additional Notes	It is not certain whether the subscriptions attached to this privilege are indicative of a council.
Bibliography	Pontal, *Die Synoden*, 209

Location	Unknown
Date	679
Size	Unknown
Provinces Represented	Arles, Trier, others?
Sources	Agatho, ep. 3 (PL 87)
Additional Notes	Some have read the three Frankish subscriptions attached to the Council of Rome (680), convoked by Pope Agatho, as evidence for a Gallic council e.g. "Felix humilis episcopus sanctae ecclesiae Arelatensis, legatus venerabilis synodi per Galliarum provinciae constituti." It also has been argued that this passage should instead read "synodus per Galliarum provincias constituta," although Riedinger's 1984 edition of the acts of the Third Council of Constantinople maintains the original wording (I.149).
Bibliography	Hefele, *Histoire*, III.1.476

Location	Arles
Date	ca. 682
Size	Unknown
Provinces Represented	Arles, others?
Sources	Mansi XI.1045–6 (re. MS Lucca BC 490)
Additional Notes	Hefele and Leclercq doubt the veracity of this council.
Bibliography	Hefele, *Histoire*, III.1.547

Location	Rouen
Date	682
Size	16 bishops
Provinces Represented	Rouen (4), Tours (2), Rheims (1), Sens (1), Trier (1), Bordeaux (1), Unknown (6)
Sources	*Vita Ansberti*, ch. 18 (MGH SRM V)
Additional Notes	The veracity of this council has been questioned.
Bibliography	Hefele, *Histoire*, III.1.546; Pontal, *Histoire*, 228; Kölzer et al, *Die Urkunden der Merowinger*, II. 598–9, II.608–9, II.628

Location	Unknown
Date	683
Size	9 bishops, 2 abbots, 1 presbyter, 1 archdeacon, 1 deacon
Provinces Represented	Arles
Sources	Privilege of Groseaux (Pardessus, no. 401)
Additional Notes	It is not certain whether the subscriptions attached to this privilege are indicative of a council.
Bibliography	Pontal, *Die Synoden*, 209

Location	Le Mans
Date	683
Size	32 bishops, 1 abbot, 1 archdeacon, 1 of unknown rank
Provinces Represented	Lyons (2), Sens (4), Rheims (5), Vienne (1), Bourges (2), Tours (3), Unknown (15)
Sources	Privilege of Notre-Dame in Le Mans (Pardessus, no. 451)
Additional Notes	It is not certain whether the subscriptions attached to this privilege are indicative of a council.
Bibliography	Pontal, *Die Synoden*, 209

Location	Meaux
Date	690

Size	Unknown
Provinces Represented	Unknown
Sources	*Die Urkunden der Merowinger*, no. 131 (Theuderic III)
Additional Notes	Theuderic refers to the "consilio ponteficum vel obtimatum nostorum villa noncopanti Latiniaco, que ponitur in pago Meldequo..." The implications of 'consilio' are debatable. This is perhaps a *concilium mixtum*.

Location	Rheims
Date	692
Size	Unknown
Provinces Represented	Unknown
Sources	Privilege of Montier-en-Der (Pardessus, no. 423)
Additional Notes	It is not certain whether this privilege (lacking subscriptions) was produced by a council.
Bibliography	Pontal, *Die Synoden*, 210

Location	Sens
Date	695
Size	9 bishops
Provinces Represented	Lyons (2), Sens (4), Bourges (1), Unknown (2)
Sources	Privilege of Saint-Colombe (Deschamps, *Le Moyen Age* 25, 160–5)
Additional Notes	It is not certain whether the subscriptions attached to this privilege are indicative of a council.
Bibliography	Pontal, *Die Synoden*, 210

Location	Chatou
Date	696
Size	14 bishops
Provinces Represented	Lyons (1), Sens (5), Rouen (1), Rheims (1), Tours (2), Bordeaux (2), Unknown (2)
Sources	Privilege of Notre Dame of Blois (Pardessus, no. 435)
Additional Notes	It is not certain whether the subscriptions attached to this privilege are indicative of a council.
Bibliography	Pontal, *Die Synoden*, 210

Location	Utrecht
Date	697

Size	Unknown
Provinces Represented	Unknown
Sources	Pseudo-Marcellinus, *Vita Suuiberti* (Leibnitz, *Scriptores Brunsvicensium*, II.222–42)
Additional Notes	Hefele and Leclercq call this council an invention.
Bibliography	Hefele, *Histoire*, III.1.590

Location	Unknown
Date	Late 7th Century
Size	Unknown
Provinces Represented	Sens, others?
Sources	*Vita Faronis Episcopi Meldensis*, ch. 110 (MGH SRM V)
Additional Notes	This pseudo-council supposedly deposed Faro's fictional successor Bishop Datlevertus of Meaux. On Datlevertus, see MGH SRM V, p. 174.

Location	Liege (2)
Date	708/56
Size	Unknown
Provinces Represented	Cologne
Sources	*AASS* Nov. I (792–3)
Additional Notes	The editors of the *Acta Sanctorum* conclude that "there is no plausible evidence" that Saint Humbert held the synods in question.
Bibliography	Hefele, *Histoire*, III.1.596–7

Location	Tongres (2)
Date	708/56
Size	30 bishops (Tongres II)
Provinces Represented	Cologne
Sources	*AASS* Nov. I (792–3)
Additional Notes	The editors of the *Acta Sanctorum* conclude that "there is no plausible evidence" that Saint Humbert held the synods in question.
Bibliography	Hefele, *Histoire*, III.1.596–7

Location	Rouen
Date	711/15
Size	Unknown number of bishops and secular nobles
Provinces Represented	Rouen, others?
Sources	*Vita Dagoberti III*, ch. 8 (MGH SRM II)

Additional Notes	This account from the hodgepodge *Vita Dagoberti III* (9th–11th cent.), draws from the language and content of the *Annales Mettenses Priores* and the *Gesta Abbatum Fontanellensium*. Moreover, the reference to Abbot Hugo of Fontenelle is anachronistic; Hugo did not take office until after Dagobert III's death (ca. 723; see *Gesta Abbatum Fontanellensium*, IV).
Bibliography	Carozzi, "La Vie de Saint Dagobert de Stenay," 225–58; Dierkens, "Note sur un Passage de la Vita Dagoberti," 259–70

Location	Utrecht
Date	719
Size	Unknown
Provinces Represented	Unknown
Sources	Pseudo-Marcellinus, *Vita Suuiberti* (Leibnitz, *Scriptores Brunsvicensium*, II.222–42)
Additional Notes	Hefele and Leclercq reject the council's authenticity.
Bibliography	Hefele, *Histoire*, III.1.597

Location	Strasbourg
Date	728
Size	4 bishops, 3 abbots, 1 presbyter, 2 archdeacons, 2 deacons, 2 *comites*, 1 *dux*, 1 tribune, 8 of unknown rank
Provinces Represented	Mainz, others?
Sources	Privilege of Murbach (Pardessus, no. 543)
Additional Notes	It is not certain whether the subscriptions attached to this privilege are indicative of a council.

Location	Danube Valley or Augsburg
Date	732/40
Size	Unknown
Regions Represented	Bavaria and Alamannia
Sources	Gregory III, eps. 44–5 (MGH Epistolae III)
Additional Notes	Hartmann argues that this council, which the Pope requested Boniface to hold among the Bavarians and Alamanni, never took place. He argues the canons credited by Werminghoff (pgs. 51–3) to a Bavarian Synod ca. 740/50 were written closer to 800.

Bibliography	Hefele, *Histoire*, III.2.806–14; Hartmann, *Die Synoden der Karolingerzeit*, 89–90

Location	Unknown
Date	745
Size	Unknown
Regions Represented	Unknown
Sources	Boniface, ep. 60 (MGH Epistolae III)
Additional Notes	Although Hartmann includes this council, Jarnut argues that no synods were held in the Frankish Kingdom between 745 and 747. The council apparently dealt with specific judicial cases as well as the issue of the restitution of ecclesiastical property.
Bibliography	Hefele, *Histoire*, III.2.844–50, 861–73; Hartmann, *Die Synoden der Karolingerzeit*, 59–60; Jarnut, "Bonifatius," 26

Location	Germania
Date	746
Size	Unknown
Regions Represented	Germania
Sources	Ludger, *Vita S. Gregorii Trajectensis*, ch. 9 (Mabillon, AASS OSB III.2.294)
Additional Notes	This pseudo-council was supposedly a *concilium mixtum*.
Bibliography	Hefele, *Histoire*, III.2.884–5

Location	Unknown
Date	747
Size	13 bishops?
Regions Represented	Kingdom of Carloman
Sources	Boniface, eps. 78, 82? (MGH Epistolae III)
Additional Notes	Hartmann suggests that the bishops mentioned by Pope Zacharias in his epistle (no. 82) to Boniface may have attended this council. Jarnut argues that no synods were held in the Frankish Kingdom between 745 and 747.
Bibliography	Hefele, *Histoire*, III.2.893–903; Hartmann, *Die Synoden der Karolingerzeit*, 60–3; Jarnut, "Bonifatius," 26

Location	Mainz
Date	753/4

Size	Unknown
Regions Represented	Kingdom of Pippin
Royal Involvement	Lull was ordained "cum decreto Pippini regis" and with "consensu principis Pippini"
Sources	*Vita Tertia Bonifatii*, ch. 7; *Vita Quarta Bonifatii Auctore Moguntino*, ch. 7 (*Vitae Sancti Bonifatii*, ed. Wilhelm Levison)
Additional Notes	This council was said to have elected Lull as Boniface's successor as bishop. In regards to its reliability, Hefele observes "Malheureusement les renseignements que nous donnent sur ce concile les anciens biographes de saint Boniface, laissent beaucoup à désirer; ils sont même parfois très incertains."
Bibliography	Hefele, *Histoire*, III.2.926

Location	Unknown
Date	755
Size	Unknown
Regions Represented	Kingdom of Pippin
Sources	Capitulary of Pippin (MGH Capitularia I, p. 31–2)
Additional Notes	Of this capitulary, Hartmann writes: "Daher muß fraglich bleiben, ob dieser Text als Erzeugnis einer Synode angesehen werden darf"
Bibliography	Hartmann, *Die Synoden der Karolingerzeit*, 67–8

Location	Les Estinnes
Date	756
Size	Unknown
Regions Represented	Kingdom of Pippin
Sources	Council of Quierzy (758)
Additional Notes	Hefele and Leclercq call this council apocryphal.
Bibliography	Hefele, *Histoire*, III.2.940

Location	Constance
Date	758/9
Size	Unknown
Regions Represented	Alamannia
Sources	Walahfrid Strabo, *Vita Othmari*, chs. 4–6 (MGH SS II).
Additional Notes	This council reportedly deposed Abbot Othmar of St. Gall
Bibliography	Hefele, *Histoire*, III.2.944–5

Location	Bourges
Date	767–8
Size	Unknown
Provinces Represented	Bourges, others?
Sources	Fredegar, *Chronica* (Continuation), ch. 50
Additional Notes	According to the continuator of Fredegar's chronicle, King Pippin spent the period between Christmas and Epiphany in Bourges "per consilio episcoporum vel sacerdotum." It is unclear whether this is a reference to a synod (It is included as such in Mansi XII.678–9).

Location	Rouen
Date	Unknown
Size	Unknown
Provinces Represented	Rouen, others?
Sources	Vienne ms. 2198, Paris; Bibl. St. Genevieve ms. 166
Bibliography	Hefele, *Histoire*, III.1.287–9; Pontal, *Histoire*, 241–3.
Additional Notes	This derivative set of canons has been dated to, among other periods, the reign of Clovis II and the later ninth century. Their relation to a real council is dubious.

APPENDIX C

CALENDAR OF COUNCILS*

January	February	March
	Eauze (551): February 1	Les Estinnes (743): March 1 Soissons (744): March 2
April	**May**	**June**
Germany (742): April 21	Lyons (583): Day unknown Orléans (639/41): Day unknown Clichy (636): May 1 Orléans (538): May 7 Orléans (541): May 14 *Auxerre (586/606):* Mid-May Compiègne (757): May 18 Marseilles (533): May 26	Toul (550): June 1 *Unknown 2 (588): June 1* Arles (524): June 6 Clichy (654): June 22 Valence (583/5): June 22 Orléans (533): June 23 Arles (554): June 29
July	**August**	**September**
Paris (653): July 1 Orange (529): July 3 Orléans (511): July 10 Ver (755): July 11		*Bourges (ca. 643): September 1* Paris (573): September 11 Epaone (517): September 15 Mâlay-le-Roi (679/80): September 15 *Unknown (675): Mid-September* Clichy (626/7): September 27

(*Continued*)

Appendix c (*Cont.*)

October	November	December
Verdun (590): Beginning of October	Mâcon (581/3): November 1	
Paris (614): October 10	*Auxerre (586/606): November 1*	
Mâcon (585): October 23	*Unknown 1 (589): November 1*	
Chalon (647/53): October 24	Vaison (529): November 5	
Orléans (549): October 28	Carpentras (527): November 6	
	Clermont (535): November 8	
	Metz (590): Mid-November	
	Tours (567): November 18	

* Councils with questionable authenticity or synodal status are not included. Councils in italics were officially convoked, but were not necessarily held.

ECCLESIASTICAL PROVINCES AND BISHOPRICES OF MEROVINGIAN GAUL

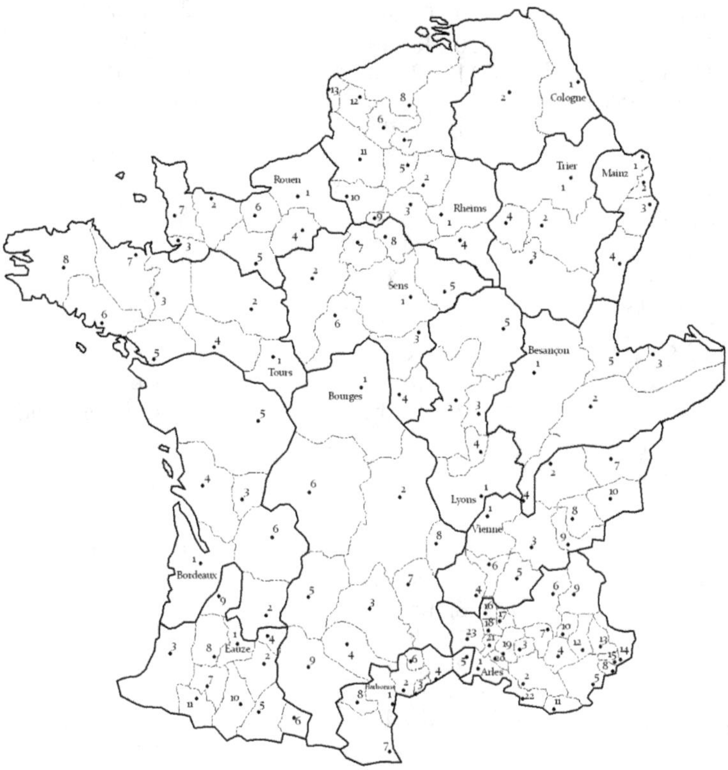

——— Ecclesiastical Provinces

------- Approximate Boundary of *civitas*

Numbers - Bishoprics Keyed to Metropolitans

1. **Arles**
2. Aix-en-Provence
3. Apt
4. Riez
5. Fréjus
6. Gap
7. Sisteron
8. Antibes
9. Embrun
10. Digne
11. Toulon
12. Senez
13. Glandève
14. Cimiez/Nice
15. Vence
16. St-Paul-Trois-Chateaux
17. Vaison
18. Orange
19. Carpentras
20. Cavaillon
21. Avignon
22. Marseilles
23. Uzès

1. **Besançon**
2. Avenches

1. **Bordeaux**
2. Agen
3. Angoulême
4. Saintes
5. Poitiers
6. Périgueux

1. **Bourges**
2. Clermont (-Ferrand)
3. Rodez
4. Albi
5. Cahors
6. Limoges
7. Javols
8. Velay
9. Toulouse

1. **Cologne**
2. Tongres/ Maastricht

1. **Eauze**
2. Auch
3. Dax
4. Lectoure
5. St-Bertrand-de Comminges
6. Couserans (St-Lizier)
7. Lescar
8. Aire
9. Bazas
10. Tarbes
11. Oloron

1. **Lyons**
2. Autun
3. Chalon(-sur-Saone)
4. Mâcon
5. Langres

1. **Mainz**
2. Worms
3. Speyer
4. Strasbourg

1. **Narbonne**
2. Béziers
3. Agde
4. Maguelonne
5. Nîmes
6. Lodève
7. Elne
8. Carcassonne

1. **Rheims**
2. Laon
3. Soissons
4. Châlons(-sur-Marne)
5. Vermand/Noyon
6. Arras
7. Cambrai
8. Tournai
9. Senlis
10. Beauvais
11. Amiens
12. Thérouanne
13. Boulogne

1. **Rouen**
2. Bayeux
3. Avranches
4. Evreux
5. Sées
6. Lisieux
7. Coutances

1. **Sens**
2. Chartres
3. Auxerre
4. Nevers
5. Troyes
6. Orleans
7. Paris
8. Meaux

1. **Tours**
2. Le Mans
3. Rennes
4. Angers
5. Nantes
6. Vannes
7. Corseul
8. Osismes (Carhaix)

1. **Trier**
2. Metz
3. Toul
4. Verdun

1. **Vienne**
2. Geneva
3. Grenoble
4. Alba/Viviers (Vivarium)
5. Die
6. Valence
7. Martigny(Valais)/ Sion
8. Tarentaise
9. Maurienne
10. Aosta

BIBLIOGRAPHY

Editions, Translations, and Synopses of Gallo-Roman and Frankish Conciliar Acta

Acta Conciliorum et Epistolae Decretales, ac Constitutiones Summorum Pontificum, edited by Jean Hardouin. Paris: Ex Typographia Regia, 1714–1715.

Canones Apostolorum et Conciliorum: Saeculorum IV, V, VI, VII, edited by Hermann Bruns. Berlin: Typis et Sumptibus G. Reimeri, 1839.

Les canons des conciles mérovingiens (VIe–VIIe siècles). SC 354. Translated by Jean Gaudemet and Brigitte Basdevant-Gaudemet. Paris: Editions du Cerf, 1989.

Conciles gaulois du IV siècle. SC 241. Translated by Jean Gaudemet. Paris: Editions du Cerf, 1977.

Concilia aevi Karolini. MGH Leges, Sectio III, Tomus II. Edited by Albert Werminghoff. Hanover: Hahn, 1906.

Concilia aevi Merovingici. MGH Leges, Sectio III, Tomus I. Edited by Friedrich Maassen. Hanover: Hahn, 1893.

Concilia Antiqua Galliae, edited by Jacques Sirmond. Aalen, Germany: Scientia, 1970 (orig. 1629).

Concilia Galliae: A.314–A.506. CCSL 148. Edited by Charles Munier. Turnhout: Brepols, 1963.

Concilia Galliae: A.511–A.695. CCSL 148A. Edited by Charles de Clercq. Turnhout: Brepols, 1963.

Concilia Omnia, edited by Petrus Crabbe. Cologne: Petrus Quentel Excudebat, 1538.

Conciliorum Omnium, edited by Laurentius Surius. Cologne: Apud Geruuinum Calenium and Hæredes Iohannis Quentelij, 1567.

Hefele, Karl Joseph Von. *Conciliengeschichte*. Freiburg im Breisgau: Herder, 1873–90. French edition: *Histoire des conciles d'après les documents originaux*. Edited and translated by Henri Leclercq. Paris: Letouzey et Ané, 1907–1952. English translation: *A History of the Councils of the Church*. Translated by William R. Clark. Edinburgh: T. and T. Clark, 1883–96.

Die Konzilien der Karolingischen Teilreiche 843–859. MGH Leges, Sectio III, Tomus III. Edited by Wilfried Hartmann. Hanover: Hahn, 1984.

Die Konzilien der Karolingischen Teilreiche 860–874. MGH Leges, Sectio III, Tomus IV. Edited by Wilfried Hartmann. Hanover: Hahn, 1998.

Konzilien und Synoden im spätantiken Gallien von 314 bis 696 nach Christi Geburt, translated by Josef Limmer. Frankfurt: Peter Lang, 2004.

Sacrorum Conciliorum Nova et Amplissima Collection, edited by Giovanni Domenico Mansi. Paris: H. Welter, 1901–27 (orig. 1759–98).

Sacrosancta Concilia ad Regiam Editionem Exacta, edited by Philippe Labbe and Gabriel Cossart. Paris: Imprentis Societatis Tipographicae Librorum Ecclesiasticorum, 1671–1672. Nicholas Coleti ed. 1728–33.

Additional Primary Sources

Ado of Vienne. *Sancti Adonis Chronicon*. PL 123. Edited by J. P. Migne. Paris: Garnier Brothers, 1879.

Ammianus Marcellinus. *Ammianus Marcellinus (Rerum Gestarum Libri)*. Edited and translated by John C. Rolfe. Cambridge, MA: Harvard University Press, 1935–9.

Annales Mettenses Priores, edited by Bernhard Simson. Hanover: Hahn, 1905. Partial English translation in *Late Merovingian France*, ed. Paul Fouracre and Richard Gerberding. Manchester: Manchester University Press, 1996.

Annales Regni Francorum. MGH SRG I. Edited by Friedrich Kurz. Hanover: Hahn, 1895. English translation in *Carolingian Chronicles*. Translated by Bernhard Scholz. Ann Arbor: University of Michigan Press, 1970.

Auvray, Lucien, ed. "Documents parisiens tires de la Bibliothèque du Vatican." *Mémoires de la Société de l'histoire de Paris et de I'Ile de France* 19 (1892): 12–7.

Avitus of Vienne. *Opera*. MGH AA VI.2. Edited by Rudolf Peiper. Berlin: Weidmann, 1883. English translation: *Avitus of Vienne: Letters and Selected Prose*. Edited and translated by Danuta Shanzer and Ian Wood. Liverpool: Liverpool University Press, 2002.

Baudonivia. *Vita Sanctae Radegundis Liber II*. MGH SRM II. Edited by Bruno Krusch, 77–395. Hanover: Hahn, 1888.

Bede. *Historia Ecclesiastica Gentis Anglorum*. Edited by Bertram Colgrave and R. A. B. Mynors. Rev. ed. Oxford: Clarendon Press, 1992.

Bertram of Le Mans. *Das Testament des Bischofs Berthramn von Le Mans vom 27. März 616*. Edited by Margarete Weidemann. Mainz: Verlag des Römisch-Germanischen Zentralmuseums, 1986.

Boniface. *S. Bonifatii et Lulli Epistolae*. MGH Epistolae III. Edited by Ernst Dümmler. Berlin: Weidmann, 1892. English translation: *The Letters of Saint Boniface*. Translated by Ephraim Emerton. New York: Columbia University Press, 1940.

Capitularia Regum Francorum. MGH Leges II.1. Edited by Alfred Boretius. Hanover: Hahn, 1883.

Chartae Latinae Antiquiores. Vols. 13–19 (France). Edited by Albert Bruckner and Robert Marichal. Olten: U. Graf, 1954–2004.

Codex Theodosianus, edited by Theodore Mommsen and Paul M. Meyer. Berlin: Weidmann, 1905. English translation: *The Theodosian Code and Novels and the Sirmondian Constitutions*. Translated by Clyde Pharr. New York: Greenwood Press, 1952.

Coens, Maurice, ed. "Les vies de Saint Cunibert et la tradition manuscrite." *Annalecta Bollandiana* 47 (1929): 338–67.

Columbanus. *Columbae Sive Columbani Abbatis Luxoviensis et Bobbiensis Epistolae*. MGH Epistolarum III. Edited by Wilhelm Gundlach. Berlin: Weidmann, 1892.

Concilium Universale Constantinopolitanum Tertium, edited by Rudolf Riedinger. Berlin: Walter de Gruyter, 1984.

Deschamps, Paul, ed. "Critique du privilège épiscopal accordé par Emmon de Sens à l'Abbaye de Sainte-Colombe (660, 26 Août)." *Moyen Age* 25 (1912): 160–5.

Desiderius of Cahors. *Epistulae S. Desiderii Cadurcensis*. Edited by Dag Norberg. Uppsala: Almquist and Wiksell, 1961.

Diplomata, Chartae, Epistolae, Leges Aliaque Instrumenta ad Res Gallo-Francicas Spectantia. Edited by J. M. Pardessus. Aalen: Scientia Verlag, 1843–9.

Donatus. *Vita Ermenlandi*, MGH SRM V. Edited by Wilhelm Levison, 674–710. Hanover: Hahn, 1910.

Eddius Stephanus. *Vita Wilfridi Episcopi Eboracensis*. MGH SRM VI. Edited by Wilhelm Levison, 163–263. Hanover: Hahn, 1913.

Einhard. *Vita Karoli Magni*. MGH SRG 25. Edited by Oswald Holder-Egger. Hanover: Hahn, 1911. English translation in *Two Lives of Charlemagne*. Translated by Lewis Thorpe. London: Penguin Books, 1969.

Eleutherius of Tournai. *Sermones*. PL 65. Edited by J. P. Migne. Paris: Garnier Brothers, 1844–64.

Epistolae Arelatenses Genuinae. MGH Epistolae III. Edited by Wilhelm Gundlach. Berlin: Weidmann, 1892.

Epistolae Austrasicae. MGH Epistolae III. Edited by Wilhelm Gundlach. Berlin: Weidmann, 1892.

Epistolae Merowingici Collectae. MGH Epistolae III. Edited by Wilhelm Gundlach. Berlin: Weidmann, 1892.

Eusebius of Caesarea. *Ecclesiastical History*. Edited by H. J. Lawlor. Translated by Kirsopp Lake and J. E. L. Oulton. London, W. Heinemann, 1926–32.

Fausti Aliorumque Epistulae ad Ruricium Aliosque. MGH AA VIII. Edited by Bruno Krusch. Berlin: Weidmann, 1887.

Flodoard of Rheims. *Historiae Remensis Ecclesiae*. MGH SS XXXVI. Edited by Martina Stratmann. Hanover: Hahn, 1998.

Formulae Merowingici et Karolini Aevi. MGH Leges V. Edited by Karl Zeumer. Hanover: Hahn, 1886.

Fredegar. *Chronica*. MGH SRM II. Edited by Bruno Krusch. Hanover: Hahn, 1888. English translation: *The Fourth Book of the Chronicle of Fredegar*. Translated by J. M. Wallace-Hadrill. London: Thomas Nelson and Sons, 1960.

Gesta Abbatum Fontanellensium, edited and translated by Pascal Pradié. Paris: Les Belles Lettres, 1999.

Gesta Episcoporum Autissiodorensium, edited and translated by Michel Sot, Guy Lobrichon, and Monique Goullet. Paris: Belles Lettres, 2002.

Gesta Episcoporum Virdunensium. MGH SS IV. Edited by George Pertz, 36–51. Hanover: Hahn, 1841.

Gesta Treverorum. MGH SS VIII. Edited by George Pertz, 111–260. Hanover: Hahn, 1848.

Gratian. *Decretum*. Corpus Iuris Canonici I. Edited by Emil Friedberg. Leipzig: Bernhardi Tauchnitz, 1879.

Gregory I, Pope. *Registrum Epistularum*. CCSL 140. Vols. 1–2. Edited by Dag Norberg. Turnhout: Brepols, 1972. English translation: *The Letters of Gregory the Great*. Edited and translated by John R. C. Martyn. 3 vols. Toronto: Pontifical Institute of Medieval Studies, 2004.

Gregory of Tours. *Decem Libri Historiarum*. MGH SRM I.1. Edited by Bruno Krusch and Wilhelm Levison. Hanover: Hahn, 1937–51. English translation: *History of the Franks*. Translated by Lewis Thorpe. London: Penguin Books, 1974.

——. *Liber in Gloria Confessorum*. MGH SRM I.2. Edited by Bruno Krusch. Hanover: Hahn, 1885. English translation: *Glory of the Confessors*. Translated by Raymond Van Dam. Liverpool: Liverpool University Press, 1988.

——. *Liber in Gloria Martyrum*. MGH SRM I.2. Edited by Bruno Krusch. Hanover: Hahn, 1885. English translation: *Glory of the Martyrs*. Translated by Raymond Van Dam. Liverpool: Liverpool University Press, 1988.

——. *Liber de Passione et Virtutibus Sancti Iuliani Martyris*. MGH SRM I.2. Edited by Bruno Krusch. Hanover: Hahn, 1885. English translation in Raymond Van Dam. *Saints and Their Miracles in Late Antique Gaul*. Princeton: Princeton University Press, 1993.

——. *Liber Vitae Patrum*. MGH SRM I.2. Edited by Bruno Krusch. Hanover: Hahn, 1885. English translation: *Lives of the Fathers*. Translated by Edward James. Liverpool: Liverpool University Press, 1985.

——. *Libri de Virtutibus Sancti Martini Episcopi*. MGH SRM I.2. Edited by Bruno Krusch. Hanover: Hahn, 1885. English translation in Raymond Van Dam. *Saints and Their Miracles in Late Antique Gaul*. Princeton: Princeton University Press, 1993.

Hincmar of Rheims. *Epistulae*. MGH Epistulae 8.1. Edited by Ernst Perels. Berlin: Weidmann, 1939.

——. *De Ordine Palatii*, edited by Thomas Gross and Rudolf Schieffer. Hanover: Hahn, 1980.

——. *Vita Remigii Episcopi Remensis*. MGH SRM III. Edited by Bruno Krusch, 239–349. Hanover: Hahn, 1896.

Isidore of Seville. *Epistolae*. PL 83. Edited by J. P. Migne. Paris: Garnier Brothers, 1862.

——. *Etymologiae*. Edited by W. M. Lindsay. 2 vols. Oxford: Clarendon Press, 1911. English translation: *The Etymologies of Isidore of Seville*. Translated by Stephen A. Barney, W. J. Lewis, J. A. Beach, and Oliver Berghof. Cambridge: Cambridge University Press, 2006.

Jonas of Bobbio. *Vitae Columbani Abbatis Discipulorumque Eius Libri Duo Auctore Iona*. MGH SRM IV. Edited by Bruno Krusch, 1–152. Hanover: Hahn, 1902.

Justinian. *Novellae*. Corpus Iuris Civilis III. Edited by Rudolf Schöll and Wilhelm Kroll. Berlin: Weidmann, 1990–5. English translation: *The Civil Law*. Vol. XVII. Translated by S. P. Scott. Cincinnati: Central Trust Co., 1932.

Die Konzilordines des Früh- und Hochmittelalters, edited by Herbert Schneider. Hanover: Hahn, 1996.

Leges Alamannorum. MGH Leges V.1. Edited by Karl Lehmann and Karl August Eckhardt. 2nd ed. Hanover: Hahn, 1966. English translation: *Laws of the Alamans and Bavarians*. Translated by Theodore John Rivers. Philadelphia: University of Pennsylvania Press, 1977.

Leges Baiwariorum. MGH Leges V.2. Edited by Ernst Maria Augustin Schwind. Hanover: Hahn, 1926. English translation: *Laws of the Alamans and Bavarians*. Translated by Theodore John Rivers. Philadelphia: University of Pennsylvania Press, 1977.

Lex Ribuaria. MGH Leges III.2. Edited by Franz Beyerle and Rudolf Buchner. Hanover: Hahn, 1954. English translation: *Laws of the Salian and Ripuarian Franks*. Translated by Theodore John Rivers. New York: AMS Press, 1986.

Liber Historiae Francorum. MGH SRM II. Edited by Bruno Krusch. Hanover: Hahn, 1888. English translation: *Liber Historiae Francorum*. Translated by Bernard S. Bachrach. Lawrence, KS: Coronado Press, 1973.

Linder, Amnon, ed. *The Jews in the Legal Sources of the Early Middle Ages*. Detroit: Wayne State University Press, 1997.

——. *The Jews in Roman Imperial Legislation*. Detroit: Wayne State University Press, 1987.

Ludger of Münster. *Vita Sancti Gregorii Trajectensis*. AASS OSB III.2. Edited by Jean Mabillon. Venice: 1733–38.

Marculfi Formularum, edited by Alf Uddholm. Uppsala: Eranos Förlag, 1952. English translation: *The Formularies of Angers and Marculf: Two Merovingian Legal Handbooks*. Translated by Alice Rio. Liverpool: Liverpool University Press, 2008.

Marius of Avenches. *Chronica*. Edited and translated by Justin Favrod. Lausanne: Cahiers Lausannois d'Histoire Médiévale, 1993.

Miliaria Imperii Romani. Corpus Inscriptionum Latinarum XVII.2. Edited by Gerold Walser. Berlin: Walter de Gruyter, 1986.

Notitia Galliarum. MGH AA IX.1. Edited by Theodore Mommsen. Berlin: Weidmann, 1892.

Odorannus of Sens. *Chronicon*. PL 142. Edited by J. P. Migne. Paris: Garnier Brothers, 1880.

Pactus Legis Salicae. MGH Leges IV.1. Edited by Karl August Eckhardt. Hanover: Hahn, 1962. English translation: *Laws of the Salian and Ripuarian Franks*. Translated by Theodore John Rivers. New York: AMS Press, 1986.

Passio Desiderii Episcopi Viennensis II. MGH SRM III. Edited by Bruno Krusch, 638–45. Hanover: Hahn, 1896.

Passiones Leudegarii Episcopi et Martyris Augustodunensis. MGH SRM V. Edited by Bruno Krusch, 249–362. Hanover: Hahn, 1910. English translation in *Late*

Merovingian France, ed. Paul Fouracre and Richard Gerberding. Manchester: Manchester University Press, 1996.

Passio Praeiecti Episcopi et Martyris Arverneni. MGH SRM V. Edited by Bruno Krusch, 212–48. Hanover: Hahn, 1910. English translation in *Late Merovingian France*, ed. Paul Fouracre and Richard Gerberding. Manchester: Manchester University Press, 1996.

Die Peutingersche Tafel, edited by Konrad Miller. Stuttgart: F. A. Brockhaus, 1962.

Pseudo-Anastasius Bibliothecario. *Epitome Chronica Casinensis*. Rerum Italicarum Scriptores II. Edited by Lodovico Antonio Muratori. Milan: Typographia Societatis Palatinae, 1723–51.

Pseudo-Marcellinus. *Vita Suuiberti*. Scriptores Brunsvicensium II. Edited by Wilhelm Leibnitz. Hanover: N. Foersteri, 1707–11.

Regino of Prüm. *Das Sendhandbuch des Regino von Prüm*. Edited and translated by Hermann Wasserschleben and Wilfried Hartmann. Darmstadt: Wissenschaftliche Buchgesellschaft, 2004.

Ruricius of Limoges. *Epistulae*. MGH AA VIII. Edited by Bruno Krusch. Berlin: Weidmann, 1887. English translation: *Ruricius of Limoges and Friends: A Collection of Letters from Visigothic Gaul*. Edited and translated by Ralph Mathisen. Liverpool: Liverpool University Press, 1999.

Rutilius Namatianus. *De Reditu Suo*. In *Minor Latin Poets II*. Edited by J. Wight Duff and A. M. Duff. Cambridge, MA: Harvard University Press, 1934.

Sidonius Apollinaris. *Poems and Letters*. Edited and translated by W. B. Anderson. Cambridge, MA: Harvard University Press, 1936–65.

Sisebut. *Vita vel Passio Sancti Desiderii Episcopi Viennensis*. MGH SRM III. Edited by Bruno Krusch, 630–7. Hanover: Hahn, 1896. English translation in *Lives of the Visigothic Fathers*. Translated by A. T. Fear. Liverpool: Liverpool University Press, 1997.

Die Urkunden der Merowinger, edited by Carlrichard Brühl, Theo Kölzer, Martina Hartmann, and Andrea Stieldorf. Hanover: Hahn, 2001.

Venantius Fortunatus. *Opera Poetica*. MGH AA IV.1. Edited by Friedrich Leo. Berlin: Weidmann, 1881. English translation: *Venantius Fortunatus: Personal and Political Poems*. Translated by Judith George. Liverpool: Liverpool University Press, 1995.

——. *Vita Albini Episcopi Andegavensis*. MGH AA IV.2. Edited by Bruno Krusch, 27–33. Berlin: Weidmann, 1885.

Vita Agili Abbatis Resbacensis. AASS Aug. VI, 574–84.

Vita Ansberti Episcopi Rotomagensis. MGH SRM V. Edited by Bruno Krusch, 613–41. Hanover: Hahn, 1910.

Vita Apollinaris Episcopi Valentinensis. MGH SRM III. Edited by Bruno Krusch, 194–203. Hanover: Hahn, 1896.

Vita Aunarii Episcopi Autissiodorensis, AASS Sept. VII, 97–8.

Vita Aviti Episcopi Viennensis. MGH AA VI.2. Edited by Rudolph Peiper, 177–81. Hanover: Hahn, 1883.

Vita Baboleni. Recueil des historiens des Gaules et de la France III.569 D. Edited by Martin Bouquet. Paris: V. Palmé, 1804–1904.

Vita Balthildis. MGH SRM II. Edited by Bruno Krusch, 477–508. Hanover: Hahn, 1888.

Vita Betharii Episcopi Carnoteni. MGH SRM III. Edited by Bruno Krusch, 612–19. Hanover: Hahn, 1896.

Vita Boniti Episcopi Arverni. MGH SRM VI. Edited by Bruno Krusch, 110–39. Hanover: Hahn, 1913.

Vita Caesari Episcopi Arelatensis. MGH SRM III. Edited by Bruno Krusch, 457–501. Hanover: Hahn, 1896.

Vita Dagoberti III Regis Francorum. MGH SRM II. Edited by Bruno Krusch, 509–24. Hanover: Hahn, 1888.

Vita Dalmatii Episcopi Ruteni. MGH SRM III. Edited by Bruno Krusch, 543–9. Hanover: Hahn, 1896.
Vita Eligii Episcopi Noviomagensis. MGH SRM IV. Edited by Bruno Krusch, 634–761. Hanover: Hahn, 1902. English translation in *Medieval Hagiography: An Anthology*, ed. Thomas F. Head. Translated by Jo Ann McNamara. New York: Garland, 2000.
Vita Eucherii Episcopi Aurelianensis. MGH SRM VII. Edited by Wilhelm Levison, 41–53. Hanover: Hahn, 1920.
Vita Faronis Episcopi Meldensis. MGH SRM V. Edited by Bruno Krusch, 171–203. Hanover: Hahn, 1910.
Vita Melanii Episcopi Redonici. MGH SRM III. Edited by Bruno Krusch, 370–6. Hanover: Hahn, 1896.
Vita Nicetii Episcopi Lugdunensis. MGH SRM III. Edited by Bruno Krusch, 518–24. Hanover: Hahn, 1896.
Vita Nivardi Episcopi Remensis. MGH SRM V. Edited by Bruno Krusch, 157–71. Hanover: Hahn, 1910.
Vita Rigoberti. MGH SRM VII. Edited by Wilhelm Levison, 58–80. Hanover: Hahn, 1920.
Vita Rusticulae sive Marciae Abbatissae Arelatensis. MGH SRM IV. Edited by Bruno Krusch, 337–51. Hanover: Hahn, 1902.
Vitae Sancti Bonifatii, edited by Wilhelm Levison. Hanover: Hahn, 1905.
Walahfrid Strabo. *Vita Galli Confessoris*. MGH SRM IV. Edited by Bruno Krusch, 280–337. Hanover: Hahn, 1902.
——. *Vita Othmari*. MGH SS II. Edited by George Pertz, 41–7. Hanover: Hahn, 1829.
Wettinus. *Vita Galli Confessoris*. MGH SRM IV. Edited by Bruno Krusch, 256–80. Hanover: Hahn, 1902.

Scholarly Works

Amidon, P. R. "The Procedures of Cyprian's Councils." *Vigiliae Christianae* 37 (1983): 328–39.
Amory, Patrick. "Meaning and Purpose of Ethnic Terminology in the Burgundian Laws." *Early Medieval Europe* 2, no. 1 (1993): 1–28.
Arjava, Antti. "The Survival of Roman Family Law After the Barbarian Settlements." In *Law, Society, and Authority in Late Antiquity*, ed. Ralph Mathisen, 33–51. Oxford: Oxford University Press, 2001.
Avril, Joseph. "L'institution synodale et la législation épiscopale de temps carolingiens au IVe Concile de Latran." *Revue d'histoire de l'Eglise de France* 89, no. 223 (2003): 273–307.
Bachrach, Bernard. *Anatomy of a Little War: A Diplomatic and Military History of the Gundovald Affair (568–586)*. Boulder: Westview Press, 1994.
——. "Carolingian Military Operations: An Introduction to Technological Perspectives." In *The Art, Science, and Technology of Medieval Travel*, ed. Robert Bork and Andrea Kann, 17–29. Aldershot: Ashgate, 2008.
——. "Charles Martel, Mounted Shock Combat, the Stirrup, and Feudalism." *Studies in Medieval and Renaissance History* 7 (1970): 47–75.
——. *Early Carolingian Warfare*. Philadelphia: University of Pennsylvania Press, 2001.
——. *Early Medieval Jewish Policy*. Minneapolis: University of Minnesota Press, 1977.
——. "The Jewish Community of the Later Roman Empire as Seen in the *Codex Theodosianus*." In *To See Ourselves as Others See Us*, ed. Jacob Neusner and Ernest Frerichs, 399–421. Chico, CA: Scholars Press, 1985.
——. *Merovingian Military Organization, 481–751*. Minneapolis: University of Minnesota Press, 1972.

——. "Was the Marchfield Part of the Frankish Constitution?" *Medieval Studies* 36 (1974): 178–85.

Barion, Hans. *Das fränkisch-deutsche Synodalrecht des Frühmittelalters*. Bonn: Ludwig Röhrscheid Verlag, 1931.

Barnes, Timothy. *Athanasius and Constantius*. Cambridge, MA: Harvard University Press, 1993.

——. *Constantine and Eusebius*. Cambridge, MA: Harvard University Press, 1981.

Barnwell, P. S. "Emperors, Jurists and Kings: Law and Custom in the Late Roman and Early Medieval West." *Past and Present* 168 (2000): 6–29.

——. "Kings, Nobles, and Assemblies in the Barbarian Kingdoms." In *Political Assemblies in the Earlier Middle Ages*, ed. P. S. Barnwell and Marco Mostert, 11–28. Turnhout: Brepols, 2003.

Barrow, Julia. "Ideas and Applications of Reform." In *The Cambridge History of Christianity*, vol. 3, ed. Thomas F. X. Noble and Julia M. H. Smith, 345–62. Cambridge: Cambridge University Press, 2008.

Basdevant-Gaudemet, Brigitte. "Le Bible dans les canons des conciles mérovingiens." In *Bibel und Recht: Rechtshistorisches Kolloquium 9.–13. Juni 1992 an der Christian-Albrechts-Universität zu Kiel*, ed. Jörn Eckert and Hans Hattenhaur, 51–67. Frankfurt: Peter Lang, 1994.

——. "L'évêque, d'après la législation de quelques conciles mérovingiens." In *Clovis: Histoire et mémoire*, ed. Michel Rouche, 471–94. Paris: Presses de l'Université de Paris–Sorbonne, 1997.

——. "Les évêques, les papes, et les princes dans la vie conciliaire en France du IVe au XIIe siècle." *Revue historique de droit français et étranger* 69 (1991), 1–16.

Batiffol, Pierre. "Le règlement des premiers conciles africains." *Bulletin d'ancienne littérature et d'archéologie chrétiennes* 3 (1913): 3–19.

Baumgart, Susanne. *Die Bischofsherrschaft im Gallien des 5. Jahrhunderts*. Munich: Editio Maris, 1995.

Beaujard, Brigitte, Paul-Albert Fevrier, et al. *Province ecclésiastique de Lyon (Lugdunensis Prima)*. Topographie Chrétienne des Cites de la Gaule IV. Paris: De Boccard, 1986.

Beck, Henry G. J. *The Pastoral Care of Souls in South-East France During the Sixth Century*. Rome: Apud Aedes Universitatis Gregorianae, 1950.

Beech, George. "Prosopography." In *Medieval Studies: An Introduction*, ed. James M. Powell, 185–226. 2nd ed. Syracuse, NY: Syracuse University Press, 1992.

Bischoff, Bernhard. *Latin Paleography*. Translated by Dáibhí O. Cróinín and David Ganz. Cambridge: Cambridge University Press, 1990.

Bouchard, Constance. *Those of My Blood: Constructing Noble Families in Medieval Francia*. Philadelphia: University of Pennsylvania Press, 2001.

Brennan, Brian. "The Career of Venantius Fortunatus." *Traditio* 41 (1985): 49–78.

Bretholz, Bertold. "Die Unterschriften den gallischen Concilien des 6. und 7. Jahrhunderts." *Neues Archiv der Gesellschaft für ältere deutsche Geschichtskunde* 18 (1892): 529–47.

Brown, Peter. *Poverty and Leadership in the Later Roman Empire*. Hanover, NH: University Press of New England, 2001.

——. *Power and Persuasion in Late Antiquity: Towards a Christian Empire*. Madison: University of Wisconsin Press, 1992.

——. *The Rise of Western Christendom*. 2nd ed. Oxford: Blackwell, 2003.

Brundage, James. *Medieval Canon Law*. New York: Longman, 1995.

Brunner, Heinrich. *Deutsche Rechtsgeschichte*. 2nd ed. Munich: Duncker und Humblot, 1906–28.

Buck, Thomas Martin. *Admonitio und Praedicatio: Zur religiös-pastoralen Dimension von Kapitularien und kapitulariennahen Texten (507–814)*. Frankfurt: Peter Lang, 1997.

Bullough, Donald. "The Career of Columbanus." In *Columbanus: Studies of the Latin Writings*, ed. Michael Lapidge, 1–28. Woodbridge: Boydell Press, 1997.

Burnouf, Joelle. "Towns and Rivers, River Towns: Environmental Archaeology and the Archaeological Evaluation of Urban Activities and Trade." In *Post-Roman Towns, Trade and Settlement in Europe and Byzantium*, ed. Joachim Henning, 165–80. Berlin: Walter de Gruyter, 2007.

Cardot, Fabienne. *L'espace et le pouvoir: Étude sur l'Austrasie mérovingienne*. Paris: Publications de la Sorbonne, 1987.

Carozzi, Claude. "La Vie de Saint Dagobert de Stenay: Histoire et hagiographie." *Revue belge de philologie et d'histoire* 62, no. 2 (1984): 225–58.

Caspar, Erich. *Petrus Diaconus und die Monte Cassineser Fälschungen*. Berlin: Verlag von Julius Springer, 1909.

Casson, Lionel. *Travel in the Ancient World*. Paperback edition. Baltimore: Johns Hopkins University Press, 1994.

Champagne, J., and R. Szramkiewicz. "Recherches sur les conciles des temps mérovingiens." *Revue historique de droit français et étranger* 49 (1971): 5–49.

Charles-Edwards, T. M. *Early Christian Ireland*. Cambridge: Cambridge University Press, 2000.

Chevallier, Raymond. *Roman Roads*. Translated by N. H. Field. Berkeley: University of California Press, 1976.

Classen, Peter. "Fortleben und Wandel spätrömischen Urkundenwesens im frühen Mittelalter." In *Recht und Schrift im Mittelalter*, ed. Peter Classen, 13–54. Sigmaringen: Thorbecke, 1977.

——. "Kaiserreskript und Königsurkunde, Diplomatische Studien zum römische-germanischen Kontinuitätsproblem, II. Teil." *Archiv für Diplomatik* 2 (1956): 1–115.

Claussen, M. A. *The Reform of the Frankish Church: Chrodegang of Metz and the Regula Canonicorum in the Eighth Century*. Cambridge: Cambridge University Press, 2004.

Clercq, Charles de. *La législation religieuse franque de Clovis à Charlemagne (507–814)*. Louvain: Bureaux du Recueil Bibliothèque de Université, 1936.

Coates, Simon. "Venantius Fortunatus and the Image of Episcopal Authority in Late Antique and Early Merovingian Gaul." *English Historical Review* 115, no. 464 (2000): 1109–37.

Collingwood, R. G. *An Autobiography*. Oxford: Oxford University Press, 1939.

——. *The Idea of History*. Oxford: Clarendon Press, 1946.

Collins, Roger. *Charlemagne*. Toronto: University of Toronto Press, 1998.

——. *Fredegar*. Authors of the Middle Ages. Vol. IV.2. Aldershot: Variorum, 1996.

——. "Law and Ethnic Identity in the Western Kingdoms in the Fifth and Sixth Centuries." In *Medieval Europeans*, ed. Alfred P. Smyth, 1–23. New York: St. Martin's Press, 1998.

——. "Pippin III as Mayor of the Palace: The Evidence." In *Der Dynastiewechsel von 751*, ed. Matthias Becher and Jorg Jarnut, 75–91. Münster: Scriptorium, 2004.

Constable, Giles. "*Nona et Decima*: An Aspect of Carolingian Economy." *Speculum* 35, no. 2 (1960): 224–50.

Coulon, Gérard. *Les Voies Romaines en Gaule*. Paris: Errance, 2007.

Cubitt, Catherine. *Anglo-Saxon Church Councils c. 650–c. 680*. London: Leicester University Press, 1995.

Daly, William M. "Clovis: How Barbarian, How Pagan?" *Speculum* 69, no. 3 (1994): 619–64.

Davies, Luned Mair. "*Statuta Ecclesiae Antiqua* and the Gallic Councils in the *Hibernensis*." *Peritia* 14 (2000): 85–110.

Davies, Wendy, and Paul Fouracre, eds. *The Settlement of Disputes in Early Medieval Europe*. Cambridge: Cambridge University Press, 1986.

De Jong, Mayke. "Charlemagne's Church." In *Charlemagne: Empire and Society*, ed. Joanna Story, 103–35. Manchester: Manchester University Press, 2005.

Depreux, Philippe. "L'expression 'Statutum est a Domno Rege et Sancta Synodo' annonçant certains dispositions du Capitulaire Francfort (794)." In *Das Frankfurter Konzil von 794: Kristallisationspunkt karolingischer Kultur*, ed. Rainer Berndt, I.81–101. Mainz: Selbstverlag der Gesellschaft für Mittelrheinische Kirchengeschichte, 1997.

Devroey, Jean-Pierre. "Juifs et Syriens a propos de la géographie économique de la Gaule au Haut Moyen Age." In *Peasants and Townsmen in Medieval Europe: Studia in Honorem Adriaan Verhulst*, ed. Jean-Marie Duvosquel and Erik Thoen, 51–72. Ghent: Snoeck-Ducaju and Zoon, 1995.

Devroey, Jean-Pierre, and Christian Brouwer. "La participation des Juifs au commerce dans le monde franc (VIe–Xe siècles)." In *Voyages et voyageurs à Byzance et en Occident du VIe au XIe siècle*, ed. Alain Dierkens, Jean-Marie Sansterre, and Jean-Louis Kupper, 339–74. Geneva: Droz, 2000.

Dierkens, Alain. "Note sur un passage de la *Vita Dagoberti*: Dagobert II et le domaine de Biesme." *Revue belge de philologie et d'histoire* 62, no. 2 (1984): 259–70.

Dierkens, Alain, and Patrick Périn. "Les sedes regiae mérovingiennes entre Seine et Rhin." In *Sedes Regiae (ann. 400–800)*, ed. Gisela Ripoll and Josep M. Gurt, 267–304. Barcelona: Reial Academia de Bones Lletres, 2000.

Dill, Samuel. *Roman Society in Gaul in the Merovingian Age*. London: Macmillan and Co., 1926.

Drew, Katherine. "The Barbarian Kings as Lawgivers and Judges." In *Life and Thought in the Early Middle Ages*, ed. R. S. Hoyt, 7–29. Minneapolis: University of Minnesota Press, 1967.

Dubois, Jacques. "Les listes épiscopales témoins de l'organisation ecclésiastique et de la transmission des traditions." In *La christianisation des pays entre Loire et Rhin (IV–VII siècle)*, ed. Pierre Riché, 9–23. Paris: Éditions du Cerf, 1993.

Duchesne, Louis. *L'Eglise au VI siècle*. Paris: Fontemoing & Co., E. de Boccard, Successeur, 1925.

——. *Fastes épiscopaux de l'ancienne Gaule*. Vols. 1–3. Paris: Albert Fontemoing, 1907–15.

Dumézil, Bruno. *Les racines chrétiennes de l'Europe*. Paris: Fayard, 2005.

Durliat, Jean. *Les finances publiques de Dioclétien aux Carolingiens (284–889)*. Sigmaringen: Jan Thorbecke Verlag, 1990.

Dussen, W. J. van der. *History as a Science: The Philosophy of R. G. Collingwood*. The Hague: Martinus Nijhoff Publishers, 1981.

Ebling, Horst. *Prosopographie der Amtsträger des Merowingerreiches: Von Chlothar II (613) bis Karl Martell (741)*. Munich: Fink, 1974.

Egmond, Wolfert S. Van. *Conversing with Saints: Communication in Pre-Carolingian Hagiography from Auxerre*. Turnhout: Brepols, 2006.

Engels, Donald. *Alexander the Great and the Logistics of the Macedonian Army*. Berkeley: University of California Press, 1978.

Ewig, Eugen. "Beobachtungen zu den Bischofslisten der merowingischen Konzilien und Bischofsprivilegien." In *Spätantikes und fränkisches Gallien*, ed. Hartmut Atsma, vol. 2, 427–55. Munich: Artemis Verlag, 1979.

——. "Beobachtungen zu den Klosterprivilegien des 7. und frühen 8. Jahrhunderts." In *Spätantikes und fränkisches Gallien*, ed. Hartmut Atsma, vol. 2, 411–26. Munich: Artemis Verlag, 1979.

——. *Die Merowinger und das Frankenreich*. Stuttgart: W. Kohlhammer, 1988.

——. "Milo et Eiusmodi Similes." In *Spätantikes und Fränkisches Gallien*, ed. Hartmut Atsma, vol. 2, 189–219. Munich: Artemis Verlag, 1979.

——. "Das Privilig des Bischofs Berthefrid von Amiens für Corbie von 664 und die Klosterpolitik der Königin Balthild." In *Spätantikes und Fränkisches Gallien*, ed. Hartmut Atsma, vol. 2, 538–83. Munich: Artemis Verlag, 1979.

——. "Résidence et capitale pendant le Haut Moyen Age." *Revue historique* 230 (1963): 25–72.

——. "Saint Chrodegang et la reforme de l'Eglise franque." In *Spätantikes und fränkisches Gallien*, ed. Hartmut Atsma, vol. 2, 232–59. Munich: Artemis Verlag, 1979.

Fear, Andrew. "The Ghost of Saint Desiderius." *La Corónica* 29, no. 2 (2001): 79–93.

Fichtenau, Heinrich. *The Carolingian Empire*. Translated by Peter Munz. Oxford: Blackwell, 1957.

Firey, Abigail. "Carolingian Ecclesiology and Heresy: A Southern Gallic Juridical Tract Against Adoptionism." *Sacris Erudiri* 39 (2000): 253–316.

——. "Ghostly Recensions in Early Medieval Canon Law: The Problem of the *Collectio Dacheriana* and Its Shades." *The Legal History Review* 68, nos. 1–2 (2000): 63–82.

——. "Lawyers and Wisdom: The Use of the Bible in the Pseudo-Isidorian Forged Decretals." In *The Study of the Bible in the Carolingian Era*. ed. Celia Chazelle and Burton Van Name Edwards, 189–214. Medieval Church Studies 3. Turnhout: Brepols, 2003.

Fischer, Joseph, and Adolf Lumpe. *Die Synoden von den Anfängen bis zum Vorabend des Nicaenums*. Paderborn: Ferdinand Schöningh, 1997.

Fleury, Jean. *Recherches historiques sur les empêchements de parenté dans le mariage canonique*. Paris: Recueil Sirey, 1933.

Fontaine, Jacques. "King Sisebut's *Vita Desiderii* and the Political Function of Visigothic Hagiography." In *Visigothic Spain: New Approaches*, ed. Edward James, 93–129. Oxford: Clarendon Press, 1980.

Fouracre, Paul. *The Age of Charles Martel*. Harlow: Pearson Education, 2000.

——. "Eternal Light and Earthly Needs: Practical Aspects of the Development of Frankish Immunities." In *Property and Power in the Early Middle Ages*, ed. Wendy Davies and Paul Fouracre, 53–81. Cambridge: Cambridge University Press, 1995.

——. "Merovingian History and Merovingian Hagiography." *Past and Present* 127 (1990): 3–38.

——. "The Nature of Frankish Political Institutions in the Seventh Century." In *Franks and Alamanni in the Merovingian Period: An Ethnographic Perspective*, ed. Ian Wood, 285–316. Rochester: Boydell Press, 1998.

——. "'Placita' and the Settlement of Disputes in Later Merovingian Francia." In *The Settlement of Disputes in Early Medieval Europe*, ed. Wendy Davies and Paul Fouracre, 23–43. Cambridge: Cambridge University Press, 1986.

——. "The Work of Audoenus of Rouen and Eligius of Noyon in Extending Episcopal Influence from the Town to the Country in Seventh-Century Neustria." *Studies in Church History* 16 (1979): 77–91.

Fouracre, Paul, and Richard Gerberding, eds. *Late Merovingian France*. Manchester: Manchester University Press, 1996.

Fournier, Paul, and Gabriel Le Bras. *Histoire des collections canoniques en Occident depuis les Fausses Décrétales jusqu'au Décret de Gratien*. Vol. 1. Paris: Recueil Sirey, 1931.

Fowler-Magerl, Linda. *Clavis Canonum: Selected Canon Law Collections Before 1140*. Hanover: Hahn, 2005.

Frakes, Robert M. "The Manuscript Tradition of the *Lex Dei*." *Zeitschrift der Savigny-Stifung für Rechtsgeschichte* 124 (2007): 290–304.

Friedrich, Johann. "Die *Vocati Episcopi* Erchanfried und Otkar der Passauer und der Oadalhart episcopus der Freisinger Urkunden." *Sitzungsberichte der philosophisch-philologischen und historischen Classe* 1 (1882): 313–48.

Fuhrmann, Horst. "The Pseudo-Isidorian Forgeries." In *Papal Letters in the Early Middle Ages*, ed. Detlev Jasper and Horst Fuhrmann, 135–95. Washington, DC: Catholic University of America Press, 2001.

Fustel de Coulanges, N. D. "Étude sur l'immunité." *Revue historique* 22–3 (1883): 249–90, 1–27.

Gaastra, Adriaan. "Penitentials and Canonical Authority." In *Texts and Identities in the Early Middle Ages*, ed. Richard Corradini, Rob Meens, Christina Pössel, and Philip Shaw, 191–203. Vienna: Verlag der Österreichischen Akademie der Wissenschaften, 2006.

Ganshof, François Louis. "A propos du tonlieu sous les Merovingiens." In *Studi in onore di Amintore Fanfani*, ed. Gino Barbieri, I.291–315. Milan: Giuffrè, 1962.

——. "The Church and the Royal Power in the Frankish Monarchy Under Pippin III and Charlemagne." In *The Carolingians and the Frankish Monarchy: Studies in Carolingian History*, trans. Janet Sondheimer, 205–39. Ithaca, NY: Cornell University Press, 1971.
——. *Frankish Institutions Under Charlemagne*. Translated by Bryce Lyon and Mary Lyon. Providence: Brown University Press, 1968.
——. "L'immunité dans la monarchie franque." In *Les liens de vassalité et les immunités*, 2nd ed., 171–216. Bruxelles: Editions de la Libraire Encyclopédique, 1958.
——. "The Impact of Charlemagne on the Institutions of the Frankish Realm." *Speculum* 40, no. 1 (1965): 47–62.
——. "Les liens de vassalité dans la monarchie franque." In *Les liens de vassalité et les immunités*, 2nd ed., 153–69. Bruxelles: Editions de la Libraire Encyclopédique, 1958.
——. *Recherches sur les capitulaires*. Paris: Sirey, 1958.
——. "La tractoria: Contribution à l'étude des origines du droit de gîte." *Tijdschrift voor Rechtsgeschiedenis* 8 (1928): 69–91.
Ganz, David. "Bureaucratic Shorthand and Merovingian Learning." In *Ideal and Reality in Frankish and Anglo-Saxon Society*, ed. Patrick Wormald, Donald Bullough, and Roger Collins, 58–75. Oxford: Blackwell, 1983.
——. "The Ideology of Sharing: Apostolic Community and Ecclesiastical Property in the Early Middle Ages." In *Property and Power in the Early Middle Ages*, ed. Wendy Davies and Paul Fouracre, 17–30. Cambridge: Cambridge University Press, 1995.
——. "On the History of Tironian Notes." In *Tironische Noten*, ed. Peter Ganz, 35–51. Wiesbaden: Otto Harrassowitz, 1990.
——. "Roman Manuscripts in Francia and Anglo-Saxon England." *Settimane di Studio del Centro Italiano di Studi Sull'Alto Medioevo* 49, no. 1 (2002): 607–47.?
García Moreno, Luis. "Les relations entre l'Église des Gaules et l'Église d'Espagne du Ve au VIIe siècle: Entre suspicion et méfiance." *Revue d'histoire de l'Église de France* 90, no. 224 (2004): 19–54.
Gaudemet, Jean. "A propos du C. 12 du Concile de Macon (1er Novembre 583)." *Mémoires de la Société pour l'histoire du droit et des institutions des anciens pays bourguignons comtois et romands* 13 (1950/1): 277–82.
——. *L'Église dans l'Empire Romain (IVe–Ve siècles)*. Histoire du droit et des institutions de l'Église en Occident III, ed. Gabriel Le Bras and Jean Gaudemet. Paris: Sirey, 1958.
——. *Église et cité: Histoire du droit canonique*. Paris: Cerf/Montchrestien, 1994.
——. *La formation du droit séculier et du droit de l'Eglise aux IVe et Ve siècles*. Paris: Sirey, 1957.
——. *Les sources du droit canonique VIIIe–XXe siècle*. Paris: Les Éditions du Cerf, 1993.
——. *Les sources du droit de l'Eglise en Occident*. Paris: Éditions du Cerf/Editions du C.N.R.S., 1985.
——. "Les statuts épiscopaux de la première décade du IXe siècle." In *Proceedings of the Fourth International Congress of Medieval Canon Law*, ed. Stephan Kuttner, 303–49. Vatican City: Biblioteca Apostolica Vaticana, 1976.
——. "Survivances romaines dans le droit de la monarchie franque du Vème au Xème siècle." In *La formation du droit canonique médiéval*. London: Variorum, 1980.
Gauthier, Nancy. "Le réseau de pouvoirs de l'évêque dans la Gaule du Haut Moyen-Age." In *Towns and Their Territories Between Late Antiquity and the Early Middle Ages*. The Transformation of the Roman World 9, ed. Gian Pietro Broglio, Nancy Gauthier, and Neil Christie, 173–207. Leiden: Brill, 2000.
Geary, Patrick J. *Aristocracy in Provence: The Rhône Basin at the Dawn of the Carolingian Age*. Philadelphia: University of Pennsylvania Press, 1985.
——. *Before France and Germany: The Creation and Transformation of the Merovingian World*. Oxford: Oxford University Press, 1988.

——. "Extra-Judicial Means of Conflict Resolution." *Settimane di studio del Centro Italiano di studi sull'alto Medioevo* 42, no. 1 (1995): 569–605.
Geisel, Christof. *Die Juden im Frankenreich*. Frankfurt: Peter Lang, 1998.
Gelzar, Heinrich. *Ausgewählte kleine Schriften*. Leipzig: B. G. Teubner, 1907.
George, Judith. "Poet as Politician: Venantius Fortunatus' Panegyric to King Chilperic." *Journal of Medieval History* 15:1 (1989): 5–18.
——. *Venantius Fortunatus: A Latin Poet in Merovingian Gaul*. Oxford: Clarendon Press, 1992.
Gérard, Pierre. *Histoire des Francs d'Austrasie*. 2nd ed. Bruxelles: J. Rosez, 1865.
Gerberding, Richard. *The Rise of the Carolingians and the Liber Historiae Francorum*. Oxford: Clarendon Press, 1987.
Geuenich, Dieter. *Geschichte der Alemannen*. Stuttgart: Verlag W. Kohlhammer, 1997.
Godding, Robert. *Prêtres en Gaule mérovingienne*. Bruxelles: Société des Bollandistes, 2001.
Goetz, Hans-Werner. "Karl Martel und die Heiligen: Kirchenpolitik und Maiordomat im Spiegel der spätmerowingischen Hagiographie." In *Karl Martell in seiner Zeit*, ed. Jörg Jarnut, Ulrich Nonn, and Michael Richter, 101–18. Sigmaringen: Jan Thorbecke Verlag, 1994.
Goffart, Walter. *The Le Mans Forgeries*. Cambridge, MA: Harvard University Press, 1966.
——. "Old and New in Merovingian Taxation." *Past and Present* 96 (1982): 3–21.
Gottlieb, Gunther. "Die formalen Bestandteile in der Überlieferung der gallischen Konzilien des 4. und 5. Jahrhunderts." *Annuarium Historiae Conciliorum* 16, no. 2 (1984): 254–63.
Graboïs, Aryeh. "Un mythe fondamental de l'histoire de France au Moyen Age: le roi David, précurseur du roi très chrétien." *Revue historique* 287, no. 1 (1992): 11–31.
Grierson, Philip. *The Coins of Medieval Europe*. London: Seaby, 1991.
Griffe, Élie. *La Gaule chrétienne à l'époque romaine*. Vols. 1–3. Paris: A. et J. Picard, 1947–57.
Grubbs, Judith Evans. *Law and Family in Late Antiquity: The Emperor Constantine's Marriage Legislation*. Oxford: Clarendon Press, 1995.
Guillot, Olivier. "La justice dans le royaume franc à l'époque mérovingienne." *Settimane di Studio del Centro Italiano di Studi Sull'Alto Medioevo* 42, no. 2 (1994): 653–731.
Guterman, Simeon. *The Principle of the Personality of Law in the Germanic Kingdoms of Western Europe from the Fifth to the Eleventh Century*. New York: Peter Lang, 1990.
Halfond, Gregory. "All the King's Men: Episcopal Political Loyalties in the Merovingian Kingdoms." *Medieval Prosopography* (forthcoming).
——. "*Cum Consensu Omnium*: Frankish Church Councils from Clovis to Charlemagne." *History Compass* 5, no. 2 (2007).
——. "*Patrimoniolum Ecclesiae Nostrae*: The Papal Estates in Merovingian Provence," *Comitatus* 38 (2007): 1–18.
Halphen, Louis. *Charlemagne et l'empire carolingien*. Paris: Éditions Albin Michel, 1947.
Halsall, Guy. *Settlement and Social Organization: The Merovingian Region of Metz*. Cambridge: Cambridge University Press, 1995.
Hannig, Jürgen. *Consensus Fidelium*. Stuttgart: Anton Hiersemann, 1982.
Harries, Jill. "Church and State in the *Notitia Galliarum*." *The Journal of Roman Studies* 68 (1978): 26–43.
——. *Law and Empire in Late Antiquity*. Cambridge: Cambridge University Press, 1999.
Hartmann, Wilfried. "Der Bischof als Richter nach den kirchenrechtlichen Quellen des 4. bis 7. Jahrhunderts." *Settimane di Studio del Centro Italiano di Studi Sull'Alto Medioevo* 42, no. 2 (1994): 805–37.

——. "Conciles et synodes." In *La Neustrie: Les pays au nord de la Loire de Dagobert à Charles le Chauve (VIIe–IXe siècles)*, ed. Patrick Périn and Laure-Charlotte Feffer, 115–7. Rouen: Musées et Monuments Départementaux de Seine-Maritime, 1985.

——. "Die Konzilien in der vorgratianischen Zeit des Kirchenrechts." In *Proceedings of the Ninth International Congress of Medieval Canons Law*, ed. Peter Landau and Joers Mueller, 259–86. Vatican City: Biblioteca Apostolica Vaticana, 1997.

——. "Konzilien und Geschichtsschreibung in karolingischer Zeit." In *Historiographie im frühen Mittelalter*, ed. Anton Scharer and Georg Scheibelreiter, 481–98. Vienna: R. Oldenbourg, 1994.

——. "Konzilsprotokolle aus karolingischer Zeit." *Annuarium Historiae Conciliorum* 15, no. 2 (1983): 260–1.

——. "Laien auf Synoden der Karolingerzeit." *Annuarium Historiae Conciliorum* 10, no. 2 (1978): 249–69.

——. *Die Synoden der Karolingerzeit im Frankenreich und in Italien*. Paderborn: Ferdinand Schöningh, 1989.

——. "La transmission et l'influence du droit synodal carolingien." *Revue historique de droit français et étranger* 63 (1985): 483–97.

——. "Zu einigen Problemen der karolingischen Konzilsgeschichte." *Annuarium Historiae Conciliorum* 9, no. 1 (1977): 6–28.

Hauck, Albert. *Kirchengeschichte Deutschlands*. 8th ed. Berlin: Akademie Verlag, 1954.

Heinzelmann, Martin. "L'aristocratie et les évêchés entre Loire et Rhin jusqu'à la fin du VII siècle." In *La christianisation des pays entre Loire et Rhin (IV–VII siècle)*, ed. Pierre Riché, 75–90. Paris: Éditions du Cerf, 1993.

——. *Bischofsherrschaft in Gallien*. Munich: Artemis Verlag, 1976.

——. "Bischof und Herrschaft vom spätantiken Gallien bis zu den karolingischen Hausmeiern. Die institutionellen Grundlagen." In *Herrschaft und Kirche*, ed. Friedrich Prinz, 23–82. Stuttgart: Anton Hiersemann, 1988.

——. "Gallische Prosopographie, 260–527." *Francia* 10 (1982): 531–718.

——. *Gregory of Tours: History and Society in the Sixth Century*. Translated by Christopher Carroll. Cambridge: Cambridge University Press, 2001.

——. "Prosopographie et recherche de continuité historique: L'exemple des V–VII siècles." *Mélanges de l'École française de Rome: Moyen Age-Temps Modernes* 100, no. 1 (1988): 227–39.

Hen, Yitzhak. "The Annals of Metz and the Merovingian Past." In *The Uses of the Past in the Early Middle Ages*, ed. Yitzhak Hen and Matthew Innes, 175–90. Cambridge: Cambridge University Press, 2000.

——. *Culture and Religion in Merovingian Gaul A.D. 481–751*. New York: E. J. Brill, 1995.

——. "Educating the Clergy: Canon Law and Liturgy in a Carolingian Handbook from the Time of Charles the Bald." In *De Sion Exhibit Lex et Verbum Domini de Hierusalem: Essays on Medieval Law, Liturgy, and Literature in Honor of Amnon Linder*, ed. Yitzak Hen, 43–58. Turnhout: Brepols, 2001.

——. "Knowledge of Canon Law Among Rural Priests: The Evidence of Two Carolingian Manuscripts from Around 800." *Journal of Theological Studies* 50, no. 1 (1999): 117–34.

Herlihy, David. "Church Property on the European Continent." *Speculum* 36, no. 1 (1961): 81–105.

Herrin, Judith. *The Formation of Christendom*. Princeton: Princeton University Press, 1989.

Herrmann, Elisabeth. *Ecclesia in Re Publica: Die Entwicklung der Kirche von pseudostaatlicher zu staatlich inkorporierter Existenz*. Frankfurt: Peter Lang, 1980.

Hess, Hamilton. *The Early Development of Canon Law and the Council of Serdica*. Oxford: Oxford University Press, 2002.

Heuclin, Jean. "Le Concile d'Orléans de 511, un premier concordat?" In *Clovis: Histoire et mémoire*, ed. Michel Rouche, 435–50. Paris: Presses de l'Université de Paris-Sorbonne, 1997.

——. *Hommes de Dieu et fonctionnaires du roi*. Villeneuve d'Ascq: Septentrion, 1998.

Hinschius, Paul. *Kirchenrecht*. Vol. 3. Berlin: I. Guttentag, 1869–97.

Hoffmann, Hartmut, and Rudolf Pokorny, eds. *Das Dekret des Bischofs Burchard von Worms*. Munich: Monumenta Germaniae Historica, 1991.

Holmberg, Erik. *Zur Geschichte des Cursus Publicus*. Uppsala: A. B. Lundequistska Bokhandeln, 1933.

Hove, Alphonse Van. *Prolegomena*. 1945 edition. Commentum Lovaniense in Codicem Iuris Canonici, vol. I, tom. I. Mechelen: H. Dessain, 1945.

Hubert, Jean. *L'architecture religieuse du Haut Moyen Âge en France*. Paris: Imprimerie Nationale, 1952.

Hubert, Jean, Jean Porcher, and W. F. Volbach. *Europe in the Dark Ages*. Translated by Stuart Gilbert and James Emmons. London: Thames and Hudson, 1969.

Humfress, Caroline. *Orthodoxy and the Courts in Late Antiquity*. Oxford: Oxford University Press, 2007.

Hummer, Hans. *Politics and Power in Early Medieval Europe: Alsace and the Frankish Realm, 600–1000*. Cambridge: Cambridge University Press, 2005.

Imbert, Jean. "Disciplina et communio à l'époque carolingienne." In *Comunione Interecclesiale Collegialita': Primato Ecumenismo*, ed. Giuseppe d'Ercole and Alphonso M. Stickler, II.519–46. Rome: LAS, 1972.

——. "Le pouvoir législatif dans l'Eglise carolingienne." Mélanges offerts à Pierre Andrieu-Guitrancourt. *L'année canonique* 17 (1973): 589–601.

——. *Les temps carolingiens*. Vol. 1. Histoire du droit et des institutions de l'Église en Occident V, ed. Gabriel Le Bras and Jean Gaudemet. Paris: Editions Cujas, 1994.

Innes, Matthew, "Charlemagne's Government." In *Charlemagne: Empire and Society*, ed. Joanna Story, 71–89. Manchester: Manchester University Press.

——. *State and Society in the Early Middle Ages: The Middle Rhine Valley, 400–1000*. Cambridge: Cambridge University Press, 2000.

James, Edward. "*Beati Pacifici*: Bishops and the Law in Sixth-Century Gaul." In *Disputes and Settlements: Law and Human Relations in the West*, ed. John Bossy, 25–46. Cambridge: Cambridge University Press, 1983.

——. *The Franks*. Oxford: Basil Blackwell, 1988.

——. *The Origins of France: From Clovis to the Capetians, 500–1000*. New York: St. Martin's Press, 1982.

——. "Septimania and Its Frontier: An Archaeological Approach." In *Visigothic Spain: New Approaches*, ed. Edward James, 223–41. Oxford: Clarendon Press, 1980.

Jarnut, Jörg. "Bonifatius und die fränkischen Reformkonzilien (743–748)." *Zeitschrift der Savigny-Stiftung für Rechtgeschichte: Kanonistiche Abteilung* 66 (1979): 1–26.

Jasper, Detlev. "The Beginning of the Decretal Tradition." In *Papal Letters in the Early Middle Ages*, ed. Detlev Jasper and Horst Fuhrmann, 1–133. History of Medieval Canon Law, ed. Wilfried Hartmann and Kenneth Pennington. Washington DC: The Catholic University of America Press, 2001.

Jones, A. H. M. "Church Finance in the Fifth and Sixth Centuries." *Journal of Theological Studies* XI (New Series), no. 1 (1960): 84–94.

——. *The Later Roman Empire*. Norman, OK: University of Oklahoma Press, 1964.

Jones, A. H. M., J. R. Martindale, and J. Morris, eds. *The Prosopography of the Later Roman Empire*. Vol. 1. Cambridge: Cambridge University Press, 1971.

Jonkers, E. J. "Die Konzile und einige Formen alten Volksglaubens im fünften und sechsten Jahrhundert." *Vigiliae Christianae* 22, no. 1 (1968): 49–53.

Kaiser, Reinhold. "Les évêques et leurs pouvoirs." In *La Neustrie: Les pays au nord de la Loire de Dagobert à Charles le Chauve (VIIe–IXe siècles)*, ed. Patrick Périn and Laure-Charlotte Feffer, 99–101. Rouen: Musées et Monuments Départementaux de Seine-Maritime, 1985.

——. "Steuer und Zoll in der Merowingerzeit." *Francia* 7 (1979): 1–17.

Katz, Solomon. *The Jews in the Visigothic and Frankish Kingdoms of Spain and Gaul.* Cambridge, MA: Medieval Academy of America, 1937.

Kay, Richard. "Mansi and Rouen: A Critique of the Conciliar Collections." *The Catholic Historical Review* 52, no. 2 (1966): 155–85.

——. Review of *Histoire des conciles mérovingiens*, by Odette Pontal. *Speculum* 67, no . 4 (1992): 1030–2.

Keller, Hagen. "Fränkische Herrschaft und alemannisches Herzogtum im 6. und 7 . Jahrhundert." *Zeitschrift für die Geschichte des Oberrheins* 85 (1976): 1–30.

Kéry, Lotte, ed. *Canonical Collections of the Early Middle Ages (ca. 400–1140).* History of Medieval Canon Law, ed. Wilfried Hartmann and Kenneth Pennington. Washington DC: The Catholic University of America Press, 1999.

Klingshirn, William. *Caesarius of Arles: The Making of a Christian Community in Late Antique Gaul.* Cambridge: Cambridge University Press, 1994.

——. "Charity and Power: Caesarius of Arles and the Ransoming of Captives in Sub-Roman Gaul." *Journal of Roman Studies* 75 (1985): 183–203.

Klöckener, Martin. "Eine liturgische Ordnung für Provinzialkonzilien aus der Karolingerzeit." *Annuarium Historiae Conciliorum* 12 (1980): 109–82.

Köbler, Gerhard. *Wörterverzeichnis zu den Concilia aevi Merovingici.* Lahn-Giessen: Distler, 1977.

Kolb, Anne. "Transport and Communication in the Roman State: The Cursus Publicus." In *Travel and Geography in the Roman Empire*, ed. Colin Adams and Ray Laurence, 95–105. London: Routledge, 2001.

Kratochwil, Friedrich. *Rules, Norms, and Decisions.* Cambridge: Cambridge University Press, 1989.

Kroell, Maurice. *L'immunité franque.* Paris: Librairie Nouvelle de Droit et de Jurisprudence, 1910.

Kuttner, Stephan. "The Scientific Investigation of Mediaeval Canon Law." *Speculum* 24, no. 4 (1949): 493–501.

Lebecq, Stéphane. "Entre antique tardive et très Haut Moyen Age: Permanence et mutations des systèmes de communications dans la Gaule et ses marges." *Settimane di Studio del Centro Italiano di Studi Sull'Alto Medioevo* 45, no. 1 (1997): 461–501.

——. "The Role of the Monasteries in the Systems of Production and Exchange of the Frankish World Between the Seventh and the Beginning of the Ninth Centuries." In *The Long Eighth Century*, ed. Inge Lyse Hansen and Chris Wickham, 121–48. Brill: Leiden, 2000.

Le Bras, Gabriel. *Prolégomènes.* Histoire du droit et des institutions de l'Eglise en Occident T. 1. Paris: Sirey, 1955.

Leighton, Albert C. *Transport and Communication in Early Medieval Europe, AD 500–1100.* Newton Abbot: David and Charles, 1972.

Lemarignier, Jean-Francois. "Quelques remarques sur l'organisation ecclésiastique de la Gaule du VIIe à la fin du IXe siècle principalement au nord de la Loire." In *Recueil d'articles rassemblés par ses disciples: Structures politiques et religieuses dans la France du Haut Moyen Age*, 65–100. Rouen: Publications de l'Université, 1995.

Le Roy, Yves. "Les conciles gaulois et le Décret de Gratien." *Revue historique de droit français et étranger* 62 (1984): 553–75.

Lesne, Emile. "Les diverses acceptions du terme 'beneficium' du VIIIe au XIe siècle." *Revue historique de droit français et étranger* series 4, no. 3 (1924): 5–56.

——. *La hiérarchie épiscopale: Provinces, métropolitains, primats en Gaule et Germanie.* Lille: Facultes Catholiques, 1905.

——. *Histoire de la propriété ecclésiastique en France.* Vols. 1–6. Lille: Rene Giard, 1910–43.

Levillain, Léon. "Notes sur l'immunité mérovingienne." *Revue historique de droit français et étranger* series 4, no. 6 (1927): 38–67.

Levison, Wilhelm. *England and the Continent in the Eighth Century*. Oxford: Clarendon Press, 1946.

Levy, Ernst. *West Roman Vulgar Law: The Law of Property*. Philadelphia: American Philosophical Society, 1951.

Lifshitz, Felice. *The Name of the Saint: The Martyrology of Jerome and Access to the Sacred in Francia, 627–827*. Notre Dame: University of Notre Dame Press, 2006.

Linger, Sandrine. "L'écrit à l'époque mérovingienne d'après la correspondance de Didier, évêque de Cahors (630–655)." *Studi Medievali* series 3, 33.2 (1992): 799–823.

Lippert, Woldemar. "Die Verfasserschaft der Canon gallischer Concilien des V. und VI. Jahrhunderts." *Neues Archiv der Gesellschaft für ältere deutsche Geschichtskunde* 14 (1889): 9–58.

Loening, Edgar. *Geschichte des deutschen Kirchenrechts*. Strasbourg: Verlag Karl J. Trübner, 1878.

Lotter, Friedrich. "La crainte du prosélytisme et la peur du contact: Les juifs dans les actes des synodes mérovingiens." In *Clovis: Histoire et mémoire*, ed. Michel Rouche, 849–79. Paris: Presses de l'Université de Paris-Sorbonne, 1997.

——. "Sind christliche Quellen zur Erforschung der Geschichte der Juden im Frühmittelalter weitgehend unbrauchbar?" *Historische Zeitschrift* 278, no. 2 (2004): 311–27.

——. "Totale Finsternis über 'Dunklen Jahrhunderten.' Zum Methodenverständnis von Michael Toch und seinen Folgen." *Aschkenas* 11 (2001): 215–32.

——. "Zur sozialen Hierarchie der Judenheit in Spätantike und Frühmittelalter." *Aschkenas* 13 (2003): 333–59.

Lumpe, Adolf. "Zur Geschichte der Wörter *Concilium* und *Synodus* in der antiken christlichen Latinität." *Annuarium Historiae Conciliorum* 2, no. 1 (1970): 1–21.

Maassen, Friedrich. *Geschichte der Quellen und der Literatur des canonischen Rechts im Abendlande*. Graz: Akademische Druck-U. Verlagsanstalt, 1870.

MacMullen, Ramsay. *Voting About God in Early Church Councils*. New Haven: Yale University Press, 2006.

Magnou-Nortier, Elisabeth. "A propos des rapports entre l'Eglise et l'état franc: La lettre synodale au Roi Théodebert (535)." In *Societa, Istituzioni, Spiritualita: Studi in Onore di Cinzio Violante*, vol. 1, 519–34. Spoleto: Centro Italiano di Studi Sull'alto Medioevo, 1994.

——. "Étude sur le privilège d'immunité du IVe au IXe siècle." *Revue Mabillon* 60, no. 297–8 (1984): 465–512.

——. "Les évêques et la paix dans l'espace franc (VIe–XIe siècles)." In *L'évêque dans l'histoire de l'Eglise: Actes de la septième rencontre d'histoire religieuse tenue à Fontevraud les 14 et 15 Octobre 1983*, 33–50. Angers: Presses de l'Université d'Angers, 1984.

——. "Existe-t-il une géographie gaulois des courants de pensée dans le clergé de Gaule au VIe siècle?" In *Grégoire de Tours et l'espace gaulois*, ed. Nancy Gauthier and Henry Galinié, 139–57. Tours: Revue Archéologique du Centre de la France, 1997.

——. "Remarques sur la genèse du *Pactus Legis Salicae* et sur le privilège d'immunité (IVe–VIIe siècles)." In *Clovis: Histoire et Mémoire*, ed. Michel Rouche, 495–538. Paris: Presses de l'Université de Paris-Sorbonne, 1997.

Malkiel, David. "Jewish–Christian Relations in Europe, 840–1096." *Journal of Medieval History* 29 (2003): 55–83.

Markus, R. A. "From Caesarius to Boniface: Christianity and Paganism in Gaul." In *The Seventh Century: Change and Continuity*, ed. J. Fontaine and J. N. Hillgarth, 154–72. London: The Warburg Institute, 1992.

——. *Gregory the Great and His World*. Cambridge: Cambridge University Press, 1997.

Martindale, J. R., ed. *The Prosopography of the Later Roman Empire*. Vols. II and III. Cambridge: Cambridge University Press, 1971–92.

Mathisen, Ralph. "Between Arles, Rome, and Toledo: Gallic Collections of Canon Law in Late Antiquity." *'Ilu: Revista de Ciencias de las Religiones* 2 (1999): 33–46.

——. *Ecclesiastical Factionalism and Religious Controversy in Fifth-Century Gaul.* Washington DC: Catholic University of America Press, 1989.

——. "Episcopal Hierarchy and Tenure in Office in Late Roman Gaul: A Method for Establishing Dates of Ordination." *Francia* 17/1 (1990): 125–40.

——. "A Reconstruction of the List of Subscriptions to the Council of Orange." *Annuarium Historiae Conciliorum* 19, no. 1 (1987): 1–12.

——. *Roman Aristocrats in Barbarian Gaul.* Austin: University of Texas Press, 1993.

——. "The Second Council of Arles and the Spirit of Compilation and Codification in Late Roman Gaul." *Journal of Early Christian Studies* 5, no. 4 (1997): 511–54.

——. "Syagrius of Autun, Virgilius of Arles, and Gregory of Rome: Factionalism, Forgery, and Local Authority at the End of the Sixth Century." In *L'Église et la mission au VIe siècle*, ed. Christophe de Dreuille, 260–90. Paris: Éditions du Cerf, 2000.

Maurin, Louis, Brigitte Beaujard, et al. *Province ecclésiastique de Bordeaux (Aquitania Secunda).* Topographie Chrétienne des Cites de la Gaule X. Paris: De Boccard, 1998.

Mayeux, M. R. "Les biens de l'Eglise considérés comme patrimoine des pauvres à travers les conciles occidentaux du VIe siècle." In *Inspiration religieuse et structures temporelles*, 139–209. Paris: Les Éditions Ouvrières, 1948.

McCormick, Michael. *The Origins of the European Economy.* Cambridge: Cambridge University Press, 2001.

——. "Pippin III, the Embassy of Caliph al Mansur, and the Mediterranean World." In *Der Dynastiewechsel von 751*, ed. Matthias Becher and Jorg Jarnut, 221–41. Münster: Scriptorium, 2004.

McKitterick, Rosamond. *The Carolingians and the Written Word.* Cambridge: Cambridge University Press, 1989.

——. *Charlemagne.* Cambridge: Cambridge University Press, 2008.

——. *The Frankish Church and the Carolingian Reforms, 789–895.* London: Royal Historical Society, 1977.

——. *The Frankish Kingdoms Under the Carolingians.* London: Longman, 1983.

——. *History and Memory in the Carolingian World.* Cambridge: Cambridge University Press, 2004.

——. "History, Law and Communication with the Past in the Carolingian Period." *Settimane di Studio del Centro Italiano di Studi Sull'Alto Medioevo* 52, no. 2 (2004): 941–79.

——. "Knowledge of Canon Law in the Frankish Kingdoms Before 789: The Manuscript Evidence." In *Books, Scribes, and Learning in the Frankish Kingdoms, Sixth–Ninth Centuries.* Brookfield, VT: Variorum, 1994.

——. "Some Carolingian Law-Books and Their Function." In *Books, Scribes, and Learning in the Frankish Kingdoms, Sixth–Ninth Centuries.* Aldershot: Variorum, 1994.

McNamara, Jo Ann, and Suzanne F. Wemple. "Marriage and Divorce in the Frankish Kingdom." In *Women in Medieval Society*, ed. Susan Mosher Stuard, 95–124. Philadelphia: University of Pennsylvania Press, 1976.

Meens, Rob. "The Oldest Manuscript Witness of the *Collectio Canonum Hibernensis.*" *Peritia* 14 (2000): 1–19.

——. "Reforming the Clergy: A Context for the Use of the Bobbio Penitential." In *The Bobbio Missal: Liturgy and Religious Culture in Merovingian Gaul*, ed. Yitzhak Hen and Rob Meens, 154–67. Cambridge: Cambridge University Press, 2004.

——. "The Uses of the Old Testament in Early Medieval Canon Law: The *Collectio Vetus Gallica* and the *Collectio Hibernensis.*" In *The Uses of the Past in the Early Middle Ages*, ed. Yitzhak Hen and Matthew Innes, 67–77. Cambridge: Cambridge University Press: 2000.

Mikat, Paul. *Die Inzestgesetzgebung der merowingisch-fränkischen Konzilien (511–626/27)*. Paderborn: Ferdinand Schöningh, 1994.

——. *Die Inzestverbote des Dritten Konzils von Orléans (538): Ein Beitrag zur Geschichte des Frankischen Eherechts*. Opladen: Westdeutscher Verlag, 1993.

——. *Die Judengesetzgebung der merowingisch-fränkischen Konzilien*. Opladen: Westdeutscher Verlag, 1995.

Mommsen, Theodor. *Römisches Staatsrecht*. Graz: Akademische Druck-U. Verlagsanstalt, 1952–3.

Moore, Michael Edward. "La monarchie carolingienne et les anciens modèles irlandais." *Annales* 51, no. 2 (1996): 307–24.

——. "A Sacred Kingdom: Royal and Episcopal Power in the Frankish Realms." PhD diss., University of Michigan, 1993.

Mordek, Hubert. *Bibliotheca Capitularium Regum Francorum Manuscripta*. Munich: Monumenta Germaniae Historica, 1995.

——. "Bischofsabsetzung in spätmerowingischer Zeit: Justelliana, Bernensis, und das Konzil von Mâlay (677)." In *Papsttum, Kirche und Recht im Mittelalter: Festschrift für Horst Fuhrmann zum 65. Geburtstag*, ed. Hubert Mordek, 31–53. Tübingen: Max Niemeyer, 1991.

——. "Die Collectio Vetus Gallica, die älteste systematische Kanonensammlung des fränkischen Gallien." *Francia* 1 (1973): 45–61.

——. "Kanonistische Activität in Gallien in der Ersten Hälfte des 8. Jahrunderts." *Francia* 2 (1974): 19–25.

——. "Karolingische Kapitularien." In *Überlieferung und Geltung normativer Texte des frühen und hohen Mittelalters*, ed. Hubert Mordek, 25–50. Sigmaringen: Jan Thorbecke Verlag, 1986.

——. *Kirchenrecht und Reform im Frankenreich: Die Collectio Vetus Gallica, die älteste systematische Kanonessammlung des fränkischen Gallien*. Berlin: Walter de Gruyter, 1975.

——. "Die Rechtssammlungen der Handschrift von Bonneval: Ein Werk der karolingischen." *Deutsches Archiv für Erforschung des Mittelalters* 24, no. 2 (1968): 339–434.

Mordek, Hubert, and Roger Reynolds. "Bischof Leodegar und das Konzil von Autun." In *Aus Archiven und Bibliotheken: Festschrift für Raymund Kottje zum 65*, ed. Hubert Mordek, 71–92. Frankfurt: Peter Lang, 1992.

Morelle, Laurent. "Les actes de précaire, instruments de transferts patrimoniaux (France du Nord et de l'Est, VIIIe–XIe siècle)." *Mélanges de l'Ecole Française de Rome: Moyen Age* 111, no. 2 (1999): 607–47.

Morrison, Karl. *Tradition and Authority in the Western Church: 300–1140*. Princeton: Princeton University Press, 1969.

——. *The Two Kingdoms: Ecclesiology in Carolingian Political Thought*. Princeton: Princeton University Press, 1964.

Müller, Heribert. "Kunibert von Köln." *Rheinische Lebensbilder* 12 (1991): 7–23.

Munier, Charles. "L'ordo de celebrando concilio wisigothique." *Revue des Sciences Religieuses* 37 (1963): 250–71.

Murray, Alexander C. "Chronology and the Composition of the *Histories* of Gregory of Tours." *Journal of Late Antiquity* 1, no. 1 (2008): 157–96.

——. "Immunity, Nobility, and the Edict of Paris." *Speculum* 69, no. 1 (1994): 18–39.

——. "'*Pax et Disciplina*': Roman Public Law and the Merovingian State." In *Proceedings of the Tenth International Congress of Medieval Canon Law*, ed. Kenneth Pennington, Stanley Chodorow, and Keith H. Kendall, 269–85. Vatican City: Biblioteca Apostolica Vaticana, 2001.

Nelson, Janet. *Charles the Bald*. London: Longman, 1992.

——. "Legislation and Consensus Under Charles the Bald." In *Politics and Ritual in Early Medieval Europe*, 91–116. London: Hambledon Press, 1986.

——. "Literacy in Carolingian Government." In *The Uses of Literacy in Early Mediaeval Europe*, ed. Rosamond McKitterick, 258–96. Cambridge: Cambridge University Press, 1990.
——. "The Merovingian Church in Carolingian Perspective." In *The World of Gregory of Tours*, ed. Kathleen Mitchell and Ian Wood, 241–59. Leiden: Brill, 2002.
——. "National Synods, Kingship as Office, and Royal Anointing." *Studies in Church History* 7 (1971): 41–59.
——. "On the Limits of the Carolingian Renaissance." *Politics and Ritual in Early Medieval Europe*, 49–67. London: The Hambledon Press, 1986.
Noble, Thomas F. X. "Gregory of Tours and the Roman Church." In *The World of Gregory of Tours*, ed. Kathleen Mitchell and Ian Wood, 145–61. Leiden: Brill, 2002.
Nonn, Ulrich. "Merowingische Testamente: Studien zum Fortleben einer römischen Urkundenform im Frankenreich." *Archiv für Diplomatik* 18 (1972): 1–129.
Noy, David. *Jewish Inscriptions of Western Europe*. Paperback edition. Cambridge: Cambridge University Press, 2005.
Oehler, Klaus. "Der *Consensus Omnium* als Kriterium der Wahrheit in der antiken Philosophie und der Patristik." *Antike und Abendland* 10 (1961): 103–29.
Orlandis, José, and Domingo Ramos-Lissón. *Die Synoden auf der Iberischen Halbinsel biz zum Einbruch des Islam (711)*. Paderborn: Ferdinand Schöningh, 1981.
Pakter, Walter. "Les esclaves chrétiens des juifs: Troisième Concile d'Orléans (538)." *Archives Juives* 21, nos. 1–2 (1985): 3–4.
——. *Medieval Canon Law and the Jews*. Ebelsbach: Verlag Rolf Gremer, 1988.
Palanque, J. R., and Delaruelle, E. "Le rôle temporel de l'Eglise du IVe siècle au VIIe siècle." In *Inspiration religieuse et structures temporelles*, 77–106. Paris: Les Éditions Ouvrières, 1948.
Patzold, Steffen. "Créer un grade ecclésiastique: Métropolitains et archevêques du royaume franc (VIIIe–IXe siècles)." Hiérarchie, ordre et mobilité dans l'Occident médiéval (400–1100). Conference, Auxerre, France, 2006.
Paxton, Frederick. "*Bonus Liber*: A Late Carolingian Clerical Manual from Lorsch." In *The Two Laws: Studies in Medieval Legal History Dedicated to Stephan Kuttner*, ed. Laurent Mayali and Stephanie A. J. Tibbetts, 1–30. Washington DC: Catholic University of America Press, 1990.
Peyroux, Catherine R. "Canonists Construct the Nun: Church Law and Women's Monastic Practice in Merovingian France." In *Law, Society, and Authority in Late Antiquity*, ed. Ralph Mathisen, 242–55. Oxford: Oxford University Press, 2001.
Picard, Jean-Charles. "La fonction des salles de réception dans le groupe épiscopal de Genève." *Rivista di archeologia cristiana* 65, nos. 1–2 (1989): 87–104.
Picard, Jean-Charles, Brigitte Beaujard, et al. *Province ecclésiastique de Sens (Lugdunensis Senonia)*. Topographie Chrétienne des Cites de la Gaule VIII. Paris: De Boccard, 1992.
Pietri, Luce. *La ville de Tours du IVe au Vie siècle: Naissance d'une cite chrétienne*. Paris: École Française de Rome, 1983.
Pietri, Luce, and Jacques Biarne. *Province ecclésiastique de Tours (Lugdunensis Tertia)*. Topographie Chrétienne des Cites de la Gaule V. Paris: De Boccard, 1987.
Pontal, Odette. *Les conciles de la France capétienne jusqu'en 1215*. Paris: Cerf, 1995.
——. *Histoire des conciles mérovingiens*. Paris: Éditions du Cerf, 1989. German edition: *Die Synoden im Merowingerreich*. Paderborn: Ferdinand Schöningh, 1986.
——. "Survivances païennes, superstitions et sorcellerie au Moyen Age d'après les décrets des conciles et synodes." *Annuarium Historiae Conciliorum* 27/8 (1995–6): 129–36.
Pössel, Christina. "Authors and Recipients of Carolingian Capitularies." In *Texts and Identities in the Early Middle Ages*, ed. Richard Corradini, Rob Meens, Christina Pössel, and Philip Shaw, 253–74. Vienna: Verlag der Österreichischen Akademie der Wissenschaften, 2006.

Prinz, Friedrich. "Columbanus, the Frankish Nobility, and the Territories East of the Rhine." In *Columbanus and Merovingian Monasticism*, ed. Howard B. Clarke and Mary Brennan, 73–87. Oxford: B.A.R., 1981.
——. *Frühes Mönchtum im Frankenreich*. Munich: R. Oldenbourg, 1965.
Prou, Maurice. *La Gaule mérovingienne*. Paris: Société Française d'Editions d'Art, 1897.
Quentin, Henri. *Jean-Dominique Mansi et les grandes collections conciliaires*. Paris: E. Leroux, 1900.
Réal, Isabelle. *Vies de saints, vie de famille*. Turnhout: Brepols, 2001.
Reuter. Timothy. "Assembly Politics in Western Europe from the Eighth Century Through the Twelfth." In *The Medieval World*, ed. Peter Linehan and Janet L. Nelson, 432–50. London: Routledge, 2001.
——. "Kirchenreform und Kirchenpolitik im Zeitalter Karl Martells: Begriffe und Wirklichkeit." In *Karl Martell in seiner Zeit*, ed. Jörg Jarnut, Ulrich Nonn, and Michael Richter, 35–59. Sigmaringen: Jan Thorbecke Verlag, 1994.
Reymond, Maxime. "La charte de Saint Sigismond pour Saint-Maurice d'Agaune 515." *Zeitschrift für Schweizerische Geschichte* 6 (1926): 1–60.
Reynolds, Roger. "The Isidorian *Epistola ad Massonam* on Lapsed Clerics: Notes on Its Early Manuscript and Textual Transmission." In *Grundlagen des Rechts: Festschrift für Peter Landau zum 65. Geburtstag*, ed. Peter Landau and R. H. Helmholz, 77–92. Paderborn: Ferdinand Schöningh, 2000.
——. "The Organization, Law and Liturgy of the Western Church, 700–900." In *The New Cambridge Medieval History*, vol. 2, ed. Rosamond McKitterick, 587–621. Cambridge: Cambridge University Press, 1995.
——. "Unity and Diversity in Carolingian Canon Law Collections: The Case of the *Collectio Hibernensis* and Its Derivatives." In *Carolingian Essays: Andrew W. Mellon Lectures in Early Christian Studies*, ed. Uta-Renate Blumenthal, 99–135. Washington, DC: The Catholic University of America Press, 1983.
Reynolds, Susan. *Fiefs and Vassals*. Oxford: Oxford University Press, 1994.
Rhijn, Carine van. *Shepherds of the Lord: Priests and Episcopal Statutes in the Carolingian Period*. Turnhout: Brepols, 2007.
Riché, Pierre. "Columbanus, His Followers, and the Merovingian Church." In *Columbanus and Merovingian Monasticism*, ed. Howard B. Clarke and Mary Brennan, 59–72. Oxford: B.A.R., 1981.
——. *Daily Life in the World of Charlemagne*. Translated by Jo Ann McNamara. Philadelphia: University of Pennsylvania Press, 1978.
——. *Education and Culture in the Barbarian West: Sixth Through Eighth Centuries*. Translated by John J. Contreni. Columbia, SC: University of South Carolina Press, 1976.
Rosenthal, Joel. "The Public Assembly in the Time of Louis the Pious." *Traditio* 20 (1964): 25–40.
Rosenwein, Barbara. "Impossible Cloisters: Gregory of Tours and Episcopal Exemption." In *The World of Gregory of Tours*, ed. Kathleen Mitchell and Ian Wood, 181–97. Leiden: Brill, 2002.
——. *Negotiating Space: Power, Restraint, and Privileges of Immunity in Early Medieval Europe*. Ithaca, NY: Cornell University Press, 1999.
——. "Property Transfers and the Church, Eighth to Eleventh Centuries: An Overview." *Mélanges de l'Ecole Française de Rome: Moyen Age* 111, no. 2 (1999): 563–75.
Rouche, Michel. "La matricule des pauvres: Évolution d'une institution de charité du Bas Empire jusqu'à la fin du Haut Moyen Age." In *Études sur l'histoire de la pauvreté*, vol. 1, ed. Michel Mollat, 83–110. Paris: Publications de la Sorbonne, 1974.
Sainio, Matti Antero. *Semasiologische Untersuchungen: Über die Entstehung der christlichen Latinität*. Helsinki: Finnische Literaturgesellschaft, 1940.
Sainte-Marthe, Denis de, et al. *Gallia Christiana*. Vols. 1–16. Farnsborough, UK: Gregg International, 1970. First published 1856–99 by V. Palmé in Paris.
Schieffer, Theodor. *Winfrid-Bonifatius und die christliche Grundlegung Europas*. Freiburg: Verlag Herder-Freiburg, 1954.

Schmid, Karl, and Otto Oexle. "Voraussetzungen und Wirking des Gebetsbundes von Attigny." *Francia* 2 (1974): 71–122.
Schmitz, Hermann. "Die Tendenz der Provinzialsynoden in Gallien seit dem 5. Jahrhundert und die römischen Bussbücher." *Archiv für katholisches Kirchenrecht* 65 (1894): 21–33.
Schröder, Isolde. "Zur Rezeption merowingischer Konzilskanones bei Gratian." In *Papsttum, Kirche und Recht im Mittelalter: Festschrift für Horst Fuhrmann zum 65. Geburtstag*, ed. Hubert Mordek, 233–50. Tübingen: Max Niemeyer, 1991.
Schubert, Hans von. *Staat und Kirche in den arianischen Königreichen und im Reiche Chlodwigs*. Munich and Berlin: Druck und Verlag von R. Oldenbourg, 1912.
Schüssler, Heinz Joachim. "Die fränkische Reichsteilung von Vieux-Poitiers 742 und die Reform der Kirche in den Teilreichen Karlamanns und Pippins." *Francia* 13 (1985): 47–112.
Seyfarth, Erich. *Fränkische Reichsversammlungen unter Karl dem Grossen und Ludwig dem Frommen*. Borna-Leipzig: Buchdruckerei Robert Noske, 1910.
Sieben, Hermann Josef. *Die Konzilsidee in der Alten Kirche*. Paderborn: Ferdinand Schöningh, 1979.
Smyth, Matthieu. "Les canons conciliaires de la Gaule, témoins des responsabilités liturgiques épiscopales en Occident." *Revue de droit canonique* 49, no. 2 (1999): 259–77.
Socii Bollandiani, ed. *Bibliotheca Hagiographica Latina Antiquae et Mediae Aetatis*. Brussels: Socii Bollandiani, 1898–1901.
Sohm, Rudolph. *Kirchenrecht*. Leipzig and Munich: Verlag von Duncker and Humblot, 1892–1923.
Spilling, Herrad. "Die Sprache des Konzils." In *Das Frankfurter Konzil von 794: Kristallisationspunkt karolingischer Kultur*, ed. Rainer Berndt, II.699–727. Mainz: Selbstverlag der Gesellschaft für Mittelrheinische Kirchengeschichte, 1997.
Stein, Peter. *Regulae Iuris*. Edinburgh: Edinburgh University Press, 1966.
Sternberg, Thomas. *Orientalium More Secutus*. Münster: Aschendorff, 1991.
Stickler, Alphonso M. *Historia Iuris Canonici Latini*. Torino: Pontificium Athenaeum Salesianum, 1950.
Stocking, Rachel L. *Bishops, Councils, and Consensus in the Visigothic Kingdom, 589–633*. Ann Arbor: University of Michigan Press, 2000.
Stroheker, Karl Friedrich. *Der senatorische Adel im spatantiken Gallien*. Tübingen: Alma Mater Verlag, 1948.
Sullivan, Richard. "The Carolingian Age: Reflections on Its Place in the History of the Middle Ages." *Speculum* 64, no. 2 (1989): 267–306.
Suntrup, Aloys. *Studien zur politischen Theologie im frühmittelalterlichen Okzident*. Münster: Ascherendorff, 2001.
Tengström, Emin. *Die Protokollierung der Collatio Carthaginensis*. Göteborg: Göteborg University, 1962.
Theurillat, Jean-Marie. "L'Abbaye de Saint-Maurice d'Agaune des origines à la réforme canoniale, 515–830." *Vallesia* 9 (1954): 1–128.
Toch, Michael. *"Dunkle Jahrhunderte": Gab es ein jüdisches Frühmittelalter?* Trier: Arye-Maimon-Institut für Geschichte der Juden, 2001.
——. "Jews and Commerce: Modern Fancies and Medieval Realities." In *Il Ruolo Economico delle Minoranze in Europa Secc. XIII–XVIII*, ed. Simonetta Cavaciocchi, 43–58. Florence: Le Monnier, 2000.
——. "The Jews in Europe, 500–1050." In *The New Cambridge Medieval History*. Vol. 1. Ed. Paul Fouracre, 547–70. Cambridge: Cambridge University Press, 2005.
——. "Mehr Licht: Eine Entgegnung zu Friedrich Lotter." *Aschkenas* 11 (2001): 465–87.
Turner, C. H. "Arles and Rome: The First Developments of Canon Law in Gaul." *The Journal of Theological Studies* 17 (1916): 236–47.
Ullmann, Walter. "Public Welfare and Social Legislation in the Early Medieval Councils." *Studies in Church History* 7 (1971): 1–39.

Van Dam, Raymond. *Leadership and Community in Late Antique Gaul*. Berkeley: University of California Press, 1985.
Verhulst, Adriaan. *The Carolingian Economy*. Cambridge: Cambridge University Press, 2002.
Verlinden, Charles. *L'esclavage dans l'Europe médiévale*. Vol. 1. Brugge: De Tempel, 1955.
Vessey, Mark. "The Origins of the *Collectio Sirmondiana*: A New Look at the Evidence." In *The Theodosian Code*, ed. Jill Harries and Ian Wood, 178–99. Ithaca, NY: Cornell University Press, 1993.
Vogel, Cyrille. *Introduction aux sources de l'histoire du culte chrétien au Moyen Age*. Spoleto: Centro Italiano di Studi Sull'Alto Medioevo, 1975.
——. "Pénitence et excommunication dans l'Eglise ancienne et durant le Haut Moyen Age: Perspective historique." *Concilium* 107 (1975): 11–22.
——. "Primatialité et synodalite dans l'Église locale durant la période anteniceene." In *Aspects de l'orthodoxie: Structures et spiritualité*, 53–66. Paris: Presses Universitaires de France, 1981.
——. "Les sanctions infligées aux laïcs et aux clercs par les conciles gallo-romains et mérovingiens." *Revue de droit canonique* 2, nos. 1–3 (1952): 5–29, 171–94, 311–28.
Voigt, Karl. *Staat und Kirche von Konstantin dem Grossen bis zum Ende der Karolingerzeit*. Stuttgart: W. Kohlhammer, 1936.
Vollrath, Hanna. *Die Synoden Englands bis 1066*. Paderborn: Ferdinand Schöningh, 1985.
Wallace-Hadrill, J. M. *The Frankish Church*. Oxford: Clarendon Press, 1983.
——. *The Long-Haired Kings*. London: Methuen and Co., 1962.
Weidemann, Margarete. "Bischofsherrschaft und Königtum in Neustrien vom 7. bis zum 9. Jahrhundert am Beispiel des Bistums Le Mans." In *La Neustrie: Les pays au nord de la Loire de 650 à 850*, ed. Hartmut Atsma, I.161–193. Sigmaringen: Jan Thorbecke Verlag, 1989.
——. *Kulturgeschichte der Merowingerzeit nach den Werken Gregors von Tours*. Mainz: Verlag des Römisch-Germanischen Zentralmuseums, 1982.
Wemple, Suzanne F. *Women in Frankish Society*. Philadelphia: University of Pennsylvania Press, 1981.
Werminghoff, Albert. "Zu den fränkischen Reformsynoden des 8. Jahrhunderts." *Neues Archiv der Gesellschaft für ältere deutsche Geschichtskunde* 32 (1907): 221–36.
Werner, Karl F. "Important Noble Families in the Kingdom of Charlemagne." In *The Medieval Nobility*, ed. and trans. Timothy Reuter, 137–202. New York: North Holland Publishing, 1979.
——. "Liens de parenté et noms de personne: Un problème historique et méthodologique." In *Famille et parenté dans l'occident médiéval*, ed. Georges Duby and Jacques Le Goff, 13–18 and 25–34. Rome: École française de Rome, 1977.
Weyl, Richard. *Das fränkische Staatskirchenrecht zur Zeit der Merovinger*. Breslau: Verlag von Wilhelm Keobner, 1888. Reprint, Aalen: Scientia Verlag, 1970.
White, Stephen D. *Custom, Kinship, and Gifts to Saints: The Laudatio Parentum in Western France, 1050–1150*. Chapel Hill: University of North Carolina Press, 1988.
Wickham, Chris. *Framing the Early Middle Ages*. Oxford: Oxford University Press, 2005.
Wiel, Constant Van De. *History of Canon Law*. Louvain: Peeters Press, 1991.
Wieruszowski, Helene. "Die Zusammensetzung des gallischen und fränkischen Episkopats bis zum Vertrag von Verdun (843) mit besonderer Berücksichtigung der Nationalität und des Standes." *Bonner Jahrbücher* 127 (1922): 1–83.
Winroth, Anders. *The Making of Gratian's Decretum*. Cambridge: Cambridge University Press, 2000.
Wolfram, Herwig. "Karl Martell und das Fränkische Lehenswesen." In *Karl Martell in seiner Zeit*, ed. Jörg Jarnut, Ulrich Nonn, and Michael Richter, 61–78. Sigmaringen: Jan Thorbecke Verlag, 1994.

——. *The Roman Empire and Its Germanic Peoples*. Translated by Thomas Dunlap. Berkeley: University of California Press, 1997.

Wood, Ian. "Administration, Law, and Culture in Merovingian Gaul." In *The Uses of Literacy in Early Medieval Europe*, ed. Rosamond McKitterick, 63–81. Cambridge: Cambridge University Press, 1990.

——. "The Code in Merovingian Gaul." In *The Theodosian Code*, ed. Jill Harries and Ian Wood, 161–77. Ithaca, NY: Cornell University Press, 1993.

——. "Disputes in Late Fifth- and Sixth-Century Gaul: Some Problems." In *The Settlement of Disputes in Early Medieval Europe*, ed. Wendy Davis and Paul Fouracre, 7–22. Cambridge: Cambridge University Press, 1986.

——. "Early Merovingian Devotion in Town and Country." *Studies in Church History* 16 (1979): 61–76.

——. "The Ecclesiastical Politics of Merovingian Clermont." In *Ideal and Reality in Frankish and Anglo-Saxon Society*, ed. Patrick Wormald, Donald Bullough, and Roger Collins, 34–57. Oxford: Basil Blackwell, 1983.

——. "Forgery in Merovingian Hagiography." In *Monumenta Germaniae Historica: Schriften* 33. Fälschungen im Mittelalter V (1988): 369–84.

——. "The Franks and Papal Theology, 550–660." In *The Crisis of the Oikoumene*, ed. Celia Chazelle and Catherine Cubitt, 223–41. Turnhout: Brepols, 2007.

——. "Fredegar's Fables." In *Historiographie im frühen Mittelalter*, ed. Anton Scharer and Georg Scheibelreiter, 359–66. Vienna: R. Oldenbourg, 1994.

——. "Incest, Law, and the Bible in Sixth-Century Gaul." *Early Medieval Europe* 7, no. 3 (1998): 291–303.

——. *The Merovingian Kingdoms: 450–751*. London: Longman Group, 1994.

——. *The Missionary Life: Saints and the Evangelization of Europe, 400–1050*. London: Longman, 2001.

——. "Prelude to Columbanus: The Monastic Achievement in the Burgundian Territories." In *Columbanus and Merovingian Monasticism*, ed. Howard B. Clarke and Mary Brennan, 3–32. Oxford: B.A.R., 1981.

——. "Roman Law in the Barbarian Kingdoms." In *Rome and the North*, ed. Alvar Ellegard and Gunilla Åkerström-Hougen, 5–14. Jonsered: Paul Åströms Forlag, 1996.

——. "Teutsind, Witlaic, and the History of Merovingian Precaria." In *Property and Power in the Early Middle Ages*, ed. Wendy Davies and Paul Fouracre, 31–52. Cambridge: Cambridge University Press, 1995.

Wood, Susan. *The Proprietary Church in the Medieval West*. Oxford: Oxford University Press, 2006.

Wormald, Patrick. "The *Leges Barborum*: Law and Ethnicity in the Post-Roman West." In *Regna and Gentes*, ed. Hans-Werner Goetz, Jörg Jarnut, and Walter Pohl, 21–53. Leiden: Brill, 2003.

——. "*Lex Scripta* and *Verbum Regis*: Legislation and Germanic Kingship from Euric to Cnut." In *Early Medieval Kingship*, ed. Peter Sawyer and Ian Wood, 105–38. Leeds: University of Leeds, 1977.

——. *The Making of English Law: King Alfred to the Twelfth Century*. Oxford: Blackwell, 1999.

INDEX

www.ingramcontent.com/pod-product-compliance
Lightning Source LLC
LaVergne TN
LVHW010631300926
849162LV00001B/127